CULTURAL AWARENESS, SENSITIVITY AND COMPETENCE

Michael Winkelman, Ph.D., M.P.H.
Arizona State University

ACKNOWLEDGEMENTS

This text has benefited from the teaching experiences I have had at Arizona State University and in the California State University Statewide Nursing Program. I thank the many students whose experiences have helped me to understand the difficulties in adapting to the challenges of working cross-culturally. I also thank Elizabeth McNeil for her line editing and suggestions for improving the text, and Marsha Schweitzer for her editing assistance.

Exclusive marketing and distributor rights for
U.K., Eire, and Continental Europe held by:

Gazelle Book Services Limited
Falcon House
Queen Square
Lancaster
LA1 1RN
U.K.

eddie bowers publishing co., inc.
P. O. Box 130
Peosta, Iowa 52068 USA

www.eddiebowerspublishing.com

ISBN 1-57879-064-6

FORWARD

This is a textbook you will want to keep and use throughout your career. The helping professions have long valued cultural awareness, sensitivity and competence. In social work this is reflected in the National Association of Social Workers Code of Ethics and the Council on Social Work Education Curriculum Policy Statement. The helping professions know the importance of culture and ethnicity in the helping process with individuals, families, groups, communities and organizations. Theories of human development in the social environment and all forms of practice are clearly interwoven with cultural implications. Whether taught to a specific course or integrated throughout the curriculum we recognize the significance of culture and try to assure that its content is appropriately addressed. Even as the helping profession acknowledges the importance of practicing in an ethnically sensitive manner, we recognize the lack of theoretical practice literature and research on these issues. There is a critical need to articulate true ethnic sensitive and cultural practice. We live in societies characterize by cultural pluralism -- the existence of different cultures living side-by-side. This cultural pluralism makes the dynamics of interpersonal relations more challenging and requiring that we learn how to relate effectively to people who may behave, think and feel differently from our own personal and cultural expectations. The necessity of relating effectively to people of other cultural groups increases the difficulties in client worker relations for many of the helping professions -- social workers, physicians and nurses, psychologists and counselors, educators and many others.

The laudable goal of cultural sensitivity in practice requires the development of knowledge and skills necessary for cultural competence. Unfortunately, available texts fail to adequately provide the theory, knowledge, skills and models necessary for culturally competent practice and understanding culture as a strength. Ethnic sensitive practice has received only minimal coverage leaving students and practitioners with inadequate information on this topic.

Because the helping professions have not had a knowledgeable base significant for cultural awareness, sensitivity and competence, they have had to drawn heavily on sociology and psychology. Input from cultural anthropologists has been limited even though this is perhaps the greatest resource for understanding and applying cultural competence. This book provides the basic conceptual framework for understanding people of other cultures and working effectively with them. Perspectives from social work and other helping professions including psychology, counseling, health-care and communication are integrated to provide an outline for engaging in the process of self-assessment and personal development necessary for cultural competence. The text is designed to move the individual from cultural embeddedness -- a normal ethnocentrism -- towards an appreciation of the importance of understanding and working with the perspective of people from other cultures. The self-assessment exercises and text material is designed to lead the student on a course towards cultural awareness developing cultural sensitivity and understanding the basis to develop cross-cultural competence.

Dr. Michael Winkelman of Arizona State University, provides a clear and comprehensive treatment of cultural awareness, sensitivity and competence necessary for the helping professions. Through a number of models and presentation of cross-cultural work issues in the professional areas of social work education, social work in schools, health services, public health, child welfare, and criminal justice this book provides the reader with a detailed understanding of the content, skills and knowledge necessary for cultural competence. Dr. Winkelman's own cross-cultural competence is reflected in his skillful entry in to the world of social work and the helping professions. His insightful analysis of how we practice is articulated throughout a host of settings. This is indeed a textbook that students, faculty and practitioners will return to often as they work with a multitude of cultural groups which enrich and provide a vibrant tapestry for our important work.

PREFACE

Today we live in societies characterized by cultural pluralism— the existence of different cultures living side by side. This cultural pluralism makes the dynamics of interpersonal relations more challenging, requiring that we learn how to relate effectively to people who may behave, think and feel differently from our own personal and cultural expectations. The necessity of relating effectively to people of other cultural groups increases the difficulties in client relations for the many different helping professions— social workers, doctors and nurses, psychologists and counselors, educators, and many others.

This book provides the basis conceptual frameworks for understanding people of other cultures and working effectively with them. Perspectives from anthropology, communication, psychology, sociology, cross-cultural medicine and education are integrated to provide guidelines for engaging in the processes of self-assessment and personal development necessary to be culturally competent.

This text is designed to help move the individual from cultural embeddedness— a normal ethnocentrism— towards appreciation of the importance of understanding and working with the perspectives of people from other cultures. The self-assessments, exercises and text material is designed to set you on a course of moving towards cultural awareness, developing cultural sensitivity, and understanding the bases from which you may develop cross-cultural competence.

The need for people to develop these cultural skills is becoming increasingly apparent within our society and around the world. All too often cultural differences create insurmountable barriers to effective social and political relations. Most humans are trapped in a "cultural encapsulation" in which they are unable to understand others points of view and work effectively with them. This text is designed to help you begin to overcome these limitation and move towards being a culturally competent global citizen.

CULTURAL AWARENESS, SENSITIVITY AND COMPETENCE

TABLE OF CONTENTS

Chapter 3

Culture, Biology and Socialization: The Psychocultural Model 60

Chapter 4

Cultural Systems Models 100

CHAPTER 1

CULTURAL COMPETENCE IN THE HELPING PROFESSIONS

Overview

This chapter explains why practitioners in social service, health, educational and other helping professions must address the roles culture and ethnicity play in their work. Culture is examined in relation to the overall functions, skills and competencies of helping professionals and the specific requirements of generalist social work practice. The cultural competencies required of helping professionals are illustrated through a review of the knowledge base required. The role of culture and cultural perspectives is examined in terms of cultural strengths perspectives, cultural systems approaches and the cultural sensitivity and competence required for professional effectiveness. The reader is provided with an opportunity to assess his/her cultural sensitivity and development of cross-cultural competence. Distinctions among different degrees of cultural sensitivity and competence are introduced, along with their personal, interpersonal and organizational benefits.

Objectives

Explain the role culture competence plays in the helping professions
Illustrate the social skills and cultural competencies required of helping professionals
Describe the benefits of cultural strengths perspectives and cultural systems approaches
Engage the reader in self-assessment of his/her preparedness for cultural sensitivity and competence
Introduce the overall aspects of development of increased cultural sensitivity and competence
Present the personal, interpersonal and organizational benefits of cultural sensitivity

Chapter Outline

Introduction: Understanding Cultural Diversity
Culture in Generalist Social Work Practice and the "Helping Professions"
    Culture in the Process-Stage Approach
    Strengths Perspectives and Cultural Sensitivity
        Cultural Systems Perspectives
Cross-Cultural Awareness, Sensitivity, Competence and Proficiency
Aspects of Cultural Competence Capacities and Development
Cross-Cultural Learning and Training
    Benefits of Cross-Cultural Skills and Cultural Knowledge
Overview of the Text
    Basic Conceptual Distinctions for Culturally Pluralistic Societies
References and Additional Readings
Self-Assessment 1.1: Cross-Cultural Adaptation
Self-Assessment 1.2: Culture and Personal Style
Self-Assessment 1.3: Social Interaction Styles

INTRODUCTION: UNDERSTANDING CULTURAL DIVERSITY

The U.S. has experienced increasing interest in its cultural pluralism in recent years, a diversity of cultures that makes personal, social and institutional relations more complex and challenging. Cross-cultural difficulties are particularly prevalent in the "helping professions" — social work, psychology, education, nursing, medicine and other human services. Cultural differences play a part in the effectiveness and quality of client interactions, making the development of cultural competency a professional responsibility. Members of ethnic minority groups experience conflicts, misunderstanding and alienation in relationships with social service institutions, creating additional challenges for helping professionals. The reality of cultural pluralism means helping professionals need to develop intercultural relations skills and adapt culture-specific approaches sensitive to client background. Cultural sensitivity and competence require personal adaptations to manage the challenge of cultural differences and develop intercultural relations skills to provide professional services in spite of ethnic and cultural differences.

Cultural pluralism has been an ignored reality of the U.S., in spite of the fact that the coexistence of distinct ethnic groups has been a characteristic of this country since its colonial period (Winkelman 1998). U.S. political and social philosophies have been dominated by a "melting pot" ideology that has insisted diverse immigrants would lose their distinctive culture and "melt" into the Anglo Saxon Protestant European culture. In contrast to this ideology is the persistent reality of diverse ethnic groups. The culturally pluralistic nature of U.S. society is more appropriately characterized as an obviously diverse "Salad Bowl" rather than an undifferentiated "Melting Pot." The melting pot ideology demanded assimilation while simultaneously discriminating against some ethnic groups, thereby maintaining social boundaries and denying certain groups access to assimilation and resources.

Although there has been an increased concern with the issues specific to ethnic minority groups, the helping professions have been slow to address these issues within the professional curriculum. Lum (1996) points out the lack of cultural, multicultural and ethnic material in social work practice texts, leaving students with inadequate information on how to develop intercultural skills and knowledge. Basic texts on social work practice emphasize the need to develop a variety of skills and knowledge relevant to working with minority individuals and communities. The Council on Social Work Education requires curriculum content addressing the differences among the populations served, specifically the use of assessment processes and intervention skills appropriate to clients' cultural backgrounds. The new generations of social work practice texts have brought ethnic issues into focus. But the new generation of social work texts recognizing the need for cross-cultural training has not provided the material necessary for learning how to develop cultural competence.

This book contributes to the development of cultural competence in client relations by addressing generic issues affecting helping professionals and others involved in understanding and effectively managing cross-cultural differences. Working with cultural difference is essential in all of the helping professions and life in general in culturally pluralistic societies. This makes cultural foci central to assessment and the identification and implementation of appropriate cultural interventions that utilize client strengths. Cross-cultural perspectives and skills are necessary to meet the professional obligations of social workers and other helping professionals, augmenting the traditional approaches by providing broader and more inclusive models for addressing the role of culture in professional-client relationships.

A central purpose of this text is to provide educational material relevant to developing intercultural skills and the cultural knowledge necessary for learning how to develop a culturally sensitive practice. Developing cross-cultural competence requires many kinds of knowledge, including knowledge of the cultural nature of self and others and the roles of culture in human development, behavior, communication and understanding. A foundation for culturally sensitive and competent approaches requires understanding of:

* Cultural determinants of human development, behavior and personality;
* Individual and group dynamics of intergroup relations;
* Cultural systems perspectives on the influences affecting relations of providers and clients; and
* Professional skills for adapting to cultural differences.

Cultural understandings include knowledge of many aspects of culture: socialization influences from community and the wider society; ethnic group history and its effect on the present; population characteristics; family and community organization; macro-level social and economic effects upon behavior; communication and behavioral interaction patterns; value and belief systems; non-conscious influences on self and behavior; cognitive and affective influences upon behavior; and world views.

This text provides guidelines for incorporating culturally aware, sensitive and competent approaches into the education and practice of those in social work and other helping professions. The present work rejects the deficit approaches often taken in addressing cultural pluralism, instead emphasizing the skills that make cultural pluralism an asset and benefit. Cultural perspectives focused on cultural strengths help overcome the historical psychoanalytic and sociological perspectives in social work theory and practice that traditionally viewed cultural differences in terms of pathology and deviance. Cultural perspectives provide the basis for a cultural awareness and competency approach in which one learns about cultural resources and the processes of intergroup relations and develops skills for addressing the difficulties presented by cultural differences.

This text teaches intercultural adaptation skills and perspectives, facilitating personal movement from a natural ethnocentric cultural embeddedness towards ethnorelative perspectives based upon knowledge of and effective adaptation to other cultures. Cross-cultural approaches provide a basis for integrating multiple perspectives, creating a cross-cultural synergism that enriches the possibilities for all involved. Cross-cultural perspectives and intercultural relations skills provide a basis for continually adapting professional practice to achieve intercultural effectiveness. The material in this book helps bridge the gap between professional cultures and ethnic cultures by providing an understanding of the general dynamics of culture and intercultural relations. The primary foci addressed are:

* The nature of race, ethnicity and culture;
* The effects of culture upon human development and differences;
* Understanding cultural systems and the psychocultural dynamics of ethnicity;
* The dynamics of intergroup relations; and
* Assessing personal development for cross-cultural competency and adaptation.

Addressing cultural differences and developing ethnic sensitivity and competence is not merely an issue for providers' relations with their clients. The increasing diversity of society and work produces cultural differences among social workers and organizations, making cross-cultural assessments and development an essential element of effective staff relations in agencies and organizations. This book contributes to the development of culturally sensitive social work practice by addressing generic barriers to cross-cultural awareness and the adaptation and learning processes involved in the development of the cultural sensitivity and competence. Culture needs to be central to assessment, collaboration to utilize client strengths and identifying and implementing appropriate cultural interventions to ameliorate environmental conditions producing individual and collective problems. Helping professionals can use this material to assess their cross-cultural skills and increase the perspectives necessary for developing culturally sensitive task-centered and problem-solving interventions at both individual and institutional levels.

CULTURE IN GENERALIST SOCIAL WORK PRACTICE AND THE "HELPING PROFESSIONS"

The helping professions face common concerns in addressing how individual well being is produced in relationship to the "environment." This "environment" is not merely physical, but fundamentally cultural, which includes economic, familial, community, class, political and religious dimensions, and their effects upon the physical environment. The classic bases for addressing culture in social work practice was addressed in an article by Bartlett (1958, republished 2003), "Working Definition of Social Work Practice," in which she described the many dimensions of the cultural environment that must be addressed to assure healthy functioning. Bartlett further developed the focus upon the environment in her book *The Common Base of Social Work Practice* (1970). Social work addresses the interdependence between the person and the environment in social functioning, providing the foundation for the person-in-environment model that characterizes social work today. Bartlett also characterized social work as depending upon values, purposes, knowledge, methods and perspectives provided by other social science disciplines, including anthropology, psychology and sociology.

The social skills and cultural competencies required of social workers are illustrated in Bartlett's consideration of the areas of knowledge about humans and their societies and cultures (summarized and paraphrased from Bartlett 2003:269):

1) Economic, social, cultural and interpersonal influences upon human development
2) The social psychology of providing and receiving help
3) Patterns of expression, especially feeling and non-verbal communication
4) The effects of group processes upon individuals
5) The effects of cultural heritage, especially religious and spiritual beliefs
6) The interactional processes of groups
7) The internal processes of communities, including their social resources
8) Social service resources and their organization and procedures
9) The practitioner's awareness of how emotions and attitudes affect relations with others.

Bartlett's nine points involve five broad categories related to culture and social relations:

1) Socialization processes (1, 5)
2) Cultural Self-awareness (1, 9)
3) Cultural systems (7, 8)
4) Interpersonal and group dynamics (2, 3, 4, 6)
5) Social work organization and culture (7, 8).

The effectiveness of the considerations that Bartlett offered for social work and the other helping professions has been recently examined (see *Research on Social Work Practice* 13(3):2003). Some limitations in Bartlett's classic considerations reflect substantial changes in society in the ensuing decades. Nonetheless, the basic conceptualizations offered by Bartlett have withstood the test of time and will continue to guide the profession as they are extended to address new complexities produced by in multicultural societies. The increasing awareness of cultural diversity in the U.S. means that social workers also need to develop knowledge of the culture of a variety of ethnic groups, and effectively deal with cultural differences (see Risler, Lowe & Nackerud 2003). The helping professions increasingly are addressing cultural differences between providers and clients. This increased focus on cultural differences and emphasis on cultural awareness, responsiveness, sensitivity and competence in understanding and responding to client cultures. A focus upon cultural differences has highlighted the importance of understanding culture itself, as well as the numerous levels of social life through which cultural influences are manifested.

The focus on the individual emphasized in Bartlett's concerns is now seen as too limiting to address the communal dimension of well being and the stronger emphasis on interdependence emphasized in many cultures. The person-in-environment model has been refined to include an emphasis on the particulars of a person's "situation," understanding the individual's circumstances within the broader sociocultural environment. This interdependence leads to a greater emphasis on a systems approach in addressing the multiple social and cultural determinants of human health and social functioning. Human needs are not merely biologically determined, but are also produced and shaped by culture. The focus on the individual so prevalent in Western society has to be expanded in the helping professions to a focus on changing the social environment to assure that the needs of individuals, as well as groups and communities, are met to assure healthy functioning. This means that a greater emphasis needs to be placed upon understanding cultural systems and how they change (Risler, Lowe & Nackerud 2003). Understanding person-in-environment requires an appreciation of cultural systems and societies, through the determination of answers to questions, such as: What are they? How are they organized and structured? What are their components? Answers to these kinds of questions illuminate the dynamics of the individual in situation in environment.

Recognition that effects upon the individuals may derive from environments and personal situations has required an increased focus upon how individuals can change their situations and environments. This emphasis has given greater importance to the empowerment of the individual, refocusing the classic approach in which the helping professional is seen as providing the focus for initiating change. Helping professionals need to give greater attention to how to help the individual client manage the environmental and situational forces that affect well being. This means the helping professionals need a good understanding of community organization and dynamics. The ability to resolve clients' problems is increasingly dependent upon the practitioner's ability to address economic, political and other social factors that impact well being.

Sallee (2003) review the competencies of generalist social work practice, illustrating their roles in enabling the helping professional to:

* Affect relationships between people and social institutions;
* Assess problems and determine available options;
* Enhance coping and problem-solving capacities;
* Link people to resources and services;
* Intervene effectively on behalf of vulnerable populations;
* Promote effective and humane operation of services;
* Improve organizations to make them responsive to consumers.

These competencies are dependent upon the social worker's ability to place the consumers' concerns within a multiple-level system; acquire relevant information and analyze it to develop and implement an intervention; understand other cultures' perspectives; develop cultural sensitivity and competence; and work with groups in producing effective change for clients by re-integrating them into the resources of their own cultures and communities.

Sallee (2003:354) illustrated the range of skills that underlie the competencies of a generalist in regard to knowledge required of the client's culture. These skills include:

---

* Addressing problems from the perspectives of the client's strengths;
* Building partnerships with clients and their families and other community groups and services;
* Understanding, respecting and practicing within the client's cultural system;
* Being knowledgeable and respectful of and sensitive and responsive to the client's culture;
* Providing services based upon a commitment to the client's cultural system and working within that environment; and
* Empowering clients through partnerships that incorporate their families, groups and communities, building upon natural support systems.

Culture in the Process-Stage Approach

The elements of the classic social work process-stage approach — problem background knowledge, problem identification and assessment, development of intervention plans and termination — are all based in culture. Culture frames what clients view as problems, the environment within which the client's behavior should be assessed and the resources that can be utilized for intervention.

Social workers' preparation for involvement with clients is basically a cultural assessment, focusing upon understanding the community and identifying the cultural structures and elements. These aspects of the community profile include: historical and geographic features; demographic characteristics; the technological and economic infrastructure; family organization and roles; class influences; social institutions and their relations to family and community life; and patterns of feeling, thinking and behaving. This range of

factors is part of the broader psychocultural model presented in Chapter 3.

Identifying the problem requires both culturally sensitive social interaction skills, as well as understanding the clients' circumstances within their culture's perspective. Social interaction patterns involve a range of behaviors, including communication styles, interpersonal space, self-disclosure norms, eye contact and a wide range of other social rules. The ability to interpret cultural behaviors accurately is essential for engaging the client. Cultural perspectives on the presumptive problem are central for identifying the actual source of the difficulties and decentering the personal biases of the social worker and those of the social work institutions and broader society, which focus on individual responsibility. Cultural systems perspectives help to identify the systemic external social factors that create the focal problem and its consequences for the individual.

Resolving problems requires an understanding of the client's perspective on the putative problem and the realistic and acceptable solutions from the perspective of the individual and his/her social group. Plans to resolve problems are likely to be unsuccessful if the client and his/her cultural group do not consider them appropriate. A final resolution of the problem and termination of the encounter must consider not only agency goals, but must also include cultural concerns and the continued relationship between client and community.

Strengths Perspectives and Cultural Sensitivity

A culturally sensitive approach to social work practice is exemplified in the strengths perspective (see Cowger 1994; Saleebey 1996), which has been developed to replace the traditional social work approaches focused upon client dysfunction. Rejecting the traditional notions of deficit and pathology, the strengths perspective emphasizes addressing client problems by focusing upon the personal strengths and cultural resources that can assist in enhancing life opportunities. The strengths approach focuses upon the client's cultural system and its goals and values, building a helping relationship based upon mutual respect and collaboration. A key focus of the strengths approach is upon social empowerment, understanding clients' personal and environmental context to assist them in gaining control over their lives and choices. This requires knowledge of the cultural dimensions of their lives and their relationships and access to resources of the broader society.

The strengths perspective necessarily embodies advocacy, since it requires that the client be assisted in addressing the consequences of the inequitable distribution of societal resources. Compensating for inequality requires not only removing social barriers to access but also focus it upon resources within their cultural system that may be used to empower people. This focus upon strengths must, by necessity, consider cultural resources and traditions that give people meaning and organization to their lives. This cultural focus strengthens people's sense of community, a necessary component of healthy psychological functioning. Strengths perspectives must focus upon the integration of individuals within their communities, a significant aspect of the emotional life of individuals and an important aspect of overall well being. This connection of individual and community is an inherently empowering process.

The guidelines Cowger (1994) suggests for strengths perspectives are largely focused upon cultural understandings. These include the client's perspectives or "understanding of facts" and his/her wants. Their personal and environmental strengths are largely derived from family and kinship networks, other significant relationships in their immediate community and social lives, as well as a variety of community organizations. Planning with the client and making assessments and goals a joint activity based in mutual agreement helps reinforce the empowerment of the individual at personal and cultural levels. By explicitly incorporating the client's goals and desires, the social worker can enhance client motivation for change within a culturally relevant framework. This collaborative relationship creates an investment on the part of the client This perspective also enhances the development of

realistic plans by assuring that the client's culturally based objectives and willingness to change are incorporated within the goals.

Helping professionals have been primarily concerned with micro-level interventions; factors affecting the relationship of the individual to the macro-level institutions are also crucial to assure that institutions are responsive to individual and community needs. The meso-level focus on interaction between levels requires knowledge of both ethnic community institutions and the macro-level institutions of the broader society. Respect of clients is central to the helping relations. Respect requires knowledge and understanding of the client's cultural systems and the client's perspectives and conditions. Knowledge of cultural structures and processes is essential for the effectiveness of helping relationships; ignorance of cultural dynamics places any intervention at risk of failure, and the client at a disadvantage because of inappropriate and insensitive services. Effectiveness in the helping process requires adaptation to culturally specific help-seeking patterns.

In addition to the traditional social work practice skills, a culturally sensitive approach and culturally competent practice requires a range of skills and knowledge. Devore and Schlesinger (1991) provide a model for ethnically sensitive social work practice which emphasizes the interaction of "layers of understanding," the problem solving endeavor of social work and its professional values and the ethnic realities. These ethnically sensitive skills and knowledge include:

---

* Knowledge of determinants of human behavior, especially the impact of culture;
* Human life cycle development, social roles and personality;
* Self-awareness of one's own cultural influences;
* An awareness of the cultural values of the social work profession;
* A positive valuation of cultural diversity;

(continued)

* Openness to learning about cultural differences;
* Knowledge of characteristics of cultural groups;
* Understanding of cultural subsystems (e.g., family, work, community, etc.);
* The ability to access community resources;
* Understanding of immediate and distant influences upon clients' behaviors;
* Recognition of the influences of cultural perceptions, values and priorities on behavior and self-concepts; and
* An ability to adapt social work skills to clients' culturally specific needs.

Effective social work practice requires the integration of knowledge about the cultural lifestyle and social class influences upon ethnic groups. This involves the integration of the traditional sociological and psychological approaches within cultural perspectives in assessment and intervention processes. While culture is only one of many influences upon individual behavior, other major influences (e.g., age, sex, education, occupation, family status, etc.) are themselves mediated by cultural influences. Understanding cultural reality is essential for culturally sensitive practice because culture is the matrix within which individuals develop their beliefs, values, motivations, life and work orientations, coping styles and identity. A central aspect of this cultural reality is created in family and community, where language and tradition provide influences on individual identity and self-concept. Family and community contexts provide the most significant influences on client perceptions and definitions of problems; and the keys to change are located within the family and community.

Cultural competence requires cultural self-awareness, skills in intercultural relations and knowledge about cultural groups served. Cultural self-awareness includes recognition of one's own cultural influences upon values, beliefs and judgments, as well as the influences derived from the professional's work culture. Awareness of the effects of these personal and professional influences upon client relations is necessary for developing a culturally sensitive approach. Without self-awareness, biases will be unconsciously imposed and client self-determination will be compromised. The commitment of the social work profession to equal treatment of all groups requires an approach which is not "color blind," but, rather, is sensitive to the particular situations of each individual, including the impact of the client's culture upon their lives. Developing culturally competent professional services begins with assessments of one's cross-cultural knowledge, beliefs, attitudes, skills and experiences.

Cultural Systems Perspectives

Social work and the other helping professions address cultural knowledge with general systems perspectives. These cultural systems approaches, reflected in the "biopsychosocial" perspective, provide a broad framework for addressing the many different factors that affect behavior and affect the social worker's ability to understand the person-in-situation. These cultural systems perspectives are derived from ecological approaches that have conceptualized the environment broadly in terms of relationships among family, community, work place, other formal organizations and the broader social systems.

Cultural systems perspectives enhance the approaches of helping professionals by providing models for linking the individual and his/her behavior to the adaptation to numerous environments. The wide range of contributory influences on conditions emphasizes that problems occur in relationship to broader environments. This cultural perspective is expanded in the psychocultural model (Whiting & Whiting 1975), used in Chapter 3 as a central organizing perspective for knowledge about both ethnic cultural realities and the broader systems that have effects upon them (see also Chapter 4). Human behavior is influenced by many factors, including the material, social and ideological environments.

Cultural systems approaches provide important correctives, avoiding the deficit, pathology and deviance approaches characteristic of earlier models. This helps change traditional views of the problems associated with ethnic group. In contrast to the perspectives of pathology and deviance, the psychocultural approach explicitly recognizes the causal influences in structural factors from the broader society's social and physical environments. The psychocultural and cultural systems perspectives provide the structural context for identifying important influences for solving problems, particularly cultural coping processes that reinforce cultural strengths perspectives. Systems perspectives help in overcoming the "blaming the victim" approach inherent in psychoanalytic and deviance approaches within the justice system, instead locating the problem in the interdependent relations between the individual and numerous cultural and social influences. This enables development of more appropriate intervention strategies that address the numerous subsystems that affect the client and his/her behaviors and opportunities.

CROSS-CULTURAL AWARENESS, SENSITIVITY, COMPETENCE AND PROFICIENCY

Understanding what is necessary to manage effectively cultural differences has evolved from recognition of the importance of awareness of other cultures to a realization that more sophisticated skills are necessary. The need for a culturally sensitive approach requires that helping professionals assess their own competencies to determine areas of needed development. A self-assessment is provided here for readers to assess their intercultural attitudes, beliefs, behaviors and accomplishments (see "Self-Assessment 1.1: Cross-Cultural Development").

Mere awareness of other cultures needs to be supplemented with knowledge of cultural patterns of behavior and how to effectively adapt to them. Knowledge of culture and intercultural processes and a range of intercultural skills are also necessary to effectively manage cultural differences. Cultural competence involves personal, interpersonal and organization skills that enable people to work effectively with the various cultural groups they serve. Cultural competence includes behaviors, attitudes and policies that effectively address cultural effects, overcoming cultural differences through employment of intercultural skills (Chin 2000). Cultural competency has three major dimensions:

1) Knowledge of the general dynamics of culture and cross-cultural relations;
2) Skills in intercultural adaptation and relations; and
3) Culture specific knowledge of behaviors and beliefs of specific groups.

The ability to deal effectively with cultural issues in clinical settings can be conceptualized in terms of a three-factor model involving capacity level, specialty area and specific cultural groups (Castro 1998). Cultural capacity levels range from destructiveness (ethnocentrism), incapacity and blindness, through cultural sensitivity, competence and proficiency. Cultural sensitivity portrays an awareness of cultural differences and a response to them, while competence involves the capability to deal with cultural references effectively. Proficiency involves the ability to transfer cross-cultural knowledge and skills to others.

An individual's cross-cultural development and capacities vary across specialty areas (e.g., assessment, intervention and research), across different ethnic groups and even within ethnic groups (e.g., one may be competent in relations with younger Mexican Americans but lack sensitivity in dealing with elderly Mexican Americans). General cultural competency involves recognition of the impacts of culture on the clinical encounter and an ability to apply cultural knowledge, cultural resources (e.g., translators, interpreters), intercultural skills and reflective thinking to resolve difficulties presented by cultural differences. Intercultural competency is an aspect of general cultural competency, an awareness of the dynamics of cross-cultural interactions and the ability to adopt perspectives that facilitate those interactions. These generic skills include a perspective of cultural relativism and conflict resolution and cross-cultural negotiation skills. Specific cultural competencies refer to relational abilities in regard to particular cultural groups (e.g., Mexican Americans). Specific cultural competencies require long periods of time to develop and are generally beyond the reach of providers unless they are native members of the culture or have spent long periods of time engaged with the culture in both professional relations and everyday life. Providers are generally more likely to learn how to incorporate aspects of cultural knowledge into culturally aware or sensitive care rather than develop true cultural competency and proficiency.

Hogan-Garcia (1999) emphasizes addressing barriers to cultural competency at personal, interpersonal and organizational levels.

Overcoming these three barriers requires a cultural systems approach, cultural self-awareness and insider perspectives on other cultures' orientations. Effectively adapting to other cultures requires use of knowledge of cultural influences and an awareness of common barriers to effective intercultural relations and communication. Effective adaptation involves the use of knowledge and interpersonal skills to overcome cultural conflicts and barriers through an integration of knowledge of intercultural dynamics with persons and self-awareness.

Cultural awareness and sensitivity involves adaptation to other cultures through knowledge of specific cultural information and the ability to address general barriers to effective cross-cultural relations. Cultural competence involves greater personal skills that enable people to work effectively with other cultural groups. Cultural competence is viewed as including behaviors, attitudes and policies that effectively address cultural differences and provide intercultural skills

---

Aspects of Cultural Competence Capacities and Development

Three Factors in Cultural Capacity (adapted from Castro 1998)
Capacity Level
Specialty Area
Specific (Sub)Cultures

Capacity Levels
Ethnocentric — Ignorance of and dislike of other groups
Contact — Initial learning leading to development or withdrawal
Awareness — Recognition of importance of cultural differences
Acceptance — Appreciation of differences of other cultures
Sensitivity — Capable of culturally appropriate behaviors
Competence — Works effectively with other cultures
Proficiency — Capable of teaching cultural competence to others

Specialty Areas
Clinical Care
Community Intervention
Teaching
Research
Management

(Chin 2000). Many authors (e.g., Hogan-Garcia 1999; Chin 2000; Chrisman & Zimmer 2000) who examine cultural competence in clinical skills coincide in emphasizing the importance of personal, interpersonal and organizational levels of competence:

---

* Personal, including cultural self-awareness and cross-cultural adaptation skills;
* Interpersonal, particularly, clinical skills and intercultural relations abilities; and
* Knowledge of cultural systems and organizational culture and their impacts on behavior.

CROSS-CULTURAL LEARNING AND TRAINING

The fundamental concept for developing effective intercultural relations is culture, which represents the learning fundamentally responsible for human behavior, particularly its variations between groups. Culture shapes or determines virtually everything that characterizes us human beings — our thoughts, feelings, beliefs, behavior, communication, etc. Understanding ethnic groups and their patterns of behavior requires an appreciation of the nature of cultural influences upon behavior. Realization of cultural effects is necessary for developing greater tolerance of those who are culturally different and acquiring a basis for adapting to them through developing new perspectives appropriate for understanding culturally different others. An ability to successfully negotiate the more complex relations created by a culturally pluralistic U.S. society and world is necessary today. The internationalization of economy and politics and the "global village," combined with changing demographic trends, means that there is no escaping cross-cultural relations in the world today. Success requires that we understand our own cultural attitudes and

beliefs, and acquire skills for more effectively addressing cross-cultural relations.

But how we should address this reality remains a conflictive issue, and the rhetoric often leaves the mistaken impression that there are no established ways to adapt to intercultural relations. There are empirical bases for cross-cultural education and intercultural effectiveness. Anthropology and cross-cultural communication studies provide a body of experiences, knowledge and perspectives about intercultural relations and cross-cultural understandings. These cross-cultural understandings provide perspectives that can help move management of ethnic and cultural differences from a controversial "politically correct" education to a basis from which to develop cross-cultural skills and knowledge. Anthropological concepts such as culture, ethnicity, race, inheritance, enculturation, socialization and acculturation, as well as understandings of the processes of cross-cultural adaptation, provide essential perspectives for intercultural relations and adaptation to a culturally pluralistic society. Cross-cultural adaptation requires the use of both general cultural orientations to generic aspects of cross-cultural contact and specific cultural orientations to the features of contemporary cultures. Successful cross-cultural training must combine a variety of methods in order to integrate new cultural self-awareness; modify attitudes, beliefs and feelings; and achieve behavioral changes.

Knowledge about the nature of intercultural relations and means for establishing cross-cultural skills are necessary to achieve ethnically sensitive relations. A social learning approach that combines cognitive and behavioral strategies is necessary for developing cross-cultural competency. A cognitive orientation directs one towards successful adaptation strategies, and behavioral skills provide for effective personal and social relations. Acquisition of cross-cultural skills and competencies requires a number of forms of cross-cultural learning. Cognitive and "classroom" learning is a necessary but inadequate basis for establishing competent interactions with people in other cultures.

Effective cross-cultural training requires many forms of learning, including cognitive, emotional and behavioral components. Development of cross-cultural capabilities involves forms of resocialization requiring direct social interaction and new social relations for learning and support; new reference groups for modeling behavior and self; an altered social identity and new social roles; and new cultural knowledge, attitudes and perceptions. These learned abilities are acquired through cross-cultural orientations that teach more effective ways to relate to people of other cultures. They involve both general cultural orientations to the general intercultural dynamics involved in cross-cultural interaction and adaptation; as well as specific cultural orientations to the nature of individual cultures.

A general cross-cultural orientation covers the general dynamics of intercultural interactions, providing perspectives for developing productive and less-stressful relations with members of different cultures by understanding the dynamics of cross-cultural contact and adaptation. This book provides an introduction to the cognitive aspects of a general cross-cultural orientation. A central aspect of general cross-cultural orientation is an understanding of the culturally relative nature of beliefs and behavior. This perspective provides a basis for acceptance of other cultures as meaningful and rational. Another important aspect is development of cultural self-awareness, particularly of one's values, prejudices and beliefs. Effective intercultural relations require an awareness of one's cultural biases that can block acceptance and understanding of other cultures. Specific cross-cultural orientations provide information about a particular culture, region or ethnic group, covering information such as the group's history, cultural system, normative social behavior, politics, beliefs and other information necessary for successful adaptation to interpersonal interaction with people from that culture. The companion to this text provides specific cross-cultural orientations to major U.S. ethnic groups.

A wide range of methods and procedures are employed in training people for cross-cultural

interaction. These include cognitive instruction from books and lectures; self-assessments of values, communications styles, relational modes and other aspects of social interaction patterns; behavioral practice in alternate patterns of behavior; and structured exercises and interaction to process cross-cultural experiences and analyze them for future use. While human relations or sensitivity training approaches are also useful, used alone, without appropriate support and debriefing, they can create stress and psychological breakdown through the elicitation of previous traumatic and unresolved experiences. Although sensitivity training can provide insight, it does not necessarily lead to development of appropriate understandings and skills. A combination of many methods is necessary to integrate cognitive and experiential learning, to access feelings and unconscious cultural values and attitudes without provoking psychological crises, and to process this information for effective adaptation to cross-cultural environments. A number of complementary methods have been developed to deal with the need for intercultural training, among them self-awareness inventories; contrast American exercises; cultural assimilator or critical incident activities; case studies; and role playing and simulations (see publications from the Intercultural Press for guidelines for such training). Effective intercultural training must combine a variety of these methods: exposure to culturally different individuals, discussion of reactions to cross-cultural encounters, practice of intercultural adaptation skills and engaging in culturally specific forms of behavior and communication. Ultimately, ethnically sensitive skills and cross-cultural competence only come through immersion and functioning in other cultural groups.

Benefits of Cross-Cultural Skills and Cultural Knowledge

Success in learning about and adaptation to other cultures provides a number of advantages, enhancing the well being of providers and their clients and the effectiveness of their institutions.

Benefits include:

Personal
* Increased awareness of unconscious cultural influences on one's behavior;
* Reduced stress through better adaptation to cultural differences;
* Reduced provider frustration and burnout, and enhanced coping;
* Expanded options for our own lives and behaviors;
* Enhanced appreciation of the value of cultural diversity;
* Enhanced understanding of non-verbal communication; and
* Better relations with clients.

Client and Community Relations
* Reduction of conflict and misunderstandings;
* More effective communication with clients;
* More client disclosure and cooperation;
* Better recognition of client psychocultural dynamics and conflicts;
* Appreciation of sociocultural and other environmental effects upon clients;
* Better understanding of client problems and community needs;
* Enhanced service delivery to clients and communities;
* More effective management and overcoming of client resistance;
* Reduced client dissatisfaction, non-compliance and withdrawal/dropout;
* More appropriate assessment, problem solving and development of goals and objectives; and
* Enhanced empowerment.

Agency Operations
* Better adapted agency goals and practices to facilitate effectiveness of service delivery;
* More effective outreach;
* Better utilization of agency and community resources;
* Better community support; and
* Reduced time to termination.

OVERVIEW OF THE TEXT

The text is organized to address the major understandings of culture required for cultural awareness and sensitivity in social work and other helping professions. The information provided in this book will neither make you culturally competent nor inform you about how to address specific clients. Rather, it provides general information about the nature of cross-cultural differences and the successful approaches for developing cross-cultural competence. Applying them to achieve such competence is up to you.

Chapter 2, "Race and Ethnicity" introduces and addresses the concepts of race, ethnicity and culture, showing the inadequacy of race as a biological or scientific construct and its inability to explain intergroup differences. The concept of ethnicity, focused upon cultural identity, provides a better perspective for addressing the variable nature of groups and intergroup relations. Different forms of ethnic identity adaptation in multicultural contexts are illustrated.

Chapter 3, "Culture, Biology and Socialization: The Psychocultural Model" illustrates some of the basic relationships between culture and human behavior, examining the relationship of culture to human biology and needs. The socialization of human needs and the range of effects of the socialization process are reviewed, with specific attention to sex and gender, psychosocial and cognitive development and communication and relational styles. The psychocultural model is introduced to illustrate the myriad of cultural and social factors that affect the development of cultural identity and behavior, producing both common group psychodynamics as well as within group variation.

Chapter 4, "Cultural Systems Models" examines the applications of cultural systems models in the helping professions. The intricacies of cultural systems and their effects upon behavior are examined, with a focus on infrastructure, the material aspects of work and economic systems; structure, the social organization established by family, kinship and other groups and intergroup dynamics, particularly ethnic class stratification; and ideological elements, the cultural influences found in language, socialization processes, values, religion and expressive culture.

Chapter 5, "Process Dynamics of Intergroup Relations," <u>examines the structural and process dynamics of intergroup relations, the regular patterns resulting from interaction between cultures</u>. These include cultural conflict and shock; ethnocentrism and other in-group versus out-group dynamics; prejudice and discrimination; attribution processes; segregation and integration; and a variety of individual and group accommodations, including acculturation, assimilation and amalgamation.

Chapter 6, "Cross-Cultural Awareness, Sensitivity and Competence," <u>addresses the general dynamics of cross-cultural development in the context of cultural competence</u>. These developments are placed in the context of relinquishing ethnocentric perspectives and developing perspectives of ethnorelativism that enable better understanding of other cultures and adaptation to them. These changes are discussed in terms of the transformations of the self that occur in the process of becoming bicultural and multicultural.

Chapter 7, "Developing Cross-Cultural Competence," <u>provides a range of specific guidelines for developing cross-cultural perspectives</u> <u>and competence</u>. These include anthropological perspectives of culture, socialization and cultural relativism, as well as a number of specific strategies such as developing self and other cultural awareness; managing emotional reactions, including culture shock; identifying cross-cultural conflict and problem solving; overcoming emotional and personal resistance to change; developing personal and social relations and knowledge of social interaction rules; and developing a multicultural self.

Chapter 8, "Cross-Cultural Work in the Helping Professions," <u>provides an overview of the many areas in which the helping professional must address cultural factors to carry out his/her professional responsibilities competently</u>. These include involvements and applications in areas of education, health services, psychology and child welfare, criminal justice and management and occupational social work.

Basic Conceptual Distinctions for Culturally Pluralistic Societies

The terms society, culture, subculture and ethnicity are similar, yet, for our purposes, they denote some important distinctions. Society refers generally to group patterns of human association. Society is the principles, norms and arrangements that provide order and regularity in human life through the coordination of individuals into groups, based upon a complementary integration of different roles. The organizational structures of societies involve principles that structure groups and their behavior, a system of status and roles, shared norms and values and institutions. A society is typically a geopolitical entity, a recognized sociopolitical organization dominating a geographical region with some degree of self-determination in economic and political spheres. A society may be based on a single cultural group; however, modern world societies tend to represent the linkages of several cultural groups in interdependent relationships. The largest societies are those represented by nation-states, in which generally one cultural group is dominant and imposes its cultural forms upon the institutions and organizations of the society. Most of the nations of the world are characterized by cultural pluralism, a condition in which a society has a number of different cultural groups living together within its boundaries and institutions. Multicultural is used to refer to people who have two or more cultural backgrounds.

The term *culture* refers to group patterns of learned behavior, as well as groups that share these common patterns of behavior. The concept of culture differs from that of race which has mistakenly been thought to be based upon biology (see Chapter 2). Culture also differs from *ethnicity*, which is one's identity with respect to social and cultural reference groups. This distinction between cultural patterns of behavior and ethnicity emphasizes recognition of variation among group members resulting from differing levels of acculturation influences from other groups. A *subculture* refers to a subdivision within a cultural group into a subgroup with some distinctive patterns of learned behavior. Subcultures may result from internal differentiations within a culture (e.g., based upon gender, occupation, class) or from acculturation and assimilation between cultural groups, resulting in partially shared cultural patterns. Some major U.S. ethnic cultures (e.g., Mexican Americans and numerous Native American subcultures) reflect the outcome of acculturation of what were once distinct cultural groups to the influences of the dominant European American society and its cultural patterns. Similarly, the *cultural* influences derived most immediately from one's family and community need to be distinguished from *social* influences derived from the broader society. Cultural and social influences are often confused, as when the social consequences of poverty are mistakenly believed to be a characteristic of a specific culture, or when failure to attain success within the broader society's educational system is misinterpreted to imply that members of a cultural group do not value education.

Cultures are not homogeneous groups with all members the same; rather, cultures have a number of dimensions of variation. Cultures can be conceived as consisting of a number of nested or inclusive levels or organizations with increasingly specialized or exclusive features, ranging from broad national and ethnic cultures to narrower regional, business and occupational levels of culture. A society (i.e., country) may have a national culture with considerable similarity throughout the country, which nonetheless has a variety of regional cultures (e.g., the classical U.S. regional cultures of North and South, or the more recent East Coast and West Coast). The national culture is shared to varying degrees by ethnic cultural groups that have historical origins distinct from the national culture (e.g., Mexican Americans). Within the national culture, and within cross-cutting regional cultures, are a variety of specialized organizational cultures as found in business or professional subcultures. Professionals also have their own culture, exemplified in practices such as medical culture and social work, as well as more specialized occupational cultures (e.g., the cultural practices of physicians versus nurses).

The concept of subcultures is important for social workers and other members of the helping professions. In addition to the widely recognized ethnic subcultures that professionals need to understand, there is also the national culture of the U.S. that has shaped the nature of professional practices, including social work and medicine. Social work practice is based in an organizational subculture, and is differentiated into some specialized subcultures (e.g., the practices of a social worker engaged in probation activities in the criminal justice system as opposed to those of the person working as a clinical social worker). Social workers also have to engage with a variety of other professional subcultures (e.g., correctional systems, physicians, nurses).

In the modern world, a nation and its society generally encompass a number of different cultures. The distinction between society and culture is not just analytic, but empirical and practical as well. Even if a society is created through the power and institutions of a single culture, the specific social grouping or society thus formed includes inputs from and interactions among many different cultures. Modern societies are dependent upon other cultures and social systems, both internally and externally. While a single cultural group may dominate the social and political institutions of these multicultural societies, other cultural groups exist within the society in a variety of conditions: assimilation, accommodation, acculturation, segregation and cultural pluralism. The other cultural groups within the society accommodate to the dominant cultural presence of the other culture, and may become subcultures if, through time, they assimilate major aspects of the dominant culture.

The terms multicultural, cross-cultural, intercultural and culturally pluralistic are often used as if they are synonyms. Cross-cultural and intercultural are used here to refer to interactions or relations between people of different cultural groups.

A variety of intercultural skills are necessary for effectively dealing with cultural differences found in culturally pluralistic societies. The information provided in this book cannot inform you regarding how to interact specifically with any particular client. Rather, it provides general knowledge about the nature of cross-cultural interactions and how to adapt to them more effectively with intercultural skills.

REFERENCES AND ADDITIONAL READINGS

Bennett, M. 1993. Toward Ethnorelativism: A Developmental Model of Intercultural Sensitivity. In: M. Paige, ed. *Education for the Intercultural Experience,* Pp. 21-71. Yarmouth, Maine: Intercultural Press.

Bartlett, H. 2003. Working Definition of Social Work Practice. Research on Social Work Practice. 13(3):267-270. Originally published in *Social Work* 3(2):5-8.

Bartlett, H. 1970. The Common Base of Social Work Practice. New York: National Association of Social Workers.

Castro, F.G. 1998. Cultural Competence Training in Clinical Psychology: Assessment, Clinical Intervention and Research. In: A.S. Bellack and M. Hersen (Eds.), *Comprehensive Clinical Psychology* (10):127-140.

Chin, J. 2000. Viewpoint on cultural competence: Culturally competent health care. *Public Health Reports* 115:25-33.

Chrisman, N. J., and Zimmer, P. A. (2000). Cultural competence in primary care. In: P. V. Meredith and N. M. Horn (eds.), *Adult Primary Care,* pp.65-75. Philadelphia: W.B. Saunders.

Cowger, C.D. 1994. "Assessing Client Strengths: Clinical Assessment for Client Empowerment." *Social Work* 39(3):262-270.

Devore, W. and E. Schlesinger. 1991. *Ethnic-Sensitive Social Work Practice (3rd edition).* New York: Merrill.

Edwards, R., Editor-in-Chief. 1995. *Encyclopedia of Social Work 19th Edition.* Washington, D.C.: National Association of Social Workers Press.

Germain, C. and A. Gitterman 1980. *The Life Model of Social Work Practice.* New York: Columbia University Press.

Hogan Garcia, M. 1999. The Four Skills of Cultural Diversity Competence. U.S.: Brooks/Cole Wadsworth.

Kelley, C. and J. Meyers. 1992. *Cross-Cultural Adaptability Inventory.* Minneapolis: National Computer Systems.

Landon, P. 1995. *Generalist and Advanced Generalist Practice.* In: Edwards *Encyclopedia of Social Work 19th Edition,* pp. 1101-1108. Washington, D.C.: National Association of Social Workers Press.

Lum, D. 1996. *Social Work Practice and People of Color.* Pacific Grove: Brooks/Cole Publishing Co.

Meyer, C. (ed.) 1983. *Clinical Social Work in an Ecosystems Perspective.* New York: Columbia University Press.

Mickelson, J. 1995. *Advocacy.* In: Edwards *Encyclopedia of Social Work 19th Edition,* pp. 95-100. Washington, D.C.: National Association of Social Workers Press.

Paige, M., ed. 1993. *Education for the Intercultural Experience.* Yarmouth, Maine: Intercultural Press.

Risler, E., L. Lowe and L. Nackerud. 2003. Defining Social Work: Does the Working Definition Work Today? *Research on Social Work Practice.* 13(3):299-309.

Sallee, A. 2003. A Generalist Working Definition of Social Work: A Response to Bartlett. *Research on Social Work Practice* 13(3):349-356.

Saleebey, D. 1996. The Strengths Perspective in Social Work Practice: Extensions and Cautions. In: *Social Work* 41(3):296-305.

Whiting, B. and J. Whiting. 1975. *Children of Six Cultures A Psycho-Cultural Analysis*, Cambridge, Mass.: Harvard University Press.

Winkelman, M. 1998. *Ethnic Relations in the U.S.* Dubuque: Eddie Bowers Pub.

NOTES

29. NO/YES   Everyone should have to learn about the cultures of American minority groups.

30. NO/YES   I behave in different ways depending upon whom I am with.

31. NO/YES   Islam is just as moral as Christianity or Buddhism.

32. NO/YES   People who practice animal sacrifice as part of their religion should be put in jail.

33. NO/YES   Cultures in which people eat dogs and cats are really evil.

34. NO/YES   Other cultures' values are as worthy of respect and tolerance as my own values.

35. NO/YES   There are no universal standards for evaluating what is right or wrong.

36. NO/YES   Americans would be better off if we adopted some practices from other cultural groups.

37. NO/YES   In Muslim cultures women should generally appear in public only with their faces covered.

38. NO/YES   I have been able to show that I can view reality from the perspective of another culture.

39. NO/YES   There are many different cultural definitions of reality and morality that are equally valid.

40. NO/YES   It is important to me to be able to speak more than one language.

41. NO/YES   I have incorporated aspects of other cultures into my life and behavior.

42. NO/YES   I have established close friendships with people from other cultures.

43. NO/YES   You can relate better if you know a person's age, racial identity, education and social class.

44. NO/YES   My culture makes me really different from the people with whom I regularly associate.

45. NO/YES   I do not identify with the traditions of my parents and grandparents.

46. NO/YES   I would be embarrassed if my friends found out about the cultural background of my family.

47. NO/YES   I feel like I have a "split personality," that I am a different person at home than I am at work or school.

48. NO/YES   Some aspects of my parents' or grandparents' culture embarrass me.

49. NO/YES   Sometimes I feel like there are two different cultures fighting inside me.

50. NO/YES   I sometimes feel like I am "putting on an act" in order to fit in with others.

51. NO/YES   I feel more comfortable when I am with people from a culture different than my own.

52. NO/YES   I use the language and cultural behaviors in everyday life of groups other than my birth culture.

53. NO/YES   People in another cultural group have "adopted" me, considering me to be their own.

54. NO/YES   I can feel totally comfortable being in a culture different from my birth culture.

55. NO/YES   I can feel like a totally different person when I am with people of a different culture.

56. NO/YES   The way in which I evaluate a situation and behave depends upon who is involved.

57. NO/YES   There is no objectivity; I create my own reality.

58. NO/YES   I do not adhere to the values and beliefs of any one culture.

59. NO/YES   Whether or not something is immoral depends on the situation and who does it.

NOTES

60. NO/YES   Who I am depends upon whom I am with.

61. NO/YES   Clients should be required to use English when seeking social services.

62. NO/YES   Services provided by employees of public agencies should always be provided in "English only."

63. NO/YES   I have an ability to work effectively with clients from a cultural group different from my own.

64. NO/YES   Policies of social work agencies ought to reflect the expectations of the cultural groups they serve.

65. NO/YES   Public agencies should use the same procedures for dealing with clients of all ethnic groups.

66. NO/YES   Public service organizations should be required to hire personnel at all levels of the organization that reflect the ethnicity and culture of the community.

67. NO/YES   I have solicited suggestions from community groups on how to improve my professional practice.

68. NO/YES   Public agencies should support the alternative health services in their communities.

69. NO/YES   Community groups ought to have a say in the policy and practices of social service organizations.

70. NO/YES   Social service agencies should have advisory and review boards that include representatives from all of the major ethnic groups in their service area.

71. NO/YES   Public agencies should translate written materials into the major languages of their community.

72. NO/YES   Social service agencies should provide services in the language most comfortable to their clients.

73. NO/YES   I engage in activities to make sure the rights of minority groups are protected from discrimination.

74. NO/YES   Developing cultural sensitivity in staff is the responsibility of government organizations.

75. NO/YES   I have trained people to use knowledge of culture to understand others, communicate empathy and use relevant skills in working with people from another culture.

NOTES

SELF-ASSESSMENT 1.1

SCORING

For each answer on your self-assessment, assign the value of "0" for No and "1" for Yes. Write the answer (0 or 1) to each question in the space beside the question number. Then add up the totals of your answers for each line, convert your answers where instructed and add the subtotals for an overall score for each scale.

Scale N = N1 + N2 = _____ (N Range = 0 to 12) **Normal/Ethnocentric;** Higher values indicate higher levels of ethnocentrism
N 1 = #1___ +#2___ +#4___ +#5___ +#6___ +#8___ +#9___ +#10___ +#11___ + #12____ = _____(N1)
N 2 = #3___ + #7___ = _____*   *If 0, N2= 2; If 1, N2 = 1; If 2, N2=0   + _____ (N2)
                                                                             = _____ N

Scale U = U1 + U2 = _____ (U Range = 0 to 11) **Universalism;** Higher values indicate universalist assumptions rather than recognition of the importance of cultural principles
U1 = #13___ + #14___ +15___ + #17___ + #19___ + #21___ + #22___ + #23___   = _____ (U1)
U2 = #16___ + #18___ + #20___ = _____*If 0, U2= 3; If 1, U2 = 2; If 2, U2=1; If 3, U2= 0 _____ (U2)
                                                                             = _____ U

Scale AC = B + V = _____ (AC Range 0 to 12) **Acceptance;** Higher values indicate higher levels of acceptance of other cultures
B1 = #24___ + #25___ + #26___ + #29___ + #30___   = _____ (B1)
B2 = #27___ + #28___* *If 0, B2= 2; If 1, B2 = 1; If 2, B2=0   + _____ (B2)
V1 = #31___ + #34___ + #35___ =   + _____ (V1)
V2 = - #32___ + #33___* *If 0, V2= 2; If 1, V2 = 1; If 2, V2=0   + _____ (V2)
                                                                             = _____ AC

Scale AD = E + P = _____ (AD Range 0 to 8) **Adaptation;** Higher values indicate higher levels of adaptation to other cultures
E = #36___ + #37___ + #38___ + #39___   = _____ E
P = #40___ + #41___ + #42___ + #43___   = + _____ P
                                                                             = _____ AD

Scale M = _____ (M Range 0 to 8) **Marginalized;** Higher values indicate higher levels of experiencing a *marginalized* biculturalism
M = #44___ + #45___ + #46___ + #47___ + #48___ + #49___ + #50___ + #51___   = _____ M

Scale B = B1 + M = _____ (B Range 0 to 12) **Bicultural;** Higher values indicate higher levels of biculturalism
B1 = #52___ + #53___ + #54___ + #55   = _____ (B1)
                                                                             + _____ (M)
                                                                             = _____ B

Scale I = _____ (I Range 0 to 5) **Integrated;** Higher values indicate higher levels of ethnorelativism
I = #56___ + #57___ + #58___ + #59___ + #60___   = _____ I

Scale C = C1 + C2 + I = _____ (P Range 0 - 10) **Cultural Competence;** Higher values indicate higher levels of cultural competence
C1 = #63___ + #64___   = _____ (C1)
C2 = #61 + #62 + #65___* *If 0, C2= 3; If 1, C2 = 2; If 2, C2=1; If 3, C2= 0 + _____ (C2)
                                                                             + _____ (I)
                                                                             = _____ C

Scale P (P Range 0 to 10) **Cultural Proficiency;** Higher values indicate higher levels of cultural proficiency
P = #66___ +#67___ +#68___ +#69___ +#70___ +#71___ +#72___ +#73___ +#74___ +#75___ = ____**P**

<u>NOTES</u>

SELF-ASSESSMENT 1.2

CULTURE AND PERSONAL STYLE

1. What are the cultural groups other than your own with which you have frequent contact?

2. What is the source of your knowledge about the principal cultural groups of the U.S.?

3. What do you consider to be the most important cultural groups in the U.S.? Why?

4a. What is your cultural background? _____

4b. What are the most important characteristics of your culture(s)?

5. What aspects of your behavior reflect your cultural influences?

6. How do your dress and appearance reflect your culture's norms?

7. What are styles of dress of other cultures that you feel appropriate for yourself?

8. How does your culture affect the way in which you interact with others?

9. What is your "cultural style" of interaction?

10. Do you have a personal style you consider to be different from your culture's normative patterns?

<u>NOTES</u>

SELF-ASSESSMENT 1.3

CLASS EXERCISE: SOCIAL INTERACTION STYLES

Divide your class up into three groups, A, B and C. Each group should only read their own assigned roles defined below. Triads of students are then formed with one member each from groups A, B and C. All participants in the triad have the same assignment, carried out through the manners described in their roles. After approximately 10 minutes of the exercise, stop, reconvene the entire group and discuss the problems you faced and why.

Assignment:
All of the groups have the assignment of interacting to develop a consensus plan regarding how to prioritize and implement cross-cultural communication training in your workplace, classroom or dorm.

Role A
Your role is to make sure your group stays focused on the assignment of developing strategies for implementing cross-cultural training in your workplace. Keep the group focused on the job; avoid trivialities and personal issues. Maintain a professional atmosphere and formality, and discourage distractions and digressions. Take charge of the group, if necessary, and assure that everyone makes a contribution to your consensus statement on strategies. You have 10 minutes to complete your task, including prioritizing your group's strategies.

Role B
The real purpose of this exercise is to see how much the members of the group know about each other's personal experiences in of cross-cultural communication. Your role is to "warm up" the group, making sure that everybody in the group knows each other. Find out about each participant's personal and cultural background and his/her personal experiences in cross-cultural relations. Make sure that everybody in the group contributes to the plan, and keep individuals from dominating or withdrawing. Don't let people manipulate your personally or invade your space, but, if necessary, use teasing and humor to loosen them up or draw them out.

Role C
You are the support person in the group. You keep your personal business to yourself. You follow the group's consensus rather than lead, but encourage the ideas proposed by others. To support the points that other people make, provide examples by telling stories about cross-cultural incidents that you have witnessed (or make them up). Support suggestions made by others, but don't let them make you responsible for proposing ideas. Show your support non-verbally, using close interpersonal distance, smiling and reassuring touches.

Discussion
1. Was your group able to accomplish its goals? Why or why not?

2. Based on the interactions in your group, what can you conclude about the interactional style adopted by the other members?

3. Do these styles reflect cultural styles with which you are familiar?

4. Did particular styles clash with you? Have you experienced such conflicts before?

NOTES

NOTES

CHAPTER 2

RACE AND ETHNICITY

Overview

This chapter presents an understanding of the differences between race and ethnicity. The original conceptualization of race as a distinct biological species has been rejected with modern scientific studies of population differences. These classic racial beliefs are corrected with the actual patterns of biological differences among humans. The human differences that are perceived as racial are re-interpreted in terms of ethnicity, how relations within cultural groups and in distinction to other groups in society are used to produce social classifications. A variety of ways in which individuals form their identity in response to multiple cultural influences are examined, along with the impacts of minority status on self-esteem and identity. The impacts of multiple cultural influences in the development of biculturalism are presented.

Objectives

Distinguish the bases for the differences between race and ethnicity
Review the original concepts of race and why they lack scientific validity
Present modern scientific understandings of population differences and racial differences
Introduce the concept of ethnicity as an alternative to racialized conceptualizations
Illustrate how ethnic identity is formed in relations with one's own cultural group and others in society
Illustrate a variety of ways in which individuals form their identity in response to multiple influences
Examine the impacts of minority status on self-esteem and identity

Chapter Outline

Introduction: Differentiating Race and Ethnicity
The Concept of Race
    Race in Historical Perspective
    Modern Concepts of Race
    Skin Color and Racial Distinctions
    Racism and Ideology
Ethnicity
Classic Perspectives on Ethnicity
    Ethnic Categories
    The Construction of Ethnicity
Acculturation and Stages of Ethnicity Identity Development
Types of Intercultural Adaptation
Minority Ethnic Identity Development
Dominant Groups' Development of Ethnic Awareness
Summary: Self and Identity in Cross-Cultural Perspective
References and Additional Readings
Self-Assessment 2.1: Racial and Ethnic Identity

INTRODUCTION: DIFFERENTIATING RACE AND ETHNICITY

Effective adaptation to intercultural relations requires an understanding of the differences among the concepts race, ethnicity and culture and how they relate to biology and learning. Common meanings of these words often conflict with the scientific meanings and evidence. Intergroup differences are often attributed to the effects of race, which is falsely presumed to represent biological factors. The common belief that race reflects biological differences lack a scientific basis. Meanings historically implied by the concept of race emphasized biologically distinct groups of humans with unique and common biological traits that exclusively differentiate them from other human groups. This is false. Almost all human genetic material is shared in common, and the differences which do exist between racially defined human groups are statistical, not absolute. Furthermore, differences in the frequency with which genes occur in various groups are not causally related to differences in behavior or other capabilities. The groups called races have their differences in culture — learned behavior and learned beliefs.

Cultural concepts determine what are viewed as races — and these cultural concepts do not correspond to the presumed biological reality. Race is a distracting term in interethnic relations because it implies a basis for intergroup differences that do not in fact exist. Race is a cultural concept, not a biological group. Insufficient attention has been focused on understanding the learned cultural bases of intergroup differences. The consequence is often tragically manifested in intercultural relations, where actions inspired by the beliefs in the biological races have led to discrimination, violence, subjugation, slavery and even genocide. Ashley Montague called race the "most dangerous myth" of humanity because of its destructive influence upon human relations. Effective cross-cultural relations require examination of the effect of cultural factors, and not confusing their influences with falsely presumed genetic ones.

An alternative to the concept of race is that of ethnicity. Ethnicity is concerned with how people are identified with respect to their culture of origin and other significant reference groups. This identity is variable, even for people of the same cultural background. Ethnicity is an identity constructed with respect to both one's own cultural background and with respect to other significant groups in society. This relationship to multiple reference groups provides for a number of different aspects of personal identity. Cross-cultural exposure and culturally pluralistic societies produce a variety of options for the construction of identity. While the nature of the contact and relations between cultures structures individual adaptations, group-level relations do not completely determine the nature of individual adaptations to cross-cultural contact. Within any given group a wide range of different individual adaptations may be achieved. This chapter examines some of the different individual adaptations to intergroup contact and the consequences of these different adjustments for the individuals involved. While there is individual variability within a culture in terms of the adaptations of cross-cultural relations, these different types of adaptations show cross-cultural regularities, the consequences of the process dynamics of intercultural relations. These structural aspects affecting individual adaptations to cross-cultural relations are produce by a variety of impacts of culture upon self, and may lead to a variety of ethnic, bicultural, multicultural and global identities. Understanding these culturally based aspects of identity require an appreciation of the nature of culture and its effects upon behavior, the focus of the following chapter.

THE CONCEPT OF RACE

The term "race" is an important part of the vocabulary commonly used to discuss differences between groups of people, but "race" implies conditions contrary to scientific evidence. Race is a concept that historically implied biologically different groups, but the notion of a group with unique and shared biological traits that exclusively differentiate that group from other so-called racial groups is false. Cultural concepts determine what is viewed as a race and do not reflect an underlying biological reality.

Race in Historical Perspective

The conceptualization of different races began in the context of Western contact with peoples of Africa, Asia and the Americas. Early racial classifications were generally directed towards providing some meaning to the differences. An early influential racial classification of the 1700s divided humanity into five principal groups, conveniently labeled by distinctions of skin color: Black, Brown, Red, Yellow and White. While this schema had no basis in biology or genetic variation, its popularity and representation of popular thinking created a legacy that persists until today. Racial classifications were ultimately used to justify political ideologies of dominance and exploitation of others on the basis of the claimed natural superiority of the race of the people who made the typologies. Conceptualizations of presumed racial differences among humans were refined as species differences in the development of Western classification of different species of animals.

Pseudo-Scientific and Political Racism

The belief in multiple biological origins for modern humans was developed by what was called the polygenists (poly = multiple; genesis = origins) movements in the 19th century. The polygenist belief in multiple origins of humanity was bolstered by a search for evidence that would provide a scientific basis for racism. This view of multiple origins of humanity ran counter to both religious belief in a single creation and the evolutionary thought inspired by Darwin. Both of these traditions view all humans as having common origins. Pseudo-scientific work was done to find support for the belief that the racial differences among humans were the consequence of primordial physical differences between the races. Cranial features such as skull shape, size and thickness were examined to argue that group differences in these physical measurements

directly reflect mental capacity and evolution. But absolute brain size is insignificantly related to intelligence among modern humans (Brues 1977). Furthermore, *Homo neanderthalensis* had an average brain size exceeding that of modern humans, but with clearly inferior cultural accomplishments.

The lack of relationship between brain size and intelligence did not deter investigations, since the assumption of biological variation between human groups reflected the contemporary social and political trends. Political and intellectual movements concerned with the social implications of race were strong in Europe and the U.S. during the later part of the 19th century and early part of the 20th century. The attitude about race was developed in response to explaining the different other, particularly dark-skinned people, and providing justifications for the political policies of governments and actions of individuals. The rise of racial ideology and political action to segregate society on the basis of race was associated with the defense of the trade and the practice of slavery, rather than the period of initial contact with Africans. The development of racial attitudes was expanded in conservative reactions to the loss of aristocratic power represented in the French Revolution and the end of slavery in the U.S. The same racial ideology provided a justification for both domestic and international political orders. While European Americans sought a rationale for the repression of newly freed slaves, the European nations sought justification for their exploitation and military dominance in their colonies around the world. The notion of inherent biological differences between the Europeans and other races became increasing compelling to the Europeans as their industrialization and accumulation of material goods and destructive power increased the perception of their superiority to other groups. Beliefs that biological differences determined cultural achievements were used for political interests, opposing immigration and rights for non-whites, passing legislation against what were classified as interracial marriages on the false grounds that they produced inferior offspring.

Scientific Approaches to Race

The modern cultural anthropology response to the pseudo-science of polygenist ideology was found in Franz Boas's classic *The Mind of Primitive Man*, which addressed the inappropriateness of many of the supposed scientific demonstrations of the biological basis for racial differences. Boas's work emphasized the distinctiveness of the concepts of race, language and culture, providing the groundwork for a modern sense of culture in the recognition of the nature of cultural characteristics and effects. Boas's data was instrumental in showing that the presumed inferiority of Eastern European immigrants (as opposed to Western Europeans) was the consequence of environmental factors (diet) rather than innate characteristics.

The anthropological investigations of the relationship of biological features to racial classification included not only the obvious traditional features such as skin, eye and hair color, but also examined a wide range of other genetically determined features, including dentition, enzymes, blood types, serum proteins, hemoglobin, nasal index and skeletal features. Specific emphasis has been given to anatomical features and blood type. As the actual measurement and analysis of physical characteristics of humans from different groups increased, the concept of a few primary races had to be modified to recognize secondary races and sub-races. As characteristics of biological features that differed between individuals were subjected to more precise measurement and assessment, the concept of biologically distinct races became more tenuous. The idea of homogeneous populations with distinct genetic characteristics shifted to a recognition that human populations have an admixture of genetic traits thought to be characteristic of other groups.

The notion of a racial group composed of genetically homogeneous and distinct ideal types of an individual could not persist in the face of the considerable biological variation that existed within all of the socially recognized races. Such recognition is not to deny that physical differences among *groups* of people exist in terms of the frequency of specific genetic traits. However, these groups defined in terms of statistical frequencies include within them considerable internal differences. These differences are so great that some individuals that they include more closely approximate the ideal types of other races rather than the one to which they are socially assigned. For instance, many Blacks or African Americans have more biological heritage from European or White ancestry than African ancestry. In spite of the preponderance of European genetic heritage (as much as 87% or more) in some individuals, they are still socially identified as Black. Similarly, people in the U.S. often consider people from subcontinent India Black, while their gene pool and ancient origins are related to European populations. The classic concept of Caucasian included people from India, while most white people in the U.S., who would be classified as Caucasians, would not consider people from India to be white.

Anthropologists dispute the appropriateness of the term race, feeling that there are no biological races within the species *Homo sapiens* ((Lieberman, Stevenson & Reynolds 1989). Race does not represent a concept that has been validated by scientific research. The distribution of biological characteristics in human populations precludes any division into races. All members of the species *Homo sapiens* are members of an open genetic system in the sense that all members can interbreed because their genes are interchangeable. Such interbreeding potential undermines the notion of biological distinctiveness. The common conceptions of race are typically based upon superficial features (skin, eye and hair color) rather than underlying biological patterns and configurations. Most of the commonly recognized racial features are not determined by specific genes, but by a combination of genes. Races represent cultural beliefs and social conventions which may be elevated by legal statuses, but they fail to represent the basis for the fundamental differences between groups of people.

Modern Concepts of Race

While the biological basis for races has never been scientifically established, legal, social, administrative and political concepts of races have been and continue to be widely utilized. An examination of some of the legal concepts serves to illustrate how such classifications are cultural or social, not biological. Legal definitions of race, particularly those defining the Negro or African ancestry group, have had an important role in intergroup relations in the U.S. Legal definitions of being a Negro have included criteria such as 1/8 or 1/16 Negro heritage, that is, having one Negro great-grandparent or great-great-grandparent. Other statutes have specified any "recognizable Negro ancestry," leaving to social conventions to determine what constitutes "recognizable Negro ancestry."

The U.S. National Center of Health Statistics had employed until recently a "racial code" for the classification of individuals according to race. The racial code table is reproduced below (see Table 2.1). What can be seen in the racial classification for offspring of mixed parentage is that the criteria employed are social designations, not biological ones. For instance, in all cases of a white father and a different race code for the mother, the child is always assigned to the racial code of the mother. A parallel situation prevails for the children of white mothers with fathers of a different race code; here the race of the father is assigned to the child. Whenever a mixed offspring is produced, it is denied membership in the "white" race. In the case of a Negro (or American Indian) father, the race code for the child is Negro (or American Indian), regardless of the race code of the mother, except if she is Hawaiian. Similar inconsistencies abound, illustrating that racial coding in the U.S. has been on the basis of social conventions rather than any real consideration of biological or cultural factors specific to the individual so coded.

While the biological concept of a race has been rejected, the notion of race representing ancient breeding populations persists. The long-standing core groupings include Mongoloid, Australoid (Archaic White), Caucasoid and Negroid. However, these broad groupings immediately fail to account for the characteristics of many groups of people. For instance, the Pygmies and Bushmen of Africa do not correspond to the broad physical profile characteristic of other members of the Negroid group. Other racial typologies begin with a greater number of primary races, but all have to recognize the need for indefinitely further divisions in order to achieve relatively homogeneous groups. These efforts have led some to create 200 categories to organize all of the exceptions to the primary races. Still within each of these groupings are substantial differences, the need for divisions into further races and sub-races, and people with combinations of characteristics that contradict conventional notions about racial characteristics and boundaries. For instance, included in the Caucasoid race are people whose skin color ranges from the lightest to dark pigmentations. Some Caucasoid groups, such as those from India and Pakistan, have much darker skin than many Africans and African Americans, and may be considered "Blacks" in the U.S.

A typology of nine geographic races is provided by Garn (1971). These regionally (or geographically) delimited collections of breeding populations largely correspond to continental areas. These geographic races are further subdivided into thousands of local races. While the relative frequencies of specific genes may serve to differentiate such populations at the level of local contrasts, they do not identify or cause the factors used to determine the socially relevant racial distinctions. The distinctions made regarding races differ from culture to culture. This sociocultural nature of racial distinction does not undermine their importance and power. Beliefs are real in their consequences, with the consequent social actions having greater effects than any actual physical differences. In the sociological sense, races are those groups of people who are believed by themselves or by others in society to constitute a distinct group. The lack of biological validity of distinctions is immaterial to the social reality of race.

NATIONAL CENTER OF HEALTH STATISTICS RACIAL CODE

CODE FOR FATHER'S RACE	CODE FOR MOTHER'S RACE									
	1	2	3	4	5	6	7	8	0	9
	CODE FOR CHILD'S RACE[a]									
1 White	1	2	3	4	5	6	7	8	0	1
2 Negro	2	2	2	2	2	6	2	2	2	2
3 Indian	3	3	3	3	3	6	3	3	3	3
4 Chinese	4	4	4	4	4	6	4	4	4	4
5 Japanese	5	5	5	5	5	6	5	5	5	5
6 Hawaiian	6	6	6	6	6	6	6	6	6	6
7 Other Non-white	7	7	7	7	7	6	7	7	7	7
8 Filipino	8	8	8	8	8	6	8	8	8	8
9 Guamian	0	0	0	0	0	6	0	0	0	0
0 Unknown	1	2	3	4	5	6	7	8	0	A

[a] Where races of both are unknown or not stated, the race of the child is based upon the last known race of ancestors.

Table 2.1 National Center of Health Racial Codes for Offspring

An Alternative to Race: The Cline

Since the concept of race as originally conceived as a biological category has been shown to lack a scientific basis, what are the alternatives for organizing information about biological differences among humans? An alternate biological concept is the cline, the varying frequency of a single genetic trait across a geographical area. The systematic analysis of single traits permits determination of the relationship of the trait to ecological conditions, population movements and other factors. The cline shows that the concept of races is arbitrary since discrete geographical boundaries for genetic traits do not exist. The discordance of variation of different traits is why classification of people into races characterized by combinations of distinct genes is not possible. Human variation at the group level can only be described in terms of different frequencies of genes, not their absolute presence or absence. But even trying to define racial groups on the basis of relative gene frequencies in the populations is problematic. What specific genes are to be considered relevant for this classification, and what percentage of the gene in the population is relevant? Ten percent? Fifty percent? Ninety percent? There are neither natural determinants of which genes should be used for the purposes of racial classification nor percentages of the population that should have the gene to make it a marker of a "racial" group. Any group defined on the basis of a specific gene would include people who consider themselves to be of different races, as well as exclude people who consider themselves to be of the same race. Ultimately, the number of races depends upon the definition of race one employs.

In an effort to reconcile the term race with the knowledge about actual biological variation, Brues defines a race as "a division of a species which differs from other divisions by the frequency with which certain hereditary traits appear among its members" (Brues 1977:1). But such a definition is insufficient on several grounds. Most patterns of biological variation (e.g., molar patterns, blood types) are not used to classify people into racial groups and, furthermore, could not, since they cross so-called racial groups. Furthermore, the racial traits or characteristics that are "found to differ in frequency of occurrence or degree of development between races are also found to differ among individuals within races....[T]here is no single characteristic that is shared by all individuals of one race and denied to everyone else. Still less is there any single simple quality, which one race possesses and another does not, that bestows... physical and behavioral traits on some people and not on others" (Brues 1977:7). While members of an identified race may share certain traits in common more often than they do with members of other designated races, this is not true for all members of a race.

Skin Color and Racial Distinctions

Differences in skin color are a primary basis from which racial distinctions have been made, exemplified in white versus black, brown, red, yellow. The factors responsible for skin color illustrate why this factor does not provide a basis for biological distinctions of race. A microscopically thin pigment-bearing layer of skin determines skin color. The color of skin, as well as hair and eyes, is determined by the same substance — melanin. Melanin granules are found in two forms, eumelanin, which produces skin coloration, including all brown and black shades of color, and phaeomelanin, which is responsible for red hair. These forms of melanin are also found in many other mammals. The melanin granules are produced by melanocytes that are located in the deep (germinative) layer of the epidermis. The number of melanocytes is approximately the same for all different colors of skin, but the amount of melanin produced and the way in which it is distributed does vary. Light-skin persons produce melanin slowly, while dark skin individuals produce much more melanin and more rapidly. Individuals with darker skin also have their melanin granules more evenly distributed. This greater dispersion absorbs light more effectively and thereby produces a darker skin color. Thus the differences in whites and blacks, in those with light versus dark skin, are not with respect to the absence and presence of a genetic characteristic determining skin color. Both those with light skin and those with dark skin have the same pigment-producing cells. Classifying people into different races on the basis of skin color is basically the same thing as classifying people into different races based upon the thickness or rate of growth of their hair.

There are no discrete separations between persons of different colors of brown and black skin and those with lighter skin. Differences in intensity of skin coloration result from the interaction of sunlight exposure with the body's melanocyte cells. Differences in skin color found among the diverse peoples of the world reflect the operation of this single factor, with minor variations in color and tone also provided by near-surface blood vessels and carotene in the diet. The differences in skin color reflect the mediation of two different bodily processes through the intensity of pigmentation, one providing for protection from the sun's ultraviolet radiation, the other providing for the production of vitamin D. Exposure to the sun's ultraviolet radiation can cause serious burning of the skin. Exposure to the sun results in the stimulation of melanin production and its movement towards the surface of the skin, where it provides protection against the sun and reduces painful burns. The importance of this protective response is represented by the (ancient) distribution of skin pigmentation. People living nearest the equatorial zones where ultraviolet radiation is the most intense have had the darkest-pigmented skin as a protection. Dark skin also prevents over-production of vitamin D in areas where intense equatorial sunlight increases ultraviolet radiation and overproduction of Vitamin D that can cause calcium buildup in body tissues, kidney failure and circulatory, joint and other health problems.

The distribution of lighter-pigmented skin reflects a complementary process. People living in the northernmost areas of the globe face a risk of vitamin D insufficiency, since the limited sunlight both reduces ultraviolet radiation and creates the demand for additional clothing that limits the skin's exposure to ultraviolet radiation. Dark-colored skin with larger amounts of melanin would further reduce the amount of ultraviolet radiation absorbed and vitamin D produced. The traditional explanation regarding the selective pressure for lighter-skin individuals was postulated to involve the mediating effects of the lack of vitamin D, which can result in a disease called rickets. Rickets leads to a weakening of bones and can produce difficulties in childbirth. Therefore, light-colored skin can be adaptive in these more extreme regions in order to assure sufficient ultraviolet absorption and vitamin D production. Additional selective mechanisms for light skin in northern regions may result from a greater propensity for frostbite on dark-skinned individuals. Thus skin pigmentation and color represent different adaptations to contrasting environmental conditions.

Human Biological Diversity

Admixtures of biological traits are found in all areas of the world and within all socially recognized races. Even features like blood type, blood proteins and other biochemical variations show regional tendencies but not an exclusive racial distribution. So while human breeding populations that are largely endogamous (in-group marriage) are clearly present, it is equally clear that these populations interbreed and have done so throughout time. Estimates of isolation and differentiation of these breeding populations range from 35,000 to 1 million years before the present. Skin color differences in the various human populations have probably been part of the hominid populations since climatic dispersions began over one million years ago. Comparison of North American and Asian populations sheds light on Asian, African and European differentiation. The probable dates of Asian and American Indian differentiation some 15,000 to 30,000 years ago are indicated by the periods of glaciations. Strong genetic similarities remain between the two populations in terms of epicanthic fold, dry ear wax, hair form and color, molar (tooth) patterns and blood types, more similarities than between any of the other major "racial" populations in the world. To account for the typical differences between the populations of Europeans, Africans and Asians requires much more time, probably requiring an isolation of ancient breeding populations for at least 100,000 years.

Racism and Ideology

While race as a category of human beings and racism as a form of discrimination are normally considered to be separate issues, the lack of scientific basis for the concept of race helps to reveal the racist basis of the belief in races. The belief in races contributes to racism, and may be considered a form of racism because it prejudicially imputes to people and groups inherent characteristics and qualities.

Racism is an ideology, a set of beliefs that considers some genetic biological basis to be the cause of the inferior capabilities or behaviors typical of individuals from a specific cultural group. Racism is also considered by some to include the use of these beliefs by a powerful group to facilitate and justify the oppression of another group. The belief in races and the practices of racism are generally used to justify an unequal distribution of power, resources and rights in a society. Racism normally focuses upon certain real or imagined traits of a group (which are generally viewed negatively) and considers them to be determined by genetic constitution, but without any evidence of actual genetic differences or causal linkages of genes and behavior. Racism against other groups is generally combined with a belief in the inherent biological superiority of the dominant group and the insurmountable gap between the superior and inferior groups. The supposed inherent biological nature of the differences is used as an ideology and a social justification for maintenance of these differences in social life, particularly in terms of power. The ideology of racism is also used to justify why it is necessary to maintain the social barriers, the norms, beliefs, prejudices and discriminatory treatments necessary to perpetuate the separation of the so-called racial groups. Racism as an ideology fails to acknowledge the importance of the social and cultural environments that affect achievement. Racism does not consider how economic opportunity or educational opportunities are denied by the structural conditions of society and the intercultural relations that the dominant group maintains.

The strongest forms of racism are associated with societies in which there are very obvious physical appearances distinguishing groups and strong differences in political power between the groups. Slavery tends to have racism associated with its justification, and indeed the slave systems tend to have the strongest ideologies of racism. Colonization is also strongly associated with racist ideologies, and indeed racism is often used as an explicit justification for colonial exploitation.

Racist beliefs are found throughout the world and across history. The power of racism in the U.S. in the 20th century is in part due to the powerful influences of 19th-century intellectual developments that have been called "scientific racism." The development of scientific racism

occurred in the interaction of developing evolutionary science and the emergence of political philosophies justifying colonialism. The reality of interspecies biological differences was used as a model to discuss the differences between different groups of humans. The presumed biological differences were used as a justification for differential treatment of groups. Racist beliefs justified treating those considered to be biologically inferior in a different manner, considering it a "natural" outcome of biological superiority of the dominant social groups. Justification of slavery, colonization, class inequality and other forms of exploitation were derived from the beliefs in biologically different races with different capabilities, and consequently different rights. Social stratification and domination were given "scientific" legitimacy based upon the assumption of the reality of races and the presumed effect upon potentials and behavior.

Some have suggested that racism only be applied to the ideologies espoused by those in the positions of dominance in intergroup relationships. There certainly is a different dimension to the beliefs in races and espousal of racism when it is elevated as a principle of societal differentiation by those in positions of power. But similar beliefs and attitudes about racial differences and racial-behavioral linkages are also expressed by subordinated groups. The subordinated groups may also believe they themselves are biologically inferior, incorporating the dominant ideology; or they may deny the legitimacy of the dominant ideology and support an ideology of racism in the beliefs in their own biological superiority that will enable them to someday come to dominate their current oppressors. Whether from a position of power or subordination, the beliefs of inherent biological differences in human groups is an impediment to intercultural relations.

Since the concept of races as traditionally conceived — a biological category — is contrary to fact, and since these false beliefs are themselves harmful to the groups so labeled, the belief in races can be seen as being in and of itself racist. Historical development of the concept of race was motivated by the need for justifying political and economic subordination of racially identified groups of people. Similar political agendas are proposed today on the basis of falsely construed notions of race. Abandoning the unqualified use of the term race helps to focus attention on sociocultural causes of group behavior and characteristics.

Post-Modern Concepts of Race

In final analysis, what is race? In a curious way, scientific approaches have come to endorse a "philosophical" concept of race. This is the notion that race is a "social construction," a set of beliefs held by people that produce major consequences for their social relations. While conceived as biological categories, the groups designated as "races" reflect a cultural concept — social criteria for grouping people — rather than some distinctive biologically defined groupings. The continued use of the term race in science is with a different set of meanings than originally associated with the term. Races are statistical aggregates, groups that differ in the relative frequency of traits rather than in their absolute presence or absence. In terms of its original intent to designate human subspecies or groups with unique and homogeneous biological characteristics, the concept of race is unscientific. Its continued use is misleading, given its original denotations and connotations. However, the social definitions of race do continue to provide the basis for ascribing certain characteristics or imposing limitations on this socially defined category of "other"/outsider. Beliefs about race are powerful determinants of behavior and relations. Consequently, race cannot be ignored, because people's responses to those labels produce real social consequences. How can we address this social reality of race while rejecting its biological basis? The approach is to utilize an alternative to the concept of race, that of ethnicity. Ethnicity is the constructed identity of people who are members of a socially recognized cultural group. This definition often includes ideas about racial origins and identity, derived from the history and culture of the group.

ETHNICITY

Ethnicity has become an alternative conceptual framework for race, one directly linked to cultural rather than biological factors. While the shift from the term "race" to that of "ethnicity" has not changed many peoples' conceptualizations about the nature of the referents of these terms, this shift is a fundamentally different conceptualization about the social nature of intergroup differences. The repetitive changes in the problematic U.S. Census's racial and ethnic categories in recent decades reflects the difficulties in developing a social consensus regarding the appropriate classification of groups, and changing perspectives on their meaning. Yet an understanding of the nature of ethnicity is the only viable route for making sense of the numerous dimensions of variation in human identity and behavior.

Classic Perspectives on Ethnicity

There are a wide variety of uses of the term ethnicity. But cross-cutting a variety of conceptualizations, it represents people's notions about the concepts of self-identity in relationship to the inclusive "other" — our people or group with whom we personally and socially identify. Ethnic groups are socially recognized groups with salient differences with respect to other groups in society. Ethnic groups generally maintain their boundaries and differences on the basis of in-group behavior producing geographical segregation and socially and culturally salient distinctions in language, dress, physical appearance and other easily recognized differences by the ethnic group, as well as by others. Ethnic groups maintain a culture or subculture, a group history and social and behavioral characteristics generally linked to a national background of the ancestors of the immigrants.

Ethnic groups' sense of identity may be reinforced by any number of physically, behaviorally, socially or culturally salient distinctions in comparison to other groups in society. Prominent sources of ethnicity are derived from national background (e.g., Mexican American), regional identifications (e.g., Southerner), and religious membership (e.g., Protestant, WASP, Jewish, Black Muslim). Other sources may include occupation, gender, sexual identity or virtually any salient dimension of difference that contributes to a collective sense of identity as a group: a specific language; recognized values and beliefs, sometimes including religion; specific social and behavioral patterns; social roles; preferred emotional states; and other cultural values, beliefs and practices.

Ethnic groups and ethnic identity play an important role in the relations between people. Such ascribed membership often shapes the ways in which individuals perceive one another. Learned attitudes about the other ethnic groups have prominent effects upon social perceptions and behaviors and differentiation of the in-group from out-groups. The greater the difference between an ethnic group and the dominant groups in society, the more likely it is that ethnic identity will be at the focus of conflict between the groups and identity within the group. Such differences tend to strengthen the boundaries between the groups and the ethnic group identity of the individuals from the respective groups. For many, ethnicity is also defined by exclusion from being accepted as a member of the dominant society. This is part of the consequence of minority status in which prejudice and discrimination prevent identification with the ideal characteristics of the European American. This ascribed membership shapes individuals' relations to those in other groups. Ethnic categorization may even be imposed by external groups upon diverse groups of people who share no sense of inclusive commonality (e.g., mixed race, colored). Ethnic groups tend to serve as a fundamental reference group in society, the social category from which one takes one's own personal characteristics. These ethnic characteristics play a fundamental role in social and psychological attachments and definitions of self, providing a sense of common membership, identity or consciousness, a sense of group belonging, nationhood or some other sense of shared ancestry. The concept of ethnicity involves collective identity, the intersection of the individual psychosocial characteristics and the collective cultural influences. The sense of ethnic identity is not just a function of one's cultural behaviors and sense of self-identity, but also the constraints and attributions derived from others in society. Other groups may ascribe the salient characteristics of ethnic identity. Ethnicity involves how individuals identify themselves as persons in relationship to some others in a context of many others.

Ethnic subcultures are maintained through diverse mechanisms. One mechanism underlying ethnic groups derives from the common cultural traits (or belief in such traits) that help create a sense of community membership and identity. This common cultural, national or historical background claimed by an ethnic group may be fictive rather than actual. That is, the actual cultural characteristics may be less important to ethnicity than what people perceive to be the case. For the individual, ethnic categorization provides an important sense of identity with strong emotional components. Ethnicity may be asserted or ascribed without the presence of cultural characteristics. People may be considered a member of an ethnic group without an actual cultural heritage. One frequent characteristic of ethnicity is its ascription by members of society in a way that forces other members of society to accept a particular ethnic status. For instance, people from India in the U.S. may be considered to be Blacks in spite of having no relationships to the African American culture.

Ethnicity may be defined as a consequence of distinct characteristics and processes. Keefe (1989) has suggested that there are three principal ways of characterizing ethnicity. She calls these processual, perceptual and empirical approaches. The processual approach characterizes ethnicity as an identity emerging in social and political processes of negotiation in contact and interaction between groups. The perceptual view of ethnicity examines the meanings that groups attribute to themselves and others and how the attributed meanings affect subsequent interactions. The view of ethnicity as an empirical phenomenon is concerned with the actual groups and the differences between them. The focus is upon the measurement of traits and patterns that characterize and distinguish ethnic groups. If we are to understand the nature of ethnicity we must address all three aspects of ethnicity: the processes of interaction, the perceptions of groups and their actual characteristics.

Ethnicity derives from the collective dimensions of individual identity, the individual's personal cultural background, and influences derived from broader societal relations. The foci for construction of ethnicity are: (1) the self as social being, (2) the self with reference to the inclusive other (culture) and (3) the self in contrastive reference to other social models of self and collective relations (society). The linguistic roots of "ethnic" also point to its current use as a means of designating an identity-based cultural group with close and long-standing ties, as well as with reference to groups with whom one does not identify. The linguistic origins of the word "ethnic" include the social "other" who is not identified as self and the collective other with whom one shares a common identity. The source of ethnic is in the Greek word *ethnikos*. This term was used to refer to foreign national groups, being derived from *ethnos*, a people or nation. The proto Indo-European root of ethnic is *seu*. The meanings of *seu-* include a reflexive pronoun of the third person (e.g., herself), blood relatives and various referents to a social group as an entity in the sense of "we ourselves" (*American Heritage Dictionary* 1538-1539). The roots of ethnic in a reflexive pronoun suggest the recognition of self in relationship to others. *Seu* is also the root of the word ethic, referring to the principles of right and wrong conduct that comes from culture. The roots of ethnic reflect its use as a means of designating an identity based upon both a cultural group and in contrast to others in society with whom one does not identify. These identifications are social criteria that play an important role in our concepts of "right" and "wrong."

Ethnic Categories

The commonalities with the experiences of similar others create the characteristics that link people as ethnic groups. Yet common cultural characteristics with a group do not determine a person's ethnic identity. Ethnic identity is often problematic, requiring that we understand that ethnic labels may not be appropriate in spite of simple external evidence that suggests a person is a member of a specific ethnic group (e.g., "But you look Black" or "Of course he's Hispanic; his last name is Martinez!"). An *ethnic category* may take precedence over actual ethnic identity. Ethnic categories, the official stereotyped or official designations for different groups of people (e.g., Caucasian, White, Black or Asian), have often been used in a way that overlooks what the group affiliation means for individual identity. The different cultures grouped together as Hispanics or Asians may not feel a sense of common identity. The categories commonly used to classify people according to race or ethnicity tends to tell us relatively little about the actual cultural and personal characteristics of many of those to whom they are applied. Indeed the very labels used may be disputed, for instance rejecting the terms "Hispanic" or "Negro."

How does one determine the ethnicity of others? A variety of principles and processes may serve to determine ethnic identity. In the U.S. government's determinations of ethnicity, the general practice has been to accept the individual's self-definition as provided in a formal declaration. Such claims may be challenged when the claimant's characteristics depart from the dominant stereotype of their ethnic, racial or social classification. Just as the governmental racial classification is riddled with errors and contradictions, self-identified ethnicity is not unproblematic either. Members of ethnic groups will also dispute ethnic identity of individuals who claim to be members. Native American tribal definitions, federally recognized Native Americans and self-identified Native Americans constitute overlapping but not identical groups. The disputation of ethnicity in the African American community is also an important issue. While historically African Americans of light skin color may have attempted to "pass" as whites in the broader society, today we find an opposite phenomenon. Similarly, some light-complected African Americans who ethnically and culturally identify with their group nonetheless find themselves rejected by members of the African

American community on the basis of their "whiteness." Puerto Ricans who have traditionally claimed "white" status while recognizing that "everyone has a black grandmother" may find their ethnic identity as white Hispanics challenged by Americans who consider them to be Blacks. Dark-skinned individuals of contemporary African cultural background may, upon arriving in the U.S., find themselves considered to be "Black" even when their cultural experiences and identities have nothing in common with African Americans.

We cannot do without categories and labels, but we must recognize ethnic categories as social constructions rather than natural entities, with differentiated internal structures rather than a homogeneity. People who may "obviously" seem to be members of a race or ethnic group may have little or no identity with that group. Heterogeneity, the differences within a group, undermines any simplistic effort to identity behavior patterns and psychodynamics on the basis of categorical ethnic group membership. Nonetheless, "ethnic categories will continue to be needed because of the importance of exploring and understanding the many differences associated with aspects of ethnicity" (Phinney 1996:924). In spite of its problematic nature, ethnicity remains as one of the most crucial aspects of collective identity in the modern world. This reflects the multidimensional nature of ethnicity and its importance in social relations.

The Construction of Ethnicity

While some aspects of ethnic identity may be derived passively from the exposure to one's cultural group, the sense of ethnic identity is primarily created in interaction with others and their beliefs and attributions. The unique sense of one's ethnicity requires some contrastive experience, something that is "not self" for the ethnically derived self-characteristics to be revealed. Ethnicity is not merely given by virtue of culture or family background, but constructed in relations with others. Actual cultural characteristics may be less important to ethnic identity than people's perceptions. Ethnicity may be asserted without the presence of cultural

characteristics, but rather based in a sense of historical connectedness. For some, ethnicity may be defined by exclusion as a member of the dominant society (e.g., denied the classification as white). The negotiated and constructed nature of ethnicity is exemplified in "symbolic ethnicity," a phenomenon of strong ethnic identity in spite of little direct cultural involvement or background. This often reflects broader contextual factors that shape the salience and centrality of ethnic identity for the individual in relationship to others in society.

The importance and nature of ethnicity varies among group members, rather than being simply a categorical construct. Rather than a passive acceptance of the cultural identity of parents, children may model themselves on their parents and others, but in a reactive rather than strictly imitative process, with each generation reinterpreting and reinventing it's ethnic identity. Ethnicity is "the interweaving of cultural threads from different arenas . . ., a matter of finding a voice or style that does not violate one's several components of identity . . . , a pluralistic, multidimensional, or multifaceted concept of self as a crucible for a wider social ethos of pluralism" (Fischer 1986:230, 196). Fischer reviews contemporary ethnic autobiographies to illustrate this multidimensional emergent representation of the ethnic self, emphasizing ethnicity's deeply rooted emotional component, based on processes analogous to dreaming and transference (Fischer 1986:195-96). The ethnic self emerges as a form of implicit knowledge about one's essential being that is experienced as an influence originating and operating from outside of oneself.

Ethnic identity goes beyond one's sense of personal self, with one's sense of identity affected by historical and external social factors. Ethnicity is not strictly a function of group socialization, but an effort motivated by the individually and collectively felt needs for self-identity in relation to a group. The erosion of historical tradition, public cohesion and social connectedness characteristic of modern society heightens this need for renewal and self-definition. "[T]he ethnic search is. . . seeing others against a background of ourselves, and ourselves against a background of others" (Fischer 1986:199). This role of the social "other not self" in ethnic identity is more importance for those of minority status because of its powerful effects upon self-formation and identity. This minority status and the associated prejudice, discrimination and deprivations can have powerful impacts upon the individual. Mechanisms of secondary socialization from the broader social and political institutions and intergroup relations have powerful roles in shaping the self and personal identity.

The multiple social others, of one's own cultural other and the broader social other of a culturally differentiated society, can produce a duality within the personality, sometimes-irreconcilable aspects of one's self. This "twoness" reflecting the influences of both one's own culture and the broader society, a sense of multiple selves, is illustrated in Fischer's analysis of Black autobiographies which develop multiple selves or alternative selves constructed in explicit contrast to the dominant ideologies of the broader society. Different selves provide different voices, the presentation of alter egos and different identities. The multiplicity of selves is also reflected in the contextual variation in the use of ethnic group labels by the same person (e.g., Latino, Hispanic, Mexican, Chicano). Self-identity labels of a person may even shift across ethnic groups (e.g., white, Latino, newyorican) as a function of context.

Culture's largely unconscious aspects that are "invisible to the subject" reflects the ethnocentric perception of the commonplace cultural occurrences as universal and natural. It is the contact with the other, the culturally different, that helps to force to awareness characteristics of the self. The contact with the cultural other provides a point of reference for assessing one's own nature. Phinney (1996) illustrates this in analysis of the agreement in accounts of the global characteristics of American ethnic groups (e.g., interdependence and collective orientations), showing that they reflect the opposite of the characteristics of the dominant European American culture (e.g., value on independence and individualism). This illustrates the necessity of an explicit comparative approach rather than one unaccountably and unconsciously biased by one's own cultural perspectives.

Development of this awareness of one's point of reference requires a cultural and historical approach, as well as a comparative cross-cultural approach that illustrates the unique nature of a specific culture as well as its differences in relation to other groups.

Phinney (1996) points out that, to assess the implications of ethnicity, it is essential to "unpack" culture to "explain cross-cultural differences in terms of specific antecedent variables" (p. 920). Assessment of ethnic identity involves a number of dimensions of acculturation and considerations of the strength of identification with or commitment to the ethnic group identity, cultural norms and values and the experiences associated with minority status. Assessments of the psychological impacts of ethnicity include strength of identification, the evaluation of its personal significance, one's broader societal relations and experiences associated with minority status such as prejudice, discrimination and powerlessness. Phinney also emphasizes that "ethnic identity can be conceptualized as a process: individuals progress from an early stage in which one's ethnicity is taken for granted, on the basis of attitudes and opinions of others or of society; through a period of exploration into the meaning and implications of one's group membership; to an achieved ethnic identity that is not necessarily a static end point of development; individuals are likely to reexamine their ethnicity throughout their lives and thus may re-experience earlier developmental stages" (Phinney 1996:923). These stages of ethnic identity may be superseded in the development of bicultural and multicultural identities (see Chapter 6).

Ethnicity is a multidimensional construct with variable impacts upon the psychology of the members of the group and a number of dimensions of variation along which its members differ. The effects of ethnic group membership on psychological characteristics of individuals are variable, as individuals have variant social, interpersonal, emotional and cognitive relations within a culture. To understand ethnicity, one must examine the cultural and social systems within which it is produced, as described in the following chapters.

Summary: Race Versus Ethnicity Versus Culture

The concepts of race, ethnicity and culture are often used interchangeably. While all are social constructs, their differentiation is important, especially since race is often used with a biological implication. The differences between race and ethnicity can be seen most clearly when we contrast the biological inheritance of individuals with the socially designated racial category. What stands out in many cases is the discrepancy between a person's socially recognized race, the actual biological heritage of the person and his/her cultural background and experiences. In the U.S., the presence of any genetic heritage of African origins has been typically sufficient for racial classification as a Negro, Black or African American. The presence of as little as 1/16 African heritage has served as both a social and legal standard for determining African origin ethnic labeling in the U.S. Biologically a person may be 80-90% of European (Caucasian) genetic heritage and 10% African genetic heritage and still be typically seen as a Black person. This is because any extent of skin pigmentation has been used as a social marker to designate "blackness." People from India, Australia, the Middle East and other parts of the world have been considered "black" in the U.S. and treated as such, often forcibly assimilating them and their descendants to Black America. Some people of identifiably African American parents do not appear so themselves, yet they consider themselves to be African American. Other people appear African American but do not identify themselves as such.

Ethnicity as opposed to culture refers to how one views one's identity. A person may have a Hispanic name but not have a Hispanic identity. Even without a cultural background as a member of an ethnic group, a person may nonetheless have a strong identity with that group. A fifth-generation descendant of Mexican immigrants may have little in common culturally with Mexicans but, nonetheless, have a strong ethnic identity as a Chicano and a strong pride in Mexican culture and history. A blond blue-eyed third-generation descendant of European immigrants living in Mexico may look Nordic, but be culturally and ethnically Mexican in every respect. One's own ethnicity and how one views one's social identity may conform to or differ from one's culture of origin or how one is viewed racially by others. For instance, in the U.S., Jews are viewed as a single ethnic group regardless of their diverse cultural origins, languages and even denominations. Within Israel, a number of different Jewish ethnic groups are recognized. Furthermore, in Israel, the American Jew is considered to be an American. Some Americans whose great-grandparents had cultural roots in Asia no longer have any cultural identity with or knowledge of these ancient roots. Yet because of their physically salient features like slanted eyes, they are typically considered by others to be a Japanese or other Asian nationality. Cultural stereotypes ascribe to them an ethnic identity they do not actually have but can not escape socially. This diversity of people and identities within standard racial and ethnic categories requires that we understand the variety of ways in which people may identify themselves with respect to the cultural groups to which they are exposed. To understand appropriately these effects of groups upon identity, the following material illustrates people's variable responses to others in the formation of ethnic identity.

ACCULTURATION AND STAGES OF ETHNICITY IDENTITY DEVELOPMENT

The influences on an individual from his/her own culture and other institutions of society can produce a variety of different adaptations in identity and psychology. When people live in a context of influences from more than one culture, there are a variety of possible forms of acculturation, or change. Oppressive and discriminatory institutions can induce a negative outcome in subordinated people, but their cultural institutions can also provide a variety of mechanisms for adaptation and maintenance of self.

Theories of the individual ethnic identity derived from intercultural contact have often emphasized a few set stages of development, a progressive sequence of adaptations typically towards assimilation (e.g., see discussion of Gordon's theory of assimilation in Chapter 6). While there are no fixed stages that all people must pass through in the process of cross-cultural adaptation, there are typical patterns. The structural dynamics of cross-cultural contact produce regular patterns of individual psychocultural adaptation. Identical social circumstances and similar cultural backgrounds can produce as variant adaptations as encapsulation and isolation, nativism, marginalization or mediation, depending upon the goals and resources of the individual. But recurrent patterns in individual self-adaptation to cross-cultural relations are also revealed in studies of the typical patterns of development of ethnic awareness and response to intergroup contact among minority groups, especially African Americans (Cross 1971; Thomas 1971); and the stages of "racial consciousness development" among European American counselors and counselor trainees (Helms 1985; Ponterotto 1988). The individual generally moves from conditions of ethnic encapsulation and a lack of self or other cultural awareness; to various phases of reaction to the other, possibly including extreme ethnic antagonism, self-hate or integration; through various stages of ethnic clarification, and cross-cultural understanding and appreciation; to various forms of biculturalism; and potentially on to a range of multicultural and situation specific identities.

Types of Intercultural Adaptation

There is not a single outcome for identity in contact between ethnic groups since there are many influences and opportunities in adaptation. Group-level cross-cultural adaptations are crucial for understanding the nature of individual adaptations, but while the nature of intergroup relations structures the consequences for individuals, group-level relations do not completely determine the nature of the individual's adaptations to the inter-cultural context. Individual adjustments vary as a function of many influences, including individual goals, community dynamics

and societal factors. But overall patterns do exist, ones in which cross-cultural adaptation of minority and majority group members show cross-cultural regularities. Intercultural contact produces a variety of different kinds of adaptations, exemplified in isolation, passing, marginality, mediation and multiculturalism.

Ghettoization and Isolation

Some theories of ethnic identity development emphasize an initial effort to "pass" or assimilate as a member of the dominant society, but the predominant trend tends to be the opposite. New immigrants tend to seek social and personal support in communities from their country of origin. Individuals in this initial phase of cross-cultural adaptation may attempt to isolate themselves from the dominant society rather than acculturate. This isolation may be achieved by living within an ethnic enclave and maintaining personal and work relationships primarily with those of their own cultural group. Minority members who opt for isolation from the dominant society may do so with different psychological reactions. Some may accept the segregated role and the dominant society's negative attitudes towards their ethnic group, possibly leading to self-hatred and perpetration of negative stereotypes about their own ethnic group. A sense of learned helplessness may be associated with the feeling that the dominant society's prejudices and control of resources may permanently confine the person to a life of poverty and discrimination. Others may accept segregation while rejecting the dominant society's negative stereotypes. This may be accompanied by a deliberate separation in order to avoid contact with the members of the dominant society in an attempt to maintain a positive self-concept within the relations provided by their own ethnic group. While this stage is not typically applied to the members of the dominant culture, they too may attempt to isolate themselves from other cultural groups in society.

Passing

Passing refers to a phenomenon in which the individual rejects their culture of origin, and embraces another culture, an effort at assimilation. Passing generally involves an attempt to appear assimilated when major aspects of the person's characteristics are from a different cultural background, not the dominant society into which they attempt to pass. Passing may involve denial of ethnic identity with their culture of origin, even deprecating that culture in the process of trying to achieve acceptance by the dominant society. This phase may be expected of immigrants, but more likely occurs in later generations. Passing is normally more prevalent among the offspring of immigrants who attempt to deny their parents' culture. This may be accompanied by a withdrawal from contact with their own culture of origin. Such individuals may express hatred of and dislike for their group of origin, and even feel self-hatred because of personal characteristics related to that group.

Nativistic Reactions

At any point in the process of acculturation the individual may feel a need to intensify identity with their culture of origin and reject contact with other cultures. This may be manifested in a variety of ways: racism, nationalism, separatism, rebellion and cultural pluralism. Normally, this nativistic phase follows a period of attempted learning about the other culture and develops as a reaction to the rejection of others. The minority individual may reject the dominant culture, or dominant group members may want to avoid further contact with minorities. Individuals in this phase of ethnic adjustment may engage in social and political action to raise the consciousness and strengthen the identity of other members of their own cultural group, or to promote racism and discrimination against others. Nativism emphasizes in-group ties and traditions, while the dominant culture is rejected. Within the U.S., such reactions have been manifested in the recent past in the Black Power movement, the MECHA and La Raza (Chicano) movement among Mexican Americans, the American Indian Movement and a resurgence of the new "white ethnics" as a defensive reaction against other ethnic groups.

Marginality

The marginalized person was characterized as a cultural hybrid in Stonequist's (1937) classic *The Marginal Man*. Stonequist described the marginalization syndrome as a consequence of an alienated sense of culture membership in which the individual is insufficiently integrated into two different cultural identities, with conflict between the two and confusion in personal identity. Marginality occurs as a consequence of incomplete adaptation; neither culture is thoroughly and completely accepted or acquired by the individual. The person finds him/herself vacillating between the two cultures in conflict and identity confusion, or conversely alienated from both cultural systems and identities. This marginalized position leaves the person insufficiently socialized to the deep moral commitments of either culture. The marginalized person cannot accommodate to the contradictory demands created by the two groups, nor find comfort in the identity and social relations provided by either. Marginality may be addressed by attempting to completely deny one's minority culture past, making an effort to pass into the dominant culture. Such identification may have great emotional costs as parts of one's emotional life and past are denied in the effort to acquire a new ethnic identity. Efforts to resolve marginality through dominant culture identification may be unsuccessful as the members of the dominant society use ethnic cues such as dress, accent, place of residence, skin color, hair texture or other easily recognized features as a means of continued discrimination, thwarting the individual's effort to legitimate a dominant culture identity.

Mediators and Middlemen

Mediators are bicultural people who have effectively integrated both cultures into their personal identity. The interaction of the two cultures may be mediated through a true integration of two different cultural selves, or through a compartmentalization of the person's life. The mediator may have friends, intimate relations and social interaction with members of both cultural groups, but the primary relations in the two cultural groups can remain completely segregated. Some mediators have been "middlemen minorities." These may be represented by entire ethnic groups who occupy social and economic status between the dominant group and the most subordinated groups. Their "middleman" position literally refers to their role as intermediaries linking the two strata of society. They may be merchants serving as business representatives for the lower strata in interactions with the dominant group, or may occupy positions as traders, money lenders, guarantors or in other professional services. Middlemen are generally valued because they provide services for both sectors, shielding the upper strata from contact with the lower, and providing the lower strata with services and goods available from the dominant sector of society. This position can be subject to scapegoating and discrimination for many reasons derived from the intermediary status (convenient to blame for systemic problems, associated with low-status people, accused of exploitation, etc.). In the U.S., Jewish people have played this middleman role, serving as store owners in poor areas and engaging in money-lending activities which had been historically developed as a service to Christians who prohibited money lending by members of their own community. In contemporary times, Asians have increasingly occupied some of the middleman roles both in the U.S. and in other parts of the world. The worldwide diaspora (dispersion, distribution) of the Chinese as a middleman group in business and economic activities of many nations exemplifies this role.

Multiculturalism and Globalism

Multiculturalism is a condition in which individuals are capable of relating effectively to people of two or more cultures and are capable of appropriate participation in substantial aspects of the cultural life of two or more cultural groups. Multiculturalism involves a range of skills and perspectives that allow effective relations with people from many cultural groups. Multiculturalism and related global perspectives represent personal identity development beyond the ethnic and national models. This global identity does not necessarily abandon ethnic or national identities, but rather encompasses them within a broader perspective. Globalism represents a recognition of the dependence upon one another and the benefits that can accrue from a synergistic integration of the complementary potentials provided by different cultures. Globalism as an identity is manifested in a variety of international movements and non-governmental organizations that address issues such as human rights, ecological degradation, preservation of the ozone layer and rain forests and a variety of other human, social and ecological issues that collectively threaten the planet. The dynamics of this cross-cultural development of self are addressed in Chapter 6.

Minority Ethnic Identity Development

By the early 1970s, several theories of ethnic identity development had been elaborated from a focus upon the characteristics of African Americans and their adaptations to the dominant society. Thomas's (1971) model suggested that the Black person began with identity confusion created by the definitions of the dominant society. This requires withdrawal from the dominant society to reexamine and understand the processes of becoming and being a Black in America. This realization leads to an effort to learn about Black cultural heritage and to develop relationships that expand understanding and connections with the Black experience. Finally, the Black person may transcend previous psychological limitations in identifying with all of humanity. Cross's (1971) model of the Negro-to-Black Conversion Experience saw development as following a progressive sequence of stages. Like Thomas's model, Cross's initial Pre-Encounter stage is characterized by a devaluing of Black identity, followed by an Encounter stage in which the individual begins to develop an awareness of Black identity. This gives way to an Immersion stage in which there is an effort to maintain an exclusive adherence to Black ideals and total immersion within Black culture. When the Black is comfortable with Black identity, the stage of Internalization has been reached in which comfortable relations with other cultures are then again possible and a healthier mental adjustment can occur. Counselors and educators (e.g., Atkinson, Morten & Sue 1983; Banks 1987) have taken these ideas of Black ethnic awareness development and expanded them into a more general model of the adaptations of minority groups in general. While some differences exist between them, they reflect basic commonalities in processes and perspectives, as illustrated in the following.

Minority Ethnic Identity Development Sequences

Conformity/Acceptance/Psychological Captivity.
A limited cultural self-awareness, weak and negative self and ethnic identity and a dependence upon and preference for dominant cultural values.

Dissonance.
Cultural confusion and conflict with conformity to the ideals of the dominant culture.

Resistance and Ethnic Encapsulation/Immersion.
Voluntary separatism and ethnic ethnocentrism with a new pride in ethnic group identity developed to challenge and reject the dominant culture.

Introspection/Identity Clarification/Redefinition.
New autonomous identity develops that rejects previous ethnocentric ethnic models and identities, and addresses cross-cultural conflicts in identity and responsibilities in a manner that manifests self-acceptance and positive interethnic relations.

Internalization and Synergistic Awareness.
A new self-fulfilled cultural identity is securely incorporated; acceptance of other cultures and interethnic relations. Some models (e.g., Banks 1987) proposes that these self-acceptance achievements may be followed by a range of cross-cultural developments.

Bi-ethnicity
Capable of effective functioning in two cultures, both of which are integrated into one's identity.

Multiethnicity
Capable of functioning in interaction with numerous cultures with ethnic identity dependent upon the social interaction context.

Globalism
Universalistic values and human principles.

DOMINANT GROUPS' DEVELOPMENT OF ETHNIC AWARENESS

Similar patterns of cross-cultural adaptation to awareness of self and other cultural influences and identity are found among members of dominant cultural groups. Models of "racial consciousness development" for European Americans derive from studies (Helms 1985; Ponterotto 1988) of the changes that occur for European Americans learning about counseling of other ethnic groups, confronting their society's legacy of racism and prejudice and attempting to deal with its implications and their personal responsibility. These stages may be more generally applicable to members of the dominant culture who come into intense and sustained interaction with and learning about other cultures in their society.

Helms (1985) suggests a five-stage theory similar to the Cross model for Blacks' identity development. European Americans may begin in a pre-exposure stage of limited awareness of other groups and little understanding of the nature of ethnic and cultural differences, including the nature of one's own culture. Such people are unaware of ethnicity and cultural characteristics, stating, "I don't have any cultural characteristics. I'm just a normal American!" Contact with other cultures to learn about them may lead to a Disintegration stage in which the European American individual recognizes the role of white racism in society and the practices of prejudice and discrimination against other groups. This knowledge and awareness can lead in two directions, what Helms calls Paternalism vs. Reintegration. A sense of guilt and an effort to compensate and protect ethnic minorities and their interests may lead to a paternalistic posture, or conversely produce a reaction leading to the Reintegration phase that attempts to avoid contact with other ethnic groups and intensifies exclusive relations with European American culture. Hostility towards out-groups may increase, although the individual may eventually develop a greater awareness of the other groups and the need to accept them. If feelings of reintegration are weak, a stage of Pseudo-Independence may emerge, where the person accepts the minority group members and begins to learn more about their cultures. The person at the stage of Pseudo-Independence has knowledge of other cultures, they still tends to view them ethnocentrically, in terms of the person's own culture and values. The final stage in Helms's developmental schema is that of Autonomy, in which the person is knowledgeable about other cultural groups and is capable of accepting and respecting the importance of cultural differences. The person accepts other cultures at cognitive, emotional and behavioral levels and makes an effort to establish relationships with people of other cultural groups as a continued part of the intercultural learning and growth process.

Ponterotto (1988) confirms the major aspects of Helms's model of development in analyzing the experiences of European American counselor trainees. A Pre-Exposure stage of ignorance of cross-cultural issues and a failure to consider historical and contemporary racism and its effects is transformed through contact to a stage of Exposure. In exposure, the individual is confronted with the realities and consequences of racism and prejudice, which forces an examination of group values and individual responsibility. This increasing awareness and recognition of responsibility and the sense of guilt it produces may be dealt with in different ways. This involves opposing options, what Ponterotto called the Zealot-Defensive. In this stage, the individual may take a paternalistic approach in an effort to compensate and protect ethnic minorities, a zealot approach focused upon remedying past wrongs and current injustices by helping repressed groups.

Or instead, the reaction may be one of a defensive reintegration — a reaction in which the person withdraws from contact with these distressing experiences with other ethnic groups, retreating to his/her own cultural enclave. These two options may ultimately be resolved and superseded in an Integration stage, characterized by a reduction of defensiveness and the development of appreciation of other cultures. This involves accepting cultural differences, establishing relationships with the members of other cultural groups and continuing the intercultural learning and growth process.

Majority Ethnic Awareness Development Stages

1) *Pre-Exposure/Contact Stage.*
Ethnocentric, limited self and other cultural awareness; naive "color blindness" or belief in the sameness of people from all cultures.

2) *Exposure/Contact/Disintegration Stage.*
Confrontation with realities and consequences of racism and prejudice and group responsibility.

3a) *Zealot-Paternalism.*
Compensation and protection; accepting responsibility for helping repressed groups and remedying past wrongs and current injustices;
OR
3b) *Defensive-Reintegration.*
Out-group avoidance and hostility, withdrawal into cultural encapsulation.

4) *Pseudo-Independence.*
Acceptance of others, but with persistent ethnocentrism, even hostility.

5) *Autonomy/Integration.*
Knowledgeable about and acceptance of and respect for other cultural groups; recognizes importance of cultural differences; cross-cultural learning as part of personal growth.

SUMMARY: SELF AND IDENTITY IN CROSS-CULTURAL PERSPECTIVE

These patterns of cultural identity formation derived from cross-cultural studies and ethnic psychology illustrate some of the fundamental aspects of identity adaptation to cross-cultural relations. The presence of multiple reference groups means that there are multiple aspects of identity. Hecht (1993) provides a multidimensional view to identity within the framework of a communications model that examines four major dimensions of identity: communal, social (relational), role (enacted) and individual. The communal level of identity is that provided by a group of people bound together in ethnic or cultural identity. The communal aspects of identity have their self-referent in selected aspects of collective life and cultural past and a notion of membership in a select in-group. Identity includes the enactment of relationships between people in the cultural community, producing levels of identity created through social roles. These aspects of identity derive from a communicative process involving the exchange of messages between people to express their identities derived from their relationships. The relationship aspects of identity are those that are constructed in the process of social interaction, which serve to define people's identities in terms of their relationships with others. The individual's identity includes self-cognitions, a self-concept or self-image and feelings about self, all influenced by the other levels of identity. As humans change and broaden their relationships with others, reference groups for modeling their identities can become increasingly complex.

Multicultural experiences and perspectives inevitably lead to the development of new aspects of the self and identity. But the ways in which identity and the self are conceived vary widely. Self-concept represents how it is that one conceptualizes and perceives of oneself as a person, and is necessarily embedded in an indigenous psychology (see Chapter 3). Social identity is a part of self-concept derived from the ways in which social group membership(s) affect the individual's self-concept. This social identity underlies ethnic or cultural identity, based upon a sense of awareness and appreciation of psychological membership in a specific cultural group and in contrast to other groups.

The final desirable ethnic identity development depends upon values, assumptions and preferences. Theories of ethnic identity development have been criticized for assuming assimilation as the normal outcome of ethnic development. Other have pointed to the stages of biculturalism and multiculturalism, an acculturation involving the maintenance of ethnic identity rather than its loss. If the desired outcome of ethnic development is an ethnic identity in which the individual has a well-developed awareness of one's own cultural and ethnic characteristics and is strongly committed to exclusively maintaining them, then biculturalism and multiculturalism may not be part of ethnic identity development. But if we desire cross-cultural competency, then some form of bicultural development is inevitable, as explored in Chapters 6 and 7.

Cultural pluralism in the contemporary U.S. requires that we understand the nature of these cultural differences. The notion that these differences in races are biological has structured intergroup relations in the past, with those consequences still affecting people today. An important step in overcoming this legacy of racism is in developing understanding of the important differences among the various groups in society primarily as derived from culture. To this end, the next chapter provides models for understanding the nature of cultural influences upon behavior and identity. The influences of culture upon individual development and identity involve a range of factors related to how one integrates a variety of cultural influences. The sources of cultural influences are addressed in Chapters 3 and 4, with the material in Chapter 5 addressing group-level dynamics. Chapter 6 examines individual development, and Chapter 7 explains how one can engage in a cross-cultural development process that provides increasingly sophisticated skills for managing intercultural differences.

REFERENCES AND ADDITIONAL READINGS

Atkinson, D., G. Morten and D. Sue. 1983. *Counseling American Minorities: A Cross Cultural Perspective.* Dubuque, Iowa: Wm. C. Brown.

Bandlamudi, L. 1994. "Dialogics of Understanding Self/Culture." *Ethos* (22):160-193.

Banks, James. 1987. *Teaching Strategies for Ethnic Studies.* Boston: Allyn and Bacon.

Boas, Franz. 1911(1965) *The Mind of Primitive Man. New York: Free Press.*

Brues, A. 1977. *People and Races.* Prospect Heights: Waveland.

Cross, W. 1971. "The Negro-Black conversion experience: toward a psychology of Black liberation." In: *Black World* 20:13-27.

Fischer, M. 1986. "Ethnicity and the Post-Modern Arts of Memory." In: J. Clifford and G.E. Marcus. *Writing Culture.* Berkeley: University of California Press.

Garn, S. 1971. *Human Races.* Springfield, Ill.: Charles Thomas.

Glazer, N. and D. Moynihan. 1979. *Beyond the Melting Pot.* Cambridge: MIT Press.

Gordon, M. 1964. *Assimilation in American Life.* New York: Oxford University Press.

Hallowell, A. 1974. *Culture and Experience.* Philadelphia: University of Pennsylvania Press.

Hecht, M. 1993. "2002 — A research odyssey: towards the development of a communication theory of identity." *Communication Monographs* 60:76-82.

Helms, J. 1985. "Towards a theoretical explanation of the effects of race upon counseling." *The Counseling Psychologist* 12:153-165.

Hoopes, D. 1979. "Intercultural communication concepts and the psychology of intercultural experience." In: M. Pusch, ed. *Multicultural Education: A Cross-cultural Training Approach.* pp. 10-38.

Keefe, S., ed. 1989. *Negotiating Ethnicity: The Impact of Anthropological Theory and Practice.* Washington, D. C.: American Anthropological Association.

Lieberman, L., B. Stevenson and L. Reynolds. 1989. "Race and anthropology: a core concept without consensus." *Anthropology and Education Quarterly* 20:67-73.

Marger, M. 1991. *Race and Ethnic Relations American and Global Perspectives.* Belmont, CA.: Wadsworth.

Montagu, A. 1964. *The Concept of Race.* New York: Free Press.

Phinney, J. 1991. "Ethnic identity and self-esteem: a review and integration." *Hispanic Journal of Behavioral Sciences* 13(2):193-208.

Phinney, J. 1996. "When We Talk About American Ethnic Groups, What Do We Mean?" *The American Psychologist.* 51(9):918.

Ponterotto, J. 1988. "Racial consciousness development among White counselor trainees: a stage model." *Journal of Multicultural Counseling and Development.* 16:146-156.

Spindler, L. 1962. "Menomini women and culture change." *American Anthropology Association Memoir,* p. 91.

Stocking, G. 1982. *Race, Culture and Evolution.* Chicago: University of Chicago Press.

Stonequist, E. 1937. *The Marginal Man.* New York: C. Scribner & Sons.

Terpstra V. and K. David. 1991. *The Cultural Environment of International Business.* Cincinnati: South-Western Pub.

Thomas, C. 1971. *Boys No More.* Beverly Hills: Glencoe Press.

Winkelman, M. 1998. *Ethnic Relations in the U.S.: A Sociohistorical Cultural Systems Approach.* Dubuque: Eddie Bowers Publishing, Inc.

NOTES

Other Ethnic Groups

What are some of the other ethnic and cultural groups with which you have the most frequent contact?

What are some of the principal characteristics of these groups?

What are some aspects the social behavior of these other groups that differ from what is the norm in your cultural group?

What cultural or social factors create those aspects of their group behavior which you noted?

Which ethnic groups do you feel particularly positive towards? Why?

Which ethnic groups do you have uneasy feelings toward? Why?

NOTES

<u>NOTES</u>

CHAPTER 3

CULTURE, BIOLOGY AND SOCIALIZATION: THE PSYCHOCULTURAL MODEL

Overview

This chapter introduces the concept of culture and the socialization processes that impose its effects upon humans. These socialization influences are shown to produce both similarities and differences within cultures. The psychocultural model is presented as a framework for organizing information about the many social and cultural influences upon development, including the influences of culture upon biology and behavior. The psychocultural model provides a framework for analyzing the effects of culture upon personality and self-formation, the essence of ethnicity. Frameworks for analyzing ethnicity are provided by anthropological approaches to personality and self embodied in the culture's indigenous psychology.

Objectives

Introduce the basic aspects of culture and their relationship to human biology
Describe the basic processes of socialization and the influences of culture upon behavior
Illustrate the socialization influences of culture and the cultural production of intracultural variation, or within-group differences, from multiple influences from the social and cultural environments
Present models for describing culture's effects upon behavior and personality
Illustrate cultural effects upon life cycle human development and cognition
Present the basic aspects of the psychocultural model as a framework for addressing the many influences involved in the socialization process
Introduce anthropological approaches to ethnicity, personality, self and indigenous psychologies

Chapter Outline

Introduction
The Concept of Culture
    Culture, Biology and Human Needs
Effects of Socialization
    Unconscious Cultural Acquisition
    Behavioral Determinism
    Cultural Adaptation and Integration
    Socialization and Deviance
    Intracultural Variation
    The Ecology of Human Development
The Psychocultural Model
    The Socialization of Biology
    Life Cycle Human Development in Cross-Cultural Perspective
    Culture and Cognition
Anthropological Approaches to Ethnicity
    Personality and Self
    Indigenous Psychologies
    Social Roles and Cultural Self
References and Additional Readings
Self Assessment 3.1: Socialization Experiences

INTRODUCTION

Human behavior is a function of many factors in which species' general genetic bases develop under a variety of ecological, social, cultural and situational influences. Understanding the determinants of human behavior is essential for professional competence in social work practice and the other helping professions, providing a basis for making culturally sensitive service adaptations. The traditional psychosocial perspectives of social work have addressed differences from the pathological perspectives of psychiatry and medicine and the social deviance perspectives of sociology. More recently, differences have been addressed from ecological and cultural systems perspectives that provide a more appropriate perspective for understanding cultural differences in human behavior. Ethnic sensitivity and competence require broader conceptualizations of cultural influences that recognize the role of culture as a positive influence affecting social and psychological dynamics.

This chapter illustrates a range of cultural influences on behavior. The concept of culture provides a broader basis for understanding the nature of race, ethnicity and other factors related to group differences in behavior. Culture, the learned patterns of behavior shared by a group, affects virtually everything that humans do, including producing their perceptions and beliefs regarding race, the content of their ethnic identities, and their everyday behavior. Culture is an organizing concept for understanding both the nature of specific groups and the differences between them. All human behavior is shaped or determined by culture, from the manifestation of basic capacities and needs, to the social conventions that make possible our everyday interactions. These socialization influences often operate unconsciously, but in pervasive ways that affect behavior, personality, identity and intergroup relations.

The Concept of Culture

Culture is the core concept for understanding the fundamental source of human behavior and the basis of social life. Culture has been defined in a variety of ways, but common core concepts underlie the varying definitions of culture. These are that culture is learned human behavior and beliefs which are shared by groups of people, learned through intergenerational transmission of information and used as the basis for adaptations to human problems and needs.

Culture is a "blueprint" or program for what humans do. Culture may be embodied in objects (artifacts), represented in ideas or reflected in behavior and biological responses. Culture is an invisible teacher and controller of humans. It creates thoughts, feelings, beliefs and behavior, frequently totally outside of the consciousness and deliberate intentions of the individual. Culture gives meaning to the world, behaviors, relationships and communication. Culture determines how to relate to the environment and other groups. The fundamental role of culture in human life can be appreciated by recognition of the many human activities and societal functions that culture enables humans to meet.

Basic Functions of Culture

Human Survival
Classification of the World
Interpretation of Behavior
Solutions to Problems
Socialization
Developmental Canalization
Reproduction and Family Organization
Social Organization and Control
Motivation and Legitimization
Provide Values and Behavior

Personal Factors Affected by Culture

Gender and Identity
Language and Communication
Values and Priorities
Beliefs and Attitudes
Dress and Appearances
Social Behavior
Thought and Learning
Emotional Expression

Culture as a System

Culture involves an integrated system of interrelated practices and institutions that organize, regularize, stabilize and integrate human behavior across diverse domains of experience and activity. Cultural systems address the universal needs of humans and the functions of their groups. Culture involves a number of subsystems described in Chapter 4. Cultures involve systems integrated around common values and principles that guide and organize the various institutions that sustain groups. These common principles provide a holistic perspective on a culture and provide an understanding of the principles guiding behavior across diverse situations. An understanding of cultural systems and their global dynamics, as well as their influences upon human behavior and development, is necessary for cultural competence.

Culture, Biology and Human Needs

A basic problem for all of the human sciences is determining the relative importance of biological and cultural influences upon behavior and thereby reconciling the universals of human nature with the diversity of human cultural manifestations. This has been discussed as the "nature-nurture debate" over the genetic versus social determinants of behavior. The real issue is the necessary interaction of genetic potentials and learning, understanding cultural influences and learned behavior as basic to human nature. While recognition of cultural influences provides a basis for the rejection of many aspects of biological determinism, cultural perspectives do not deny biological influences upon human behavior. Human nature is based upon a unique biology, but one that humans share irrespective of their cultural background. There are biological factors to which all cultures must respond and which set important limits on the types of adaptations humans make. For humans, culture and biology have been and continue to be interacting systems. Cultural capabilities are themselves dependent upon a specialized biology for learning. Culture is also intimately involved in structuring and regulating biological functioning. An interactive

feedback loop between culture and biology integrated both together in human evolution and continues to function in contemporary human development. Biologically based processes make possible the acquisition of culture within the social learning environment of other humans of the individual's group, transforming the biological human organism into a cultural being. The acquisition of human behavior — perceptual skills, language, cognitive abilities and personality — is a result of the interaction of biology and culture.

While unique human biology provides the basis for humans' abilities to acquire culture, biology alone cannot create what is recognized as the unique capabilities of humans. The fundamental role of culture in creating human beings is illustrated in the unfortunate cases of children subjected to extreme social isolation during early formative years. These extreme isolation cases, often referred to as "feral" or "wolf" children deprived of years of contact with normal social interaction and opportunities and so do not manifest the physical and social behaviors associated with normal humans. Prolonged deprivation (2 to 6 years) may take the individual beyond the period of plasticity ("window of opportunity") during which normal development for some aspects of human behavior (e.g., language skills) can ever take place. Humans do have biologically based behaviors, once called "instincts" (species-characteristic behaviors), but even these require a normal social-ecological context for their development. Furthermore, many of biologically based behaviors, like free soiling (indiscriminate defecation) and non-seasonal sexuality, are strongly controlled by culture.

All complex human behavior depends upon an intimate interdependence and combination of both biological and cultural potentials. In examining the interaction of the two, we generally find that biology provides the basic capacities that enable us to acquire skills, while culture provides the processes for acquiring those skills related to specific tasks and behaviors. Thus, while biology is crucial to the human capacity for behavior, culture provides the necessary programming that enables capacities to develop and determines the particular patterns of behavior through which they are realized. The unique differences in behavior between groups derive from the cultural or learned bases. On the other hand, the universal features characteristic of people in all cultures are normally found to be based in biology. Even when biologically based factors determine behavior (e.g., the need to eat), culture determines what we eat, when we eat, how we eat and even aspects of our physiological responses to the cultural cues about eating.

Culture and Human Needs

The way in which cultures and individuals respond to biological needs must be incorporated into any complete picture of human development and difference. A central approach to understanding human behavior is from the perspectives of *human needs*, "that which is necessary for either a person or a social system to function within reasonable expectations, given the situation that exists" (Johnson 1992:4). Charlotte Towle's (1965) classic conceptualization of human needs in her *Common Human Needs* reflects fundamental anthropological conceptualizations of the major aspects of cultural systems: physical aspects, including food and shelter; relationships with others and the opportunities for emotional and cognitive development; and provision for spiritual needs, embodied in the ideological aspects of culture. While such needs are universal, they are met in culturally specific ways. Basic needs are manifested through derived or secondary needs, culturally constructed needs (e.g., not any food, but only specific ones, will fulfill our need to eat). Johnson elaborates a model within the framework of Maslow's hierarchy of needs, which moves from material bases meeting physiological needs and safety through social needs for belonging, comfort and self esteem and on to cognitive needs for understanding. However, Maslow's emphasis on self-actualization reflects a Western egocentric bias not shared by many cultures that emphasize social embeddedness and group realizations. Biologically based needs — food, excretion, sleep, social role specialization and reproduction — are met in highly variable ways in different cultures. These different approaches to meeting needs can produce cross-cultural conflict,

especially in child-care settings (see Gonzales-Mena 1993).

EFFECTS OF SOCIALIZATION

The relationships of culture to behavior involve processes of socialization and enculturation. Socialization involves learning the basic social and mental skills necessary for functioning in human society, including language, role expectations, values, beliefs and customary ways of thinking, feeling and acting. Enculturation refers to the socialization into the patterns and expectations of a specific culture. The many different aspects socialization processes involve the interaction of biological, psychological, social and cultural factors. These processes instill cultural influences in personality and identity.

Socialization and Enculturation

Through exposure to others, infants simultaneously undergo a socialization process in which they learn generic aspects of being human (social interaction, role taking, language, etc.), and a more specific enculturation process in which they learn generic human capabilities in culturally specific forms (e.g., a specific language, particular family roles, etc.). Socialization responds to innate human needs (e.g., nutrition, protection, affection), while enculturation provides the culturally specific ways in which the needs are met, as well as providing culturally derived needs to be met and managed. Socialization also involves a two-way interaction, or guided participation (Rogoff 1990), in which the child is an active participant in self-socialization and has reciprocal effects upon others.

Primary and Secondary Socialization

The distinction between primary and secondary socialization processes contrasts the initial influences in the primary group, generally the parents and other primary caretakers, from the subsequent broader influences from society. These early primary socialization experiences are very important to the formation of personality and the development of the secure attachment necessary in the development of later relationships. As the child develops an understanding of social expectations, this provides the basis for relationships beyond the family. The child begins to develop an understanding of society in general — the "generalized other" — the notion that there is a general set of expectations that others in society have about one's behavior. Children become increasing exposed to secondary socialization as their relationships move beyond the family to child care centers, schools, after-school programs, sports activities, clubs and peer groups. Many different influences guide human development. Parenting styles are a central early feature of the socialization process that varies widely between cultures. Other individuals and institutions of the society eventually supplant parental influences, to varying degrees. Understanding differences between primary and secondary socialization relationships is central to addressing the person-in-situation, an ecological and cultural context. The processes of socialization involve both informal and as formal learning settings in most cultures. Informal learning settings in many cultures emphasize *scaffolding* in the learning processes, where competent adults assist cognitive development through direct support and guidance in task completion and problem solving. While the informal learning processes are generally primarily based in family settings and personal engagement utilizing observation, modeling and imitation, the formal socialization processes typified in school systems that introduce new modes of learning focus upon information transfer in the vocal-aural mode. The formal learning processes may not have effective linkages with prior family-based learning styles, creating a gap in the child's ability to transfer effectively information in the formal settings.

The effects of socialization and enculturation are characterized by a number of principles that reflect the ways in which biological, interpersonal and group influences structure the development of the human organism. Central to these effects are unconscious effects of the socialization processes; cultural determination of

behavior, including gender; and cultural adaptation or integration of the individual. Even patterns of deviance, while often seen as violating cultural expectations, are also a product of cultural influences. Cultural effects also produce within-group differences, rather than the common effects of cultures upon their members creating a single kind of person. Appropriate use of cultural information includes recognition that cultural processes produce intracultural (within-culture) variation.

Unconscious Cultural Acquisition

The cultural patterns of behavior acquired through processes of socialization and enculturation lead to both universal patterns of behavior and the acquisition of the patterns characteristic of one's specific cultural group. These learning processes are made possible by the biologically based learning capabilities of humans and their immersion in a sociocultural context. The processes by which humans acquire culture include the principles of introjection and identification, reinforcement and modeling described by Freudian, behaviorist and social learning traditions, respectively (Williams 1983). All of the different ways of learning share an important basis in the unconscious aspects of acquisition of human culture.

Much of what humans learn as cultural beings is based upon processing of material in ways that are outside of conscious awareness and deliberate intention. Language acquisition is a prime example. Language is one of the most complex (if not the most complex) systems of knowledge which humans possess. During primary language acquisition in childhood, it is, however, acquired without much deliberate attention and application of the learner. Young children exposed regularly to speakers of several different languages will acquire competency in all those languages at the same time without deliberate instruction. Through unconscious learning, we acquire the complex cultural system of language and the intricate phonetic, phonemic, morphemic, syntactic and semantic rules that construct the language. But in spite of this implicit knowledge of the structural components of language that humans have acquired, most remain incapable of detailing the productive or generative laws of the native tongues that they use on a daily basis. Rules of language remain largely unconscious, outside of intellectual awareness.

Many aspects of social interaction, including the basic rules in interactive and communicative behavior, are acquired partially or completely unconsciously in fundamental ways. The styles with which people walk, their postures and gestures, eye contact practices, interpersonal space dynamics and many other aspects of routine behavior and social interaction are acquired without deliberate attention paid to the learning process or manifestations in behavior. People of different cultures often try to maintain different interpersonal (proxemic) distances between themselves during interaction, based on their own cultural norms. This is frequently manifested as an intercultural conflict. However, the participants often have no knowledge or awareness of the basis for the conflict. For instance, in social interaction North Americans tend to keep others "at arm's length," while Mexicans tend to maintain a closer interpersonal distance. North Americans often feel that Mexicans are "pushy" or "in their face," while Mexicans often view Americans as "cold" and "distant." Neither party is generally aware of the different proxemic rules or how they unconsciously shape perceptions.

Behavioral Determinism

Cultural systems of beliefs and priorities shape, guide and often determine one's patterns of behavior. Such a perspective does not deny the notion of free will. It does however suggest that whether or not people think that they have a free will and the ways in which they might attempt to express that free will are consequences of cultural learning. In spite of the widespread evidence of cultural influences upon behavior, many people in the U.S. still tend to lead their lives with a sense of free will and individual determination of behavior. This is because many of the influences of culture are manifested as unconscious constraints and compulsions. It also reflects a widespread American ideal that we are "unique individuals" — every last one of us. The

influences that culture has upon behavior tend to be implicit, since they are so widely shared and internalized. One example I frequently use with my classes illustrates the pervasive cultural influences on classroom behavior. In spite of the diverse cultural origins of the students in my classes and their unique individual socialization and learning experiences, they behave in remarkably similar manners. Their diversity in cultural background and socialization apparently has little impact on what they do in the classroom. They typically sit, quietly and attentively (most of them), with paper and writing instruments, taking notes of the lecture. The remarkable conformity and consistency of behavior that emerges in the classroom reflects cultural compulsions towards standard forms of social behavior. The social context of classrooms evokes common patterns of behavior from all of these distinct individuals. Not only does culture provide specific compulsions towards conforming behavior, it also provides important constraints on what people do. Students do not show up in my classes dressed in string bikinis, loin clothes, Greek togas or formal dress. While they might wear such attire in other contexts, cultural constraints on what is appropriate in classroom settings restricts their classroom behavior.

Culture and socialization provide powerful compulsions towards conformity with what is expected by the social group. The compulsions towards conformity not only create uniformity in social behavior, but also conformity to the demands of authorities in individual interactions and small-group settings. Some of the classic experiments in social psychology by Milgram (1975) and Asch (see Rock 1990) illustrated this cultural pressure towards conformity. Milgram's experiment involved subjects recruited to what they thought was a role as an experimental assistant in a learning experiment. The subjects' stated role was to provide response prompts with a word list, to check the "subject's" learning and to administer shocks when they made a mistake. Subsequent mistakes required an increase in the intensity of shocks. While the experimental subjects were isolated from direct contact with the subject learning the list (actually an accomplice of the experimenter), they could hear what were cries and protests as shock levels increased. Many subjects persisted in administering what they thought were dangerous and lethal levels of shocks in spite of the other person's apparent protest. When subjects paused to ask if they should continue, the experimenter's response as to whether they understood what was expected of them was sufficient social pressure to convince most subjects to continue, implicitly conforming to cultural expectations about relationships to authority. Asch studied less violent but equally persuasive social influences upon conformity. In his experiment, subjects were asked to judge the relative length of three lines with differences that were sufficiently great to make judgment of differences unproblematic. Unknown to the actual experimental subjects, the other "subjects" making judgments of the lines' length were actually confederates of the experimenter. The confederates in the room with the actual subject were instructed to make erroneous but consistent judgments among themselves about the relative lengths of the lines. The actual subjects were normally overwhelmed by the social consensus. Although they knew it to be erroneous, the subjects generally reported their judgments in agreement with the majority.

Culture has numerous and pervasive compulsions upon behavior. While people may experience the world as unique individuals and feel that they make decisions based upon their own free will, rather than from some cultural determination, their behavior is always framed by cultural learning and experiences. Cultural learning provides the options from which people may choose, and the broad frameworks within which people engage in behavior, constrained by the cultural assumptions about what is possible. Even deviants follow cultural norms for their behavior. The influences of culture are so pervasive that even when someone decides to deviate, or if a person becomes mentally ill, the person still follows cultural patterns of deviance and illness. The cultural influences on mental illness are widely recognized as "cultural bound syndromes" or "folk illnesses" which are specific to particular cultural groups. Even standard or universal psychiatric syndromes (e.g., paranoia) have culture-specific features that reflect how culture affects the content of behavior.

Cultural Adaptation and Integration

These common behaviors of members of a culture reflect patterns of cultural adaptation. Cultural adaptation refers to processes of both an individual and group nature. Adaptation refers to the adjustment of groups to their environment and individuals to their cultures. The concept of cultural adaptation reflects the balance between cultural systems and their environments. Cultural integration refers to the consistency of principles, values and structures across the different institutions and contexts of the culture, and consistency of norms and behavior across the various members of culture. This consistency reflects a cultural core, characteristics which people of a culture share in common. The common cultural influences upon the members of the culture and the adaptation of the individual personality to the patterns of the culture provides for an integration of individuals into the culture. The consistency of the same behaviors, values, and principles across diverse members of a cultural group reflects individual adaptation to and integration within a culture. However, as cultures and societies become more complex, they tend to develop greater internal differentiation and less integration, and have a lesser degree of integration across their members in terms of common patterns in their behavioral adaptations.

LeVine (1973) proposed that cultures create the need for four distinct aspects of adaptation for the individual's personality. The child care environment and the customs that guide parent-child interaction are in part an adaptation of the child-rearing practices to ecological pressures. The adaptation of child-rearing practices to ecological pressures are manifested in the typical differences in child-rearing practices of lower-class as versus middle-class parents. A second adaptation involves those factors created by the parental behaviors established through deliberate aspects of the socialization process. The use of parental guidance, rewards and punishments shapes children's behavior toward actual and ideal adult behavior. A third aspect of adaptation involves the secondary adaptations of self-image and personality to the normative roles, attitudes and behaviors required of adults. This may involve a strengthening of principles of behavior initiated in childhood socialization, or may represent radical departures from childhood principles, for instance, when initiation rites terminate childhood patterns and initiate adult ones. This secondary socialization (e.g., schools, military, peers, work, initiation, etc.) and its influences may be quite distinct from those of family. The fourth aspect of personality adaptation involves the adaptation of the aggregate personality characteristics of the population, including conformance with the ideal patterns represented in the expressive systems and rewarded by society.

Socialization and Deviance

Socialization of the individual to the specific institutional goals of a society creates an adaptation of the personality to meet these socially and culturally imposed goals. The expectations about appropriate behavior, coupled with rewards and punishments, are considered to provide the motivations for acquiring and adhering to the culturally expected patterns of behavior. But in addition to conformity, societies are also characterized by deviation, where people fail to meet normative expectations or deliberately flaunt them. These deviant patterns are also important aspects of understanding societal values and ideals for people. The different personality types, including non-normative profiles and social dynamics, serve to differentiate and delineate the intracultural patterns and internal differences in psychocultural dynamics. The patterning and normative nature of deviance indicates that it reflects intracultural diversity that must be included within a model of group social psychology. Individuals who do not conform to the ideal or expected norms for behavior also experience cultural and psychocultural patterning. These occurrences of deviation follow typical patterns, reflecting cultural processes that lead to patterns of deviation. The cultural patterning of deviance provides a characterization of what the society values and feels is most important. The relationship of deviant behavior to social norms illustrates that deviance is often an exaggeration of the normative expectations of social life, as well as a protest against what are perceived as the excesses of normative behavior. Deviance may also point to the breakdown of norms as a consequence of dysfunctional societal institutions. The relationship of the particular deviant behaviors to cultural meanings provides additional perspective on normative core value orientations. Deviance can reflect a number of different population dynamics; with the patterns of deviance helping to clarify the culture's expectations for individual personality and how they are achieved. The incidence and psychosocial dynamics of deviance and behavioral disorder and illness provide important information about social values, social integration and patterning and the conditions of dysfunction. The procedures for remedying deviance, particularly the therapeutic systems and their ideology of illness and cure are important sources of information about the indigenous conceptions of group psychodynamics.

Intracultural Variation

Culture provides an understanding of the common patterns of behavior that characterize a group, including behavior, personality, social roles, etc. But while culture provides the basis for commonalities, it does not create a single type of individual. Cultures are characterized by numerous sources of internal variation, including differences in men's and women's roles, between generations, in occupational specializations, between class positions, in family roles, etc. Culture does not permit exact prediction of behavior but rather an understanding of the range of typical variation and possible normative and alternative patterns that an individual may adopt. Culture also provides a basis for understanding the different patterns of behavior that its members may adopt. These include behaviors that related to different positions (statuses) within the culture and the associated behaviors (roles). For example, these include different expectations of fathers in different cultures. Patterns of deviance within a culture also follow patterns; even the individuals who do not conform to the ideal or expected norms for behavior manifest typical cultural patterns of deviance.

Appropriately using cultural information requires a differentiation of stereotypes from normative cultural characterizations or what is typically expected within a culture. Cultural characterizations help us understand the internal complexity of a group and the typical characteristics of individuals. Culture characterizes the patterns of variation that occur within the group as well as the commonalities. The multiple social and cultural influences upon socialization require a complex model of the diverse influences of culture, including a recognition of the internal contradictions found within culture.

Ideal and Real Culture

Understanding the effects of cultural values, norms and requirements requires a differentiation between the cultural ideals and the actual, real behavioral norms. While cultures state and embody certain ideals for behavior to which members of the culture are expected to adhere, achievements of these ideals by members of the culture may vary widely. In spite of cultural compulsions towards ideals, many people in a culture do not achieve those ideals or adhere to the ideal norms. Or, the members of cultures as a whole may believe that people in general do achieve some ideal (e.g., equality) even though a large proportion of the population may actually not be afforded these opportunities. The relationship between ideals and reality is an important perspective for addressing aspects of intracultural variation.

The Ecology of Human Development

The necessity for the consideration of multiple influences upon behavior is exemplified in Bronfenbrenner's (1977, 1979, 1989) systems approach to the ecology of human development. The ecology of human development involves examination of the accommodation between developing humans and their immediate settings, including the effects of relations with broader social contexts. The nature of the settings of

interaction between the developing child and others, as well as the relationships between different settings, is crucial to individual development. These settings and their interactions are described by Bronfenbrenner as:

* Microsystem — Face-to-face settings and interpersonal relations that affect interaction with the immediate environment
* Mesosystem — Linkages between the person's different microsystem settings
* Exosystem — Linkages between social settings that include contexts beyond the person's immediate environment that affect development within immediate settings. These are exemplified in linkages of family or peer networks to social institutions such as schools or other agencies
* Macrosystem — Patterns linking micro-, meso- and exosystems of the person's culture with the broader society.

These embedded ecological systems perspectives provide important tools for the social worker's person-in-environment analysis because of the need to understand how people are linked both directly and indirectly to multiple contexts, and influenced by settings beyond their immediate experience and control. These interacting systems provide perspectives for understanding how it is that different persons in the same society, culture or community might have dramatically different socialization experiences. Consequently, Bronfenbrenner emphasizes the importance of the developmental niche, the learning environment and factors affecting developmental processes derived from the interaction among the person's everyday life settings, the childrearing customs of their family culture and the psychological structures and expectations of caretakers. These fundamental influences on development must also be understood in terms of their mesosystem linkages to other systems of influence. These multiple influences based in differential access to various systems and subsystems can be addressed within the parameters of the psychocultural model.

THE PSYCHOCULTURAL MODEL

The relationship of culture to behavior and personality is a long-standing part of anthropology (Bock 1988a; Bourguignon 1979). Psychological anthropology's models integrate a variety of perspectives to elucidate historical and contemporary factors affecting personality. This is exemplified in the conceptual framework of the *psychocultural model* by Whiting and Whiting (1995), based upon the insights obtained from decades of cross-cultural studies of the socialization process and its effects upon personality and behavior. Whiting and Whitings' psychocultural model considers the primary elements to be history, environment, the maintenance (cultural) system, the child-rearing environment, innate needs and projective systems. The psychocultural model provides a systems approach for examining the diverse ecological, familial, cultural and societal influences upon development of personality, behavior and ethnicity.

The *environment* has many influences on culture and personal development. Resource-scarce environments will affect people differently than abundant ones, and harsh and dangerous environments require parental restrictions on children to assure their safety. Cultural *history* provides the repertoire of experiences and models with which parents model their own behavior and that of their children. The *maintenance or cultural system* includes the totality of cultural and societal institutions that structure behavior and opportunities. This cultural system provides the influences upon individual and group behavior, shaping the child's *innate skills and potentials*, including needs, drives and capacities. The influences on these biological potentials are primarily exercised in the *child's learning environment*, where interactions with other members of the culture, beginning with family, serve to transmit and instill cultural influences in development. The confluence of the innate tendencies with learned behavior during childhood may interact with broader societal influences in producing the *adult personality*. This personality both reflects and projects its influences and dynamics in the *projective and expressive system* such as religion, mythology, cosmology, ritual art, etc.

The relationship of human behavior and culture is more complex that the linear model suggested, with feedback loops and interactions. Potentially, any aspect of the system can directly impact socialization and development patterns at another part of the system. Projective and expressive systems provide direct input into the child rearing environment, providing values, guidelines and instructive material about cultural beliefs and expectations. The environment may also directly impact the child-rearing environment, for example, when a harsh or dangerous external environment restricts children indoors or to other safe settings. Learning affects how the family environment and cultural system are structured and the physical environment conceived and treated.

The psychocultural model illustrates the multitude of influences that must be considered in order to appreciate the cultural influences upon personality and identity. The diverse nature of inputs to the model, as well as the options at every level of the model, provide a basis for assessing not only cultural commonalities, but also intracultural variation. That is, there will be variation among members of the same culture in terms of their socialization experiences and how they respond. These differences will result from any variety of factors: internal variation in environment, different family histories and structures, different economic opportunities, different secondary socialization experiences, different adult models, etc. Some of the most significant aspects of these models — psychohistorical perspectives, the organization of work, innate needs and expressive culture — are elaborated in the following sections and in Figure 3.1.

History
Traditions and Beliefs
Intergroup Relations

Environment
Ecosystem Relations and Adaptations
Migrations and Borrowings

Maintenance System/Cultural and Social System

Production
Subsistence and Work Patterns
Means of Production
Division of Labor

Domestic Economy
Family Organization
Kinship Patterns
Community Organization

Reproduction
Population Size
Fertility Patterns

Political Economy
Political Systems
Social Structure and Stratification
Law and Social Control

Child's Learning Environment
    Settings Occupied
    Caretaker Relations and Teachers
    Tasks Assigned
    Mother's Work

Socialization of Biological Needs
Needs, Drives and Capacities
Emotions and Attachment
Sex and Family Roles
Secondary Social Drives

Learned
Behavioral Styles
Skills and Abilities
Value Priorities
Conflicts and Defenses

Secondary Socialization
Stages of Life Cycle Development
Social Roles
Initiation and Adult Transition
Mesosystems, Exosystems and Macrosystem Relations

Individual Adult
Material and Social Organization of Behavior
Social Roles
Population Ideals and Norms

Projective/Expressive Systems
    Religious Beliefs and Practices
    Art and Recreation
    Deviance, Crime and Suicide Rates
    Indigenous Psychology

Ritual and Ceremony
Games and Play
"Culture-Bound Syndromes"

**Figure 3.1. Expanded Psychocultural Open-Systems Model
For Research on Self, Personality and Ethnic Identity**

Psychohistorical Perspectives on Psychocultural Dynamics

The need for a psychocultural systems perspective on personality is increasingly recognized in other academic fields. Gilmore (1984) points out that new perspectives needed to characterize the psychological dynamics of the other groups include the collective personality developments of groups, the relationship of the individual to the larger collectivities, the role of the family in socialization and psychohistorical explanations, collective psychological issues, and indigenous (non-Western) conceptions of personality. A serious shortcoming of the classic psychohistorical approach has been the neglect of the sociocultural and institutional environment, the economic, institutional, demographic, political and cultural contexts that shape behavior. Runyan (1988) outlines a systems approach with six levels as an alternative framework for conceptualizing psychohistory and constructing historical psychologies. These are persons, groups, organizations, institutions, social systems and international or intersocietal relations. This perspective indicates structures for assessment of the sociocultural context that shapes individual behavior.

The Organization of Work and Political Economy

Cross-cultural research indicates that central factors affecting personality formation are derived from the organization of work. The principal items in Whiting and Whiting's maintenance system and learning environment are explicitly work related: subsistence patterns, means of production, the division of labor, task assignment and mother's work patterns. The structures of materialist investigation of culture — infrastructural reproduction and production, domestic and political economy and structure (Harris 1987) — provide an organizing framework for the investigation of psychocultural characterizations from both the internal, cultural ethnic point of view and from the point of view of the dominant society as well. The fundamental work and economic interactions, work behaviors and organization, relations of means of production and division of labor provide characterizations of desired social behavior, social ideals and social ideology that create primary role identification. The universal aspects of work (Applebaum 1987) can be used as a structure for the assessment of specific aspects of workplace socialization for social behaviors and values. The work-related approach of the psychocultural model dovetails with the focus upon social structural influences on personality development. This "social structure and personality" approach focuses on the psychological characteristics of classes or roles (statuses) within a society. The importance of class-related subcultural psychologies is indicated by a broad range of findings that indicate class differences in many characteristics: achievement motivation, internal/external locus of control and behavior of people in different social strata. One's social class disposes toward different interests and motivations and varying patterns of behavior, in essence subcultural psychologies. Class differences in parental styles and value emphases (e.g., the middle class stresses authoritative styles and independence while the lower class stresses authoritarian styles and obedience) point to some substantial differences in class psychodynamics. Such a perspective leads to a focus upon class psychologies; but, rather than a strictly materialist approach, it employs what Bock (1988) calls a "positionalist" approach, which includes other criteria (e.g., ethnicity, sex, age, occupation, differential socialization) as a means of illustrating primary role identification and identifying the essential aspects of psychic integration. Similarly, social conditions may be used to infer aspects of social self and identity (e.g., repression, frustration and hostility inferred from repressive and exploitative social conditions).

Psychocultural Aspects of Expressive Culture

Expressive culture refers to those aspects of cultural activity called art, performance drama, myth, ritual, etc., which are embodied in stories, proverbs, poetry, visual arts, dance, music, ballads, myths, legends and oral traditions. Expressive culture is a source of information about cultural psychologies, especially as related to the social presentation of people and the ideals and scripts for behavior. Expressive culture provides insight regarding collective psychosocial dynamics. Expressive culture can be used as a means of understanding ethnicity because it provides an expression of group sentiments and psychodynamics. Expressive culture serves socialization functions through expression of feelings, communication of culturally important meanings, formulation and expression of social sentiment, fulfillment of psychological needs and expression of the ideals for appropriate social behavior and aspects of the social structure. Expressive culture also serves socialization functions in examples of norm violations and the resultant consequences, and serves integrative functions through expressing commonly understood meanings and evoking collective emotions and experiences. Expressive manifestations of culturally important emotions provides a perspective on the collective psychocultural dynamics of a group. Since expressive culture abstracts the unconscious representations of the culture and expresses themes and values basic to culture, it provides an important means of gaining insight into unconscious psychocultural patterns. Expressive material reflects cultural perceptions of social reality and ideas about humans' social relations with the supernatural, itself a projection of society. Religion is an important source of expressive culture and indigenous psychology. Religious beliefs provide ultimate values and justifications, determining many aspects of behavior, attitudes and values, and organizing familial, economic, social and political activities. Some of the most important aspects of the cultural conceptualization of the person are found in religious systems. Representations of humans in supernatural systems provide symbolic depictions of the social domain, societal forces and interpersonal conflicts. These perspectives derive from the recognition that the supernatural, religious and cosmological beliefs are projective systems that reflect symbolic and metaphorical modeling of personalities, selves and the forces that affect them. Religion has been called the source of culture, providing meanings, rules for social behavior and a cosmology and metaphysics (explanations about the origin and nature of the world). Religion can provide perspectives and organizing frameworks for understanding the global patterns of psychocultural dynamics and behavior since they embody ideals for individual behavior and insight into the linkages of the individual to the group. These expressive culture perspectives are elaborated in the later sections of this chapter.

Advantages of the Psychocultural Approach

Characterizations of psychocultural dynamics and ethnic identity can be constructed from the components of the psychocultural model, especially historical identifications, work organization, the child-rearing environment, the socialization of biological needs and potentials, secondary socialization, projective systems and expressive materials. These diverse foci facilitate a representation of historical models, environmental-behavioral dynamics, family and social influences, intergroup behavior and the cultural self-images constructed in cultural ideology and psychology. The psychocultural model provides mechanisms that explain the processes through which both cultural similarities as well as internal diversity are produced. The diverse inputs to the model and the variable options at every level of the model provide a basis for assessing intracultural variation. Differences within a culture can be investigated in terms of a variety of factors, including variation in social and legal status; occupational specialization and economic resource distribution; family structures, composition and dynamics; different secondary socialization experiences; different adult models; and various linguistic, communication, educational, religious and other ideological factors. Advantages of the psychocultural model for representing ethnicity and group psychologies derive from its open system approach, incorporating many conceptual and theoretical foci relating psychology and culture. The inappropriate application of outsider perspectives that fail to represent the psychocultural dynamics of other cultures are partially resolved by the use of emic perspectives, particularly representations from indigenous psychologies, cultural ideology and expressive culture. The conceptually related social structure and personality approach provides tools for constructing culturally specific forms of behavior, social self and personal and group identity. The notion of a social role or status has been a fundamental concept in the social sciences for revealing how social behavior is organized within a culture and social senses of self inculcated. This social type or status (position) and the associated responsibilities provide the linkages of the individual to sociocultural institutions, permitting social conditions to illustrate group psychology.

The Socialization of Biology

LeVine (1973, 1982) describes the processes of socialization that create the relationships of culture and personality from a Darwinian perspective that incorporates both biological and social dimensions. This perspective provides a common framework for addressing the necessity of the human personality to adapt to both the physical and sociocultural environment. The materialist approaches emphasize the need to ground our understanding of human behavior in the physical conditions of life, both in terms of the external environment (the ecology) and our biological heritage (human needs). What are significant are both the actual material conditions and how the culture represents its manifestations. These conditions are the baseline from which humans make rational decisions and adaptations, framed by cultural conceptions of what is rational and meaningful. Parents socialize their children to adapt to those environments, as well as the future environments they will face as adults. Since these adaptations involve forms of learning, the focus of the culture and personality relationship must be on these processes of learning or socialization. LeVine suggests that these learning and socialization processes can be approached through a number of types of information: institutional goals, the normative institutional rules and sanctions for role performance, situational norms for managing institutional and motivational pressures, patterns of personality in social situations, personality dispositions, success in attaining institutional goals, experienced

satisfactions and frustrations of the population, and behavior disorders and deviant behavior.

LeVine proposes that cultures create four distinct aspects of adaptation for the individual's personality — environmental, primary parental socialization, secondary socialization and group adaptations to population norms. These involve adaptation of the child-rearing practices to ecological pressures; deliberate aspects of the socialization process; secondary adaptations of personality to the roles, attitudes and behaviors required for adults; and the adaptation of the aggregate personality characteristics of the population, respectively. The child-care environment and cultural customs that guide parents' interactions with children are part of an adaptation of the child-rearing practices to ecological pressures. Subsequent adaptations involve deliberate parental behaviors established in the socialization process, such as the use of rewards and punishments to shape children's behavior. A third aspect of personality development involves the secondary adaptations of self-image and social roles related to the normative roles, attitudes and behaviors expected of adults. This secondary socialization (e.g., schools, military, peers, work, initiation, etc.) may involve influences quite distinct from the primary influences of family. The fourth level of personality adaptation involves adaptation to the aggregate personality characteristics of the population. Behavior patterns of the adult population as a whole will tend to conform to the ideal patterns represented in the expressive systems and rewarded by society.

The cultural patterns of addressing biosocial needs provide insights into the culturally patterned ways of manifesting human nature. Cultural psychologies and psychodynamics are revealed in cultural patterning of universal biosocial structures, such as human needs; sex roles and the structures and roles of parents and family members; emotions and the bodily symptoms of affective reactions; life span developmental stages; daily activity rhythms; cognitive modes and their applications; conceptualization and management of illness, particularly sick roles and "culture-bound syndromes", and deviance behavior and models of heroes (see LeVine 1973/1982:226).

Needs and Drives

All cultures must address the needs and drives found in human nature. The culturally specific ways of managing these aspects of human biology provide a basis for characterizing the cultural personality and self. The socialization of primary and secondary drives and their linkages to values provide information about the motivation, prestige, rewards structures, desires, idealized selves and personality organization (LeVine 1973:226). Cultural psychodynamics are revealed in the cultural significance attached to the structuring of basic needs and the socialization of primary and secondary drives through their linkages to cultural values. Universal biosocially based features such as sex, emotions and developmental stages provide important vantage points for examining how cultural processes and characteristics provide for the construction of ethnic identity.

Emotions

Psychocultural dynamics are illustrated by the socialization of emotions and their culturally patterned manifestations. Emotions are an important focus of psychocultural socialization because they include biologically based social potentials that are always shaped by the cultural and social dynamics. Emotions are a central issue in what Levy (1983) characterizes as a universal tension between the private and public aspects of the self or person. These emotionally charged aspects of private and public self are controlled and selectively expressed in social behavior. Facial expressions of basic emotions are easily understood across cultures (Ekman & Friesen 1969, 1986; Izard 1977; Ekman 1972), indicating a biologically based affective dynamics provides a basis for emotions. The manifestations of these basic emotions and the cultural norms about their acceptable and unacceptable expressions provide information about normative and ideal cultural values for personality and behavior. Culture influences what evokes emotion, how emotions may be expressed or inhibited and the significance to others. Social aspects of affective reactions can be studied through their physical manifestations

(joyous celebrations, weeping, sexual acts, nausea/vomiting, laughing), their occurrence in festivals and in terms of cultural ideals regarding their expression and significance. Human emotions have a biological basis, but there are a number of dimensions of cultural variation, as well as culturally unique emotions. The same materials or situations can evoke very different emotional responses, and cultures also differ in terms of the emphases they place on different kinds of emotional expression. Cultures also create unique emotions, providing significant information for characterizing psychocultural dynamics. Cross-cultural differences in the patterning and social manifestations of emotions and the cultural emphases placed on different kinds of emotional expression provide information about critical aspects of cultural psychology and ethnic identity. Important aspects of the psychocultural emotional dynamics are also revealed in the development of infant attachment and parental behavior.

Gender Roles

The effects of culture upon human biology are illustrated in the distinction between sex, as a biologically based reproductive characteristic of species, versus gender, the socially and culturally determined characteristics of the different sexes. While there is a biological basis for universal differentiations of male and female behavior, the cultural determination of behavior appropriate for males and females provides the most important patterning of men's and women's behaviors. Understanding these culturally normative patterns, as well as their variation within cultural groups, is a fundamental aspect of delineating psychocultural dynamics ethnic identity and significant factors developing cultural sensitivity and competence. Cross-cultural differences between male and female behavior are referred to as the universal sex role division of labor. In all cultures, men and women have different typical primary foci in their behavior — an external (male) and domestic or internal (female). In all cultures men have been primarily responsible for activities that take them away from a home base (e.g., hunting, warfare, long-distance travel) while women have been primarily responsible for tasks compatible with the care and protection of young children. These differences reflect adaptations to conditions that optimize care and protection of young offspring, particularly breast-feeding infants. But while divisions of labor based on sex are related to biology, they are adaptations to biological differences rather than causal determinants of biology. People who cross these sex roles in modern societies illustrate that these differences are cultural adaptations rather than biological determinants. Men may care for and rear children, including feeding and performing domestic chores, while women may work outside the home. The social and technological conditions of advanced industrial societies allow for sex role adaptations distinct from those required in hunting and gathering societies. Nonetheless, there are many different cultural adaptations to sexual difference, making gender an important source of information about ethnicity and culture.

Life Cycle Human Development in Cross-Cultural Perspective

Development across the life cycle provides a number of vantage points on the nature of socialization processes and the ideals and behaviors instilled. How cultures respond to the effects of universal biological processes (e.g., birth, brain maturation stages, first menses, puberty, adult transition, marriage, menopause, senility and death) provides both a comparative perspective, as well as a focus upon the specific ways a culture addresses these needs. The cultural interpretations of universal features of life cycle development provide a point of reference from which to assess the nature of ethnic identities, as well as cultural motivations, interpretations and influences. The culturally patterned expressions managing universal developmental features of life provide a vantage point for studying social and emotional relationships and the socialization of primary emotional relationships into culturally specific forms through which they are expressed. However, life cycle development stages are not all universal, but often reflect culturally specific conceptualizations. Such culturally specific stages of development provide important perspectives on individual and group influences. The

developmental focus upon culturally defined conceptions of stages and changes, especially when certain social expectations and personality types are emphasized in formal recognition and ceremonial activities, reveals some of the most significant cultural conceptualizations of the person. Culturally defined conceptions of the life stages and the changes in identity across the stages of development in terms of social expectations provide a focus upon the development of culturally specific aspects of the personality, as well as on social roles and identity and psychocultural dynamics (see Munroe & Munroe 1975).

Developmental perspectives understand human behavior in terms of regular changes across the life span that involve growth in physical, behavioral, emotional, moral, cognitive, spiritual and other dimensions. While the stages associated with these dimensions are often characterized as universal, they are subject to powerful cultural influences and, in some cases, by cultural determinants. For instance, theories of human development have often equated puberty and adolescence, considering both to be universal. While puberty, involving hormonal and physical changes, is a universal of normal human development, adolescence is a culturally recognized stage of development found in some societies, cultures and ethnic groups and not in others. Even puberty, a physiological set of changes, is subject to extreme cultural variation in its onset, social manifestations and cultural meanings. Menarche (first menses) may occur as early as 8 or 9 years of age or be delayed until the late teens; dietary factors such as wheat and fats hasten first menses, while protein deficiencies will retard it. In some cultures, first menses is viewed as a sign of adult status and eligibility for marriage, while in others marriage may still be a decade or more away. Some cultures stigmatize it as a polluted condition requiring extended seclusion, while others treat it as a natural occurrence with little or no cultural significance.

Erikson's (1982) theory of psychosocial development is widely used to understand changes across the lifespan and the associated crises of growth as involving a set of universal sequences of developmental achievements. Gardiner, Mutter and Kosmitzki (1998) provided a range of analyses that illustrate the biases and inaccuracies that result from attempting to apply this theory derived from Western cultural norms to assessing people from other cultures. The Western biases of Erikson's theory require modifications to make it useful in other cultural settings. A culturally sensitive approach to understanding the person-in-situation requires an understanding of these ecological, cultural and niche influences.

Erikson's first two developmental crises involving trust and independence reflect universals of a trusting bond with primary caretakers, and the eventual development of a degree of autonomy from the primary bond through the development of outside relationships. But these theoretical conceptualizations also embody Western cultural biases. In some societies, development involves an increasing interdependence rather than independence. While there is an underlying human universal of attachment between the child and a significant other who helps the child feel secure, especially in threatening situations, there are recognized differences both across and within cultures in terms of attachment dynamics between parents and their offspring. Laboratory studies of these threatening situations and children's responses reveal important cross-cultural differences in how fundamental bonding is managed, as Gardiner, Mutter & Kosmitzki's (1998) review shows. Cross-national studies show major differences in the levels of secure attachment (where children do not feel threatened by strangers), differences in anxious/avoidant behaviors (where children do not try to reunite with caretakers following their absence) and anxious/resistant behaviors (where children become very distressed upon separation and even following return of caretakers). While the European American culture often concerns itself with avoidance of "spoiling" children through over-indulgence in their attachment needs, in other cultures attachment is not an issue. Rather, the constant contact of the child with a large group of caregivers creates a secure environment in which separation is never considered.

There are well-recognized cross-cultural differences in the importance of social attachments. For instance, while European American culture emphasizes and instills autonomy through many mechanisms, the value systems of other cultures maintain an emphasis on interdependence that may persist throughout life. The emphasis on autonomy exemplified by the European American child sleeping apart from the parents may not occur until years later in Japanese culture, where co-sleeping arrangements enhance social learning and interdependence as an ideal value. Erikson's emphasis on the importance of initiative and industry in subsequent developmental concerns also reflects Western cultural preferences. While such achievements require independent initiative in Western cultures, other cultures (e.g., Japan) have these qualities achieved through enhancement of the role of interdependence. Concerns about identity versus role confusion take on very different dynamics in cultures, where in contrast to the European American emphasis on self-differentiation from family and autonomous decision making, there is an emphasis on clearly defined adult transition processes (rites of passage) and adult roles that emphasize continued interdependence. Gardiner, Mutter & Kosmitzki (1998) suggest that the late adulthood developmental crises of integrity versus despair, particularly the negative outcomes, reflect the consequences of Western cultures' emphases on nuclear families, independent residence patterns and the value of youth; these factors produce isolation and alienation for the elderly. They point to the central role of these cultural factors in the reasons for crises and acceptable outcomes.

Cultural biases in theories make them of questionable applicability for understanding the situations and goals of clients from other ethnic groups.. "[I]t is clear that successful advancement through the eight stages . . . [of Erikson's stages of psychosocial development] results in the individual becoming increasingly autonomous, independent, industrious, and self-initiating. . . . [But the] progression of stages embraces the values of 'rugged individualism' and does not apply to . . . traditional cultural infrastructure, which tends to be heavily collectivistic in orientation. The values associated with the West (e.g., autonomy, independence, industriousness, and self-initiative) are replaced in Asia by interdependence, self-sacrifice, and loyalty to family and group members" (Gardiner, Mutter & Kosmitzki 1998:264). In such cultures, normal healthy development involves movement from dependence towards a greater dependence that is then transformed into an interdependence. An ecological systems perspective that examines developmental conflicts in relation to the patterns of cultural and social behavior is necessary to avoid the ethnocentric biases inherent in applying theories from one culture to another.

The universality of certain features of life and development (e.g., birth, adult status, death) provide a point of reference from which to assess the nature of ethnic realities, as well as cultural motivations and influences. However, even universal stages of development are managed in culturally specific manners. Life cycle development stages currently emphasized in American developmental psychology are not all universal; rather they often reflect culturally specific influences. Culturally specific stages of development (e.g., Bar Mitvzah, quinceañera) can provide important perspectives on individual development, especially in relationship to group influences.

Culture and Cognition

How humans perceive and conceptualize the world is a product of enculturation. Adults of different cultures are equally competent in general perceptual skills, memory, the cross-modality integration of information and reasoning processes. But cross-cultural studies show that culture and socialization have effects upon many aspects of perceptual experience and cognitive processing. Cultural influences on cognitive tendencies include differences in cognitive preferences (e.g., abstract versus concrete, field independence versus field dependence), as well as the rate of acquisition of certain cognitive tendencies and the contexts to which they are applied. Cultural patterns of cognition, including dominant learning styles, reasoning processes and judgments, provide potent sources of cross-cultural differences that need to be adapted to interpersonal relations, and especially in training programs.

A central psychological theory about cognition is Piaget's (1980) stages of cognitive development. While the major stages are found cross-culturally, attesting to their universality, there are also significant cross-cultural differences in the extent to which the stages are acquired, the age of achievement and the materials with which such competencies may be demonstrated. Widespread findings in earlier decades that suggested major cognitive deficits in cognitive competence in non-Westerners have subsequently been modified with the realization of the cultural factors and biases embedded in cognitive testing procedures and materials. For example, while European American adolescents may provide abstract reasoning and categorical classification with geometrical figures, or with mixed sets of tools, clothes and food, children in other cultures will often show functional or concrete classification with these materials (see Scribner & Cole 1974). However, when classification tests utilize culturally meaningful material (e.g., wild and domesticated animals, different types of rice), the non-European American children, exhibit abstract performance while European American children often engage in concrete classification with this unfamiliar material. Though adults from other cultures may do poorly on Western tests of intelligence and thought processes, abstract and logical thought capabilities are not lacking in their day-to-day lives — or with tests designed with culturally relevant materials and incorporating cultural (social) reasoning procedures. Such culturally sensitive perspectives need to be adopted in assessing cognitive competencies in individuals who are members of ethnic minority groups within the U.S. to avoid misinterpretation of their capabilities.

Cross-cultural studies of the stages of development proposed by Piaget often provide good evidence of developmental lags in children in many parts of the world. This points to the fundamental role of socialization experiences, learning opportunities and exposure to relevant materials and situations in the development of these cognitive capacities. Children from rural areas with limited participation in formal schooling are not as readily exposed to the relevant types of materials, settings and social interactions (e.g., commercial exchanges) as are those children in urban settings. Ecological factors are essential components of all cognitive development, with the social environment playing a crucial role in providing the circumstances leading to the valuing of and development of certain reasoning processes. These ecological factors include repeated exposure to the process of testing, which is not a "normal" behavior in most traditional pre-modern cultural settings. Participation in school settings may be a prerequisite for effective performance on many of the standard testing procedures used in assessing cognitive development by Western psychologists.

Moral Development and Reasoning

Kohlberg (1981) has proposed a widely adopted theory of the cognitive processes by which an individual evolves in terms of the justifications they offer for the decisions they make regarding moral issues. Kohlberg proposes that his theory of the stages of moral development was universally valid, but there are a number of substantial objections based in a recognition of the theory's cultural, social and gender biases. Cross-cultural studies indicate that while earlier stages may be universal (e.g., pre-conventional and the first conventional stages), even adults in some cultures may not exhibit post-conventional reasoning. Furthermore, even among European Americans, post-conventional development is not universal. Strong gender biases also exist, with females more likely to persist in conventional moral reasoning patterns based upon assumptions about the priority of social relations and the welfare of others, particularly family members. The "abstract" reasoning processes characteristic of the post-conventional stages reflect a male bias that values setting aside one's feeling and attachments — itself clearly a (questionable?) cultural belief. Comparison of Kohlberg's moral stages and their justifications with those inherent in Buddhist beliefs helps to reveal the deep-seated cultural biases that are found in his theory. Similarly, examination of social priorities in African American communities concerned with caring orientations shows the different social reference that one may adopt in making moral decisions. Gardiner, Mutter & Kosmitzki (1998) suggest that the shortcomings in Kohlberg's theory indicate the need for a systems perspective in which social participation shapes the desired nature of moral thought.

ANTHROPOLOGICAL APPROACHES TO ETHNICITY

The relationship of culture to behavior and personality is a long-standing part of anthropology (see Bock 1988a; Levine 1982; Bourguignon 1976). Psychological anthropology has been the context where the culturally unique and cross-cultural perspectives of anthropology are integrated with the psychobiological, sociocultural and other transdisciplinary understandings of human nature. The phenomena of ethnicity emerge from the intersection of the two major conceptual areas embodied in psychological anthropology: the focus of psychology upon the characteristics of the individual personality and the focus of anthropology upon the collective characteristics of groups and cultures. Ethnicity is, in essence, a relationship between the domains of psychology and culture, that is, how the characteristics of individuals and their identities relate to those of the groups with respect to which they construct their identities. Explicating ethnicity requires an examination of how individuals' sense of self, identity, behavior, affect and cognition are related to the sociocultural environment, including both the microsocial level of the individual, the macrosocial institutional levels of the broader society and the relationship between them.

While anthropologists have rejected psychological dimensions of explanation as an inappropriate reductionism, the psychobiological capacities of humans represented in the concept of personality are a necessary foundation for cultural and social processes. The interface of psychology and culture is necessary in explaining determinants of human behavior: human psychobiological nature represented in personality permits the functioning of culture, and culture permits and shapes the development of personality through socialization. Human psychology and culture are also interdependent: psychology represents the psychobiological potentials for cultural behavior, and culture provides the collective influences and support necessary for the development and manifestation of personality. The process of socialization that all humans undergo is a fundamental way biologically based universals are developed through cultural processes that provide content and meaning. Biologically based social and symbolic potentials of humans are manifested in individuals through the influences of culture. But the formation of basic psychological processes — perception, memory, emotions and behavior — requires a sociocultural framework, and reciprocally sustains and creates that framework (Heelas 1981). These psychobiological foundations are culturally structured in ways that must be understood to appreciate the nature of ethnicity and humans' cross-cultural similarities and differences. The use of cross-cultural methods and perspectives is essential for understanding the effects of culture upon personality, self, behavior and social relations. This cross-cultural approach illustrates that human psychological traits cannot be understood as strictly psychodynamic or intrapsychic phenomena, but must be understood in the social, cultural and historical contexts that elicit and shape human behavior.

Psychocultural models illustrate the numerous contexts within which culture and intercultural relations affect the development of individual characteristics. These models provide guidelines for systematically assessing ethnicity as a product of the interaction in individuals of cultural and societal influences. The differentiation of culture into subsystems provides the basis for characterizing specific cultural influences on individual behavior, group psychology and ethnic identity. A systematic framework for analysis of cultural influences upon ethnicity is provided by a psychocultural open systems perspective that incorporates the classic materialist systems approach (infrastructure, structure and superstructure) within a framework which recognizes the importance of emic perspectives in the construction of identity. Diverse cultural influences upon development are illustrated through the numerous elements of the psychocultural model, including the role of historical and environmental influences, the child-rearing environment, secondary socialization contexts, the role of work in the socialization process, domestic and political social structures, social statuses and associated roles representing aspects of the self, cultural values and ideals as models for personality and behavior and projective and expressive systems and their representation of indigenous psychologies. This approach to characterizing ethnicity utilizes what LeVine (1982) characterized as the "culture-in-personality" approach, a "personality mediation" and "two systems" view that recognizea that psychology and culture represent necessarily interrelated phenomena. Ethnicity derives from this interrelationship, through the manner in which the individual personality integrates into its identity, the multiple influences of the culture and broader social systems.

Culture-behavior dynamics can be partially described with a psychocultural open systems perspective that incorporates the classic materialist systems approach (infrastructure, structure and superstructure) within a framework that analyses situational contributions and emic perspectives on personality and meaning. The objective is to provide multilevel and multi-method guidelines for examining the nature of ethnicity — culturally shaped psychology, identity, behavior, communication and interpersonal social interaction. This open psychocultural systems approach recognizes the need to incorporate change, conflict and opposition, and views models of culture as partial representations of collective behavior. Psychocultural characteristics must be understood from a number of perspectives, including the cultural (emic) symbolic perspectives, the organization of the culture and the reciprocal relations and mutual interdependencies determined by the structural conditions (e.g., economic, political), that bind together different cultural and ethnic groups. These influences operate upon humans' biologically based capacities for representing information about self and others, reflected in the concepts of personality and self.

Personality and Self

Many terms and concepts refer to the internal dynamics and organization that provide the basis for regular behavioral patterns of the individual and that permit participation in culture. Psychobiological aspects of humans that enable cultural behavior and social life have been conceptualized in terms, such as personality, self, social roles, identity, mind, behavior and symbolism. While these human aspects are based in biological capacities, they are culturally developed and constructed, creating culturally specific (indigenous) psychologies and psychocultural dynamics. While cultural psychologies differ in their conceptual and expressive frameworks, cross-cultural linguistic evidence indicates underlying universal structures that Wierzbicka (1993) suggests may serve as a basis for developing a bias-free framework for comparing cultural psychologies. All languages contain a word referring to "person" and the concept "I," as well as a range of other concepts — thinking, knowing, doing, saying, wanting and feeling (Wierzbicka 1993). "Person" and "I" refer to two principal foci for understanding the culturally shaped psychobiological nature of the humans. Referred to as the *personality* and the *self*, these represent biologically based and socially mediated aspects that all humans develop through the processes of socialization human aspects that conceptualize and guide human behavior.

While these terms are used and defined in a number of ways in psychology, I suggest that these terms personality and self involve, respectively, the cultural conceptualizations of the nature of the person and social characteristics of a person acquired by virtue of occupying certain positions. The basic distinction is in terms of the personality providing the overall organization and systemic properties of persons that generate behavior, while the social self is how the individual is presented and identified in specific social relations. These conceptualizations provide a context within which to explore the interaction of biology, socialization and culture in the formation of the unique aspects of humans, the commonalities humans share with other members of their groups, and the similarities and differences that characterize humans from different cultures. Ethnicity is derived from the role of culture in shaping the stable patterns we call personality and self, and representing the ways in which cultures create commonalities among members of the population. Ethnicity lies at the interface of the microsocial domain of the identity of the individual and the macrosocial domain of cultural institutions.

The social self refers to a variety of interrelated aspects of human beings in social relations. The social self includes the individual as social actor and the socially presented aspects of his/her person; the person's social ideal self-presentation, based upon the internalization of social standards and the socially acceptable role behaviors; the person's sense of social identity and personal continuity; and individuals' reflexivity, their self-perception and cognition about themselves in social interaction. These capabilities are based in and dependent upon the operation of personality.

While definitions of personality differ, personality is typically used to refer to the overall organization and dynamics of humans' activities, the organization of perception, attitudes, beliefs, values, dispositions, drives, thoughts, etc. embodied in consistent patterns of behavior. In general, personality refers to the totality of psychological processes of humans, with a more particular focus upon the internal dynamics that provide the basis for stable consistencies underlying a person's behavior. Personality is used here to refer to the most encompassing framework for referring to the individual biologically based and culturally constructed capacities for symbolic, mental, emotional, behavioral and social participation in group life. Personality is a model used to conceptualize the internal bases of human functioning that are responsible for the regularities in behavior. The personality can be viewed as the totality of the processes that mediate between the external environment and the individual's behavioral responses. These internal mediating processes include symbolization, cognition, emotions, memory, learning, perception and others. These enable humans to interface with the external world, both physical and social, as well as their own internal symbolic maps of that world and their position within it.

Assessing Personality

Since these internal processes are not available to direct observation, their presence and functioning must be inferred from other forms of information — behavior, self-reports, expressive modalities. Personality, in this broadest sense, must be seen to include a variety of more specific and limited conceptualizations about these human capabilities, including self, social roles, identity, ethnicity, behavior, emotions, beliefs, symbolization, cognitions, etc., the processes that underlie the functioning of the human personality in culture. LeVine (1973) suggests that we must understand personality indicators — observable patterns of behavior due to internal dynamics; the personality dispositions that underlie behavioral regularities and give rise to certain goal seeking self-regulation and social adaptation; and the personality organization among the various components — cognitive, emotional, social, etc. — that contribute to the individual self-regulatory adaptive functional system. Cultural systems perspectives provide frameworks for the conceptualization of the personality and self, a synthetic process in which many different kinds of information are combined to provide an overall picture. Consequently, examination of the relationship of personality and culture should be "pluralistic" — a multi-method approach with different perspectives, both emic and etic. These multiple perspectives can approach a more complete view of the different aspects of the manifestations of the adaptive fit between the sociocultural environment of a group and the population personality characteristics. Researchers use a variety of methods to investigate the way in which the personality system and its dispositions are manifested in social behavior, reflecting the multifaceted aspects of personality and the diverse cultural means of knowing and representing knowledge.

Personality as a Projective System

An anthropological model for cultural representation of personality systems was developed from the Freudian influences. The central notion was that the individual personality mediated between different aspects of culture. In particular, the primary institutions of society (infrastructure and social structure) provided a set of formative experiences that were projected into secondary institutions (ideological or superstructure aspects such as religion, folklore, mythology, art, etc.) through the personality processes and dynamics. The underlying notion is that the society's primary institutions create a basic personality dynamic that in turn projects or expresses certain psychological content in the aspects of the secondary institutions and ideology. To understand the effects of culture upon behavior, it is necessary to address how socialization structures personality formation, which is manifested in some aspect of expressive culture — song, drama, folklore, myths, etc. These expressive manifestations of welfare not only reflect personality dynamics, but also serve as important sources of information guiding the development of personality in the process of socialization. These secondary aspects of culture provide models, ideals, alternate scenarios for behavior and depictions of the consequences of transgressions of cultural values. Projective systems themselves have to be viewed as one of the inputs into the socialization process. But in the final analysis, the understanding of personality has to be derived from the cultural conceptualization and characterizations of the person, an indigenous psychology.

Indigenous Psychologies

A primary problem that has faced psychoanalytic psychology, as well as traditional culture and psychology studies, is the naive assumption that the psychological structures and processes identified in studies in the investigator's own culture are the same as those of people in other cultures. A universally valid framework for description of the personality is rejected by evidence that most psychological theories that have been tested cross-culturally have been rejected or have had to undergo modification or restriction. The concepts of self within Western cultures involve assumptions that are not found in all other cultures. The notion of the self as something that separates each individual from others is contrasted in other cultures with a view of the self as involving an identity, social roles and patterns of behavior that link one to others and to the ancestors. Rather than the self contributing to a sense of individual uniqueness, it may provide the basis for an immersion into the social collectivity and community.

Representing psychocultural dynamics in terms of the cultural views of the person cannot be accurate if based solely upon models of Western psychology, since other cultures' conceptions of people, self, emotion, motivation and other aspects of humans are not congruent with Western conceptions of psychological structure and processes. Since the self is basically a symbolic representation for the individual and others understanding what is symbolized in these roles and presentations is key to conceptualization of the cultural psychology. The traditional dominance of the topics of personality and self by psychology has meant that Western-bound concepts have dominated the conceptualization of these constructs referring to universal human conditions and experiences. This has limited our ability to represent accurately the psychodynamics of people from other cultures, including the nature of ethnic identity.

A solution to this culture-bound limitation is the development of an emic approach, a perspective based on the culture's own representations and conceptualizations of human beings. The ideology and expressive culture are a source of information for the construction of cultural psychologies. Overcoming culture-bound limitations requires incorporation of an emic approach based upon the culture's own representations and conceptualizations of humans. Heelas (1981) pointed out that human beings require some concept of what it is to be human. To function as a human being requires that we have a psychological structuralization, which is provided by culturally derived concepts. This includes a sense of one's identity as a social being, a social self that entails statuses (positions) and roles (behavioral expectations). These cultural conceptions of the nature of humans constitute an indigenous psychology that is vital to understanding ethnicity and the relations of culture and personality. Indigenous psychology

and group psychodynamics are represented in mythology, folklore, religious beliefs, cosmology and other aspects of ideological and expressive culture.

The nature of the human world is symbolic, with even perception of the physical world mediated by symbolic forms and processes. Examination of human symbolic forms, especially as they relate to the social presentation of people, is crucial for constructing an indigenous psychology. The challenge is how we acquire and interpret such information and use it to construct a model of the personality and self of people from other cultures. The emic perspectives, the insider's point of view, is essential to creating relevant and accurate representations. The cultural superstructure, ideology, religion, values, belief system and projective systems provide representations of group behavior ideals, the aggregated or common patterns of behavior that characterize a group. Cultural representations of the world, in essence projective systems, provide the basis for understanding the nature of cultural psychologies. The role of the projective system and expressive aspects of culture in providing an understanding of personality has many manifestations: how humans and social groups are represented, how people use the projective system, social behavior with respect to expressive manifestations, and the emotional qualities associated with the beliefs and experiences.

Indigenous psychologies are embedded in the religious systems, which provide important information about cultural psychodynamics. The meanings of religious systems are part of the linkages of the individual to the collectivity and provide insight into the dynamics of the relationship of individual and group. Representations of supernatural influences and forces and their interaction with humans has been examined in anthropology as a symbolic representation of the social domain, societal forces and interpersonal conflicts. Traditional indigenous psychologies may be found embedded in these ideological systems if we use the perspective that the supernatural, religious and cosmological materials can be understood as projective systems that reflect humans' symbolic and metaphorical modeling of the different aspects of their personalities and selves and the social forces that affect them. The content of religious thought provides important evidence about salient psychodynamic issues. The emotional experiences associated with religious activities illustrate aspects of the socioemotional dynamics of the group. The study of witchcraft illustrates the usefulness of religious behavior in understanding a culture's psychosocial dynamic, since witchcraft accusations generally involve blaming another human or group for one's problems. The entire range of supernatural beliefs can serve as a source of information about collective psychological representations since they have the goal of stripping power status, etc. from the accused.

Indigenous psychologies contrast with specialist psychologies in being concerned with a much broader range of conceptions and issues, including consciousness, agency and behavior, especially as applied to self and its relationship to the world. "Indigenous psychologies . . . are the cultural views, theories, conjectures, classifications, assumptions and metaphors — together with notions embedded in social institutions — that bear on psychological topics. These psychologies are statements about the nature of the person and his relation to the world. They contain advice and injunctions about the way that people should act, should feel and how they can find happiness and success in life" (Heelas 1981:3). An indigenous psychology requires that the culture's systematic frames of reference for understanding behavior, beliefs and emotions be explicated.

As Kim and Berry (1993) emphasize with respect to indigenous psychologies, understanding the manifestations of ethnicity requires a multidisciplinary perspective, but one with a cultural framework that gives coherence and reveals meaningful patterns. Indigenous psychologies are necessary for human beings for several reasons (Heelas 1981; Lock 1981a). They fulfill three interrelated functions.

---

1) Sustain the inner self
2) Sustain and adjust the self in relationship to the sociocultural
3) Enable operations of sociocultural institutions

Indigenous psychologies provide the action schemas that organize individual and collective social life and the creation of sociocultural institutions. In their focuses upon inner self, emotions, states of consciousness, will, memories, soul and agency, the indigenous psychologies provide a system of meaning to delineate what is human nature and to link the individual to the sociocultural order, giving a personal social identity or ethnicity.

Social Roles and Cultural Self

The cultural characteristics of persons provided in personality traits must be augmented by the situational (context) and positional (social position, status or role) determinants of the manifestation of behaviors. The psychocultural dynamics represented in cultural models of the person are complemented by the focus on the social structural influences on personality and social behavior (Biddle 1986; see Bock 1988) for review of this "social structure and personality" or "positionalist" approach). The self is a socially constituted identity that develops in the context of social relations with others and the meanings they ascribe to us through their behavior and language. The concepts of social position (status or role) and role behavior (activities and responsibilities associated with the position) provide a conceptual framework for examining the cultural psychosocial dynamics, as well as the patterns of variation within a cultural social psychology.

Role theory has developed around a phenomena that is a basic feature of social life in all societies and cultures, that of the social position (status or role). The basic conceptual vocabulary of role theory was borrowed from theater and the notion that "Life is a stage, and we are all but actors," engaging in the scripts (roles) dictated by one's social status or position. Biddle suggests that core concepts are *social positions* — parts to be played, the positions allocated by society; *roles* — normative expectations about characteristic behaviors of people in certain positions; and *expectations* — scripts for behavior. The expectations include norms as to what people should do, beliefs regarding whether or not people will fulfill them and their preferences or attitudes. From this basic recognition that cultures have a number of recognized social positions have developed a range of studies on the types of positions; the associated expectations (role behaviors) with the social position; the complementary social positions and their interaction (role sets); and the use of roles in social interaction.

Researchers have developed a number of theoretical perspectives in role theory. An early functional approach analyzed the social positions and associated roles to describe the parts of the social system and how they stabilize behavior and induce conformity. While there are many shortcomings in functionalist assumptions about roles, their basic understanding of social systems as involving social positions and roles has persisted. Structural approaches have emphasized the stable social organizations created and how these direct people in certain patterns of behavior in interaction with others. Functional and structural perspectives in role theory represent an impositional view of human behavior, one in which patterns of human interaction are imposed by the roles individuals have learned and enacted in social context. But behavioral patterns are both based upon internalization of others' expectations, as well as corrected and reinforced by others who respond to the individual. Role theories have to be augmented by an understanding of the cognitive and affective processes that link the individual's social role to actual behavior. Symbolic interactionist approaches have emphasized the improvisational, volitional and undetermined aspects of behavior, while recognizing that society places constraints on such conduct. Symbolic interactionist perspectives have elaborated upon how social actors interpret their own roles and those of others. Related concepts are role taking (adopting a certain social position and associated behaviors) and the relationship of roles to self-concept, emotions and stress. The cognitive approaches to role theory have emphasized role-playing and role-taking, where the social actor imitates the roles of other social positions.

Questions about the applicability of role theory have focused upon the limitations of these models. The degree to which there is a consensus about the expectations associated with social positions, the norms for behavior, may be limited. Adherence or behavioral conformity to the ideal expectations associated with social positions is often lacking in some individuals. Even when people do conform to the expectations for behavior associated with their social position, role conflict, role ambiguity and role overload point to the less than perfect conceptualizations embodied in the structural-functional perspectives. The roles associated with social positions are subject to considerable variation in terms of their actualization by different people, with other additional roles and with different commitments to the role and its maintenance. Within American culture, the notions of social self and identity are seen as particularly distinct when we feel that one's real identity or "true self" differs from the way we have to behave in order to be accepted, get along, fit in, etc. (e.g., how one appears at work versus what you do when you go home and "let your hair down," or how we behave politely to people who disgust us but are too powerful to be directly confronted). The behaviors associated with social positions are also situationally dependent and variable. The obligated behaviors of a particular social position change with different contexts and relationships to others. Thus roles direct and constrain but do not totally determine behavior.

Social positions and the associated roles serve as the models and ideals for behavior, but individuals may not completely adhere to those ideal patterns. Even when they do adhere to the roles assigned to their positions, people certainly express individual mannerisms and characteristics when enacting a role. The concept of role distance refers to the individual's personal disaffection with the role expected from the individual by others. The role of a person may consume his/her identity, but many roles are performed out of habit, expectations, a sense of obligation or for self-serving reasons without a sense of identity or attachment to the role. Roles are not just the demands and constraints to which individuals must adapt; they are also opportunities for individuals to pursue particular positions in the effort to meet personal desires and motives — power, control, resources. Roles are possibilities that humans creatively manipulate in achieving social goals, further driving a wedge between the role and personal identity. The multiple positions and contexts in social life provide the substance of intracultural diversity in social self. The diversity of intracultural behavior is further articulated by a social class analysis and assessment of occupational positions that further differentiate behavior, social roles, social types and styles. The perspective suggested here is that these roles represent as aspects of the self, as well as aspects of the overall personality dynamics. These roles involve social aspects of the person's capabilities and behavior. The social self is not the only aspect of personal identity or motivation within the personality, which also includes aspects of behavior directed by unconscious or repressed aspects of the total capacities of the organism. While not all cultures have these same distinctions and perspectives, all human beings have a personality, in the sense of an organizational dynamic that is responsible for cohesion in thought, memories, behavior, etc., and a social self, an agglomeration of social roles that guide their relations with other human beings.

The functionalist and symbolic interactionist approaches to role theory represent the two main anthropological approaches: one based in an understanding of sociobiological universals of human cultural organization and society, and the other based in the meaning created within the context of cultural activities. While functionalist perspectives have emphasized mechanical social determination, the symbolic interaction perspective views the individual as more than just a tool for the regeneration of the society. The socialization process involves forming the individual's role identity and role behavior, as well as the self-oriented conceptual structures acquired through applying the cultural symbols, values and knowledge to self-assessment. Socialization precedes not only from the efforts of the socializers, i.e. the family, but also from the individual's own active interpretation and deliberate self-socialization. The symbolic interaction perspective reveals the mechanisms for the wide range of variation in roles by people of the same status through recognition of the range of options for action of the individual who

consciously weighs different options and creatively adapts to evolving social circumstances created by the dynamic of one's own culture of origin and its relations with other groups of the wider society. Rather than the society mechanically acting upon passive individuals, the socialization process is one of role negotiation in which each participant selects or contends for their roles from among those allowed by others. The nature of the ethnic self in relation to social other/not-self includes internalization of influences from the wider society. These are seen in their more pernicious forms as a consequence of extreme prejudice, discrimination, racism, etc.

Self and culture are interdependent; not only is self a product of culture, which constitutes and nurtures the self, but culture is a product of a community of selves, and depends upon the self for the transmission and acquisition of culture (Lock 1981a). The self and concept arose together: "the self is constituted by culture which itself constitutes the self" (Lock 1981a:22). "The self is constituted as the mind, a controlling entity [that] comes to take over control of the many relationships that have previously been entered into and established" (Lock 1981a:32). Culture entails a moral order, the norms for conduct, which requires recognition of a locus of responsibility for one's actions. This implies a self-awareness of one's own behavior and its appraisal with respect to social standards. Self-awareness is necessary for the performance of multiple roles, and requires the ability to control behavior, choose among alternatives and treat oneself as an object. This self-awareness necessary for social life is a product of sociocultural processes. It involves seeing oneself from the perspective of others within a symbolically and culturally constituted behavioral environment (Lock 1981a). The very nature of that culturally construed self plays a fundamental role in shaping the self thus constituted (Heelas 1981). Cultural models of the self provide the means of mediating internal and external worlds and defining the role of the human in the relationship between self and others. The motives for the self are provided by culture, as are the definitions of characteristics and functions of the self. Culture functions to constitute the orientations of the self that provide the structure for behavior through self-orientation, object orientation, spatio-temporal orientation, motivational orientation and normative orientation (Lock 1981a). These constitute fundamental aspects of cultural identity and psychology.

Summary

A variety of influences from one's culture and the broader society influence development and identity. These numerous effects upon identity can be better grasped by an understanding of cultural systems and how they operate. The following chapter provides a more detailed understanding of the nature of cultural systems and how they impact individual behavior.

REFERENCES AND ADDITIONAL READINGS

Applebaum, H. 1987. "Universal aspects of work." In: Applebaum, H., ed., *Perspectives in Cultural Anthropology*. Albany: SUNY Press.

Barnouw, V. 1979. *Culture and Personality, Third Edition*. Homewood, IL: The Dorsey Press.

Berry, J.W., Y.H. Poortinga and J. Pandey, eds. 1997. *Handbook of Cross-cultural Psychology: Vol. 1. Theory and Method 2nd edition*. Needham Heights, MA: Allyn and Bacon.

Biddle, B. 1986. "Recent developments in role theory." *Annual Review of Sociology* 12:67-92.

Bock, P. 1988. *Rethinking Psychological Anthropology*. New York: W.H. Freeman.

Bourguignon, E. 1976. *Psychological Anthropology*. New York: Holt, Rinehart and Winston.

Bronfenbrenner, U. 1977. "Toward an experimental ecology of human development." *American Psychologist* 32:513-531.

———. 1979. *The Ecology Of Human Development*. Cambridge, MA: Harvard University Press.

———. 1989. "Ecological systems theory." In: R. Vasta, ed., *Six theories of child development*, (6):187-250. Greenwich, CT: JAI Press.

Coles, R. 1973. *The Old Ones of New Mexico*. Albuquerque: University of New Mexico Press.

Demause, L. 1982. *Foundations of Psychohistory*. New York: Creative Roots.

Devore, W., and E. Schlesinger. 1991. *Ethnic-Sensitive Social Work Practice (3rd edition)*. New York: Merrill.

Ekman, P. 1972. "Universals and cultural differences in facial expressions of emotion." In J. Cold, ed., *Nebraska symposium on motivation*, pp. 207-283. Lincoln: University of Nebraska Press.

Ekman, P., and W.V. Friesen. 1969. "The repertoire of nonverbal behavior: Categories, origins, usage, and coding." *Semiotica 1ournal*, pp. 49-98.

———. 1986. "A new pan cultural expression of emotion." *Motivation and Emotion* (10):159-168.

Erikson, E.H. 1982. *The Life Cycle Completed*. New York: Norton.

Epstein, S. 1973. "The self concept revisited." *American Psychologist* 28:404-416.

Erchak, G. 1992. *The Anthropology of Self and Behavior*. New Brunswick: Rutgers University Press.

Gardiner, H., J. Mutter and C. Kosmitzki. 1998. *Lives Across Cultures: Cross-cultural Human Development*. Boston: Allyn and Bacon.

Gilmore, W. 1984. *Psychohistorical Inquiry A Comprehensive Research Bibliography*. New York: Garland.

Gonzales-Mena, J. 1993. *Multicultural Issues in Child Care*. Mountain View, CA: Mayfield.

Harris, M. 1987. "Theoretical principles of cultural materialism." In: Applebaum, H. ed. *Perspectives in Cultural Anthropology*. Albany: SUNY Press.

Heelas, P., and A. Lock 1981. *Indigenous Psychologies The Anthropology of the Self*. New York: Academic Press.

Hofstede, G. 1988. *Culture's Consequences, International Differences in Work Related Values*. Beverly Hills, CA: Sage Publications.

Izard, C. E. 1977. *Human Emotions*. New York: Plenum.

Johnson, L. 1992. *Social Work Practice A Generalist Approach*. Boston: Allyn and Bacon

Kim, V., and J. Berry. 1993. Indigenous Psychologies. Newbury Park, CA: Sage.

Kohlberg, L. 1981. *Essays on Moral Development*, Vol.1. New York: Harper and Row.

Levy, R. I. 1983. "Introduction: Self and Emotion." *Ethos* 11:3.

LeVine, R. A. 1973. *Culture and Personality*. New York: Aldine Publishing Company.

———. 1982(1973). *Culture, Behavior and Personality*. Chicago: Aldine.

Lock, A. 1981. "Indigenous Psychology and Human Nature: A Psychological Perspective," In: P. Heelas and Andrew Lock, pp. 183-204. *Indigenous Psychologies*. London: Academic Press.

Lonner, W. J., and R. Malpass, eds. 1994. *Psychology and Culture*. Boston: Allyn and Bacon.

Mazlish, B. 1987 "Group psychology and problems of contemporary history." In: G. Cocks and T. Crosby, eds. *Psycho/history Readings in the Method of Psychology, Psychoanalysis, and History.* New Haven: Yale University Press.

Milgram, S. 1975. Obedience to Authority: An Experimental View. New York: Harper and Row.

Munroe, R. L., and R. H. Munroe. 1975. *Cross-Cultural Human Development.* California: Brooks/ Cole

Piaget , J. (translated by Stewart Eames). 1980. Adaptation and Intelligence: Organic Selection and Phenocopy. Chicago: University of Chicago Press.

Rock, I., ed. 1990. The Legacy of Solomon Asch: Essays in Cognition and Social Psychology. Hillsdale, N.J.: L. Erlbaum Associates.

Rogoff, B. 1990. *Apprenticeship in Thinking: Cognitive Development in Social Context.* New York: Oxford.

Rohrer, J. and M. Edmonson, eds. 1964. *The Eighth Generation Grows Up.* New York: Harper and Row.

Runyan, W. 1988. "Reconceptualizing the relationships between history and psychology." In: W. Runyan, ed. *Psychology and Historical Interpretation.* New York: Oxford.

Schermerhorn, R. 1978. *Comparative Ethnic Relations.* Chicago: University of Chicago Press.

Scribner, S. and M. Cole. 1974. *Culture and Thought.* New York: Wiley.

Towle, C. 1965. *Common Human Needs.* Washington, D.C.: National Association of Social Workers.

Triandis, H., and W. Lambert, eds. 1980. *Handbook of Cross-Cultural Psychology.* Boston: Allyn and Bacon.

Upham, S. 1987. "A theoretical consideration of middle range societies." In: *Chiefdoms in the Americas,* pp.39-102. R. Drennan and Carlos Uribe, eds. Lanham, MD.: University Press of America.

Weber, M. 1904. *The Protestant Ethic and the Spirit of Capitalism.* New York: Scribner.

Whiting, B., and J. Whiting. 1975. *Children of Six Cultures: A Psycho-Cultural Analysis.* Cambridge, MA: Harvard University Press.

Wierzbicka, A. 1993. A Conceptual Basis for Cultural Psychology. *Ethos* 21(2):205-231.

Williams, T. 1983. *Socialization.* Englewood: Prentice-Hall.

21. What role did your extended family members have in your socialization?

22. What role did child-care centers have in your socialization?

23. What were the ideals that your parents had for you as a child?

24. What did it mean to be a good child?

25. What were your first significant socialization experiences outside of the family?

26. What effect did they have?

27. How did your first school experiences affect your development?

28. What do you remember the most about your primary school experiences and influences?

29. What role have outside institutions besides school played in your development (e.g., clubs, sports, churches, criminal justice system, military, etc.)?

30. What are the primary social roles you now occupy?

31. What defines or structures those roles?

32. How do they affect your behavior?

NOTES

33. How do the reciprocal influences (the other roles to which you relate) affect your behavior?

34. How you feel about yourself?

    good

35. What are the most significant factors affecting the development of your personality and character now?

    independent school

36. What are the ideals you have for yourself?

    good person

37. Where did you acquire those ideals?

    Socialization

38. How do they relate to your cultural traditions?

39. What are the emotions that you consider to be most significant in how you feel about yourself as a person?

    happy fun

40. How do these involve others?

41. What are the emotions that you consider most significant?

42. Are there emotions that you feel that you should not express?

43. Who are your role models?

NOTES

44. How do they affect your behavior and self-concept?

45. How do these models reflect your culture and its ideals?

Goal)

46. What do you consider to be the most important ideals of your culture?

47. How do they affect your behavior?

<u>NOTES</u>

NOTES

CHAPTER 4

CULTURAL SYSTEMS MODELS

Overview
This chapter presents a systems model of the basic aspects of culture that emphasizes the importance of an "open" system that accounts for conflict, change and the perspectives of members of the culture. The chapter first addresses the infrastructure and technoeconomic system, the interface with the material environment and resources and how they affect broader aspects of social relations. The cultural levels of social organization are addressed in terms of behavioral differences underlying cultural differences, with a particular focus upon family and political structures. These domestic (family) and political relations are shown to have significant impacts upon ethnic differences and relations between ethnic groups and provider organizations. The superstructure level of beliefs, world view and values illustrates the significant deliberate aspects of socialization that produce cultural differences. Assessments of personal and cultural values are provided as a focus for examining one's own cultural influences.

Objectives
Present a systems model of the basic aspects of culture — infrastructure, structure and superstructure.
Illustrate an "open" systems approach that addresses conflict, change and emic perspectives of the culture
Show how infrastructure and technoeconomic system affect broader aspects of social relations
Show how aspects of social organization produce behavioral differences among ethnic groups
Examine how family structures and political relations impact relations between ethnic groups and providers
Illustrate the importance of beliefs, world view and values in producing cultural differences
Engage the reader in assessments of personal and cultural values to enhance cultural awareness

Chapter Outline
Addressing Ethnicity and Culture within Systems Perspectives
Cultural Systems Approaches in the "Helping Professions"
    The Cultural System: The Pyramid of Culture
    Culture in General Systems Theory and Conflict Perspectives
Emic Perspectives in the Systems Approach
Infrastructure: The Technoeconomic System
    Ecology and Demography: The Population-Environment Interface
Production: Technology and Subsistence
    Economic Systems and Society
Social Organization and Structure: Domestic and Political
    Social Organization and Behavior
    Family and Kinship
    Political Structures
Politics of Intercultural Contact: Group-Level Dynamics
    Forms of Intergroup Contact
    Institutionalized Discrimination
    Group Reactions to Subordinate Status
    Social Stratification
    The Culture and Structure of Poverty

(Continued)

ADDRESSING ETHNICITY AND CULTURE WITHIN SYSTEMS PERSPECTIVES

A base for addressing cultural knowledge within social work and the other helping professions is provided by general systems perspectives. "In the quest for a theory for this broad practice base, social work education adopted notions from general and social systems theories and ecological thinking to undergird the foundation for all practice" (Landon 1995:1102). Systems approaches facilitate social work practice by providing a broader framework for the process model, including problem identification, assessment and intervention and facilitating conceptualization of the interactions involved in the helping process. Systems perspectives help overcome the "blaming the victim" approach inherent in psychoanalytic and deviance approaches, instead locating the problem in the interdependent relations between the individual and numerous cultural and social influences. This enables development of more appropriate intervention strategies that address the numerous subsystems affecting the client and his/her behaviors and opportunities.

Systems perspectives facilitate the central focus on mediating between different systems and providing a framework for the integrative use of multi-level and multi-method approaches. These cultural systems models reflect anthropological approaches to culture, and are used in medicine, nursing, public health and other branches of the human sciences. This systems approach recognizes a broad system of interlinking influences on behavior. Systems theories and perspectives involve ecological approaches (see Germain & Gitterman 1980; Meyer 1983) that have focused attention on the surrounding environment, which has effects on the person-in-situation as well as the relationships among individual, family, community, work place, other formal organizations and the broader culture and social systems.

Systems perspectives link the individual and his/her behavior to the interaction and adaptive fit with the numerous environments that impact them. These perspectives organize assessment of the numerous influences upon behavior. Understanding cultural subsystems and their interrelationships provides advantages in consideration of a wide range of sources of problems and the possibilities for their resolution. Systems perspectives also emphasize that problems are not individual and internal, but rather occur in relationship to broader environments to which people and interventions must adapt. The many subsystems provide multiple paths of intervention to maximize effectiveness. The multiple subsystems influencing behavior also call attention to the need for different foci and models for various individuals and problems, as illustrated in the psychocultural model (Whiting & Whiting 1975) presented in Chapter 3. Human behavior is over-determined by many cultural subsystems, with restrictive over determinations ranging from environmental relations and history thorough work, family, community, class and broader social and political institutions that channel development from conception through death. Like the ecological and ecosystem approaches advocated by recent works on ethnic sensitivity in social work practice (see Lum 1996; Devore & Schlesinger 1991), this psychocultural open systems approach recognizes the validity and importance of a variety of more specific and detailed models, including the classic psychosocial models. But it moves beyond them in recognition of the necessity for developing eclectic frameworks that utilize the perspectives most appropriate for specific clients, groups, situations and problems.

Cultural systems perspectives expand the recognitions found in the classic psychosocial theories of the interplay between individual and environment by providing more encompassing and more specific assessments of the nature of environmental influences. Major components of the "person-in-situation" influences are not just the immediate contextual factors, but the cultural self-reference and external societal influences that affect individual behavior, including interpretation and assessment of situations. A fundamental component of ethnic realities is the value orientations derived from personal, cultural and broader societal influences. Individual life experiences must be contextualized within both cultural and social influences upon the ethnic identity of individuals. This involves both micro and macro frameworks, provided by family- and community-based cultural reference groups, and by the external groups of the broader society within which multiple cultural groups operate. Cultural sensitivity requires that helping professionals address cultural effects, as well as the broader external social influences on the client.

Cultural systems approaches avoid the deficit, pathology and deviance approaches. Ethnic groups may be associated with problems, but these are not necessarily inherent to their cultures; they are often derived from the interaction with the broader society. In contrast to the perspectives of pathology and deviance, the psychocultural approach explicitly recognizes the causal influences in structural factors from the broader society's social and physical environments. The psychocultural approach also enables the practitioner to address problems from the client's perspective, and in terms of their

beliefs, resources, opportunities, interpersonal realities and goals. Cultural systems perspectives provide the structural context for identifying important environmental influences on problems. Cultural systems perspectives expand the recognitions found in the classic psychosocial theories of the interplay between individual and environment by providing more encompassing and more specific assessments of the nature of environmental influences. Major components of the "person-in-situation" influences are not just the immediate contextual factors, but also include external societal influences that affect individual behavior, interpretation and assessment of situations. Ethnically sensitive social work practice must address both cultural effects, as well as the broader social influences on the client.

What needs to be known about ethnic groups is not a "shopping list" of characteristics but, rather, an integrated system of knowledge. Systems theory approaches emphasize the necessity of understanding behavior as the outcome of complex interactions among many contributory factors, including interaction with social subsystems operating outside of the ethnic culture. Systems perspectives recognize outcomes are not the consequence of simple cause-and-effect sequences, but rather the product of interactive systems connected through numerous feedback loops. These interrelated systems include not only the individual and environment, but a myriad of situational, cultural and societal influences, including family, peers, school, community, political institutions and social work agencies.

CULTURAL SYSTEMS APPROACHES IN THE "HELPING PROFESSIONS"

Cultural systems models are used in many helping professions, with specific emphasis on addressing concerns particular to individual professions. These models are often referred to as environmental ecological approaches that illustrate the multiple determinants of behavior in the relationship between the physical and sociocultural environments. Cultural systems models are used in medicine, nursing, public health, community and international health and medical anthropology to identify social and cultural factors relevant to effective professional practice (see Brody 1973; Engle 1977, 1980; Blum 1983; Leininger 1984; Baer, Singer & Johnsen 1986; Salis & Owen 1998). Cultural systems perspectives recognize the environment as including not only physical conditions, but also social and cultural effects manifested in demographic, technological, economic and political effects upon the physical environment. These cultural systems approaches identify a range of fundamental cultural and social factors that affect behavior, interventions, rehabilitation and prevention efforts. Cultural systems approaches indicate specific social, economic and environmental factors that place the individual at risk and provide resources for maintaining well being. These outcomes are influenced by multiple environments, including the physical conditions of communities, the micro-level interpersonal dynamics of family and local networks, and a range of economic, social, political and ideological influences. Cultural systems models illustrate the importance of multiple levels of influence and, more importantly, the interactions across levels exemplified in Bronfenbrenner's (1979, 1989) ecological models:

---

* Interpersonal interactions in different behavioral settings (microsystems);
* Mesosystems reflecting linkages across settings (between home and school);
* Exosystems of economy and politics that impact micro- and mesosystems.

These multiple-level systems perspectives are essential in interventions because clients' behavior is not merely a function of individual dispositions or the micro-level of interpersonal interactions and resources, but how these are related through mesosystems to exosystem dynamics affecting behavior and resources. Cultural approaches illustrate the necessity of directing interventions at the various environments influencing behaviors and tailoring interventions specific to the various contexts affecting individual behavior. Producing culturally competent client interventions requires an analysis of the individual to a variety of environments, a cultural-ecological system within which the individual experiences the influences of many interactive systems.

Cultural systems perspectives in public health are exemplified in Blum's "Environment of Health" or "Force-field Paradigm" (Blum 1983; Evans & Stottart 1994), which views well being as a product of the relationships among many subsystems or fields, including:

---

* The physical environment, including sanitation, housing, toxins and the physical health care infrastructure;
* The social environment produced by family, community, work, class, schools and social networks;
* The person's lifestyle that links them to various environments;
* Medical and social services, part of the social environment; and
* The biological level of genetic contributions and tendencies.

These fields are interdependent, affecting one another and mediating human interaction with physical resources, social networks and services. Environmental influences include human impacts upon the environment (e.g., contaminants) and stressors produced by social conditions. Family mediates socialization and development of lifestyle and behavioral factors affecting well being and behavior. The model illustrates that well being is not strictly a function of disease, biology or genetics but, rather, their complex interaction with social, economic, political and other social conditions. Systems models used in public health (McLeroy, Bibeau, Steckler & Glanz 1988; Salis & Owen 1998) emphasize the need to address interrelated levels, including:

* Intra-personal (psychological);
* Interpersonal (primary groups, especially family);
* Institutions, community and culture and society.

Huff & Kline (1999) suggest five levels of assessment for culturally competent programs:

1) Demographic characteristics, including infrastructure (housing, income, occupation), structure (class, gender) and superstructure (literacy, education, religion, acculturation);
2 Epidemiological and environmental influences, including morbidity and mortality data, risks, environmental conditions, dietary practices and exposure patterns;
3) Specific cultural characteristics, including identity, self-concepts, social norms, behavioral and communication patterns;
4) Health practices and beliefs, especially as elicited through the explanatory model and illustrated in illness beliefs, sickness behaviors, and lay and folk sector activities;
5) Institutional biomedical and pubic health capacities, including levels of cultural competence, organizational development for sensitivity and service competency.

If professionals are to achieve culturally sensitive programming and culturally competent care, they must obtain and use knowledge regarding many different cultural effects upon well being, including:

* The historical and contemporary cultural impacts upon perceptions, behaviors and opportunities;
                                    (Continued)

* Cultural world views and values and their effects upon behavior and provider relations;
* Health beliefs and practices, illnesses, perceptions of diseases and help-seeking patterns; and
* Intragroup and intergroup patterns of social interaction.

The Cultural System: The Pyramid of Culture

Culture is the core concept for explaining human behavior and intergroup relations. Culture meets human needs by the coordination of a number of interrelated systems, assuring physical and social continuity, solving human problems and giving meaning to life. Culture is too complex to be described in terms of a single perspective. Anthropologists understand cultures as integrated systems of interrelated practices that organize, regularize, stabilize and integrate behavior across diverse domains. Understanding culture requires integration of knowledge about diverse aspects of human activity, experience and knowledge. This perspective of culture as an integrated interrelated subsystem of behaviors, values, principles and institutions requires an understanding of those subsystems and their interrelationships.

A basic systems model used to identify the regularly occurring features of cultural and social life was provided by Harris (1987), who characterized cultures as having three major levels:

1) Infrastructure, material institution mediating relations with the physical environment;
2) Structure, the social relations and organizations among humans;
3) Superstructure, the level of mental representations and ideas.

These three levels of human existence are recognized in many disciplines.

	Level	Function	Activity
Infrastructure	Material	Technology/Economy	Production/Reproduction
Structure	Social	Domestic and Political Organization	Interpersonal Relations
Superstructure	Mental	Behavior, Beliefs and Meaning	Communication

The infrastructure includes both human and material modes of production, the population's reproduction dynamics and its ecological relationships and the energy extraction dynamics at the basis of the cultural system. Infrastructure represents the cultural adaptations to the universal human need to organize both productive activities for subsistence and to control population dynamics. Infrastructure also interfaces with the social structure, affecting the organization of work and the accumulation and redistribution of goods. The structure of society represents the institutions to meet the human needs for ordering relationships among members of society and with respect to other societies. These organizational needs include both the domestic family sphere and the external political economy. Domestic structure includes the family organization, gender roles, family-based division of labor and extended kinship systems. The political economy includes the societal division of labor, social groups and class systems and social control and political structures. The superstructure or ideology includes mental phenomena — language, world view, religion, beliefs, values, expressive culture and personality. Among the most prominent superstructure features are language and other symbolic processes that represent the external world and its meaning and significance. Superstructure provides important input to organization of infrastructure and structural activities. Each of these three divisions of culture can be further subdivided into subsystems.

Subsystems of Cultural Organization

Infrastructure
Economic System
Subsistence Patterns
Ecology and Demography

Domestic and Political Structures
Intergroup Relations
Political Organization
Social Stratification
Community Organization
Family and Kinship

Superstructure
Ethnicity
Group Psychology
Expressive Culture
Religion and Cosmology
Culture, Socialization and Values

This tripartite perspective of the material, social and ideological organization of cultural systems is used as the framework for a "systems theory" analyzing the nature of culture and its impact upon interethnic relations. The location of the technoeconomic infrastructure at the basis of the pyramid of culture reflects its role in providing the energy basis of the culture. The technoeconomically based energy source provides possibilities for powering the culture and society. While materialist perspectives have emphasized the fundamental and deterministic role of the infrastructure, aspects of the superstructure, such as ideology and knowledge, can also determine the nature of the technoeconomic system and infrastructural adaptation. As the following sections illustrate, the ideological mental mode may be the ultimate determinant factor in terms of the future of interethnic relations. Cultural knowledge provides the creative potential to alter material conditions and adaptations. Yet material and political power structures perpetuate social relations and beliefs. Therefore, the approach will engage a "bottom-up" trajectory, with the analyses based in the technoeconomic infrastructure and its role in providing the energy bases of the culture. The organization and distribution of this energy structures other aspects of the cultural system. These social structures are also studied in their own right, with researchers cognizant of the cultural perspectives about the meaning of these institutions for their members. Intergroup relations become a primary focus in understanding the effects of power relations on society, cultures and ethnicity. Ideological factors and culture are the mediums through which material and social process are understood, manifested and transformed.

Summary

The concept of culture represents a fundamental determinant of behavior and experiences that are essential to understanding humans and their ethnic identities. The concept of culture is a primary tool for understanding both the behavior of individuals and groups, and the organizational structures within which humans live. Cultural influences are particularly powerful because of they are embedded in interdependent systems that permeate life. They are consequently largely unconscious in nature and have global effects upon behavior. Assessing the impacts of cultural influences upon self and others requires a model from which to direct inquiry into the various aspects of culture and cultural systems. This chapter provides an elaboration of the culture concept to illustrate how it can be used to assess the "environment" or "system" within which the individual operates. Culture and its influences upon behavior can be addressed through general models that differentiate aspects of cultural systems, illustrating the different areas of life in which the individual is shaped by collective forces. This chapter provides a clarification of the nature of culture through examining its principal subsystems. It elaborates the concept of culture within a cultural systems model to illustrate the diverse cultural institutions and their interactions with broader societal structures. Cultures are not merely abstract entities, but material, social and ideological systems of human organization. These different aspects of cultural systems provide for numerous influences upon human behavior. The examination of the subsystems of culture begins with the classic materialist model emphasizing infrastructure (technoeconomic and material), structure (domestic and political social organizations) and superstructure (ideology and beliefs). These are further differentiated into more specific institutions (e.g., infrastructure differentiated into demography, reproduction, subsistence, production, distribution, etc.), providing the basis for characterizing diverse cultural influences upon behavior and intercultural relations. The classic notion of the "pyramid of culture," emphasizing the fundamental role of the material basis in the energy extraction processes embedded in the infrastructure, is expanded to include consideration of the fundamental causal effects that are found in the ideology or superstructure. The concept of culture as an open system is introduced to emphasize that the conceptualization we have of culture systems must be recognized as partial, incomplete and necessarily fluid. The major aspects of cultural subsystems are examined to illustrate a variety of ways culture may impact human behavior and that should be examined in assessing the person-in-situation and ecological context.

Culture in General Systems Theory and Conflict Perspectives

Cultural systems approaches are part of general systems theory perspectives that are concerned with how systems, in general, operate and maintain stability and constancy in the face of a variety of environmental conditions. Systems approaches traditionally emphasized the structures that maintain the system, such as a society, meeting its functional needs for persistence — reproduction, food acquisition and distribution, protection, socialization, etc. In multicultural societies, these needs are met by the interaction of different groups and their mutual interdependencies. These reciprocal relationships are organizational principles that both support the overall system and constitute the hierarchies of power that control the groups in the system. The system includes the integration of subordinate ethnic or cultural groups into the economic and social relations with the dominant groups that perpetuate their exploitation.

The "open" systems perspective emphasizing a culture or society in the processes of change and balance among competing forces is a more appropriate conceptual model than the static models of structure and organism. Rather than a completely integrated system, cultures are more a balance of competing influences and forces, often in conflict. Nonetheless, the cultural systems perspective provides a global framework for incorporating the numerous dimensions of intergroup relations, including the conflicts that exist in societies.

Cultural systems are not fully integrated, but manifest conflicts, contradictions and differences. Conflicting requirements and competing priorities characterize cultural systems. Structures and organizations also appear contradictory because they are multivocal, simultaneously embodying many perspectives. Their contradiction embodies the more complete truth about cultural reality than any single statement about cultural reality could delineate and qualify. These conflicts may involve complementarities rather than contradiction. Cultures are characterized by internal diversity, heterogeneity rather than a pure homogeneity. To understand a culture, it is important to understand the multiplicity of viewpoints, the internal variations as well as the tendencies towards uniformity and commonality. One of the characteristics of culture is structural opposition of two conflicting ideals or values that represent opposing tendencies within the culture. Rather than perfectly balance and integrate all aspects of culture, societal forces keep people and groups in interaction in spite of conflict and opposing interests.

This subordination of groups within the system illustrates why the classic structural-functional antecedents of systems theory had to be modified with conflict, power and class perspectives to provide a more complete view of the dynamics of societal activity. While structural-functional approaches emphasized the integrity and continuity of systems as a whole, conflict and power approaches analyze the control of the means of production and the apparatus of power by specific groups. Uniting power and conflict perspectives within cultural systems perspectives provides a more complete analysis of the dynamics that unite groups in opposition. The power and conflict approaches force an awareness of the lack of complete closure and balance in systems, and hence the need for an "open systems" perspective.

Systems analysis and the power-conflict theories are complementary approaches to understanding the integration and segregation that characterize intercultural contact in multiethnic societies. Integration produces conflict in linking together within a society different groups pursuing incompatible objectives. The open systems approach focuses attention on the position of ethnic groups within the overall social system. The numerous points of interaction of the ethnic group with the dominant group (and other ethnic groups) in the society provide a focus for understanding the relations that maintain the different ethnic and cultural groups within a societal configuration. Thus both organizational integration and structural conflict are integral to the intergroup relations in multicultural societies. Ethnic groups in multicultural societies are bound together by social institutions and practices while at the same time engaged in economic, social and political struggles. Most resistance and conflict engendered by the subordinate groups is still compatible with their commitment to maintaining aspects of a system of exchange and intergroup reciprocity that provides the subordinate group with their subsistence and resources. But the in-group identity and loyalty that even subordinated groups feel for their culture is an implicit source of resistance to the dominant cultural system, reflecting the tensions of integration and segregation. Social institutions, conflict of purposes and the symbolic and material dimensions of interethnic relations all contribute to the social and cultural systems within which ethnic groups relate.

Emic Perspectives in the Systems Approach

Cultural systems approaches to describing cultures have classically focused on the analyst's (etic) models rather than the perspectives of the members of the culture (emic), but need not have such shortcomings. The cultural participants' models are an essential part of understanding cultural systems and intercultural relations, with the emic perspectives providing the basis for organizing understanding of the cultural system. Emic cultural perspectives are incorporated in the materialist approaches. In addition to the etic infrastructure, structure and superstructure, Harris (1987) considers the fourth major component of a sociocultural system to be the mental and emic superstructure, exemplified in language and communication. Cultural systems are built up from communication events in which speech plays a central role in coordinating infrastructure, structure and superstructure.

The relationships between ethnic groups must be understood from the cultural (emic) perspectives of each group. Intergroup relations are influenced as much by the interests and intents of the different groups as by the structural conditions of the societies in interaction. The nature of interethnic relations in societies must be understood in terms of perceived meanings, reciprocal relations, mutual interdependencies and structural conditions (e.g., economic, political, etc.). Perspectives informed by cross-cultural similarities and differences in the relationships

between ethnic groups and the associated socioeconomic and cultural conditions help place interethnic relations in context.

Systems models have emphasized etic models because of the importance of the material conditions of society. Societies require the incorporation of physical energy for their continued existence, making material conditions necessary (although not sufficient) conditions for societal functions, organization, continuity and change. But the physical and economic considerations made by a culture reflect the values and ideology of a culture that determine priorities, guide means and ends and validate the material ownership and control of resources. This makes cultural perspectives essential to understanding the dynamics of intergroup relationships. The keys to global understanding are the patterns of interrelations that link the ideological, social and material structures. This is the level of ideological culture, the patterned world views, value systems and global themes that represent the multi-level integration offered by systems perspectives.

INFRASTRUCTURE: THE TECHNOECONOMIC SYSTEM

Infrastructure is the level at which the cultural system interfaces with its physical environment. Infrastructure includes both the patterns of cultural reproduction (biological) and production (technoeconomic). The infrastructural mode of reproduction is primarily concerned with population dynamics and the factors that affect population stability and growth. Key factors include population size, fertility and reproduction patterns, health conditions and population control. The infrastructural mode of production is primarily concerned with how humans and their cultural systems extract food and energy from the environment.

Ecology and Demography: The Population-Environment Interface

Cultures are strongly influenced by the interface with the physical environment, and the institutions, particularly technology, that make this possible. Human populations and environment are an interacting ecosystem. The culture and environment are involved in a two-way interaction in which the environment shapes and limits cultural responses and the culture transforms the environment. The importance of the relationship of the society to its physical environment lies in the energy which it provides to sustain human life and activities. Human ecology, the adaptation of people to their physical environment, structures the nature of the resources, the social system, its values and political structures. Environmental factors can affect many aspects of culture. The ecological perspective on the interface of the sociocultural system with the physical environment is necessary in order to understand the nature of social structure and forms of cultural organization, as well as the influences of the environment on individual and group behavior. Cultural and social factors specify the form of technological relations and social organization within constraints imposed by the environment.

Demographic Infrastructure (Reproduction)

The characteristics of population such as its size, sex ratio, age, distribution, composition, fertility rate and birth rates, growth patterns, morbidity, mortality, population density, age distribution and physical location can all affect how a cultural group develops and relates to other cultural groups with which it has contact. Demography is important because it impacts subsistence patterns, labor supply, population growth, longevity and health. Differential reproduction rates among the ethnic groups in the population are one of the primary factors driving changes in ethnic relations in the U.S. today.

Technoeconomic Infrastructure (Production)

The technoeconomic infrastructure refers to the cultural, social and economic development of the physical environment through human technologies to extract energy and facilitate human activities and their maintenance. The infrastructure includes food production technologies, transportation facilities (roads, railways, airports, ports, bridges), communication systems (telegraph, telephone, satellite links, TV, radio, newspapers), utilities (energy production, water, electricity, gas, sewage), and industry (technology, extractive industries, distribution networks).

Sex and Reproductive Behaviors

Reproductive and sexual behaviors are biologically based, but socially elicited and culturally shaped. Sexual behaviors have significant health implications. Sexually transmitted diseases are associated with promiscuity, extramarital sexual behavior, use of prostitution and lower socioeconomic status. Norms affecting pre-marital sex, homosexuality, marriage, extramarital sex and particular sex practices all have important health implications. Pregnancy and birth are biological processes, that are profoundly shaped by culture. Cultural practices in response to pregnancy may provide support, may constitute risk factors for mother and child and can produce conflicts with providers. Knowledge of these practices is necessary for bridging patient and biomedical realities through patient and provider education. Biomedical pregnancy practices in the U.S. involve procedures not customary in other cultures: prenatal examinations, childbirth classes, ultrasound and fetal monitoring with other obstetric technologies, induction of labor, lithotomy position, etc. Ethnomedical models of pregnancy are important for biomedicine and public health since they constitute the basis from which people make decisions. Reproduction practices structure population dynamics through fertility rates affecting group size, health conditions and population growth. Culture influences demographic structure and population characteristics (e.g., sex ratio, age-distributed mortality, fertility and birth rates, morbidity, mortality, population density and distribution). These factors in turn affect many other aspects of well being, including producing risks and disease transmission factors.

PRODUCTION: TECHNOLOGY AND SUBSISTENCE

Underlying all aspects of a culture is the subsistence technology, the most fundamental aspect of the cultural system's relation with the physical environment. The technological adaptation to environment for food (subsistence patterns) and energy extraction is fundamental since it is the material basis from which all other aspects of culture are sustained. Since food acquisition is essential for human survival, the subsistence pattern is the most fundamental and important technology in all cultures. The fundamental role of subsistence patterns and activities means that they have strong effects upon other institutions of the culture and their members' behaviors. The subsistence patterns provide a fundamental determinant in the structuring of the other aspects of culture — economic systems, social organization, ideology and psychology.

Technology has important relations to the economy and socialization practices. Socialization practices play a central role in allocating access to technological knowledge; consequently, educational systems become central gateway institutions, either providing access or denying training. In most societies, technology is a complicated body of knowledge whose development and maintenance requires extensive economic resources. Technology and subsistence issues have played a central role in ethnic relations, historically as well as today. Historically, the different ethnic groups in society were deliberately incorporated into specific aspects of the technological infrastructure. For example, the English poor were brought as indentured servants to work on the plantations of the colonies, Africans were imported as slave laborers to serve the needs of plantation agricultural systems, Chinese were brought as indentured laborers and domestic servants and Mexicans were incorporated into the agribusiness of the Southwest. Today's economy is quite different, but ethnic groups still often occupy specialized niches in the overall economy. This economic specialization is sometimes by choice, but more generally reflects the global dynamic of the society, especially how opportunity and occupation are "allocated" through education, prestige systems, discrimination and other intergroup processes. Control of technology and training for control of technology often underlie significant differences in ethnic opportunity.

Economic Systems and Society

Economic systems are the societal structures and arrangements that provide the behavioral means for sustaining the material goods required by society. Economic systems interface subsistence practices and the consuming groups. Economic systems include acquiring natural resources, division and organization of labor, converting and transforming resources into goods and exchanging or distributing goods and services. Economic systems vary considerably in terms of organization, assumptions, values, behaviors, the amount of energy produced and who controls and distributes the accumulated products. A fundamental aspect of the economic system is human work. Work has a central role in organizing social activities, providing a focal point in human cooperation. As a consequence, work has a fundamental influence upon cultural institutions, from family, kinship, childrearing and socialization, to social and political organization and religious activities and principles. In simple societies, the economic systems and organization of work are closely tied to family and kinship groups. As societies become complex and stratified, the organization of work comes under the control of political or economic organizations. The classic components of economic systems — land, labor and capital — are examined below to show how culture influences the way in which they are conceived and utilized.

Land Ownership

The practice of individual land ownership is generally absent under most subsistence patterns (e.g., hunting and gathering, pastoral and horticulture). Rather than individual land ownership, there is control by kinship groups and the right of all members of the culture to access areas to gather natural foods, graze or water animals or rotate crops to new plots of land. Concepts of land ownership are collective, based upon kin or territorial groups (villages). When land ownership is collective, it is not alienable, that is, bought or sold by individuals. With intensive agriculture emerges the practice of permanent private or individual ownership of land. Under intensive agriculture, land ownership becomes a means of control of production and provides the basis for sociopolitical power. The physical and political changes that generally accompany the development of intensive agriculture have often resulted in land ownership by a political and economic elite. For instance, the creation and maintenance of irrigation systems necessary for intensive agriculture require a system of political control that tends to create and reinforce the dominance by an elite ruling class. Control of agricultural or other productive resources in stratified societies reinforces concepts of permanent land ownership by a privileged few.

Capital and Wealth

Capital, the resources used to produce other goods, is viewed, distributed and treated differently in different cultures. In simpler societies, all members have equal access to capital goods and own them. There are strong cultural values and kin pressure to share and help assure all have access to food, basic breeding stock, land, etc. Strong values on communal sharing mean that accumulation of wealth by individuals does not occur. Accumulation of goods may be inhibited by "leveling mechanisms" or by traditional cultural rules about the communal distribution based upon fair shares rather than according to labor or capital input. Obligatory generosity, feasting, bilateral inheritance and obligatory religious expenditures tend to distribute wealth from those who have it to the less fortunate. Before money, the perishable nature of resources mitigated against their accumulation and hoarding, but once money becomes a basic feature of the economy it provided for the massive accumulation of wealth and further social differentiation.

Organization of Labor and Production

Different types of organization of labor are found in subsistence versus market societies. In simpler societies, the organization of production is based in family, household and kinship groups that are not organized solely around economic functions. Since the organizational unit has other functions, the "economic unit" is not fundamentally economic and so therefore not oriented towards economic growth or the maximization of economic gains. Economic resources may be used "non-economically" in ritual or social activities. In industrial societies, production is organized by other types of organizations, businesses and corporations. These provide the basis for the organization of labor and remove it from the realm of personal relations and subsistence. Traditional economic systems provide different patterns of production and motivations for production. These may not be in response to supply and demand, or opportunities for accumulation and wealth, but may be responsive to the needs of others in a social network, religious rituals or social prestige structure. The structure and membership of the units of production based upon the family, lineage, village or community organizes production on the basis of traditional cultural social relations and conventional norms for social activities rather than upon some cost effective principles. Labor inputs may be governed by conventional social and kinship obligations more than by wage-labor principles or motivations. Work may not be for economic ends but exist, instead, as a form of social participation. In the development of industrial economies, the economic basis of society and the units of production has been removed from the family and kinship units and domestic spheres of life. The organization of production have been replaced by economic organizations in which wage labor and a money economy are controlled by an elite industrial and financial infrastructure. This infrastructure plays a powerful role in the society's political structures, which are directed toward the maintenance of economic, labor and export conditions favorable to international and foreign trade.

Distribution Systems

There are three general types of distribution systems found cross-culturally: reciprocity, redistribution and market or commercial systems. Reciprocity involves exchange without money and sometimes without direct return, for example, family or communal sharing. Reciprocity is based upon the production of individuals and small groups, with distribution based upon social obligation rather than economic motives. Redistribution involves centralized accumulation of goods by leaders and the subsequent distribution of some proportion of accumulated goods to others in society. The amount of goods acquired by some individuals increases considerably because of centralized accumulation. Market or commercial distribution systems depend upon a public exchange system, normally mediated by a monetary system. Market economies are largely regulated by supply and demand, although the government may also exercise control of exchange. Banks, states and large economic entities like partnerships and corporations come to dominate the exchanges and economy. The three systems of exchange often coexist, but generally one predominates. The control of distribution systems has been a very important factor in the nature of cross-cultural and interethnic relations. Generally, dominant groups control the market distribution systems and are able to exert control over those who are dependent upon them for the goods provided by the exchange system. For instance, in the development of relations between Native Americans and Europeans, the latter were able to introduce subsistence changes in the former through trade and provision of foods in exchange for furs. Once the Native Americans were dependent upon the Europeans for food, the Europeans were able to control the Native Americans' behavior and the price paid for their furs. The commercialization of Native American economies through government-established trading posts was a principal means of bringing Native Americans into the European American economic system, indebting them as a means of establishing control over their lands and labor.

Colonialism and Peonage

Colonialism is an economic and political system in which one society controls another society. The economic goals are to acquire raw materials and control of labor for production and markets for the distribution of goods. While symbiotic relations develop between the two societies in terms of economic transactions, the subordinated colony generally maintains some separate social and cultural existence. Colonization involves various forms of labor control and exploitation. In some cases, it involves outright slavery of the colonized populations or various forms of servitude, apprenticeship or other systems of forced labor. The control of labor and exchange and distribution of goods serve as mechanisms to exploit the colony's labor force. Societies may also practice internal colonization, where a specific internal group is exploited through the imposition of economic systems of control. This was the experience of Mexicans in what is now the U.S. Southwest, after it was seized from Mexico. Deprived of their lands, the Mexicans had to work at whatever wages were offered. These were typically just half of what was paid to the White workers who labored with them in the mines and fields.

Dual Economies or Split Labor Markets

With dual "split" economies, the organization of the economy is segregated, with different ethnic sectors of the society engaged in similar tasks, but under different conditions. The dual economy is designed to keep one segment from competing with the dominant group for economic resources. For example, U.S. laws once forbid "Negros" from working within city limits, forcing them to practice their trade in remote areas with limited opportunities. A classic basis for the dual economy involves procedures that deny certain sectors of the population access to particular work opportunities or rewards. For instance, different wage scales have been used to pay "white" workers as opposed to other ethnic groups, particularly Mexican and African Americans. The union system also provided a two-tiered employment system, where those with union privileges are paid at scales well above what the non-union laborer can earn. Systematic discrimination forbidding the entry of certain groups to unions has resulted in their being denied more remunerative work opportunities.

Universal Aspects of Human Work

Applebaum (1987) discusses a number of different aspects of work found in all cultures. In spite of the universal nature of these dimensions or features of work, the ways in which they are manifested in different cultures varies considerably. All cultures require that people work, but what they work at, how they work, who they work with, etc. are determined by culture. Additionally, cultural and economic systems differ in terms of work rights and obligations; the principles of work specialization, especially the division of labor; how value is produced, accumulated and distributed; the control of access to and the physical arrangements of work; how work norms are developed, enforced and related to social and political organization; control and use of means of production; the mastery of expert knowledge and its patterns of transmission; the social obligation of earners; the value of work in cultural life; the motivations and incentives for work; the rewards provided for work; what aspects of work provide prestige; how people are compensated for transfer of their productions and the obligations to others in terms of transfer and sharing (Applebaum 1987). These perspectives help to focus attention on the differences in work between different groups in society, identifying the cultural and ethnic aspects of labor specialization.

SOCIAL ORGANIZATION AND STRUCTURE: DOMESTIC AND POLITICAL

Social organization and social structure represent conceptualizations of the fundamental ways in which human life and behavior are organized and coordinated. Human social life is organized through conventions about behavior and institutional structures: through norms, statuses and roles, and through groups, bureaucracies and institutionalized intergroup relations. These different organizational jaspects provide a basis from which to understand how societies and cultures differ, as well as how social similarities exist in spite of cultural differences. Similar structures are maintained in different cultures and manifested in different forms of behavior.

Understanding the social behavior of people and the organization of cultures requires perspectives on both social structure and social organization. Structure is more concerned with the social, collective and institutionalized group patterns, while organization focuses on the behavioral level of interpersonal interaction. This can be conceived of as macrosocial and microsocial foci. Social structure refers to societies' institutional arrangements and practices, the societal-wide organizations and groups that create the order in society. Social structure reflects the more permanent institutionally based aspects of societal organization, and often reflects universal human social needs represented in similar institutions in different societies (e.g., subsistence patterns, economic organizations, social groups, etc.). Social organization refers to the dynamics of the interpersonal arrangements of people and the principles which guide how they function in socially appropriate patterns for their culture. Social organization refers to the integrated behaviors, norms, roles, values and beliefs that characterize the typical patterns of interpersonal interaction of a specific culture. Social organization involves the fluid and changing aspects of interaction as opposed to the more permanent institutions of society. The forms of government of the U.S. reflect social structure, while the ways of addressing and greeting people reflect social organization.

Social Organization and Behavior

Norms are the aspect of social behavior on which culture has the greatest impact. Norms are the shared standards and expectations of what people should do in specific situations. Norms may take many forms, from informal agreements and "good manners" to rules and laws. Norms vary widely between cultures and social settings, requiring that people be direct or indirect, boastful or humble, depending on culture and social setting. The importance of cultural influences on norms is in providing standards for appropriate behavior and the meanings of behavior. What is perceived of as normal, acceptable and desirable is provided by culture. The regularity of norms provides a feeling of comfort and familiarity. When societies change rapidly, or when people enter into different cultures, the norms may no longer apply, causing problems in understanding and social organization. Norm conflict refers to situations in which different norms bring a person into conflict. This is increasingly frequent in multicultural societies as different subcultural groups frequently have different norms.

Status and Roles

One of the fundamental ways in which a society regularizes behavior is through statuses and roles. A status is a position in a society or group: mother, father, boss, president, teacher, driver, etc. The role is the behavior of a person occupying a particular status and involves what they do as a requirement or expectation of the status. The norms associated with status are role requirements. The analogy between society and a sports team (football) illustrates this relationship. A team has a number of different statuses (e.g., quarterback, receiver, guard, etc.), each of which has particular expectations associated with their statuses (throws passes, catches passes, blocks, respectively). Some statuses are present in all societies (mother), while others are specific to particular cultures (e.g., chief versus chief executive officer). There may be a wide variety of manners in which role requirements for a particular status may be met. Cross-cultural differences are also found in the same status, even where the same status is present in all societies (e.g., mother, leader). The roles associated with those positions or statuses may vary dramatically from one culture or society to another. Statuses and roles help to regularize social behavior by providing expectations about how we and others should behave and respond to

one another. Humans unconsciously develop particular ideas concerning what is expected of people in terms of their status and roles based upon their cultural experiences. When people go to another culture, the tendency to expect and perceive people to be operating from the same definitions of statuses and roles creates problems and conflicts since different cultures have different definitions of statuses and roles.

Achieved and Ascribed Status

There are different ways of achieving a particular status. Generally, statuses are discussed as being either ascribed or achieved. Ascribed statuses are those that are automatically conferred upon one at birth through no choice of ones' own. Statuses such as sex, ethnic group, nationality and social class are typically ascribed. Achieved statuses are those that are earned or acquired in some way by the occupant of the status as a consequence of his/her own efforts. Achieved statuses in U.S. society are typically considered to include different interests (baseball player, stamp collector, little league coach), as well as different job classifications (manager, secretary, supervisor, dish washer). Statuses tend to have both ascribed and achieved aspects, although one tends to predominate. This interaction of ascribed and achieved statuses reflects the fact that there are considerable ascribed limitations to realizing achieved statuses. Most people cannot realistically aspire to achieve the status of the owner of a major corporation unless they have been ascribed the status of upper class. Some statuses have ascribed or achieved aspects depending upon the particular cultures. In some cultures, leadership or managerial positions are achieved, while in others they are ascribed.

Social Groups

A group refers to a number of people who have a shared pattern of interaction and feel bound together by a consciousness of kind, the "we" feeling. Groups are particularly important in understanding social behavior since groups are the fundamental form of social structure and provide the context that defines appropriate social behavior. Groups are more than just the individuals. Groups have characteristics and dynamics different than and beyond the individuals who comprise them. Understanding groups is fundamental to understanding human behavior because groups provide:

---

* The context for the socialization and development of the individual, the transmission of culture and the learning of attitudes, values and ways of behaving;
* The context for social coordination;
* The integration and differentiation of statuses and roles; and
* The context and opportunity for accomplishments that cannot be realized by individuals alone.

The most important distinction between the many different types of groups in societies has been between primary and secondary groups. Primary groups are those in which the contacts between the members are personal, emotional, intimate and face to face. Primary groups provide relationships involving personal interaction and intimate communication. The family is the principle example of primary groups. In some societies, most interaction takes place in primary groups, including friends. As societies become more complex, secondary groups come to predominate. Secondary groups are based upon utilitarian goals and impersonal interaction. In secondary groups, interaction is based upon one's value with respect to a particular skill rather than upon personal qualities of the individual. College classes, business organizations and most of the institutional settings of public social behavior occur in the context of secondary groups. Groups have important implications for all aspects of social and cultural life. A significant dimension is the extent to which social relations are based principally upon primary groups and their extensions and norms, as opposed to secondary groups and their organizational principles.

Family and Kinship

Family influences upon behavior are the most fundamental of all cultural and social influences. The family is universal and the most important primary group in all societies. The family is the basic unit of socialization in all societies, providing the fundamental social structure and organization for the care of infants. Family is the primary context for the initial transmission of social roles, cultural values, emotional dynamics and identity. In providing the primary context for development of these roles and characteristics, the family creates the fundamental patterns of relationship among people across life. Family influences have been recognized as the basic source of sex roles, identity, emotional expression, learning styles, behavioral patterns, perceptions of the broader society and virtually all aspects of personality.

While families are universal and the most fundamental socialization context for early development, the nature of their structures, roles and influences vary widely. Examination of the family structures, statuses and roles, the values and developmental influences it provides enable us to understand some of the broad social principles that characterize social behavior and communication patterns in all contexts. A significant cultural feature of families is the roles (behavioral expectations) associated with the different positions or statuses (e.g., mother, father, eldest daughter). Important differences exist in the nature of intergenerational relations, as well as the nature and function of extended kinship networks. Social work practice must consider not only actual family pattern, but also its relationship to normative cultural patterns and the view of those patterns within the broader society. While cultures have normative expectations regarding the family, there will also be significant dimensions of variation in families within any given cultural group.

Marriage Patterns

In all cultures, men and women are united in conjugal pairs. A wide variety of marriage procedures are used to form marriage partner combinations. Monogamy and polygyny are the predominant patterns while other forms such as polyandry, concubinage and forced matings also exist. Monogamy, the union of one man and one woman, is the predominant pattern of marriage in most cultures. Most cultures have had an ideal of polygyny, where a man has two or more wives. These polygynous marriages are generally social or economic arrangements. Sororal or fraternal polygyny may be practiced in order to maintain an extended family and care for children when a man's brother or his wife's sister's husband dies and leaves a family that requires care. Polyandry (fraternal) is a rare marital arrangement of one wife with several brothers as husbands. While Americans tend to emphasize the romantic and emotional aspects of marriage, marriage is more typically emphasized as a social and economic union in most societies. In many societies, the emotional, sexual and personal desires of individuals are subordinated to group interests. The social and economic aspects of marriage are reflected in processes such as choosing a mate, where arranged marriages are used to establish or reinforce social networks.

Family Structures

The family units thereby formed are composed minimally of parent(s) and offspring. Although family is universal, the particular structure of the family and its effects upon development and behavior is quite variable. The European American family norm, the nuclear family, is comprised of husband, wife and their children. This family structure is not typical in most cultures and no longer characterizes the living situation of most Americans. The more common pattern of family organization found worldwide is the extended family. The extended family consists of two or more lineally related kin of the same sex and their spouses and offspring, constituting a three-generational family structure (i.e., grandparents, parents and children). The most typical form has been the patrilineal extended family, where father-son obedience provides the authority structure and brother loyalty reinforces the male power structure. Some extended family systems may also include other kin: aunts, uncles, cousins and fictive kin. A matrilocal family structure exists in societies with matrilocal residence and matrilineal inheritance. In a matrilocal family structure, the family is an extended family based upon women's kinship ties. The local household group may consist of all descendants of a woman, including her sons and daughters, as well as her daughters' offspring, but not daughters' husbands nor sons' wives. Polygamous or compound family structures involve multiple spouses of one sex and a single spouse of the other sex. Other family structures include an attenuated or single-parent family structure. This is typically a matrifocal structure, a biological mother and her offspring without a father present.

Kinship.

Family structures provide the basis for the most important social structures in some societies. The extensions of the minimal family structures into broader networks of relations are referred to as kinship or kin networks. Kinship includes relationships between people with ties of biological inheritance (consanguineal), as well as social ties such as marriage, adoption or other fictive arrangements (affinal). In most societies, kinship is the most important social bond and governs relationships between individuals. These kinship ties form the basis for social structure in societies without hierarchical political structures. Even in complex societies, kinship systems may predominate as the most important form of local political organization. Because of their fundamental role in organizing humans, kinship systems have important social functions. Some of the principle functions of kinship systems include care and socialization of children, providing a social group for assistance and resources, creating continuity between generations establishing the principles for intergenerational transmission of rights and property and political organization and control. Kinship systems also embody other important social definitions, including sex roles and sexual division of labor, delineation of social values and social responsibilities and group and individual identification.

Unilineal descent groups (patrilineal and matrilineal) are kinship groups that determine descent (inheritance) and which share a common and exclusive group membership. The unilineal descent groups determine whom one calls upon for assistance, serve as a basis for resource control and perpetrate themselves over time. While unilineal descent groups may be traced through either men (patrilineal) or through women (matrilineal), the patrilineal form is the most common form of kinship organization. These structures not only provide linkages across generations, but also provide organizational structures for people who, though they are not lineal descendants, do have common ancestors. The functions of unilineal descent groups in non-commercial agriculture societies include basic social organization, regulation of marriage and religious, economic and political functions. Matrilineal descent groups differ from patrilineal descent groups in important ways. Matrilineal descent groups determine kinship only through related females, creating both social and residential ties among related females. Female status and power is generally much higher in matrilineal descent groups than in patrilineal descent groups. Patrilineal groups determine relationships through men, with related men living together and wives as outsiders to the group. In matrilineal societies, women may exercise political power directly through representation on councils, or they may exercise power by appointing priests, chiefs or other political leaders. The clan is a social organization created by a unilineal descent group. It includes a group of people who consider themselves to be related through descent from a common ancestor. Clans can form an important basis for political organization in society, and were utilized by some historic and contemporary Native American groups (e.g., Iroquois, Southeast groups and the Pueblos).

Political Structures

Politics refer to societal means of coordinating and regulating behavior and mobilizing support or resources to achieve goals. Political processes and structures also play an important role in the relationships between societies and ethnic groups. "Relations between ethnic groups almost always involve elements of domination and subordination: one ethnic subpopulation is able to impose its culture and institutional arrangements on another" (Aguirre &Turner 1995:43). The nature of cultural groups' political structures and their power relative to one another are primary determinants of the relationships between those groups. Political processes are achieved by the actions of groups and their imposition of laws; and through the interpersonal implementation of norms and customs. The organization of individuals into institutions establishes legitimate power or authority. There are many levels and types of political organization, and their differences have major implications for the nature of intergroup relations. Political organization may be based on families, lineages, religious organization, military organizations, nations or classes. The legitimacy of political organizations may be from custom, kinship relations, majority popular support, military power or historical precedence. Political action also occurs through the application of traditional norms and customs, for example, where beliefs about treatment of "outsiders" create particular patterns of intergroup interaction.

Levels of Sociopolitical Organization

Bands, tribes, kingdom/chiefdoms and nation-states refer to the fundamental types of sociopolitical organization. Each type of sociopolitical organization is strongly associated with a typical subsistence pattern, and consequently also associated with population size, economic system, social stratification systems, sociopolitical complexity and degree of centralization. In today's world, the highest level of sovereign political integration is the nation-states, which have subjugated and incorporated the cultures at lower levels of sociopolitical complexity. These smaller-scale political organizations are, however, relevant to understanding the historical processes of the development of interethnic relations in the U.S.

Bands.

Bands are small (typically 20 to 50 people) politically independent nomadic groups of people related through bilateral extended families. All human societies prior to about 10,000 years ago were band societies, being the fundamental social adaptation of human groups to the limitations created by the hunting and gathering lifestyle. Bands have no single authority structure or hierarchy that integrates the community or binds it with other communities. Charismatic leadership of the elders, skilled hunters or warriors, the shaman or other skilled individuals provides direction, but there is no compulsion to obey them, nor do they have the force of authority to assure compliance. Several bands may link together for seasonal activities, but there is no force integrating them into a political unit.

Tribes.

Tribes are culturally distinct populations who see themselves as descended from a common ancestor. They are generally based upon kinship relations formed through clans. The organization of tribes is generally based upon segmentary lineage systems, a hierarchy of lineages uniting various groups under mythical/historical personages. This means that the tribe is actually formed from smaller kinship groups that are generally not subject to a single overriding authority. Tribes often have an informal integration of more than one community through association based upon kinship ties, but no political power integrates these different communities. Since there is generally no formally recognized political leadership beyond the level of the lineage, the tribe is not politically integrated, and often has internal conflicts. Kinship groups tend to be the organization that has legitimate and effective authority, but a number of different kinship lineages are found within the tribe, often precluding effective integration. Tribes are generally characterized by complementary opposition, with formation of different segments dependent upon the particular confrontation within the group. Because authoritative and legitimate political leadership is lacking beyond the minimal lineage, when conflicts emerge within the larger group one looks for support among the members to whom one is related through the wider lineage structure, engendering intragroup conflict. Tribes are generally characterized by headmen who serve in leadership roles, but their holding of their positions is dependent upon group consensus and their continued competence. Headmen are generally advised by councils of lineage heads, and do not have coercive power, instead depending upon building consensus; they are often know as "talkers," reflecting their fundamental role in reaching a consensus.

Chiefdoms or Kingdoms.

Chiefdoms are political organizations based upon the legitimate authority of a single kinship group that generally has a formally recognized structure integrating different communities into a political unit. The formal ruling structure may be a council, but is generally a single individual whose position is usually hereditary and permanent, representing the head of a lineage. Chiefdoms may be unified under one chief or derive from an alliance among several chiefs. They accumulate wealth through the control of labor, taxes and redistribution systems. Chiefdoms generally have a well-defined class system, separating the chief's and nobles' lineages from the commoners. Chiefs have power to pass judgment, punish people and resolve disputes. The classic definition of chiefdoms emphasized their role as "redistributional societies with a central agency of coordination," but more recent definitions have emphasized the notion of a chiefdom as a social or administrative organization rather than an economic one. The emphasis has been on the notion of an autonomous political unit consisting of communities or villages under the permanent control of a chief and associates who form a centralized hierarchy. Existing independently of the individual who occupies it, the office or position has authority and power associated with it. Reexamination of the concept of chiefdoms has led to the recognition of a wide range of differences among pre-state societies in terms of their redistribution systems, social stratification and administrative complexity. Many of these societies have leaders who use their positions for accumulation and material wealth rather than strictly regional redistribution, while others use them to form alliances that serve as a means of integration of local and regional populations. However, the regional alliances are personal products of these leaders rather than institutionalized structures. The Iroquois Confederacy or League formed in their struggle against the European invaders provides an example of these midrange organizations. The struggle provided a context for the unification of different tribes, clans and lineages of the Iroquoian speakers. The Great Council composed of individuals from the different clans provided the basis for decision making and coordination of the distinct populations. However, the organization did not have a supreme political leader; decisions were made by consensus or no group action was taken. Since no force united the different clans and nations within the confederacy, the groups often took opposing actions.

Nation-States.

The nation-state is a geopolitical entity with three or more hierarchically integrated levels of organization and jurisdictional hierarchy beyond the local community. For example, a state might include provinces, subdivided into administrative districts, which encompass a number of towns. The state is characterized as having the supreme source of power and political sovereignty, with no superior power recognized. States form autonomous political units that generally encompassing many communities within their territories. States have a centralized form of political organization, structured in a hierarchical and bureaucratic system with a legal rational system of government. In contrast with chiefdoms, the state has specialized spheres of decision making, greater administrative technology and a greater variety of administrative and decision-making processes. States generally have control of the economy, market, foreign trade, money and tax collection, and generally exercise a monopoly on the legitimate use of force. States are characterized by class control, elites, intensive agriculture, occupational specialization and the power to draft armies, carry out war and expand and incorporate other societies or states. States have an advantage over chiefdoms and lineages in that they are able to spread indefinitely without splitting because of permanent political

institutions that can be duplicated infinitely. This is realized through extensive territorial and governmental subdivision, each smaller unit operating within the authority of a larger division that exercises control through centralization of authority. The final stages in development of nation-state coincided with European colonial expansion. During the dynastic period (1500-1815), the state emerged from the feudal system and developed into the nation-state. The objectives in forming nation- states were to include different specialized towns with a complementary specialization within a common political boundary that integrated all different sources of raw materials and labor specializations necessary for a self-sufficient economic organization. This required political adherence to entities larger than towns and led to wars of imperialism for control of raw materials. The 16th-century national economic development of European nation-states was spurred by forces that benefited from control of world markets and foreign economies, particularly those of colonies and the wealth they produced. These nation-building efforts laid the foundation for multicultural societies by the incorporation of diverse cultural groups within their boundaries. These national societies are generally characterized by a single ethnic or cultural group that dominates political power structures and the economy and provides a social ideology and normative patterns that pervade all aspects of life, even those of the dominated ethnic groups. Institutional structures also controls intergroup relations; the government may forbid its citizens from interacting with certain nations.

POLITICS OF INTERCULTURAL CONTACT: GROUP-LEVEL DYNAMICS

When extensive contact occurs between groups, there are normally both forces to keep the groups together (integration) and forces that keep them apart (segregation). While segregation and integration are often portrayed as opposing options, they are interdependent processes found in all interethnic and cross-cultural relations. All forms of long-term stable intergroup adaptations require a balance between segregation to maintain distinctiveness and integration to keep groups together. Even when societies are in conflict with each other, such as in warfare, forced labor or political subjugation, there are some forces — environmental, political, economic, etc. that hold them together in conflict. Even when societies attempt to integrate ethnic groups into the economic systems of the dominant group, they generally simultaneously maintain some forms of segregation to keep groups separate. Without some form of segregation, the distinctiveness of groups in prolonged contact would disappear in the processes of assimilation or amalgamation. While segregation is typically viewed as a process by which the dominant group separates the other groups from its spheres of activity, segregation may be self-imposed by a group. Segregation may be practiced by a subordinated ethnic or cultural group as a way of maintaining its traditions and integrity by limiting its contact with others. The segregation of ethnic communities also serves important functions in buffering them from the larger society and providing social and personal support.

Typically, the dynamics of segregation and integration are designed to maintain the power and advantages of the dominant group and the ability to extract some advantage from the subordinated group. The different types of relations that can be established in the context of intergroup contact range from extremely prejudicial intergroup dominance such as genocide (extermination), slavery and colonization through various forms of integration of the populations involved. In relations between different groups, the economic and political structural forces imposing integration and segregation create the tone of the relationships between the two groups. Many kinds of activities and motivations will bring different groups into contact with each other.

Forms of Intergroup Contact

Migration, or the movement of a population, is the most general cause of intercultural contact. It may occur for a variety of reasons. The role and effect of migration in creating interethnic relations varies with the nature of power of the migrants. One classic difference contrasts migrant subordination with migrant superordination. Under migrant superordination, the migrant groups establish supremacy through the military and political advantages they possess. Migrant superordination was characteristic of the European colonizations of the New World. Under conditions of migrant subordination, the immigrant groups are subordinated in the new society. Migrant subordination was characteristic of the conditions of the waves of immigrants to post-colonial societies of the New World during the 19th and 20th centuries as European immigrants assimilated to the New World European societies. The relatively little impact that these migrations had upon the existing communities reflected the relative differences in power of the two groups. Involuntary movement of groups may result from activities of other groups (e.g., invasion or expansion) leading to the prior group's expulsion. When a population is expanding, its growth generally provides a numerical superiority that enables the displacement of the indigenous groups. These groups may, however, be incorporated, subordinated or exterminated.

As the contrasts of migrant superordination and migrant subordination indicate, the nature of that contact has direct implications for the consequences. Schermerhorn (1978) suggests that factors important in shaping the nature of the relations between groups are the legitimacy of the integration, the cultural congruence of the groups and the common and discrepant goals of the groups in contact. Those situations with low legitimacy, high coercion and discrepant values and goals form one extreme, while legitimate relations between culturally congruent groups with common goals form the opposite end of the spectrum. The following considerations of different types of intergroup relationships starts with the most extreme — low legitimacy, high power and low cultural congruence — and proceeds to more interculturally congruence and legitimate types of relationships.

Genocide

Genocide involves the deliberate effort of one group of people to exterminate another group. Such practices have been widespread in intercultural relations, particularly associated with colonization and expropriation of lands. Genocide and extermination have been practiced at both physical and cultural levels. Physical genocide with the violent extermination of populations has led to the total disappearance of groups. Cultural genocide has also been practiced against the survivors of such campaigns of extermination, such as Native Americans. European immigrants attempted systematic genocide against the Native Americans through practices such as destroying villages by fire, massacring entire groups, introducing germs and diseases as weapons of war, and using of bounties and military organizations as direct tools of violence against the Native Americans. Cultural genocide attempts to end the process of cultural transmission to the young through prohibitions on language and cultural practices, and implemented by forced work organizations, schools, religious indoctrination, political incorporation and economic integration.

Slavery

Slavery is a practice where some people presumed to own other humans. This may extend from rights to control their labor, earnings and activities to the right over their very lives to sell them to others or put them to death. Slavery is a frequent form of labor extraction used to exploit colonialized areas. It is also used through forced migration of captives to provide labor at distance places. Slavery was practiced with Native Americans and African Americans in the history of the U.S. The Native American groups were not easily maintained in conditions of slavery, either dying or running away. Africans were more accustomed to agricultural labor and did not have friendly groups to escape to; consequently their descendants in America came to form the largest slave group in the U.S. Similar forms of servitude have been practiced against other immigrant groups to the U.S., with peonage persisting in areas of agricultural labor even in the 21st century.

Slavery is generally initiated as an economic practice when needs for labor are high. The attitudes towards the enslaved peoples then develop as justifications for maintaining their conditions of servitude and slavery. The stereotypes created as justifications generally focus upon why it is in the enslaved person's interest to be protected, how the slave group is lazy and incapable of work without direction and how the slave represents an intellectually inferior creature who requires direction, guidance and control. Negative beliefs about the enslaved group then develop, as a set of justifications and beliefs about why such relations must be maintained.

Annexation

Annexation is a process by which a nation uses military power to incorporate another area politically, often including the population living in the area. This leads to various forms of integration of the cultural group into the dominant society. The conditions of annexation may be followed by various forms of extermination, forced assimilation, colonization or other forms of expropriation (e.g., taxation, control of commerce). The power relations that characterize annexation typically result in strong status differences between the groups and the creation of boundaries between the groups to maintain the advantages of the annexing power. This is frequently represented in "internal colonies" where specific geographic areas and cultural groups of a society are subordinated politically and forced to labor under differential wage structures to provide resources in exploitative relations. The history of the U.S. includes numerous annexations of lands and populations of Native Americans, as well as the annexation of the American Southwest (Northwest Mexico) during the Mexican American War.

Colonialism

Colonialism involves the military, political, social and economic control of one society by another to gain from the exploitative relationship. Colonization involves direct control of a country by another's political apparatus, either through imposition of a political military system or through the use of an elite ethnic or social class within the society to administer the colony in the interest of the colonizers. The subjugation may be direct, as in forms of slavery and direct colonization, or indirect, where differences in technological or political systems create differences in social and economic power. While colonialism leads to the development of symbiotic relations between the two societies in terms of economic transactions, the subordinated colony typically continues to maintain separate spheres of cultural existence. The conditions of the colonized peoples are changed in the direction of the institutions and practices that favor the colonizers, particularly economic and political incorporation. An important dimension of variation in colonial systems is the differences in power, the relative preponderance of the colonists relative to the colonized peoples and the extent of their interpersonal interactions. In colonial situations characterized by a numerically smaller colonizing force, the use of power is more important and coercion becomes the principal tool of societal and intergroup integration. These conditions established the material and social foundations for interethnic relations, with power differences allowing for extreme forms of exploitation and inhumane treatment. These conditions generally result in strong group enclosure (segregation) by both groups, maintaining strong intergroup separation and giving rise to both cultural and structural pluralism. The two groups have their integration primarily in terms of the political structures that ensure compliance, and the economic structures that allow for the colonizer to extract the wealth and labor of the colonized peoples.

Reservations and Exclusion

Reservations are specific geographical locations where cultural groups are placed and restricted as more powerful groups remove them from other spheres of activity. Reservations may be core homelands for a cultural group, but more likely reflect areas the dominant group has no interest in inhabiting. The history of U.S.-Native American relations is one in which the Native Americans have been removed to reservation areas that were of little current interest to the European Americans. The Spanish missions served as similar forms of control, utilizing colonial and reservation forms of social organization. Pariahs, an outcaste group in the lowest stratum of a stratified caste system, represent another form of social integration and exclusion. The social norms of social exclusion from the mainstream dominant culture restricts many channels of access to economic resources and political power. This is generally complemented with an integration into the economic system in ways which provide benefits to the dominant groups in forms of obligatory labor relations by the pariahs. The pariah status is considered to be immutable, unchangeable by time or social action, a permanent condition of a person and his/her descendants.

Internal Discrimination

Internal cultural prejudices may also create a minority group status as a result of subcultural segregation and outgroup segregation. For instance, women have been traditionally discriminated against in the labor market, contributing to the creation and maintenance of occupational subcultures. Religious discrimination may also serve as a marker for differentiating groups and creating a subordinated outgroup within a society. Clan and kinship relations can also serve as a means of differentiating society into the power groups and the outgroups. Internal discrimination may involve patterns of selective inclusion, where members of specific groups are only allowed to work in particular segments of the economy, normally those with limited earning potential. These practices are exemplified in institutionalized discrimination.

Institutionalized Discrimination

Institutionalized discrimination refers to the ways in which prejudice and discrimination are expressed as a part of the normative practices of organizations of societies, rather than just individual dispositions. Institutionalized discrimination can be direct, where there is a deliberate intention to discriminate, or indirect, where policies created unconsciously or for other reasons have the unintended consequence of discrimination against a group. Direct institutional discrimination involves conditions under which the legal system and customary social practices of a society legitimate the denial of access to certain groups. Laws may outlaw property ownership, residence, occupational statuses, voting rights and/or other rights and opportunities on the basis of cultural or ethnic background. Directly institutionalized systems of discrimination include practices such as slavery and voting disenfranchisement, segregation of education and other social facilities and denial of civil rights. Institutionalized discrimination may also be created through informal cultural practices, the institutional acceptance of individual prejudices and behaviors that limit access.

Indirect institutional discrimination refers to structural aspects or practices that serve to perpetuate discrimination independent of, and even in the absence of, individual discriminatory intents and actions. Indirect institutional discrimination reflects the normal operation of a society and its organizations. This enables discrimination to shift from direct consideration of the characteristics of ethnicity or culture to other "objective" features such as education, previous experience, residential location, accent and professionalism, that are indirectly affected by ethnic and cultural background. When cultural factors of the dominant group determine the "objective criteria" for selection, these institutional criteria function to eliminate ethnic groups from equal access and opportunity. Unintentional institutional discrimination may occur as a consequence of an objective criterion, e.g., education, where other factors affect access to educational institutions. Criteria such as level of education, the prestige of one's school, test scores and grades, recommendations, inside information, social networks and contacts, residential location and access to decision makers may maintain institutional barriers and discrimination without specific discriminatory intent.

Laws.

Laws have been used as formal mechanisms for restricting the rights and opportunities of specific groups. Beginning in the colonial periods, laws were passed that applied specifically to "Negros"; including their status as "property," their prohibition on practicing certain occupations; their restriction from gathering together without "white" supervision; and the denial of their right to vote, testify in court or sue for damages. Immigration laws allowed only the entry of "free whites," and later specifically prohibited Chinese and other Asian groups from entering. Laws established the systems of segregation enforced against African Americans, with similar statutes excluding other "non-white" groups from the institutions and privileges of the broader society. Even when federal laws gave universal suffrage (right to vote), local laws established voting tests and citizenship tests, selectively applied to ethnic minorities, precluding their right to register to vote.

Schools.

Educational institutions provide the basis for indirect institutional discrimination. Since access to many jobs in society requires training and certification by education systems, factors that affect access to and success within schools and universities serve to create indirect institutional discrimination. The lower funding and quality of inner city schools prevents many urban ethnic minorities from receiving the preparatory training necessary to compete effectively for entrance to universities. Thus, ethnic groups may be indirectly denied access rather than being denied directly because of ethnic status. Their indirect denial due to economic, social and political factors affects participation in those experiences necessary for job selection. Cultural values embedded in the institutions and practices of schools also serve as indirect forms of institutional discrimination. Since schools emphasize criteria such as individual achievement, competition and self-reliance, ethnic groups that emphasize those values in family life will have greater school success than those groups that value group achievement, cooperation and dependency.

Gerrymandering.

Gerrymandering refers to the determination of voting district boundaries in ways to deliberately prejudice against or favor specific constituencies. Institutional discrimination occurs when the determination of voting district boundaries affects the ability of specific groups to achieve representation on political bodies. At-large representatives all elected by the entire voting population assures a disproportional representation for the majority ethnic group, depriving other groups of representation and power. When an entire city elects all council members, the dominant ethnic group can win all seats. Districts formed around ethnic group locations would provide the opportunity for representation, but long-standing districting practices (gerrymandering) have historically served to prevent this participation, and as a consequence, direct institutional discrimination.

Banking.

The necessity of funding for most business endeavors has made the financial institutions of the country and their financial policies a major source of institutionalized discrimination. Criteria for eligibility based upon factors more easily achieved by the dominant society members, such as professional degrees, college education, employment history, residential location and business location have all constituted serious institutional impediments to economic development for ethnic communities.

Group Reactions to Subordinate Status

When powerful groups establish dominant relationships over other groups, their power often allows them to determine major aspects of the intergroup interaction. However, there are, nonetheless, a number of different group reactions to the minority status created by intergroup contact. Some involve deliberate efforts to adapt, while others involve resistance. Cultural disintegration characterized by a disorganization and destruction of the cultural system and dispersal of the population is frequently found to

occur to the smaller groups in intercultural contacts. But where population sizes are more equal and regular relations develop, this may be characterized by a variety of adaptations.

Organized Protests.

Subordinated minorities may organize public activities to protest their situation. This may involve efforts to block the activities of the broader economic system (boycotts, sit-ins, disruption of traffic) or may be designed to call attention to their situation. Such efforts may force the dominant groups to respond to their needs, or may result in greater oppression. The consequences can also result in increased support for the group's plight, with alliances crossing ethnic boundaries being established. The Civil Rights movement in the U.S. was characterized by such organized protests.

Successions and Rebellions.

Successionist relations are ongoing rebellions in which a group actively resists the control exercised over them by another group. The successionist movements may operate within areas still under control by a foreign power and actively seek to terminate its control, or may involve efforts on an international scale to sway opinion and place public pressure on the group that dominates them. Within the U.S., there have been several successionist movements, including Native Americans' efforts to reject the European invaders and Mexican Americans efforts in the American Southwest to return to Mexican sovereignty.

Ethnic Revivals and Resurgent Ethnicity.

Ethnic revival movements represent ethnic group's efforts to attain rights within a society. A resurgence of ethnic identity and pride demands recognition of cultural differences, while simultaneously insisting upon receiving equal treatment, an elimination of discrimination and opportunities for structural assimilation. The ethnic revivals associated with the rise of Black Power, Brown Power or the La Raza movement and the American Indian Movement reflected resurgences. One consequence was the overall increase in ethnic consciousness, an awareness of and pride in ethnicity and recognition of the importance of cultural background. As such, these responses are also a form of group empowerment. These responses are generally concerned with maintaining cultural separateness while achieving political and economic egalitarian integration.

Social Stratification

Social stratification refers to the division of society into distinct strata in terms of access to valued dimensions of life. Social stratification is represented in the hierarchy of classes within a society, strata that differ with respect to power, income and privilege. Social Class represents a permanent division of society into distinct social groups with unequal access to important advantages. The role of these factors in the stratification system and how they are viewed differ from society to society. Social stratification is one of the most important forms of social differentiation, but one whose dimensions and meanings differ from one culture to another. Three principle types of social stratification systems are found cross-culturally: egalitarian, in which there are no permanent groups with special access; rank, in which there is equal access to economic resources and power but unequal access to prestige, with some groups having special hereditary rights; and stratified or class systems, with distinct permanent groups with unequal access to economic resources, power and prestige. Class societies may be open classes that permit movement, or closed classes or castes in which the movement of people between groups is prohibited by custom or law.

Egalitarian Societies.
Egalitarian societies are primarily hunting and gathering and some are horticulturist. In egalitarian societies, all individuals are not the same, but all have the same chance to achieve, and there are as many "positions" available as there are people capable of achieving them. Everyone has equal access to resources. There is no social stratification, since there are enough positions for everyone and no group restrictions on who may achieve the position, except by nature of sex and age. Status and prestige differences do exist, but they are based upon achievement by individuals, not ascribed as to members of a special group within the society. There are no permanent economic differences because of the difficulty in transporting and preserving accumulation, and because status is based upon sharing and giving. Some egalitarian societies have "leaders" or headmen, but they are without power to compel legitimately other members of the group.

Rank Stratification.
Rank stratification emerges in horticultural societies where there are social groups with unequal access to prestige and sometimes to power but not to economic resources. The amount and type of work done by the leader, especially subsistence activities, is frequently the same as that of other individuals in the society. The leader may accumulate considerable goods, but the prestige derived from them is usually dependent upon their redistribution. Unequal prestige is usually reflected in the position of the leader whose position is based on social inheritance. The entire society may be organized with prestige differences according to degree of relationship to the leaders' kinship system. Generally, there is no power of the leader to enforce decisions beyond immediate descendants except through influence. This type of stratification is found in groups with clan organization and political structures.

Class Societies.
Class societies have distinct social groups that control access over the means of acquiring economic resources, prestige and power. A class represents a stratum in society, a group of people with approximately the same opportunity to obtain economic resources and prestige. Class societies may vary from closed systems — e.g., castes that prohibit movement — to relatively open systems that allow movement (even if it rarely happens). In caste systems, an individual's position in society is completely ascribed at birth. Upward mobility is prohibited by law or custom that perpetuates the class through forms of endogamy (in-group marriage). Perpetuation of the caste system serves the interest of the upper castes by providing resources, cheap labor, favorable employment, prestige, access to women and other benefits. In open societies, most people also remain in the

class of birth, constituting essentially ascription on basis of class. There are strong factors favoring maintenance of class boundaries, including education, contacts and opportunities. Different classes can be seen as different subcultures, with each class showing similar life experiences, occupational roles, values, education, association, activities, buying habits, political views, etc.

Social Differentiation.
Social stratification within a society may be based upon a wide range of dimensions. Only age and sex appear to be universal distinctions, and even these are viewed quite differently. The respect given an aged person in some societies is not found in others. What is considered to be an appropriate sex role for women differs from one culture to another. The low status of women found in some societies is contrasted with their relatively equal status in other societies. Egalitarian societies and those lacking in effective political institutions beyond household tend to have higher status for women. When women maintain separate spheres of economic power and control through separate areas of influence, e.g., when they control some aspect of economic produce or trade in local markets, their status tends to be higher. In addition to age/generation and sex differentiation, other dimensions of social differentiation include ethnicity, physical features, gender identity, marital/parental status, education, disability, language, etc.

Ethnic Stratification.
Ethnic stratification refers to the stratification of society based upon or reflective of divisions derived from ethnic group membership. In societies that are ethnically stratified members of one or more ethnic groups will predominate in positions of power and the upper strata of the class system, while individuals of other ethnic groups will occupy the lowest strata. Most societies show some degree of ethnic stratification. In the U.S., white Anglo Saxon Protestants have constituted the power structure of the society and have dominated the upper class, presidency, senate and other political bodies. Other "non-white" ethnic groups have been largely excluded from the higher social strata, but may nonetheless have their own

stratification system within their ethnic group. Traditional patterns of discrimination have created what is referred to as an ethclass, reflecting the intersection of ethnicity and class status. Traditional patterns of discrimination have tended to relegate members of minority ethnic groups to lower-class structures within the wider society, regardless of their education, occupation or economic status. Inequality plays a powerful role in affecting life opportunities, and reinforces the lack of opportunity often ascribed by minority ethnic group status. Class systems are also found within specific ethnic groups. A dual stratification system, where the range of class levels (e.g., impoverished, middle, upper) are found within ethnic groups as well, characterizes many ethnic subcultures.

Social Class in Social Work.
An understanding of the nature of social class and the oppressive conditions of under-class status are of particular importance to social work practice. This is because of the traditional focus upon assistance to members of deprived groups and the powerful influences of class-derived experiences on discrimination, prejudice, opportunity, behavior and self-concept and -esteem. Appreciation of the impact of class is necessary for the development of social policies and the implementation of class advocacy programs. Class perspectives are particularly significant in understanding cultural realities and the relationships between different ethnic realities, especially those linkages between in-group cultural processes and the broader out-group societal influences. Class factors, especially membership in the under class, affect perspectives and behavior, exemplified in the view of life as controlled by external forces (external locus of control). A fundamental effect of under-class status is poverty, a recognized cause of family dysfunction, and consequently psychopathology and social maladaptation. The concept of class, especially in the context of "lower class," carries pejorative implications that Devore and Schlesinger (1991) suggest be avoided through the use of the term "under class." A central effect of under-class status is represented in the concept of the "culture of poverty."

The Culture and Structure of Poverty

The consequences of discrimination and oppression upon personality and opportunity is substantial, but the definitive partitioning of specific causality to prejudice, discrimination, stereotyping, cultural versus structural factors and many other conditions is not empirically possible. There are considerable consequences of extreme prejudices and discrimination, however. Membership in a group subject to prejudice and discrimination can create an oppressive and inescapable lifestyle of poverty for those so entrapped. Since the groups that are subjected to the greatest discrimination in this country are disproportionately represented in the impoverished classes, the conditions of poverty have to be understood as a systematic societal consequence of discrimination.

The consequences of discrimination can be seen in the systemic features of what has been called the "culture of poverty." The concept of the "culture of poverty" was introduced as a potential explanation for why poverty perpetuates itself across generations. The underlying notion is that poverty is associated with a cultural lifestyle that maintains the same values, attitudes, beliefs and behaviors generation after generation, leaving the cultural group in the same impoverished conditions. Frequently attributed to the culture of poverty are values, practices and orientations that are considered causes of poverty. These include low achievement motivation, no educational aspirations, mother dominance, father absence, family instability, present-time orientation and immediate gratification. Criticism of this notion of the culture of poverty has focused upon the inappropriateness of blaming the victim (the poor) for their economic situation rather than recognizing it to be a consequence of structural conditions that are part of a system of political and economic control exercised by the elite, not the poor. It fails to acknowledge the systemic advantages of poverty to the rich in the form of a cheap labor force and increased political power resulting from the control of a cheap labor force and the disenfranchisement of subordinated groups from political power. Criticisms of the culture of poverty explanations point out that it involves blaming the poor for their circumstances rather than recognizing the systemic features of the society that create intergenerational poverty. The culture of poverty perspective overlooks crucial causes, such as how social and cultural barriers to education and jobs perpetuate poverty and inhibit participation in the structural features of the dominant society.

Nonetheless, the culture of poverty notion does reflect the potential of the social system to create subcultural groups that persist in both non-adaptive and culturally adaptive forms of behavior that are at variance with the norms of the dominant society. Practices of discrimination keep the offspring of the poor from participation in those social settings where the norms and ideals of the dominant society are learned. The experiences of discrimination and prejudice can lead to frustration, diminished expectations, pessimism, fatalism and an alternative set of procedures for achieving culturally defined values. The effects of the social system of the dominant society in creating the conditions called the "culture of poverty" suggest that it is more appropriately conceptualized as the "social structure of poverty."

The structure of poverty refers to the multiple consequences of a lifestyle of poverty, independent of specific cultures. Its primary determinants are the lack of opportunity and access to power; its consequences include experiences of discrimination. Persistent experiences of failure in the face of such circumstances can result in despair, helplessness, resentment, low motivation and an unwillingness to continue to attempt to achieve. These structural conditions also interact with individual tendencies and adherence to poverty-oriented norms to create the systemic consequences of impoverishment. The cycle of poverty lies in structural conditions maintained by the dominant culture's prejudices and discriminations. These serve as a feedback cycle for socialization into behavior patterns and expectations of both the poor and rich that reproduce the group barriers and expectations thereby perpetuating the poverty lifestyle. The structural conditions and the adaptive values in the conditions of poverty create personality styles and behavioral traits that conflict with the personality characteristics and behavior of the middle class lifestyle, creating further barriers. Alternate behavior patterns are formed in the cultures of the subordinated minorities who are denied legitimate access to the values defined by the dominant society. Criminal activity among economically deprived groups is often a consequence of the denial of legitimate means of access to cultural values such as wealth and material comfort, making illegal behaviors avenues for economic success.

SUPERSTRUCTURE: IDEOLOGY, WORLD VIEW AND IDENTITY

Superstructure or ideology involves the non-material aspects of culture, culture in its mental and symbolic form. The superstructure or ideology includes all of the abstract cultural patterns that produce the behavior at the levels of structure and infrastructure. This includes language, beliefs, knowledge, science, religion, cosmology, expressive culture, values and thoughts. The pyramid of culture suggests a technoeconomic or material determination of social relations and ideology. The ideological system can determine the social and infrastructural arrangements as well. Culture provides knowledge of resources, the possibilities for utilization, the technologies for manipulation and how people perceive and relate to the physical environment. Beliefs may be more powerful determinants of adaptations than are the material aspects. The mental or ideological level of culture represents one of the evolutionary achievements of the human mind. The importance of ideology lies in the meaning it provides and its role in determining why and how we behave and act. What people believe to be the case about the world has a powerful influence on what they do. Ideology in the broadest sense includes the underlying and explicit values that guide behavior. Values determine how and what we see in the world — freedom fighters or terrorists, development or exploitation.

Cultures are characterized by a world view, the broad organizing frameworks and principles for understanding and relating to the environment. World view in the broadest sense includes cosmologies, values, beliefs, principles for social behavior, religion, philosophies, etc. World views represent the cognitive organizational models employed by people and how they structure the material and social behaviors. The world view provides the broad principles that underlie the meaning of social behavior. The world view of the other culture (emic perspective) is fundamental to anthropological methods for understanding other cultures and making sense of other people's behavior.

Language and Communication

All human communication processes, including emission and reception, are shaped through cultural processes. All that culture is and produces can be viewed as a system of communication and signification. Language as human communication refers to more than just the spoken and written words. Human language includes many systems of communication — verbal, non-verbal, behavioral, gestural, artistic, organizational, environmental, etc. The meaning is symbolic, going beyond the representations. It is not only what is said, but how it is said, when it is said, to whom, etc. The overview of the social interaction rules (Chapter 7) illustrates the wide range of aspects that underlie human communication. These communication systems are essential for understanding the nature of cross-cultural relations.

Language is of fundamental importance to culture since it is the major cultural communication medium, communicating shared expectations and social relations, defining social realities and serves as the major medium of socialization. Language is a fundamental necessity for entering the social and cultural realities of others. While language is the means of communication within cultures, it is also a barrier to communication between cultures. Knowledge of culture and the ability to participate effectively is "gated" by verbal language abilities and characteristics. Language serves as a guide for coding behavior and interpreting others' actions. Language influences understanding of the environment, physical objects, perception of reality, social relations and world view. In important ways, languages provide the means by which we come to perceive and understand reality. Language is one of the most powerful forces unifying or separating cultures and ethnic groups. Language plays a fundamental role in identification and is often a defining feature that separates different ethnic groups and provokes intergroup conflict. Language issues have important implications in intercultural relations, since preferred languages and social perception of the "social and political meanings" of language are influenced by the history of relations and current political ideologies.

Socialization and Education

The first and most important source of early socialization is the family system. While the family system and its extensions remain the most important source of socialization experiences throughout the lives of people from some simple societies, in most cultures secondary socialization systems take over as the most important source of influences. Whether secondary education takes the form of peer groups, age grades, school, secret societies, military training, prisons, work organizations, religious groups or numerous other sources of formal and informal education, they come to take precedence over the course and direction of one's life. If social institutions that provide this training are under the control of one of the cultural groups in society, this will likely have direct impact on the success of the other cultural groups in society. Education in the broadest sense is provided in all societies. However, the form and nature of education differs dramatically from culture to culture. In simple societies all of education occurs within the primary group — family, relatives and close friends who impart the information necessary for survival. As societies become more complex, education begins to take on a formal character. Here, special institutions separated from family begin to play a vital role in imparting information and training the individual. When education

reaches such specialization, the educational institutions play an increasingly important role in the stratification of society and the maintenance of intergroup boundaries.

Educational institutions in complex societies play important roles in the formation of interethnic relations, for a number of reasons. Educational institutions serve as gating mechanisms for access to specialized training in societies. Not only are they frequently the primary sources of technical training for the advanced technologies of the society, but they also serve as the grounds for many other types of specialized training — legal, military, political, linguistic, scientific, philosophical, etc. The educational institutions also play an important role in guiding the ideology and beliefs of a culture. In this context, they play an important role in directly shaping interethnic and intercultural relations. Education systems can serve as barriers to other groups by prohibiting their participation in education, or can facilitate their entrance and advancement in society by encouraging their participation and facilitating their progress. The role education systems have played in interethnic relations in our own society have varied considerably. The early periods of the U.S. were predominantly characterized by educational institutions that served as barriers to the effective social participation of many ethnic groups. Later, schools became institutions for the forced assimilation of groups. In the history of the U.S., the control of the educational systems by European Americans has had direct impact on the success of many other cultural groups. This cultural influence upon educational success has continued to this day. In the present era, many alternatives to the traditional educational systems and processes are being explored in order to determine what kinds of educational experiences will assure the success of the various cultural groups that have traditionally failed to achieve success in the U.S. educational systems. While culturally based institutional barriers to school success still exist for many groups, universities and their faculties have increasingly turned to the question of how their institutions may be part of the solution rather than continuing to be part of the problem. Education unquestionably can play a vital role in improving the nature of interethnic relations.

Values

Values reflect the most important aspects of a culture's beliefs, goals and expectations, indicating which states or activities are preferable to others, and guiding everyday behavior and decisions. Values provide emotionally charged priorities for decision-making and behavior because they reflect the most important aspects of a culture's beliefs, goals and expectations. Values represent the most important cultural determinants of behavior, with their violation generally creating emotionally charged responses. As a cultural embodiment of values, religion can have important impacts upon behavior by providing ultimate justifications and demanding certain social behavior. Values play a fundamental role in determining needs, feelings, perceptions, behaviors and attitudes.

People must understand their own values and orientations if they are to be effective in intercultural relations, since the numerous ethnic and cultural groups in the U.S. have values that conflict with the dominant ethos of the European American society. Development of cultural competence requires assessment of one's own cultural values and those of the other cultures with which one interacts. Recognizing others' values is essential for cultural competency because those values determine expectations and enable us to understand reasons for behavior.

Values assessments are important to identify characteristics of self and others that must be accommodated in intercultural relations. Values identify some of the most important determinants of behavior, and frequently lie at the base of unconscious motivations. Values have a strong emotional commitment, and their violation produces emotionally charged responses. Values are intertwined with one's world view, generally with an important basis in religion. As a cultural embodiment of values, religion can have important impacts upon social behavior by providing ultimate justifications, and demanding certain social relations and providing proscriptions and prescriptions about relationships to nature and other groups. Values underlie standards for action and constitute the basis of our attitudes, shaping perceptions and determining behavior. Values

determine many needs we feel, affecting motivation and productivity. Values impact communication and what is attended to. Values determine what is defined as a problem and how it should be solved.

Understanding the main values of a culture provides some global perspectives for understanding the impacts of culture upon behavior. Values reflect the overriding and widespread influences of a culture. Cultures have different values, as well as different priorities for and manifestations of the same values. There is little about the manifestation of any given value that is universal. Even those values that are universal have culturally variant manifestations — e.g., how to show respect. Values do address common areas of concern in all culture; understanding what those areas of concern are and some of the primary variants can help prepare for cross-cultural adaptation.

Kluckhohn's Basic Value Orientations

Kluckhohn (1961) developed the idea of value orientations to refer to the patterned principles, based upon cognitive, emotional and behavioral elements, which order and direct human activity in addressing common human problems. She suggested that universal to all human cultures are some basic concerns or value orientations, although the way in which cultures view these concerns and respond to them vary considerably. Kluckhohn explored five dimensions that all cultures need in order to develop value orientations:

1) Human nature
2) Human-nature relationships
3) Time orientation
4) Activity orientation
5) Human-human relationships

Human Nature.
Human nature may be viewed as having a variety of innate characteristics, which may be immutable, or conversely, potentially subject to change. Kluckhohn suggested that cultures see humans as

either basically good, basically evil or in an intermediate condition such as either neutral or both good and evil. Cultures differ in terms of whether they feel that these innate human characteristics can be changed, or if they are permanent once set in place. The Puritan ethic in the early U.S. was characterized by a view of humans as basically evil (e.g., the consequence of "original sin") but capable of change and improvement. Contemporary social science would more likely view human nature as neither good nor evil, but certainly mutable to many different forms.

Human to Nature Orientation.
The human to nature orientation refers to how humans perceive their relationships to the natural and physical world. The orientation of humans to nature tends to take one of three predominant forms:

---

1) Humans are subjugated to the forces of nature;
2) Humans are in harmony with nature; and
3) Humans have mastery over nature.

The human subjugation to nature is often viewed as a fatalistic approach to life, one in which nature, fortune and luck determine the outcome for the individual; individuals can do little about what will happen to them. The human harmony with nature orientation views humans as a part of natural processes, and a part of the balance with the whole. These humans generally try to align their lives with nature so as to function in harmony. The human mastery over nature orientation is a view in which the natural environment should be brought under the control of human interests. The control of nature through technology is a principal aspect of the American value orientation.

Time Orientation.
The concept of time orientation is concerned with how humans view the temporal focus of their activity. The primary differences suggested by Kluckhohn were the past, present and future time

orientations. While all societies have to manage issues related to the past, present and future, they often emphasize a principle time dimension in their value orientations. The past orientation considers accomplishments in the past traditions to have the most important emphasis and direction for current activities. The past time orientation is often expressed in the feeling that traditions of a distant past must be maintained. The future orientation is one that expects subsequent changes to bring fulfillment; the future is better and improved. The future time orientation generally views time as a commodity, to be used or wasted, measured and valued. Punctuality and an obsession about time is typical of the future time orientation often ascribed to Americans. The present time orientation is an emphasis upon the here and now, with little regard for time or schedules or the past or future. The present-time-oriented person generally has little clock orientation, thereby often appearing late from the perspective of future-time-oriented people. People, relationships, activities and other factors often take precedence over time orientation for the present-oriented person.

Activity Orientation.
The activity orientation is also referred to by Kluckhohn as the valued personality type. The focus of this basic value dimension is on the question of what kind of activity is most valued to humans in terms of their self-expression. This is discussed in terms of being, being-in-becoming and doing. The being orientation emphasizes spontaneous expression of the personality, an indulgence in expression and enjoyment of desires. The being approach emphasizes giving expression to what is, rather than developing the self into something different. The being-in-becoming orientation is concerned with the development of the self as an integrated whole. The being-in-becoming emphasizes acceptance of what is, both in expression of emotional desires and reasoned control. It uses processes such as detachment and meditation to contain and control desires and their expression in order to support the development of the entirety of the person. The doing orientation is characterized by a striving for betterment and change, an improvement over

existing conditions. The self is evaluated in terms of external standards and measurable accomplishments, judgments typical in the ideal of American culture.

Human Relationships Orientation.
The human relationships orientation is concerned with how humans view their relationships to other members of their social groups. These differences are discussed in terms of three dominant patterns: individualistic, lineal and collateral. While societies have to develop all three types of relationships, one pattern tends to predominate. The individualistic orientation considers the individual to be more important than the group. The individualistic orientation emphasizes individuality, self-determination and autonomy, individual responsibility, and individual rights and freedoms. The lineal and collateral orientations emphasize the group over the individual, the rights and responsibilities of and to groups instead of the inclinations of individuals. The collateral orientations emphasize the responsibilities to a contemporary extended family and social group. The relationships are generally bilateral and encompass the people with whom one feels related through bonds of kinship, setting the individual's group off from other groups within society. The lineal orientations emphasize the familial relations, either patrilineal or matrilineal exclusively, which are extended over time, incorporating a hierarchy across generations. The principles of social power are predicated upon lines of descent within the hierarchy of kinship relations that serve as a hierarchical power structure for the group.

Summary.
These different value orientations are not exclusive within a culture. All cultures need to deal with all dimensions of these basic value orientations and others. For example, while humans may feel subjugated to nature, they nonetheless need to dominate it sufficiently to acquire their subsistence needs. Or, while most groups emphasize the priority of the collectivity, they also recognize the individual's needs apart from the global needs of the group. These value orientations must be understood as providing

guidelines for recognizing dominant tendencies rather than identifying exclusive options. Understanding one's own values is necessary for effectiveness in intercultural relations since they advise of predominant sources of conflict. Recognizing others' values is essential because their values determine their expectations and interpretations of behavior, and enable us to understand the reasons for their behavior and how to adapt effectively. The values assessment at the end of the chapter are provided for several reasons. The principal ones are (1) to assess your awareness of your and your culture's most important values; (2) to reflect on the most important values in other cultures; and (3) to provide a basis for discussing with others the variation in value orientations that exist in society. To be effective, this exercise should be discussed with a culturally diverse group of people.

Religion and Cosmology

Religion is based upon a socially shared set of beliefs about the supernatural. Religion is also intimately involved in cultural values and rules for social behavior and in providing meaning or cosmology — explanations about the nature of the world. Religious beliefs provide ultimate values and justifications, serving as major social mobilizers, providing powerful justifications for action or inaction. Religion has been called a mainspring of culture — determining many aspects of behavior, attitudes and values. Religion organizes familial, economic, social and political activities and justifies behaviors. Religious systems generally embody a cosmology, explanations and beliefs about the nature of the world. As a cultural embodiment of values, religion can have important impacts upon economic and work behavior — either exciting it or serving to inhibit economic activity. The American culture's idealized separation of church and state, and church and economic activities, has not been the case throughout history. Indeed, religious organizations have provided the economic, social and political organizations for societies. Religious beliefs and motivations provide reasons for behavior that contradicts economic rationality, effecting behavior and material adaptations. Throughout the cultures of the world, religions have provided the core of cultural values and played a very important part of social and political organization. Religion is also central to intercultural conflict. The role of religion in intercultural contact reflects many factors, including religion's ability to organize people, the role of religion in justification of activities and the role of religion in providing a new world view to adjust to change.

Summary

In order to understand the relationships between culture and behavior, the overall processes of culture must be understood. The influences of culture largely operate at unconscious levels, especially in early development. These cultural influences set the basis for the perceptual and conceptual worlds, as well as material circumstances and social resources that produce the reality for the emerging human being's experiences and opportunities. This cultural system provides both for the commonalities that link its members and the differences that distinguish members of the same group. Understanding cultural influences upon ethnic identity and group psychology requires the use of a systems model that encompasses many different aspects of behavior, socialization, social influences and experiences. Cultural and social influence set the basis for behavior, sex roles and the formation of the personality through adaptation to the cultural systems and their principles and constraints.

REFERENCES AND ADDITIONAL READINGS

Aguirre, A. and J. Turner. 1995. American Ethnicity: The Dynamics and Consequences of Discrimination. Boston: McGraw-Hill.

Applebaum, H. 1987. "Universal aspects of work." In Applebaum, ed. Perspectives in Cultural Anthropology. Albany: SUNY Press.

Bock, P. 1988. Rethinking Psychological Anthropology. New York: W.H. Freeman.

Bond, M. ed. 1988. The Cross-Cultural Challenge to Social Psychology. Newbury Park, Ca.: Sage Publications.

Bourguignon, E. 1976. Psychological Anthropology. New York: Holt, Rinehart and Winston.

Cole, M. and S. Scribner. 1974. Culture and Thought. New York: Wiley.

Devore, W. and E. Schlesinger. 1991. Ethnic-Sensitive Social Work Practice (3rd edition). New York: Merrill.

Erchak, G. 1992. The Anthropology of Self and Behavior. New Brunswick: Rutgers University Press.

Gergen, K. and M. Gergen. 1981. Social Psychology. New York: Harcourt, Brace, Jovanovich.

Harris, M. 1987. "Theoretical principles of cultural materialism". In Applebaum, H. ed. Perspectives in Cultural Anthropology. Albany: SUNY Press.

Heelas, P. and A. Lock 1981. Indigenous Psychology The Anthropology of the Self. New York: Academic Press.

Kluckhohn, F. 1961. Variations in Value Orientations. Evanston, IL: Row, Peterson and Co.

LeVine, R. 1973. Culture, Behavior and Personality. Chicago: Aldine.

Munroe, R. L. and R. H. Munroe. 1975. Cross-Cultural Human Development. California: Brooks/ Cole Publishing Company.

Schermerhorn, R. 1978. Comparative Ethnic Relations. Chicago: University of Chicago Press.

Spindler, G. ed. 1978. The Making of Psychological Anthropology. New York: Holt, Reinhart and Winston.

Weber, M. 1904. The Protestant Ethic and the Spirit of Capitalism. New York: Scribner.

Wierzbicka, A. 1993. "A Conceptual Basis for Cultural Psychology." Ethos 21(2):205-231.

Williams, T. 1983. Socialization. Englewood Cliffs, N.J.: Prentice-Hall.

SELF-ASSESSMENT 4.1

CULTURE ASSESSMENT

Infrastructure Effects

How have your living locations and community affected your development, as compared to the living conditions in some of the other communities in your state?

How have economic resources affected what you have done, or not been able to do, with your life?

Have you been unable to achieve what you consider to be reasonable goals and aspirations because of the lack of economic resources? Or, how would your life have been different if you had not had adequate economic resources for your schooling?

Family Effects

Whom do you consider to be your family?

Does your family structure reflect what is typical for your culture? In what way is it typical or not?

Do you have relatives who are important but not part of your family?

<u>NOTES</u>

SELF-ASSESSMENT 4.2

VALUES ASSESSMENT

Assess how important each of the following factors are to you on the following scale:
1 = Very Important, 2 = Important, 3 = Little Importance, 4 = No Importance

	High		Low	
Health and well being	(1)	2	3	4
Care and Service to others	1	(2)	3	4
Respect for elderly	(1)	2	3	4
Traditions of my religion	(1)	2	3	4
Being sexually attractive and desirable	(1)	2	3	4
Patriotism	1	2	(3)	4
Protection and respect for women	(1)	2	3	4
Education and personal advancement	(1)	2	3	4
More time for my personal interests	(1)	2	(3)	4
Independence from authority	(1)	2	3	4
Honesty, truth and justice	(1)	2	3	4
Directness in communication	1	2	3	4
Intense frequent interaction with family	(1)	2	3	4
Punctuality	1	2	(3)	4
Having a close relationship with my boss	1	2	3	(4)
Job security in my chosen profession	1	2	(3)	4
Lots of close friendships	(1)	2	3	4
Spiritual experiences and personal growth	1	2	3	(4)
Being liked by my co-workers	(1)	2	3	4
Planning well in advance	(1)	2	3	4
A place I can call my own home	(1)	2	3	4
Experiences of harmony with nature	1	2	3	(4)
Distinct roles for men and women	1	2	3	(4)
Formal standards for behavior	(1)	2	3	4
Being able to freely express my emotions	(1)	2	3	4
Material well being	(1)	2	3	4
Time for reflection and meditation	(1)	2	3	(4)
A sense of community/cultural solidarity	(1)	2	3	4

<u>NOTES</u>

Which of these values are the most important?
1.
2.
3.
4.

How do these values affect your behavior?

What happens if others with whom you interact do not share these values?

What values are the least important to you?

Which of these values are significant values for your culture?

Are there other values that are important in your culture?

Which cultures have those values that are least important to you? What might happen if you did not respect these values?

Select three other cultures besides your own about which you know the most.
1.
2.
3.

NOTES

1. What are their most important values?
    a.
    b.
    c.

2. How do these values affect their behavior?
    a.
    b.
    c.

3. Which aspects of these value systems are most likely to conflict with your own?
    a.
    b.
    c.

Gender and Values
What are the stereotypes, ideals and behaviors that you were taught were appropriate for your gender?

Toys work

What are the stereotypes, ideals and behaviors that you were taught were appropriate for the opposite gender?

Caring

What are the gender characteristics for females in other cultures that differ significantly from your own?

Some its opp

What are the gender characteristics for males in other cultures that differ significantly from your own?

They are the women

NOTES

SELF-ASSESSMENT 4.3

VALUES ORIENTATION ASSESSMENT

The following exercises utilize Kluckhohn's value orientations and their dimensions of variation as a basis for self-evaluation. The questions are designed to help you discover your own dominant value orientations, those of your cultural or ethnic group and the orientations of other ethnic and cultural groups in society. They are designed to provoke your own thoughts and reflections on the topic and serve as a basis for group discussion.

Comment briefly on the value dimensions that are most important to you.
  1. Human nature
  2. Human-nature relationships
  3. Time orientation
  4. Activity orientation
  5. Human-human relationships

What is your view of human nature? Good, neutral, good and evil, or evil? Is it a permanent condition or changeable? Do you believe that good behavior is rewarded and bad behavior punished?

What is your orientation to nature? Subordinate, in harmony or dominant? Do you believe that you can improve your life and the world around you?

What is your predominate time orientation? Past, present or future? Are you generally on time? How do you react to people who are late? How many minutes after a set appointment time are you late?

What is your predominate activity orientation? Being, being-in-becoming, or doing? Can you sit around and just do nothing? What are your most important goals to accomplish?

NOTES

Which social relations are most important to you?
  1. Your relation to your immediate family (spouse and children or parents and siblings)?
  2. Your relations with your extended family, relatives and deceased ancestors?
  3. Your relationship to your friends and social group?

What are the principal preferred dimensions of your cultural group on each of the value orientations?
  1. Human nature
  2. Human-nature relationships
  3. Time orientation
  4. Activity orientation
  5. Human-human relationships

Are there value dimensions that have near-universal consensus within your cultural group?

Are there dimensions that are subject to considerable variation?

NOTES

NOTES

CHAPTER 5

PROCESS DYNAMICS
OF INTERGROUP RELATIONS

Overview
The typical dynamics of intergroup relations involve misunderstanding, conflict and inappropriate projections of one's own cultural assumptions (ethnocentrism). Knowledge of the typical dynamics of intergroup relations is central for adapting to cultural differences. These include the ability to reduce cultural attributions and ethnocentrism, the inappropriate prejudice and discrimination, and the psychodynamic processes, particularly defense mechanisms. A variety of individual adaptations are made to intercultural interfaces, making the dynamics of assimilation highly variable. Recognition of the societal dynamics of cultural pluralism provides skills for intercultural adaptation.

Objectives
Explain the general dynamics of intercultural contact
Illustrate how our projections of meaning, cause and responsibility affect intergroup relations
Present ethnocentrism, prejudice and discrimination as normal intergroup dynamics
Describe psychological reactions and defense mechanisms used in intergroup accommodation
Illustrate the range of acculturation responses occurring in intergroup accommodations

Chapter Outline
Introduction
Cross-Cultural Contact and Conflict
    Cultural Shock
Attribution and Interpretation
    Types of Causal Attributions
    Cultural Attribution
    Stereotypes and Cultural Characterizations
In-Group Versus Out-Group Dynamics
    Ethnocentrism
    The Ethnocentric Syndrome
Prejudice and Discrimination
    Classic and Normative Views
    Prejudice
    Discrimination
    Explanations of Prejudice and Discrimination
Psychodynamic Process in Intercultural Relations
    Minority Defense Mechanisms
    Minority Status: Psychology and Self-Esteem
    Majority Defense Mechanisms

(Continued)

INTRODUCTION

To adapt effectively to intercultural relations, it is necessary to understand the general psychological and social reactions provoked by intercultural interactions. Independent of the particular cultures involved, intercultural contact produces similar reactions and problems, what I call the "process dynamics" of intergroup relations. Contact between different cultural groups inevitably causes conflict, and ignorance of the causes of problems exacerbates the difficulties of intercultural relations. Cultural differences not only produce conflict, they also produce cultural shock, destabilizing personal reactions that can undermine adaptation efforts. Understanding how to manage culture shock experiences is important for everyone in society as intercultural contact increases. This is manifested in an increasing incidence of intercultural and interethnic violence found globally.

Effective adaptation to intercultural contact requires an understanding of the *process dynamics* involved in contact between different cultural groups. Principal aspects of the process dynamics involve the in-group-out-group dynamics, a variety of reactions (e.g., ethnocentrism, prejudice and discrimination, attribution) that occurs in relations between different groups. Relations between culturally different individuals and groups are strongly shaped by inherent process aspects of cross-cultural interaction. These are called process dynamics because they reflect the processes of relationships, rather than the content of the interactions, their functions or the intents of the actors. Understanding these group and intergroup processes or dynamics provides perspectives for more successful cross-cultural adaptation.

Central to the process dynamics of intercultural contact is conflict. When people of different cultures interact, conflict and misunderstanding is inevitable for even well-intentioned individuals. One primary reason for intercultural conflict is ethnocentrism. All cultures are ethnocentric, with their members viewing reality from their ethnic-centered point of view. This is part of the attribution processes where we give meaning to the events and others' actions based upon our relationships to them and our own cultural assumptions and experiences, not their experiences and meanings. The processes of prejudice, discrimination and stereotyping are a normal part of understanding the world. The development of cross-cultural psychology and concerns with the impacts of culture and ethnicity upon therapeutic interactions have helped reveal other dynamics that underlie relationships between people of different cultures. Because of the emotional assumptions we acquire in the socialization process, we unconsciously engage in projection and transference to other individuals and ethnic groups our own feelings based on previous experiences. Counter-transference, resistance and defensive reactions from people of the other groups with which we interact also complicate intercultural relationships. All of these processes — conflict, shock, in-group versus out-group dynamics, ethnocentrism, prejudice, discrimination, attribution, transference and other psychological reactions — are normal, automatic and inherent aspects of the relationships between different cultural groups. Consequently, effective cross-cultural adaptation requires an awareness of these processes and how to facilitate intercultural relations.

CROSS-CULTURAL CONTACT AND CONFLICT

Cross-cultural contact will not necessarily lead to harmony and positive intergroup relations. There is a naive belief that prejudice and conflict will be automatically reduced if people of different cultures have the opportunity to interact. This is not actually the case. Studies of cross-cultural contact indicate that incidental intergroup contact is more likely to increase hostility, suspicion and prejudice and conflicts derived from many different aspects of cultural difference.

There are important cultural reasons why cross-cultural contact will inevitably result in conflict. Culture provides the basis for our communication, understandings and behavior. Each culture provides different rules about communication and behavior and what they mean. Since different cultures provide different meanings for behavior, our behavior in interaction with people from other cultures will likely be misunderstood. In intercultural relations even well-intentioned individuals will inevitably find themselves in conflict with other well-intentioned individuals. Even culturally sensitive persons can find themselves in conflicts because others do not have cross-cultural perspectives and skills. For instance, consider a hypothetical first interaction between an American and Japanese businessman. Both wish to express respect and liking for the other party. As the Japanese and American step toward each other, each follow cultural protocols for the exchange polite greetings. The Japanese bows deeply while the American extends his hand to shake hands. As the Japanese's head lowers and the American's hand rises, head and hand collide. The Japanese asks himself, "Why is this American slapping me in the face while I am respectfully bowing?" The American wonders "Why is this Japanese using forehead karate on me when I offer a friendly handshake?" The behaviors and interpretations that each party brings are reasonable from their own culture, but inappropriate for the other culture. Each party is acting in a perfectly polite manner, but conflict results in spite of their good intentions.

Intercultural interactions are fraught with such misunderstandings. Conflicts can occur in any medium of communication or interaction. Hand gestures are an example. The Americans "OK" sign is an obscene gesture in Brazil. The "V for Victory" or "peace sign" is an obscene gesture in Italy. Conflicts may occur because different parties infer different meanings. The statement "Boy this is a mess!" may seem non-discriminatory, unless one feels sensitive about the potential meanings of "boy," or has reason to suspect discrimination because of the way in which "boy" has been used in the past to oppress African Americans. To reduce these potential conflicts and determine how to avoid them, it is necessary to recognize the sources of conflict. Intercultural conflicts can result from basically any of the aspects of behavior, including some of the following most common areas of conflict:

Potential Areas for Conflict in Cross-Cultural Relations

Language	Nonverbal Communication
Norms and Values	Beliefs and Attitudes
Identity and Sense of Self	Dress and Appearance
Space and Organization	Time Concepts
Interpersonal Relations	Social Behavior
Directness and Disclosure	Learning Styles
Cognitive Processes and Habits	Work Habits and Values
Management and Negotiation Styles	Organizational Behavior

Cultural Shock

The inevitable conflicts that occur in intercultural relations produce powerful psychological and emotional consequences manifested in culture shock. Cultural shock has been conceptualized as the consequence of strain and anxiety resulting from contact with a new culture and feelings of loss, confusion and impotence resulting from loss of accustomed cultural cues and social rules and a feeling of impotence from the inability to deal with the environment because of unfamiliarity with cognitive aspects and role-playing skills. Cultural (or culture) shock is a multifaceted experience resulting from numerous stressors occurring in contact with a different culture. Cultural shock is typically recognized among immigrant groups or business people on overseas assignments, but can also occur for people in their own society when cultural pluralism creates intensive contact with other cultural groups. The culturally pluralistic nature of U.S. society creates daily cross-cultural conflict and immersion, making cultural shock an important source of interpersonal stress and conflict for many people exposed to unfamiliar cultural or subcultural settings. The circumstances provoking cultural shock and the individual reactions depend upon a variety of factors, including previous experience with other cultures and cross-cultural adaptation, the degree of difference between cultures, the extent of preparation, social support networks, and individual psychological characteristics (Furnam & Bochner 1986). Serious cultural shock experiences may provoke disabling psychological crises or social dysfunctions that impede social or job performance. Effectively dealing with cultural shock requires recognition of cultural shock occurrences and implementing behaviors to overcome cultural shock. Awareness of the nature and causes of cultural shock and the typical reactions facilitates constructive intervention by providing the basis for recognition of one's own ongoing cultural shock experiences and responding with adaptive problem-solving strategies.

Causes of Cultural Shock

Cultural shock derives from both the challenge of new cultural surroundings and the loss of a familiar cultural environment, causing both psychological and physiological stress responses. Psychological reactions include emotional, interpersonal, cognitive and social components, as well as the effects resulting from changes in sociocultural relations, cognitive fatigue, role stress and identity loss.

Stress Reactions.

A normal consequence of a new environment is the experience of stress caused by both physiological and psychological factors. In a psychosomatic interaction, psychological states affect the body and its physiological reactions, which in turn increase feelings of stress, anxiety, depression and uneasiness. Cultural shock results in an increased concern with illness; a sense of feeling physically ill; a preoccupation with symptoms, minor pains and discomforts; and increased psychosomatic and physical illness from stress- induced reductions in immune system functioning (Rhinesmith 1985).

Cognitive Fatigue.

A major aspect of cultural shock and the resultant stress is cognitive fatigue, a consequence of an "information overload." The new culture demands a conscious effort to understand things processed unconsciously in one's own culture. Efforts must be made to interpret new language meanings and new non-verbal, behavioral, contextual and social communications. The change from automatic unconscious effortless behavior within one's own culture to the conscious effort and attention required to understand the new culture results in mental fatigue or "burn-out."

Role Shock.

Changes in social roles and interpersonal relations in the new culture may affect well-being and self-concept, resulting in "role shock," from loss of roles central to one's identity. Identity is in part maintained by social interactions that contribute to well-being through structuring social roles. In the new cultural setting, the prior roles are largely eliminated, leading to "role shock" resulting from an ambiguity about one's social position, the loss of normal social roles and new roles inconsistent with self-concept.

Personal Shock.
Personal shock is an aspect of cultural shock resulting from diverse changes in personal life, including loss of personal intimacy and interpersonal contact with significant others. One's self-esteem, identity and feelings of well-being and satisfaction with life are maintained within one's system of interpersonal relations. Losing this support system can lead to deterioration in one's sense of well-being and pathological manifestations such as emotional disorders and transient neurosis. Personal shock is augmented by occurrences in the new culture that violate one's personal and cultural morals, values, logic and beliefs about normality and civility. Value conflicts contribute to a sense of disorientation and unreality, increasing the sense of pervasive conflict with one's surroundings and the feeling of being emotionally assaulted.

Phases/Stages of Cultural Shock.
Differentiation of cultural shock and its resolution typically emphasizes four major stages:

---

1) The honeymoon or tourist phase;
2) The crises or cultural shock phase;
3) The adjustment, reorientation and gradual recovery phase; and
4) The adaptation, resolution, or acculturation phase.

The phases are both sequential and cyclical. The shift from crises to adjustment and adaptation can repeat as one encounters new crises, requiring additional adjustments. One may become effectively bicultural and then the adaptation phase is a permanent stage.

The Honeymoon or Tourist Phase.
The first phase of culture shock is the opposite of what we typically think of as cultural shock. The typical experiences of people who enter other cultures for honeymoons, vacations or brief business trips is initially positive. It is characterized by interest, excitement, euphoria, sleeplessness, positive expectations and idealizations about the new culture. Although there may be anxiety and stress, these tend to be interpreted positively, with the differences viewed as exciting and interesting. This is because honeymooners, vacationers and business people have experiences largely limited to institutions (hotels, resorts, business, airports) that isolate them from having to deal with the local culture in a substantial way and on its own terms.

The Crisis Phase.
The crisis phase may emerge immediately upon intercultural contact or may be delayed, but generally emerges within a few weeks. It may start with a full-blown crisis or as a series of escalating problems, negative experiences and reactions. Although individual reactions vary, there are typical features of cultural shock. Things start to go wrong, minor issues and cultural differences become irritating, leading to excessive preoccupation and increasing disappointments, frustrations, impatience and tension. One may feel helpless, confused, disliked by others or treated like a child. A sense of lack of control of one's life may lead to depression, isolation, anger or hostility. Excessive emotionality and fatigue may be accompanied by physical or psychosomatic illness. Typical feelings include that one is being taken advantage of or cheated. Becoming overly sensitive, suspicious and paranoid, with fears of being robbed or assaulted, are also typical reactions; emotional disorders and acute crisis may also occur. Severe symptoms of cultural shock may include withdrawal and excessive sleeping, compulsive eating and drinking, excessive irritability and hostility, marital and family tensions and conflicts, loss of work effectiveness, and unaccountable episodes of crying. One finds innumerable reasons to dislike and criticize the culture. Typical in this phase are reparative behaviors to help reestablish one's familiar habitual cultural patterns of behavior.

The Adjustment and Reorientation Phase.
The third phase is concerned with making an acceptable adaptation to the new culture. A variety of adjustments can be achieved: cultural learning, adjustment without adaptation or flight and isolation. If one desires to function effectively in another cultural setting, it is necessary to adjust and adapt. One develops problem-solving skills for dealing with the culture and begins to accept the culture's ways with a positive attitude. The culture begins to make sense, and negative reactions and responses to the culture are reduced as one recognizes that problems are due to the inability to understand, accept and adapt. Problems do not end during the adjustment phase, but one develops a positive attitude toward the challenge of resolving the issues necessary to function in the new culture.

The Adaptation, Resolution or Acculturation Stage.
The fourth stage involves stable adaptations in managing the new culture. There are many different adaptation options, especially given diverse individual characteristics and goals. Although full assimilation is difficult, if not impossible, one can acculturate and achieve substantial personal change and adjustment through cultural adaptation and by developing a bicultural identity. It is important to recognize and accept that an effective adaptation will lead to the development of a bicultural identity, an integration of a new culture into one's self-concept.

Summary

Adapting to culture shock requires a range of responses. Central to the adaptation process are cognitive awareness and behavior adjustments involving intercultural effectiveness skills: the ability to manage psychological stress, capabilities in communication competence and cultural empathy, and the ability to establish interpersonal relationships. Managing ones own personal, emotional and social needs are also an essential component of culture shock resolution. Undergoing development of a multicultural self is part of the process of successfully managing and overcoming culture shock (see Winkelman 1994).

ATTRIBUTION AND INTERPRETATION

The ordinary perceptual processes used for understanding relations and behavior in one's own culture are usually used to interpret behavior in cross-cultural situations. A lack of understanding of the other culture leads participants to attribute their own cultural meanings to other cultural contexts. Employing the ordinary social and cultural processes of understanding used within our own culture to understand other cultures' behavior is ethnocentrism — ethnic centeredness.

Underlying ethnocentrism, the ethnocentric syndrome, prejudice, discrimination, stereotypes and other aspects of in-group versus out-group relations, is a common psychosocial process called attribution. Attribution refers to the processes by which humans attribute or ascribe meaning to the social situations they encounter and make causal explanations of the causes of observed actions of other persons. Individuals respond as members of groups, and use an attribution process based on the tendency to divide the world into in-group versus out-group. Attribution is a normal process humans use to make sense of the world, but its habitual tendencies and applications create additional problems in intercultural relations. The attribution process is a normal process of ascribing meaning to events based on previous experience, and has direct relevance to understanding and adapting to intergroup relationships.

The research on attribution indicates both universal aspects of attribution and a range of discrete factors that affect attribution behavior. There are several different types of causal attributions based on relationships and information or knowledge. Attributions tend to be of two general types: (1) personal, those causes considered to be within the person; and (2) situational, those causes found in the environment or situation.

Acts evoke quite different attitudes and interpretations depending upon the relationship between the persons involved, in particular the in-group versus out-group dynamic and the knowledge that the percipient has about the actor.

The information at the individual's disposal, particularly its consensus, consistency and distinctiveness, has different effects depending upon the relationship with the individual observed. Three other dimensions also underlie causal attributions: the stability of behavior, the locus of causality (internal versus external) and perceived controllability (see Fletcher & Ward 1988; Jaspars & Hewstone 1982). These processes affect cross-cultural relations.

Types of Causal Attributions

Personal attributions consider causes of behavior to be the internal aspects of a person: ability, traits, disposition, character, efforts, habits, reflexes, genes, etc. *Situational attributions* consider causes of behavior to be located in the situation — social context, luck, task difficulty and environmental, ecological and cultural factors of the setting. Personal success tends to be explained in terms of internal factors — ability and efforts — while personal failure tends to be attributed to external causes such as the situation, task difficulty or luck. This is a self-serving explanation, but also reflects information available. Social psychological research shows that the typical attributions that individuals make are based upon their relationship to the actors. An egocentric group-self-serving bias is found in attribution, with different types of explanations found for in-group versus out-group behavior. Positive in-group behaviors and negative out-group behaviors are explained with attribution of internal causes, while negative in-group behaviors and positive out-group behaviors are explained by ascribing external causes. This tendency is widespread cross-culturally, but in some non-Western cultures and under specific sociocultural traditions it appears weak or at least lacking in expressed social behavior (e.g., cultural values such as group modesty will reduce positive in-groups attributions). Internalization of negative out-group stereotypes of a minority group by the same minority groups members will apparently reverse expression of some of the general attribution tendencies. Factors that have been identified which attenuate or exaggerate these tendencies include values, beliefs, particular stereotypes, sociohistorical factors and socioeconomic conditions.

In-Group versus Out-Group Attributions

The behavior of the actor or members of the actor's in-group are subjected to different rules of attribution than applied to the "other" or out-group. These are generally social situational versus personal explanations, respectively. Research shows that people typically explain their behavior and those of in-group as determined by the situation, whereas the behavior of the outsider is attributed to actors' internal characteristics and disposition. But the kinds of attributions vary depending upon whether the actor's behavior is interpreted negatively or positively. While people tend to take personal credit for their positive outcomes and to attribute negative outcomes to situational characteristics, they reverse this for out-group members. Negative behaviors of out-group members tend to be attributed to personal characteristics, while positive attributions to out-group members tend to be situational characterizations (e.g., "anyone could have done that").

Informational Bases for Attribution

The information available about the actors affects the nature of the attributions made. The amount of information available to the observer generally determines whether an individual makes a person-centered or situation-centered explanation. The fewer distinctive reasons an actor has for his/her behavior, and the fewer the reasons shared by the percipient, the more the acts are interpreted as identifying the dispositions (internal personal characteristics) of the actor. As knowledge of others increases, the tendency is to offer situational rather than personal explanations, especially for the others' shortcomings. When the context indicates the reasons for the action, there is less inclination to attribute the reason for the actions to the actors' internal dispositions. Principles used by the observer when there is limited observation and knowledge are a discounting principle and an augmentation principle. The discounting principle means that the role of a given cause is discounted to the extent that there are other plausible causes present. The augmentation principle means that when there are known constraints, costs, sacrifices or risks involved, the action is attributed to the actor more than would otherwise be done. There is a strong tendency to offer situational interpretations of others behaviors as their behavior is seen across many situations and cross-situational variability can be noted. Actors have more information on effects of setting for themselves or their own group, ergo situational explanations are more prevalent for the in-group. The cross-cultural situation is one in which the individual may have no information about the other group, and therefore perceive no reason for the groups' actions. Personal attribution is more likely to take place, and to be wrong, since individuals have good culturally based contextual reasons for their social behavior.

The internal-external dimension central to attribution theory is apparently universal, although the extent of these attribution tendencies are affected by various factors — cultural, economic, social and personal. A fundamental attribution tendency towards error is the propensity to overestimate internal causes and underestimate the external situational aspects of behavior. Some cultures tend to make extensive situational attribution, where context is used to explain behavior instead of development or motivation. Many non-Western cultures tend to emphasize the explanatory function of social roles and contextual behaviors rather than abstract traits. Concepts of the self and reasons for behavior are conceptualized in terms of specific persons and their relationships to the actor. Thus cross-cultural research shows that while the attribution tendencies do have some universal features, there are a variety of social and cultural factors affecting those tendencies.

Cultural Attribution

Attribution research has several general implications for understanding interpersonal cross-cultural misunderstandings. The better we know people, the more we evaluate on situational terms and deflect personal blame away from them.

Similar behaviors by out-group members are likely to be interpreted as personally based out of an ignorance of relevant cultural factors. The context of cross-cultural interaction must be informed by situational explanations — cultural attribution. However, people generally lack the appropriate situational information. Instead, people enter into cross-cultural interaction with preconceived notions from their own cultures and err in making normal cultural attributions that are inappropriate for interpreting the other culture's situation. The person-centered attribution process exacerbates difficulties when dealing with cross-cultural problems and conflicts. The approach of personal attribution leads to escalation of conflict. Problems could be seen as caused by personal characteristics or dispositions of individuals, or, in contrast, by the sociohistorical and cultural influences on the individual. The normal tendency to attribute personal blame or responsibility must be replaced with the correct approach, which is to attribute cultural (contextual, situational) causes.

If the meaning attributed to the behavior of an out-group member assumes that their failure to meet our expectations results from personal irresponsibility, this is a form of person attribution (the individual is deviant) on the basis of an ethnocentric assumption (the individual should act like me). A situational explanation focuses upon explanations that examine the influences of different cultural norms, customs or opportunities. If people do not shake hands, personal attribution suggests that they are not friendly, since we shake hands when we are friendly. Situational explanations would suggest there are cultural differences in norms about greeting. This cultural interpretation of different norms is more likely to lead to a positive resolution of the potential conflict by recognizing that others ascribe different meaning to behavior. Instead of being offended that the other is not friendly, we recognize that their friendliness is expressed in a different manner. It appears that attribution of person disposition is more likely to occur when there is a behavior that is out of role — i.e., when that behavior does not conform to normative expectations. However, if the other person is from another culture, then it is a mistake to attribute one's own cultural norms as a basis for evaluation. Conflict and misinterpretation can be reduced if we assume that the behavior is normal and acceptable from the other culture's point of view. This can be best achieved by consciously adopting a cultural relativist perspective and an interpretive framework that attributes cultural causes to conflict instead of personal faults.

The normal processes of attribution of meaning in situations of conflict are based upon the assumption that people act for personal reasons. The personal reasons attributed are those provided by the percipient's culture. An understanding of the cultural basis for human behavior clearly illustrates that the ways people act and the reasons they have for their behavior are derived from their own cultural background and social situation. Such understandings illustrate that the normal processes of personal attribution are erroneous, since they are based upon our own cultural assumptions rather than an understanding of the other culture's assumptions. The tendencies to engage in personal attribution are likely to exacerbate the conflict as inappropriate attribution escalates the inevitable patterns of conflict. There is an alternative.

Harmonious intercultural relations requires that we manage to suspend or bracket our normal tendencies to engage in personal attribution in intercultural interaction. Personal attribution is largely erroneous in that the reason that people from different cultures have conflicts stems from the cultural determination and interpretation of behavior, not the personal faults of individuals. Suspending the normal processes of personal attribution in dealing with out-group and cross-cultural relations is the first step in developing the appropriate culturally or situationally based attribution. This process of cultural attribution replaces the personal attribution and blaming with perspectives that recognize that behavior and conflict in cross-cultural contact is generated by different cultural principles. Cultural attribution is a conscious effort to interpret cross-cultural conflict within a perspective that recognizes that the differences in cultural perspectives will necessarily generate conflict that must be overcome. Recognition of the cultural versus personal nature of cross-cultural conflict enables

the participants to focus upon understanding the cultural basis for the conflict rather than distracting attention and escalating conflict as a consequence of personal attribution. Cultural attribution, however, requires that we overcome some deeply seated human tendencies. Key to effective implementation of the perspective of cultural attribution is an appreciation of cultural relativism and its implications for understanding behavior.

Stereotypes and Cultural Characterizations

The normal attribution processes embody important cultural components that produce problems because we are largely unaware of their cultural aspects. We assume that we have an objective factual understanding of the world without recognizing that our perceptions and understandings are deeply embedded in cultural assumptions. Our normal understandings of the world involve processes in which immediate experience is recognized as being another instance of a previous identical or similar experience, a process of assimilation. Our experiences, whether habitual or novel, are interpreted in terms of our previous categories for understanding the world. Normally even disparate events will be accommodated to our pre-existing categories and expectations, with their contradictory or incompletely comprehended characteristics ignored.

Stereotyping is one aspect of this process of viewing the world through our cultural categories and prior expectations. Stereotyping is a fundamental part of our making sense of the world and determining the meaning of events. Stereotypes involve seeing the world in terms of a set of prior expectations provided by our socialization and culture. For most social behavior, stereotyping is the normal way of behaving. As a technique of mental generalization, stereotyping facilitates social interaction in complex societies where we do not know the personal characteristics of every individual we meet. This leads us to use some distinctive features of the individual to guide how we predict their behavior and structure our interaction. This type of stereotyping underlies our habitual ways of using different forms of social interaction with those in different social statuses: children, parents, teachers, bosses, subordinates, beggars, etc. When we appropriately and correctly stereotype, and enact roles consistent with both parties' expectations, it facilitates social interaction. However, if stereotypes are incorrect, they can cause problems by keeping us from understanding the nature of the social interaction and how to respond appropriately.

Ethnic Stereotypes

One prominent use of stereotypes in intercultural relations involves the application of a specific limited characterization about individuals from another culture. Interethnic and intercultural stereotypes are based upon the assumption that all members of a culture conform to a specific set of characteristics. Generally, specific negative or exaggerated traits are selected for focus and depreciation of the other group. Ethnic stereotyping generally involves rigid preconceptions being applied to all members of a group, regardless of individual variations, and a refusal to see evidence to the contrary (attribution-discounting principle). These stereotypes about all the individual members of the other group are firmly held, discounting evidence and experiences to the contrary. Ethnic stereotypes are generally characterized by their simplicity and acceptance by the group that uses them, leading to perception of the individual members of the culture according to these preconceived stereotypes. Those who use stereotypes generally do not recognize them to be stereotypes, but rather consider them to be accurate depictions of reality. They may consider Jewish people to be shrewd without questioning whether it is accurate or applicable to all Jews. Stereotypes are maintained through selective perceptions and through other psychological and social processes. Perceptions of the other groups' behavior may be limited to only those instances that confirm stereotyped expectations. Social interactions between the groups may serve to create self-fulfilling prophecies. Projection is a frequent aspect of stereotyping, in which a group may project onto the outside group their own unacceptable characteristics. Stereotypes about

other ethnic groups are learned in the process of socialization during which information about other ethnic groups with which people have little or no contact is conveyed.

There has been long-standing discussion in the social sciences as to whether ethnic stereotypes have any validity or relevant information about cultures and individuals. Sources of stereotypes are often in observable behavior, raising the question of the extent to which stereotypes have a "grain of truth." This requires examination of the relationships of cultural behaviors to the characteristics embodied in stereotypes and the meanings of that behavior in the cultural and intercultural context. The cultural basis for behavior indicates that groups of people should exhibit common patterns of behavior that characterize the group. What relationships exist between cultural characteristics and stereotypes? The fact that people have stereotypes of groups they have never met attests to the learning of stereotypes from cultural traditions rather than cross-cultural contact. Stereotypes and their applications are shaped by cultural, personal, social, economic and political conditions. It is important not to confuse stereotypes with cultural characteristics. While some aspects of stereotypes attributed to the group may reflect actual cultural patterns, stereotypes are insensitive to their potential inapplicability and fail to recognize intracultural variation.

The emphasis that some in our society have placed upon the abandonment of stereotypes has created opposite reactions. Investigators studying characteristics attributed to different groups frequently discover that those who are asked to characterize other groups express irritation and resentment. The respondents may insist that other groups of people do not have common characteristics, that "Everyone is a unique individual." But in relating to other cultural groups, we cannot dismiss the normative cultural characteristics of the group and how they create individual and social behavior. "Color blindness" can be a form of cross-cultural ignorance and a stereotyping that "they are just like me." Cultural and intracultural differences require that we intelligently, selectively and adaptively respond to individual and cultural characteristics. At the same time, recognizing cultural characteristics must stop short of stereotyping. Stereotyping involves an inflexible attribution of characteristics. A cultural attribution recognizes that within a culture there will be numerous sources of variation including age, sex, years of residence or generations since immigration, occupation, extent of assimilation and many other aspects. Appropriate cultural characterizations are based not only upon recognition of what is characteristic of a culture, but also upon the recognition of the sources of variation. Appropriate interaction may start from accurate cultural generalizations, but must be adjusted by an ongoing assessment of the individual's characteristics.

IN-GROUP VERSUS OUT-GROUP DYNAMICS

Fundamental aspects of cross-cultural dynamics producing conflict are the typical processes found in intergroup interaction. The psychosocial dynamics provoking cross-cultural conflict are illuminated by the general social psychology of in-group versus out-group differentiation. Major aspects of intergroup contact are created by the ascribed differences that separate participants into different groups. Any noticeable difference may be used to distinguish groups and create a negative image or stereotype of "others" who are not "us." These categorizations of people as different from us heighten our sense of conflict with them.

A range of studies in social psychology illustrates this pervasive tendency to divide into groups and dislike the other groups' members. The mere separation of people into groups without a prior history of conflict is sufficient to trigger the in-group versus out-group distinction. There is a generalized norm of hostility toward out-groups and enactment of discriminatory behavior. Merely taking a homogeneous group of people and randomly separating them into competing groups is sufficient to evoke in-group versus out-group dynamics. The in-group versus out-group (us versus them) differentiation has many explanations. A basic aspect of in-group-out-group dynamics is manifested in *xenophobia*, a

dislike and fear of strangers or foreigners. The most common theories explaining in-group versus out-group dynamics have to do with factors such as competition for resources, a sense of territory and the psychology of personal space. Any of these factors can create hostility between different groups of people in contact. Whatever the specific reasons for particular cases of the differentiation of the in-group and out-group, it appears to be a fundamental sociobiological human tendency. Part of the process of socialization involves learning about the groups we accept and relate to and those that we do not. Based upon our culture, we learn the classifications of us versus them and the associated attitudes of favor and discrimination. When social circumstances present the opportunity, the preexisting attitudes are then called into play.

The scapegoat theory of prejudice suggests that categorization as an out-group member, even on the basis of arbitrary criteria, may be used as a means of projecting blame and mistreatment, and hence discharging frustration. Attributing membership in the out-group to an individual opens that person to a range of mistreatment. As illustrated in the classic studies of contrived prisoner-guard relations, deindividuation or the removal or reduction of unique individual identity of others leads to discrimination against them and abuse. The greater anonymity of the person, the more likely and extreme are others' tendencies to harm them. Deindividuated individuals feel less responsible for their actions as well. Evidence shows that if you individuate out-group members to the in-group members through providing communicative interactions, there is a lesser likelihood of discrimination. Ignorance of others leads to categorization and treatment of them as an out-group. If we do not know individual characteristics of people, then discrimination, dislike and prejudice are typical reactions.

A variety of psychological and social functions have been attributed to in-group versus out-group dynamics. This differentiation may have important social functions in creating positive self-identities for in-group members. The need for positive social identity is achieved through social comparison, embodied in the creation of an out-group and the attribution of stereotypes and prejudices. The stereotypes used to characterize the out-group may reflect the fears of the in-group and serve their need for solidarity, dominance and self-esteem. These characterizations of the out-group can serve as social explanations by attributing causes and responsibility to the out-group, blaming them for the prejudice ideas, exonerating the in-group for blame or personal responsibility and preventing loss of self-esteem for in-group members. While the in-group versus out-group dynamics may serve the group members, it undercuts the ability of the two groups to work together.

When differences are perceived to exist between groups, this evokes processes related to group identity. The groups with which we strongly identify, our "reference groups," provide the basis for personal identity. Interaction with the members of other groups evokes our own group-based identity and sets us off from them. The "other" is also interpreted with respect to their (real or assumed) reference group, which typically provides the most important aspects of our perceptions of their characteristics and identity. The ascribed reference group characteristics often determine the principal perceptions we have of other ethnically different people whom we do not know individually and personally. To be able to relate effectively with members of other ethnic and cultural groups, we have to understand how these attributed characteristics affect our perceptions and behaviors, as well as those of others, and learn how to overcome impediments to effective relations. This requires a recognition of how our culture provides us with an arbitrary sense of what is right and normal.

Ethnocentrism

Ethnocentrism literally means "ethnically centered," a perspective that one's own ethnic or cultural assumptions have universal relevance and should serve as the criteria by which all others are assessed. Ethnocentrism is a normal way of relating to the world, one in which one's own culturally acquired perspectives are unconsciously considered to be the right way to understand the world. It normally presumes that one's cultural framework is superior to all others. Ethnocentrism

also includes an attitude or ideology characterized by negative stereotyped feelings towards out-groups. Ethnocentrism uses one's own cultural values, attitudes and ideologies as a frame of reference that denies the validity of all other cultures' frames of reference. The major aspects of ethnocentrism include:

* The use of one's own cultural beliefs as a universal standard;
* The evaluation of all other groups in a hierarchy below one's own culture;
* The evaluation of differences between groups in terms of one's own standards; and
* The rejection of out-groups that fail to accept one's own standards.

All people and cultures are ethnocentric to some degree. In its simplest forms, ethnocentrism is a belief that what we have learned as members of our culture is correct. Ethnocentrism is generally extended to mean that what we have come to believe is correct and moral about the world is applicable beyond our own personal behavior. This belief in the correctness of one's own culture is a universal cultural behavior. No culture considers any and every form of behavior acceptable. To the contrary, all cultures express a belief that their own forms of behavior are preferable to and ultimately superior to the behaviors of those of other cultures. The tendency to ethnocentrism is manifested in the ways in which cultures view themselves in comparison to others. Examination of the names that many cultures have for themselves and how they contrast themselves with others illustrates this point. Many cultures have names for their own culture that translate with meanings such as "the people", "real people," "God's people," "chosen people" or "special people." In contrast, the rest of humanity is viewed as having a lesser status, often not even considered to be fully human. Terms for other cultural groups frequently include negative connotations. For instance, the Chinese language's symbolic representation for minority ethnic groups includes the symbol for animal. Only recently was this symbol designating animal officially dropped from the representations for China's own internal ethnic and cultural minorities. Ethnocentrism may be so deeply embedded in socialization and assumptions about the world that people have difficulty in seeing their ethnocentrisms and prejudices. People who express ethnocentric assessments of others frequently do not realize that they are making value judgments or that people from other cultural groups see their remarks as offensive.

Because of an increased concern with the problems of ethnocentrism, many people have come to believe not only that they should not be ethnocentric, but have gone further to believe that they are in fact not ethnocentric. Such ethnocentricity-free perspectives would mean that the person would have no values, morals or preferences about behaviors or state of affairs. A complete elimination of ethnocentrism is not possible. Ethnocentrism is a normal part of being a member of a culture. While ethnocentrism certainly is an impediment to effective intercultural and interethnic relations, it is unrealistic to expect humans to abandon totally all ethnocentrisms. The important issue is how to control the negative impact of ethnocentrisms on perceptions of and interactions with others. A fruitful approach to addressing ethnocentric tendencies is to develop an awareness of them and how they impact our perceptions, behaviors, judgments and relations with others. One way in which ethnocentrisms are manifested is in our values that serve as a source of antagonism when they are contradicted or violated. To develop an awareness of one's ethnocentrisms, it is necessary to identify one's values. Recognizing personal values puts one in a better position to see how personal ethnocentrisms are embodied and likely to be manifested in conflicts. Values assessments serve as tools for identifying one's own values and the types of situations in which conflict with others is likely to occur. Then it is possible to address those ethnocentric beliefs to achieve different types of interethnic relations. The perspectives of cultural relativism and skills in intercultural relations are also important resources in limiting the negative impact of ethnocentrisms.

Ethnorelativism

In order to supersede the limitations of ethnocentrism, it is necessary to develop a perspective called ethnorelativism. Ethnorelativism is based in the recognition of cultural relativism, i.e., the belief that the behavior of people from other cultures is reasonable and meaningful. Ethnorelativism recognizes that no universal standards for values nor norms of behavior actually exist. The ethnorelativistic perspective allows one to accept the validity of other cultures' frames of reference. Understanding behavior and effectively adapting to social relations in a multicultural society requires accepting that people will behave in accordance with different standards and beliefs. The ability to accept these differences is an important intercultural skill. The perspectives of ethnorelativism have an important counterpart in the concept of religious tolerance. Religious tolerance became necessary for social stability in more complex societies. The formation of state-level governments often required integration of diverse religious populaces within their boundaries. Religious and state power often united in an effort to eradicate those with different beliefs. Harmony within the diverse groups required that they be allowed to practice their own beliefs. Religious tolerance was the alternative to continued internal conflict between the different religious groups integrated into the state. While many of the early European settlers in the U.S. were persecuted religious groups seeking freedom of religious expression, intolerance of religious differences even continued in the American colonies. And even though the foundation of the U.S. was based on ideals and principles of religious freedom, the new nation had periods of intense religious conflict as German and Irish Catholic immigrations in the early part of the 1800s were met by Protestant intolerance, bigotry and violence. Internal stability of religiously diverse nation-states required a greater tolerance of religious differences. The same kind of tolerance of cultural difference is necessary for success in increasingly culturally pluralistic societies.

Explaining Ethnocentrism

There are many causes of ethnocentrism. The wide range of factors and situations that provoke ethnocentric reactions suggests that no one theory is likely to explain all of the causes. Relations with other groups are affected by many different social and cultural influences in socialization processes, providing for multiple aspects of ethnocentrism. Learning to be ethnocentric, to accept what is normal and right from our own culture's point of view, is a normal part of socialization and enculturation processes. Ethnocentric attitudes and beliefs are acquired as a normative part of cultural learning. Because of this, many of our ethnocentrisms are manifested without recognition of their presence. This pervasiveness of ethnocentrism suggests that it is a natural and inherent aspect of the human condition, manifested as the ethnocentric syndrome.

The Ethnocentric Syndrome

The processes of human intergroup relations are characterized by what Brown (1991) calls the ethnocentric syndrome or coalitional thinking. This ethnocentric syndrome includes a wide range of behavioral tendencies that are manifested when interacting with people considered to be the out-group. The ethnocentric syndrome includes a "double-standard" — one set of morals and values for relating to the in-group and a different set for relating to the out-group. The list below of characteristics of the ethnocentric syndrome is adapted from those outlined by Brown (1991).

The occurrence of these features in intergroup relations is so widespread as to suggest that they are universal features of relationships between in-groups and out-groups. Such universality would suggest that these ways of relating to "others" are sociobiologically based. Similar features are also found in the relationships between different groups of animals of the same species (i.e., intertribal interactions between monkeys, baboons or chimpanzees). The widespread occurrence of the features of the ethnocentric syndrome suggests that they illustrate some basic sociobiological tendencies of humans and other social animals. This is not to say that the specific behaviors are biologically determined. To the contrary, the specific content of ethnocentrisms and procedures for treating out-groups are learned. Nonetheless, we can recognize that the behaviors associated with the ethnocentric syndrome reflect deep-seated biological tendencies to separate oneself and one's reference group from similar others.

The suggestion that such widespread intergroup behaviors have a biological basis may seem to be suggesting dismal prospects for the amelioration of ethnocentrism and related ethnocentric syndrome behaviors. Resignation to the current state of affairs is not necessary. Many aspects of human behavior have a biological basis

---

Characteristics of the Ethnocentric Syndrome

Division of people into in-group and out-group	Ethical dualism (different treatment for out-group)
In-group pride	Discrimination against out-group members
Judging out-group with in-group criteria	Degrading and dehumanizing the out-group
Lack of empathy for out-group	Mistrust and fear of out-group
Mechanisms for recognizing out-group	Extreme sensitivity to out-group markers
Means of identifying in-group members	Considering out-group characteristics to be innate
Stereotyping	Ignoring out-group peoples' individuality
Exaggeration of out-group characteristics	Ignoring subordinated out-group (generally)
Ignoring out-group history	Treating out-group heroes as villains
Loss of objectivity in out-group relations	Blaming out-group for problems
Negative reciprocity, revenge against out-group	Vicious circle of antagonisms
Intensification of out-group treatment during crises	Sensitivity to out-group organization

but are controlled through socialization. These biologically based behaviors are called species-characteristic behaviors (Williams 1983). Human species-characteristic behaviors include free-soiling, rooting reflex, absolute nutritional dependence and repression of the sense of smell. These biologically based behaviors and dispositions are overcome in the process of socialization and development such that we become toilet trained, give up nursing, develop capabilities for acquiring our own food and become highly sensitized to odors, which we attempt to control. The biological basis for behavior does not imply that those factors run our lives. To the contrary, they are features that we overcome in the process of becoming human. If the ethnocentric syndrome is biologically based, perhaps it, too, will someday be controlled through socialization and learning.

PREJUDICE AND DISCRIMINATION

Prejudice and discrimination are two closely related process aspects of culture, the ethnocentric syndrome and intercultural relations. Prejudice and discrimination have been classically differentiated as attitude and behavior, respectively. Prejudices are often defined as negative attitudes toward another group. Discrimination is the negative and damaging behavior people manifest against other groups as a consequence of their prejudices. The intimate linkages of beliefs and behavior mean that prejudice and discrimination must be understood as interrelated phenomena. While prejudice and discrimination have often been characterized as deviant or abnormal behavior, they must also be understood to reflect normal aspects of culture and the interactions between people from different cultures. They are based in the ordinary processes of having values and beliefs, using them to make sense out of the world and acting accordingly. We must reject the absolute separation of discrimination and prejudice, as well as the idea that one can be totally free of prejudice and discrimination, and instead recognize how these

phenomena operate as a normal aspect of cultural life. Human behavior, whether or not deliberately discriminatory, is based upon certain presuppositions about the world and what is in it, which are in essence prejudices. To be free of prejudice would require suspending all judgments and preconceptions, and nonetheless such a suspension would also harbor certain prejudices (prejudgments) about the possibility and desirability of such action. Self-awareness of prejudice and discrimination, rather than denial of their presence, is necessary in order to keep these ordinary perceptual, cognitive and behavioral processes from detrimentally effecting intergroup relations. Awareness of one's own prejudices and an understanding of their psychosocial and cultural bases and dynamics is essential for effectively reducing their incidence, cost and consequences.

Classic and Normative Views

The classic view of the relationship of prejudice and discrimination was provided by Merton (1949), who created a typology displaying the interaction between the presence and absence of discrimination and prejudice (see Figure 5.1). The *prejudiced discriminator* is an active bigot or racist who holds negative attitudes about other groups (prejudices) and acts upon those negative beliefs (discriminates). These types of people manifest the worst of what concerns us about the effects of prejudice and discrimination upon social relations. They dislike most or all out-groups and act against them. The *prejudiced non-discriminator* was characterized as a compliant racist or timid bigot, a person who has negative attitudes about other groups, but does not act upon them to discriminate directly. These individuals are constrained by situational norms from doing that to which their prejudices predispose them. The *unprejudiced discriminator* is the fair weather liberal or reluctant liberal, someone who recognizes that certain forms of prejudicial or discriminatory behavior are wrong, but for some reason does it anyway. Situational factors, such as the presence of a reference group that expects discriminatory forms of behavior, will evoke what is the normative response. Or, fear of others'

Merton's Paradigm

Prejudice

	Yes	No
Yes	Prejudiced Discriminator "Active Bigot"	Non-Prejudiced Discriminator "Fair Weather Liberal"
Discriminates		
No	Prejudiced Non-Discriminator "Timid Bigot"	Non-Prejudiced Non-Discriminator "All Weather Liberal"

Figure 5.1 Merton's Paradigm

reactions will lead the reluctant liberals to discriminate to protect themselves. The *unprejudiced non-discriminator* or all-weather liberal is someone who is considered as lacking prejudice and refraining from detrimental discrimination. They accept the idea of social equality for all groups and attempt to assure equal treatment in their behavior.

The typology offered by Merton suggests that there are unprejudiced non-discriminators. Is this so? Is it possible to be a social being without having prejudices and discriminating among people on the basis of experiences, values and preferences? Traditionally, sociological texts on ethnic relations have suggested that it is possible for a person to be tolerant and free of prejudice and still be discriminatory in his/her thinking and behavior. As illustrations of this, sociologists may provide examples of people who are paternalistic in their behavior because they hold simplistic stereotypes of other groups. For instance, a person with economic interests in an ethnic group's labor may feel that they "have to taken care of" because the ethnic group is incapable of behaving rationally and taking care of themselves. As a consequence, they may impose certain restrictions on the group (e.g., prohibiting alcohol consumption, outlawing certain types of activities or gatherings, etc.) The rationalization is that the person may not harbor ill-will (prejudice) toward

the group, but at the same time may discriminate against the group in terms of what they think is in the group's best interest. For instance, a high school guidance counselor may feel that specific ethnic groups cannot expect to become doctors or lawyers. In what they perceive as being in the individual's best interest, the counselors schedule students from these groups into technical training programs (rather than college prep courses) because technical work is what they view as the sort of jobs people from that group do best.

The idea that we can easily become unprejudiced non-discriminators because of a commitment or desire to be so is misleading. To consider fair weather liberals unprejudiced when they recognize that their behavior is wrong but do something discriminatory anyway overlooks an important fact. It is inconsistent to claim that a person would deliberately (or unconsciously) discriminate against another group but at the same time lack any prejudices against or prejudgments about the group. If the person did not harbor some depreciating beliefs and prejudices about the other social group that ascribed to them some lower status, the person would not have conformed to expected prejudices and norms for discrimination. Given that the process of enculturation gives everyone prejudices and patterns of discrimination, it may be that the best we can hope for is some mild form of the prejudiced non-discriminator. This person recognizes he/she has learned attitudes and beliefs about other groups but attempts to keep these attitudes from being manifested as negative and discriminatory behavior that harm others or their relationships with them.

While it is important to recognize the negative and destructive aspects of prejudice and discrimination, it is counter-productive to assume that prejudice and discrimination can be completely eliminated. Prejudice and discrimination, in their most basic sense, are processes all humans use to make sense of their physical, social and cultural worlds, as part of our cultural assumptions about right and wrong. They are also part of the process of normal interpretation and social relations, the backlog of experience applied to new situations. The problems of prejudice and discrimination lie not only in their nature and intended effects, but more importantly, in their unrecognized and unacknowledged manifestations. Since social developments have led many to denounce prejudice and discrimination, people have increasingly accepted the idea that they are not. When adopting a commitment to non-prejudicial and non-discriminatory behavior, many people assume that they are no longer prejudiced and discriminatory. Such beliefs serve as a barrier to recognition of one's persistent and unconscious prejudices. Eliminating all prejudices would require a suspension of all of one's own values, beliefs and assumptions about the world, including the prejudice that elimination of prejudice and discrimination are desirable. Such total suspension of belief is unlikely. Behaving in a meaningful and informed manner in our social and cultural worlds requires that we have some assumptions in place, a system of prejudgments about the nature of the world and others. What is important in intercultural relations is the accuracy and flexibility of our assumptions.

Effectively managing the effects of prejudice and discrimination in intercultural relations requires that we recognize that they are normal aspects of intergroup relations. This recognition that prejudice and discrimination are a normal part of cultural behavior is called a normative explanation. Prejudice and discrimination are a part of the ethnocentric syndrome, derived from our cultural assumptions about right and wrong and what behavior is expected from other people. This perspective requires rejection of the notion that people can be totally non-prejudicial and non-discriminatory in their social behavior. In order to function effectively in multicultural societies, we have to learn how to overcome the effects of the ethnocentric syndrome. This means we must accept responsibility for examining our prejudices and discriminatory tendencies, assess their origins and implications and seek to modify them in ways that facilitate harmonious intercultural relations. Analysis of the unconscious nature of prejudices and the social factors guiding their perception is necessary. Since prejudices are frequently seen as accurate depictions of the world, many people who manifest prejudice are not aware that others may view their attitudes as prejudicial. This exemplifies the normative nature of prejudice, where what is learned as an objective social fact in one cultural group may be viewed a prejudicial from the point of view of another.

Prejudice

Prejudice is generally defined as involving fixed or inflexible emotionally charged attitudes and beliefs about another group. Prejudices are generally manifested in stereotyped negative and unfavorable beliefs about the out-group. Prejudicial statements are often not recognized for what they are. The victims of prejudice generally feel that the beliefs are inaccurate or complete misperceptions that ignore the individual and his/her particular qualities, and instead relate to the individual through ascribed characteristics derived from prior beliefs about the person's group. Prejudices are frequently represented in beliefs about what people think is actually the objective nature of the world, and are not recognized as prejudices by the people who hold them. For instance, one may believe that "Mexicans are lazy" without recognizing that such features are not characteristic of all members of the group, and perhaps not true of even the specific individuals so labeled. Prejudices frequently consider behaviors to be an inherent characteristic of the group rather than recognizing that they may be caused by external societal factors beyond the control of the group. For instance, lower average I.Q. scores of African Americans may be cited as "proof" of their innate cognitive inferiority without taking into consideration the relevant causal factors: cultural biases in teaching, educational funding, quality of education, biases in testing materials or other social factors that affect behavior relevant to school participation and learning. Prejudice includes positive as well as negative attitudes. Those who make prejudicial statements may view them as compliments (e.g., "Blacks are such natural athletes" or "Asians are such good workers; they are so obedient and just do what they are told"). Minority group members also hold prejudices about one another, as well as members of the dominant group.

Prejudices have been described as cognitive phenomena, a set of beliefs that ignore reality and interpose a set of negative attitudes about other persons. However, this negative reaction is more than a cognitive and mental response. Prejudice also has important emotional components, feelings that frequently lead to behavior (discrimination). It is this emotional component of prejudices that makes them so volatile in intercultural relations and a source of discriminatory behavior. Prejudices involve a system of beliefs, feelings and action orientations. Prejudices with respect to specific groups are a manifestation of a more general human tendency to "prejudge" based upon expectations and beliefs. Our perceptions of the world are based on prejudices, prejudgments about "what is," based upon what we have learned to believe and expect "should be." Prejudgment is a normal part of relating to the physical and social world through our prior expectations. Like ethnocentrism, prejudices reflect what people have learned to expect is correct, proper and true about the world. These prejudices undermine effective relations with others for a variety of reasons. They distract attention from people's actual characteristics and conditions and prevent authentic relationships. They create barriers to full utilization of the skills and potentials people have to offer. In effect, prejudices stand between us and reality, as a barrier to knowledge about others.

Since our society has emphasized the importance of abandoning prejudices, many people today believe that they have no prejudices. I frequently challenge my students who feel that they have no prejudices with the following intellectual exercise. Write an essay about how Saddam Hussien was the savior of the Islamic world, a messenger from God and the only international symbol of hope for the impoverished and exploited masses of the world. Explain how his values and behaviors manifest a religiously inspired holy mission. Then write an essay on how George W. Bush was the savior of the world and explain how his morals and values required that he oppose Hussien and his aggressions. Convincingly argue that his military invasion of Iraq and the deaths of thousands of Iraqis was a morally justified act. If you can write a completely convincing and balanced essay on the moral grounds for these two individuals and their positions, then do the same for other opposing points of view. For instance, explain the validity of radical black Islamic political ideology (e.g., Louis Farakan or early Malcom X) and white supremacist ideology (e.g., KKK, Nazi). Few people could provide such a balanced representation, much less believe in both positions with equal commitment. Your prejudices, "prejudgments" about what is right and preferable, will undoubtedly lead you to prefer one position over another. While it is unlikely that humans can totally suspend prejudices, it is possible to become aware of prejudices and learn how to reduce their effects by deliberately making an effort to suspend judgmental approaches. But the belief that we can and should do so is also a prejudice.

Targets of Prejudice

The factors that determine who may be the target of prejudice are highly variable. A wide variety of factors — historical, personal, cultural, situational, economic, structural and institutional — influence which groups may be targets and when. The groups most likely to be targets of prejudice generally are part of the prejudicial groups' cultural history and beliefs, which provide the bases for attitudes acquired in the process of socialization and used to guide subsequent encounters. Specific features that focus prejudices are the socially and culturally visible and salient symbols that differentiate groups and reinforce the in-group versus out-group boundaries. Prejudices frequently reflect the prejudiced group's identity as "symbolic actions" that represent characteristics rejected by the group. Prejudices reflect what a group denies as its own characteristics in attributing them as negative characteristics to other groups. Prejudices frequently become cultural rationalizations for maintaining structural and social conditions. For example, if the impoverished characteristics of some groups are viewed as a consequence of their stereotyped characteristics — they are lazy and do not want to work, they prefer welfare, etc. — these prejudices can serve to justify the existing conditions (e.g., inequality, discrimination), and to create practices and policies that reinforce those conditions (e.g., cutting job assistance and education programs). Situational factors have important impacts upon selection of targets of prejudice, with the most salient groups providing the most immediate focus for prejudice and discrimination. Competition focuses attention on groups viewed as depriving one's own group of resources, making them likely targets of prejudice.

Summary

While recognizing that prejudice may be treated analytically as distinct from discrimination, prejudice and discrimination are closely linked, since prejudice provides input into decisions about acts and targets of discrimination. Studying prejudice apart from discrimination is difficult since studying prejudice requires that it be given some expression. Expression means that it is manifested in some form of behavior (e.g., self-reports, test responses, etc.); technically prejudice becomes a behavior, a form of discrimination.

Discrimination

Discrimination is broadly defined as behavior, in contrast to the attitudinal predispositions represented by prejudice. But discriminatory actions are based upon a prior belief that guides action. Significant aspects of the determinants of discrimination are beliefs about another group of people and the treatment that they deserve. One prominent characteristic of discrimination is that it generally has negative impacts upon those who are subjected to it. The group discriminated against may be denied equal treatment, position, access or rights. Some sociological definitions of discrimination emphasize a power dimension to discrimination, emphasizing the importance of the differences in power that enable the discriminations of the dominant group to have a negative impact upon the subordinated group. While power is central to the detrimental effects of discrimination, prejudice must be understood as a much broader human response that is also expressed by members of subordinated groups towards the dominant group, towards other subordinated cultural groups or even towards members of their own cultural group.

Discrimination, like ethnocentrism and prejudice, is a part of the process aspects of intercultural relations, a normal part of human behavioral processes. While recognizing that the customary forms of discrimination (e.g., "prejudicial discrimination") have intentional deleterious effects upon the victim, we must understand this behavior in the broader context of human tendencies. In the most fundamental sense of "drawing a distinction," discrimination is part of all cultural systems and their means of making sense of the world. Discrimination means that we make distinctions based upon our previous experiences and value preferences. Being totally free of discriminations would require that we be totally free of values, preferences and ethnocentrisms. Not only are such totally value- and preference-free states highly unlikely, but if we were to achieve them, we would undoubtedly be charged with being discriminatory for treating out-group members the same way as the in-group. One's in-group — friends and family — certainly deserves better treatment than strangers.

Some people protest allegations that they engage in discriminatory behavior, and instead insisting that they "treat everyone the same." Such attitudes have inherent properties that are insensitive to cultural effects, and paradoxically are among the most discriminatory. Who is represented by "everyone"? How does this reference group expect to be treated? As an American? A Japanese? A person who has a handicap? A business leader? A spiritual representative? The reference group for "everyone" is tied to the speaker's sense of who they are and how they want to be treated. The preferred forms of social interaction in different cultures and subcultures are so variable as to make the notion of "treating everyone the same" a sign of extreme cultural ignorance and insensitivity. "Treating everyone the same" is inappropriate in cross-cultural relations where what is polite in one cultural context (e.g., belching, thanking the host for a good meal) is considered impolite in another cultural context. Actually "treating everyone the same," for example, politely, requires (1) discrimination between people/cultures in terms of what is considered to be polite and (2) treating people from different cultures and backgrounds differently, according to their preferences.

Normal social behavior, even within a single society or culture, requires discrimination in the broadest sense — different behavior roles for different people and situations. Discrimination provides for different (and appropriate) interaction with parents, children, bosses, subordinates, teachers, peers and others. If we failed to discriminate whether a person was an adult or child, or our boss or subordinate, the failure to discriminate appropriately would be disadvantageous and inappropriate. If you expected child-like responses from adults, or adult behavior from children, both would appropriately complain of discrimination (or failure to discriminate correctly). When children or senior citizens are given special rates or discounts, this is a form of discrimination, but one that has certain advantages for the recipient. When children are denied access or rights, or when the elderly are denied jobs because they are "too old," discrimination acts against them. Culture dictates a wide variety of necessary, desirable and customary discriminations. How do we determine what is appropriate and which are detrimental and damaging?

The emphasis on discrimination as a normal aspect of cultural interpretation and social interaction is not intended to discount the negative effects of prejudicial discrimination. The intent is to place this kind of behavior in the broader context of human actions. Concern about detrimental and negative discriminations against others must be understood in the broader context, for several reasons. The belief that people can and should be non-discriminatory leads to a denial of discrimination rather than a recognition of its perpetuation as a condition of cultural life and normal preferences. The insistence that people can and should be non-discriminatory leads to denial of one's own discriminatory behavior covered up by the denial of the persistence of discrimination. Without recognition of discrimination, one's behavior may be viewed as "objective evaluations" without recognition of how the "objective evaluations" necessarily have cultural assumptions that prejudice us towards making certain kinds of decisions and actions (discriminations). A comparison of the criteria in work performance evaluations in different countries provides the perspective to see the cultural biases in what are considered to be "objective criterion."

Rather than living under the illusion that we are abandoning all discriminations, we need to directly address the nature of our discriminations and their implications. Affirmative Action illustrates this approach. Affirmative Action programs were designed to redress the institutional and historical inequalities in many aspects of social, economic and political life. Some European Americans and white ethnics have protested against Affirmative Action as a form of "reverse discrimination." Is Affirmative Action a form of discrimination or reverse discrimination? In that Affirmative Action requires that we make distinctions among people and differentially treat them on that basis, it is a form of discrimination. Is this discrimination undesirable? The author's opinion is that it is a necessary and useful form of social discrimination, designed to redress differences caused by historical inequalities. Contemporary social conditions and institutional arrangements that are a consequence of past discrimination will not simply go away if we ignore them. Some form of discrimination, making socially relevant distinctions, is necessary if we are to redress the contemporary situations and inequalities that persist in the U.S.

Prejudicial and Ethnic Discrimination

Recognition of the culturally inevitable and normative aspects of discrimination should not distract its effects and us from concern with prejudicial discrimination. Prejudicial discrimination involves negative attitudes and detrimental behaviors that are directed towards individuals based upon stereotyped associations with their group membership and the intention to harm them through actions. Prejudicial discrimination involves the deliberate and institutional behaviors that have as their intent or consequence the denial of access or opportunity to groups of individuals based upon ascribed membership categories. Prejudicial discrimination ignores individual characteristics in favor of ascribed group characteristics as a means of assessing individuals' qualifications and the treatment to be accorded them. A prominent feature of prejudicial discrimination is ethnic discrimination, where damaging actions are taken against individuals because of their group membership, and against groups because of prejudicial judgments about their qualities. Prejudicial discrimination has played an important role in the formation of intergroup relations, class stratification and power systems in the U.S. Native Americans, African Americans, Mexican Americans, Asian Americans, women and other groups have been officially denied the rights and opportunities allowed other Americans. These discriminatory actions have even been based in laws that prohibited civil liberties, voting rights, property ownership, education, the right to testify, the right to congregate, marriage arrangements, parental rights and many other privileges afforded to other members of society. While the legal precedents for these discriminatory actions have been largely eliminated, informal norms and cultural traditions perpetuate unequal treatment in many of these areas. These group-specific prejudicial discriminations involve ethnic prejudice, negative beliefs about an ethnic group that are used to justify the differential negative treatment of their members. These ethnic prejudices are some of the most important to be addressed in establishing more conducive interethnic relations. Ethnic prejudices are particularly dangerous because they tend to focus upon negative, fear-evoking characteristics that create a tendency to legitimate discrimination, particularly violent responses against members of the ethnic group. The climate of interethnic tension characteristic of many culturally pluralistic societies is exacerbated by the unchallenged expression of ethnic prejudice.

Explanations of Prejudice and Discrimination

Research on prejudice and discrimination has identified a wide range of factors that affect or are correlated with their manifestations. The predominant foci have been the social and psychological conditions that increase prejudice and discrimination and the individual or collective functions that they serve. Some of these specific hypothesized causes include fear of strangers, scapegoating, frustration, self-reference and status enhancement, in-group bonding and values reinforcement, projection of unacceptable characteristics, political rationalizations, acquiring economic advantages and political control and other social manipulations (see Winkelman 1998). The psychological theories tend to focus on how the negative treatment of outsiders serves certain psychological needs or supports the personality structure and compensatory dynamics.

Psychological explanations of prejudice and discrimination generally emphasize functions that serve individual needs, but these dynamics are also social, in that they meet group needs as well. Social theories tend to emphasize the benefits to groups that are derived directly or indirectly from another group's subordination through prejudice and discrimination. Most societal causes of prejudice and discrimination are interrelated and serve to enhance the economic and political advantages of the dominant group. These social functions also have individual psychological consequences for the group practicing prejudicial discrimination, as well as their victims. While some aspects of prejudice and discrimination do manifest primary concerns with social exploitation or psychodynamic compensation, most aspects have interrelated psychological and social functions that reflect their functions as primary processes of human interpretation and social behavior.

While these different approaches contribute to our global understanding of the dynamics of prejudice and discrimination, they often treat the phenomena as reflecting aberrant, pathological or extreme social tendencies. This book emphasizes a contrastive perspective that prejudice and discrimination are normal beliefs and behaviors learned and reinforced in the processes of normal enculturation, socialization and social interaction, and that they may reflect a normal aspect of intergroup interaction. From this perspective, prejudice and discrimination are process phenomena of intergroup contact, normal aspects of socialization, enculturation and intergroup contact. Analysis of these phenomena must begin with the fundamental cultural learning processes that serve to define the forms and targets of prejudice and discrimination. Sociological approaches to prejudice and discrimination establish their normative and situational character. This reveals that prejudice and discrimination are part of the learned social order of beliefs and social relations. That is to say, prejudice and discrimination are normative, following the rules and socialization influences of the society.

This normative approach illustrates that prejudice and discrimination are not just the actions of a few aberrant and disturbed individuals, but patterns of behavior that are typical and widespread in society. The factors that elicit conformity to those patterns of behavior are numerous. They include the immediate social context, cultural norms for behavior, economic competition and political objectives. The necessity of the normative perspective is illustrated by the fact that stereotypes, ethnocentrisms and prejudices follow cultural patterns rather than individual psychodynamics. In fact, relatively non-prejudicial individuals placed in highly prejudicial environments (e.g., foreigners sent to South Africa) tended to develop much more prejudicial attitudes after living in that environment. Understanding prejudice and discrimination requires an assessment of the

influences that make those behaviors a normal part of socialization influences. Prejudice and discrimination are from the same types of learning and influences that create other kinds of behavior. Socialization influences forming prejudices and discriminatory behavior are often indirect, occurring through observation, participation and imitation. Prejudices and discriminatory behavior involve factors that operate largely in an unconscious fashion. Since they are learned unconsciously, those who hold and act upon them generally do not recognize prejudice and discrimination.

History is a potent source of prejudice and discrimination, since it embodies the previous experiences of interaction and conflict. Because of previous conflicts, prejudice and discrimination can persist even if the factors that initiated them are no longer present. The history of prejudice and discrimination become embedded in cultural history, beliefs and institutions that provide the patterns for future behavior. Normative perspectives focus upon explaining how the social phenomena of prejudice and discrimination are learned and manifested in each generation and their behaviors. The reasons for these phenomena being present in the first place must be understood at the level of societal forces and intergroup dynamics. But the prior precedents for discrimination and its continuation must be sought in societal factors rather than strictly psychological or cultural ones, since these phenomena are universally distributed in human societies. While the targets and cultural content of prejudice and discrimination are learned, their universal manifestations suggest that the origins of such tendencies are more basic.

Sociobiological Organization: Intergroup and Intragroup Dynamics.
The essentially universal prejudice and discrimination that exists in intergroup relations suggests that their origin is sociobiological. The widespread manifestations of prejudice, discrimination and the ethnocentric syndrome in human societies and social behavior, and similar principles of in-group versus out-group differentiation found among other social animals,

suggests that some fundamental aspects of prejudice and discrimination represent a sociobiological-based tendency. Humans and other animals apparently have an in-born tendency to differentiate their intimate primary and social groupings from other groups formed by members of the same species. The sense of identity with the "other" does not extend to all members of the species. The in-group versus out-group differentiation reflects the most fundamental aspect of this tendency to differentiate one's own group from all others. The importance of intragroup dynamics is illustrated in the effects of group size. The respective size of the groups and intensity of the interaction affects the dynamics of intergroup interaction and manifestations of prejudice and discrimination. The size of the subordinated group — either very large or very small — seems more likely to evoke reactions from the dominant group. The fundamental divisions of in-group and out-group are further utilized as a principle of differentiation within a society. The ethnocentric syndrome makes in-group versus out-group separation an important factor structuring self-perceptions and behaviors. All groups define out-groups and use this discrimination as a basis for self-definition. The out-group boundary serves as a way of increasing in-group identity and solidarity. Intensification of in-group relations and identity serves to strengthen dependence on the in-group.

Summary.
While prejudice and discrimination will persist in intergroup relations, a deliberate effort to understand one's own prejudices and reduce discriminatory behavior can improve intergroup relations. Understanding the numerous normative sources of prejudice and discrimination provides a basis for recognizing the influences on one's own life as well as on the lives of others. Self-examination provides a basis for modifying behaviors that have impeded effective intercultural relations and can set the stage for developing improved relations. Key to these achievements is a recognition and understanding of the normal processes by which humans understand their worlds.

PSYCHODYNAMIC PROCESSES IN INTERCULTURAL RELATIONS

Investigations of the impacts of culture and ethnicity upon therapeutic interactions reveal dynamics that underlie relationships between people of different cultures. These process aspects of cross-cultural relations have been discussed in the cross-cultural counseling literature in terms of the effects of projection, transference, counter-transference, resistance and defensive reactions in therapy. These same processes are also characteristic of the social interactions between members of different ethnic and cultural groups.

Projection.
Projection involves attributing to others those characteristics that are in fact derived from our own assumptions, characteristics or predispositions rather than theirs. This psychological process is a normal part of relating to the world. It involves utilizing previous learning, expectations and relations as the interpretive and emotional basis for our relationship in new situations. Our previous experience in intercultural contact is "baggage" we carry into new situations. The understandings we have of other cultural groups are derived from previous experiences and expectations that serve to structure awareness of current relations. The phenomena of projection are manifested in various aspects of cross-cultural counseling and ordinary social interactions. The manifestations of projection include transference, counter-transference and resistance. Transference and other forms of projection are likely to occur in the cross-cultural setting because of the necessity of viewing people from the other culture in terms of our own prior experiences and expectations regarding the characteristics of their cultural group.

Transference.
Transference is a concept primarily developed in the context of therapeutic relations. It is a form of projection in which an individual (client) responds to another individual (therapist) in a

manner derived from their patterns of relationships established with other significant individuals in the past. In therapy, transference is typically discussed in terms of how the client may project the father (mother) image onto the counselor. Transference of previous experiences with members of a cultural group to current interactions with members of that group is a part of the process dynamics of intercultural relations. This transference may be particularly powerful for the minority group ethnic members because of the intense emotional and oppressive experiences that many members of minority ethnic groups have in interethnic relations.

Counter-transference.

The cross-cultural counseling literature also discusses the phenomenon of counter-transference, when a counselor responds to the client based upon patterns of previous experience with similar individuals from that ethnic group. This is really the same phenomenon as transference, but the conceptual distinction has some important implications for understanding and adapting to the dynamics of intercultural relations. Being able to relate effectively to people from other cultures requires that we address not only our own transference to them, but also understand and adjust to the transferences being projected onto us by the others with whom we interact. For instance, a member of a group that has traditionally practiced discrimination against another group has to expect that initial interactions with people from that oppressed group will be strongly influenced by their expectations based upon those past experiences. This transference phenomenon is prominent in initial interactions of African Americans with European Americans when they assume that a European American holds prejudices against them until they verify the actual attitudes of the individual. Until it is clarified, the underlying assumption may be that the individual is a racist merely because of their culture of origin. To deal with the countertransference, it is necessary to approach cross-cultural interaction with self and other awareness that allows one to address the distortions in the interaction process.

Resistance.

Resistance is defined in counseling as an opposition by the client to the goals of the counselor. Cross-cultural counseling perspectives suggest that the diagnosis of resistance may be a misinterpretation. A client's apparent resistance may, in fact, reflect cultural differences in the goals to be achieved or the means of achieving them. The application of this understanding to the context of cross-cultural psychology suggests the following dictum: In cross-cultural psychology, there is no client resistance, only the failure of the therapist to understand the cultural perspectives of the client. In cross-cultural conflict, the perception of client resistance indicates our failure to understand the intercultural situation that causes conflict. Resistance has broad application in examining cross-cultural relationships. The members of the dominant culture experience a range of resistances to the demands of cross-cultural adaptation. When confronted by the experience of other cultures, languages and behaviors, one of the principle reactions of members of the dominant culture is irritation. The expectations of assimilation, conformance and integration can also be forms of resistance to the reality of multicultural society. Ethnocentrism can be a form of resistance to the cultural perspectives necessary for adapting to cross-cultural relations. Interactions between people of different cultures may not only have different cultural conceptions of the ideal goals, but may also have different cultural conceptions of the appropriate processes for achieving the same goal. The inherent cultural conflicts in cross-cultural interactions will easily lead people to assume that the other party does not wish to achieve a common goal. This assumption could be mistaken if people have differing beliefs regarding how to achieve the goal. We may resist other people's good intentions because we confuse form (manner of behaving) with substance (different goals). Successful cross-cultural relations require that we manage to overcome the inherent tendencies toward conflict and misunderstanding. One of the guidelines we can employ to achieve common ground is to assume that the other person has the same global interests and goals as our own, as well as something different and distinct. Such a perspective then enables us to lower our resistance to what may only appear to be contrary ideas, but are actually different ways of expressing or achieving a common goal.

Minority Defense Mechanisms

Defense mechanisms constitute psychological reactions designed to maintain psychological stability and integration in the face of stress. These psychological strategies are designed to protect the ego in its efforts to mediate between unconscious or personal desires, on one hand, and the demands of other forces in society on the other. Vander Zanden (1966) pointed out that because of the differences in power that characterize the relationships between dominant and minority ethnic groups, minorities use a variety of defense mechanisms to buffer their relationships with members of the dominant group. Although intercultural relations have shifted in recent decades, the reactions remain the same. Some of the psychological reactions to cultural subordination include the following:

Self-hatred.
This involves an acceptance of the dominant society's negative view of members of the minority culture, an internalization of a negative self-image of one's own group. This may be manifested in discriminatory behavior towards members of one's own culture, particularly the less assimilated, and an active dislike of aspects of one's own self.

Denial.
Individuals who find discrimination directed against their own group psychologically devastating may deny that they are members of that group. This may be manifested as an effort to "pass" as a member of the dominant group and to explicitly deny one's own cultural background. These individuals may be identified by members of their culture of origin as "apples," "coconuts," "bananas" or "Oreos," referring to the "colored" outside ethnic appearance with a "white" cultural orientation inside.

Acceptance.
This involves an outward accommodation to dominant group's definitions, attitudes and expectations about one's group. The resentment felt and one's own point of view are repressed in acquiescence to accommodate to the dominant group of the society. The experience of discrimination by the dominant society may be denied or minimized and assimilation emphasized.

Obsessive sensitivity.
Because of the frequent experience of discrimination, individuals from a subordinated group may habitually interpret the behavior of members of the dominant group as involving prejudice and discrimination. These people may "play the 'R' card," making racist accusations of everyone that disagrees with them. Neutral comments may be interpreted as having some implicit prejudice or racist message.

Ego enhancement.
In an effort to compensate for previously internalized feelings of inferiority or other experiences of discrimination, the individual proclaims that his/her own group is in fact superior to the dominant society thereby enhancing the status of his/her ethnic group and own self-esteem.

Aggression.
Direct expressions of hostility towards the dominant group may be another reaction to the experiences of prejudice and discrimination by those in subordinated ethnic groups. This aggression may be a direct reaction against those who have previously discriminated, or may be displaced onto others who are safe targets or represent the dominant group.

Knowledge of different types of defensive reactions to interethnic contact is an important intercultural effectiveness skill. Understanding these kinds of reactions prepares the individual to respond more effectively to these normal defensive responses. People's concerns can then be addressed explicitly instead of leaving the reactions as an underlying and potentially disruptive influence on relations.

Minority Status: Psychology and Self-Esteem

Minority status based upon physical or cultural characteristics easily recognized or distinguished by the dominant group can make minorities easily subjected to discrimination and prejudice. The subordinated position accompanying minority status has global impacts upon the social and psychological adaptation of members of the subordinated groups. Typically, the minority group members are held in low esteem by the dominant culture, with prejudice and discrimination further limiting access to social opportunities, economic resources and political rights. This may induce low self-esteem. Even though positive identities are created by primary relations, the negative perceptions imposed by the wider society negatively impact identity and self-esteem of members of ethnic minority groups. Those discriminated against will internalize negative images or develop defense mechanisms for dealing with the stresses of prejudice, discrimination and inequality. Even the very use of the term minorities as a self-designation may be negative because of the pejorative meanings associated with its use, the *sub*culture being below the culture. Minority status may undermine self-esteem and cultural pride. The psychological consequences for those who suffer from the imposition of a discriminatory power structure can include internalization of negative feelings about one's self and group membership. Biographical material on the life experiences of ethnic minorities, particularly African Americans, has illustrated the self-esteem problems resulting from internalization of racialized identities formed by white society. Stereotypes and discrimination imposed by the dominant society can create negative attitudes on the part of the ethnic individuals towards themselves and their ethnic group. Many models of ethnic identity development indicate a poor sense of self-esteem as an initial condition for their models of minority ethnic identity development.

Resistance to the minority labeling status is an important way of resisting such effects and asserting positive ethnic group identity. The population dynamics and growth in the U.S. indicate that the future of our nation is one in which the so-called minorities will become a majority of the nation. While recognizing objections to the use of the term "minority," the concept represents recognition of important social and psychological consequences of subordinated groups in a discriminatory society. However, such minority status does not automatically have negative consequences, as illustrated in the studies of ethnic identity and self-esteem. While much evidence substantiates negative effects upon identity produced by discrimination, having ethnic identity or being a minority group member does not necessarily entail having poor self-esteem. Although ethnic minorities are subjected to stereotypes and discrimination, not all minority group members accept and internalize the negative stereotypes projected by the dominant society. With cultural resources and social support, people have of course been able to deflect the negative image of their ethnic group and maintain positive self-esteem in spite of external negative views of their group.

Phinney (1991) reviewed research that focuses upon those aspects of ethnic identity related to high self-esteem. Factors that may affect the nature of one's ethnic identity include the extent of self-identification with the ethnic group; attitudes about and commitment to one's own group membership; evaluative attitudes about one's group; and ethnic knowledge, behavior and practices. The range of aspects of ethnic identity requires separate assessment of these different aspects in terms of their potential relationship to self-esteem. Ethnic identity as related to identification with the group can be seen as embodying a continuum. Phinney suggested that this ethnic identity continuum represent a number of dimensions of difference: variation within an ethnic population, differences in an individual's behavior across different contexts and changes within an individual across time. Phinney offered the following continuum contrasting strong and weak identities.

Ethnic Identity Continuum
Adapted from Phinney [1991]

High	Low
Strong and secure; achieved identity	Weak or diffuse identity
Involvement in ethnic behaviors	Limited involvement in ethnic behaviors
Positive group evaluation	Negative group evaluation
Prefers own ethnic group	Majority group preference
Satisfied with ethnic identity	Unhappy with ethnic group membership
Knowledgeable about ethnic group	Little interest in ethnic group
Commitment to ethnic group	Little sense of commitment to ethnic group

Figure 5.2 Ethnic Identity Continuum

Ethnicity is a multidimensional concept that includes beliefs, attitudes, feelings, behaviors, cognitions and social relations. While an individual may suffer low self-esteem due to the negative characteristics attributed to their ethnicity, some individuals maintain high self-esteem in spite of the fact that their groups are held in low esteem. By dismissing the negative evaluations as stereotypes, some minority individuals manage to remain largely unaffected by the group stigmatization. Increased self-esteem is also associated with interest in learning about one's own cultural group. Positive self-esteem has been found to be most likely associated with bicultural identities rather than a strictly monocultural ethnic identity without adaptation to the dominant culture. Phinney suggests that the best psychological outcome in multicultural contact is an identity that includes affinity with one's own group and with the mainstream society. Cross-cultural competencies are also associated with a strong sense of cultural identity and knowledge of others. Effective intergroup relations with other cultures are facilitated by a clear awareness of one's own cultural influences and a positive regard for the cultures of others. Consequently, self-esteem and ethnic identity are products of competency in managing intergroup relations in the wider society.

Majority Defense Mechanisms

Members of dominant ethnic groups also use defense mechanisms in intergroup relations. While these may include some of those characteristic of minority groups (e.g., aggression), the reactions are generally different. This is because the dominant group is, by definition, not subordinated, and does not face pressure towards self-hatred and its consequences. Members of majority groups may use tactics such as denial and acceptance, but generally with a different psychological dynamics.

The typical defense mechanisms used by members of majority groups include the typical process dynamics of intergroup relations — ethnocentrism, prejudice, discrimination, denial, projection and other ways of minimizing cultural differences (see Chapter 6). The psychodynamic processes of projection and transference are also significant defense mechanisms, particularly when European Americans' own tendencies (e.g., aggression, closed group boundaries) are attributed to minority group members. Denial often plays an important part of the attitude of majority group members. For instance, a denial of the reality of prejudice and its continued consequences for African Americans is a frequent phenomenon.

Majority group members may "historicize" concerns of other groups. For instance, they may express the sentiment that while Blacks historically suffered from slavery, that was the past, and it has no influence on Blacks (or Black-White relations) today. Persistent inequality manifested in the continued lower class status of many African Americans may be rationalized, with the poor people considered to experience failure from lack of personal effort, rather than victimization from societal and institutional discrimination.

Persistent inequality among ethnic groups (for instance the persistent of large segments of the African American population in poverty) may be blamed upon the poor. The idea that "everybody is the same," or that "everybody has the same opportunities" is often used to rationalize inequality with the perception that the poor are merely people who don't try. Such attitudes are contradicted by the fact that African Americans never had the opportunity to overcome the persistent effects of centuries of slavery and legalized discrimination.

As the ethnic power dynamics in the U.S. has shifted from unchallenged White Anglo Saxon Protestant dominance to a greater degree of cultural pluralism, European Americans may also develop new defense mechanisms. A "defensive pluralism" has been noted in the resurgence of "white" ethnicities, where some groups feel the need to enhance their sense of ethnic group identity in the face of visible efforts at ethnic elevation by minority ethnicities. Whites may express a sense of being victims of prejudice and discrimination, asserting that affirmative action and other programs designed to assure access for minorities are acting in an unfair manner against whites.

Regardless of one's particular ethnic, class and personal positions in a culturally pluralistic society, there are important ways in which we need to respond to cultural differences. These differences and adaptations are often presented to us fixed conditions, for example, integration or segregation, assimilation of separatism. But the actual options are far more complex, with many different possible accommodations to the presence of different cultures in one's formative influences.

DYNAMICS OF GROUP INTERCULTURAL ACCOMMODATION

The nature of the adjustments that are made in intercultural contact can involve a variety of different forms of group interaction and exchange of characteristics. Different balances between integration and segregation create a number of different outcomes for groups and their individual members. The relations established between different groups are represented by the concepts of acculturation, amalgamation and assimilation.

Integration and Segregation

Integration and segregation are often perceived as being opposite aspects of intercultural relations, but both are inseparable aspects of the structural processes of all intergroup relations. Stable relationships between different cultural groups incorporate these two diametrically opposed processes of integration and segregation as the means of bringing groups together and keeping them distinct. Stable intergroup interaction of two groups requires forces that bring people together (integration) and forces that keep them apart (segregation). These opposing tendencies have also been discussed as centripetal and centrifugal trends in social life (Schermerhorn 1978). Centripetal tendencies are those that involve the acceptance of common values and lifestyles and participation in the same structural features of social life (groups, associations and institutions). Centrifugal tendencies refer to those patterns of group behavior that involve a separation of the subordinated group from the dominant group. Integration and segregation may be manifested in a wide variety of different ways, depending upon many factors, including the causes of contact; the characteristics of the cultures involved; their attitudes towards one another; the relationships established between the groups and individual members; and the consequences, both individual and societal, resulting from intergroup contact.

Integration

Integration involves processes that bring different groups together. Integration usually refers to procedures designed to foster equality between the integrated groups, but some forms of integration are designed to fit another group into a specific aspect of society, for instance, an exploited labor force. Some forms of integration do not support equality, but rather establish conditions conducive to stable exploitation. Integration into a society may go hand in hand with the persistence of other forms of segregation. Schermerhorn in *Comparative Ethnic Relations* (1978), defines integration as the process by which elements of society are brought into a coordinated compliance with the objectives and activities of the dominant social groups. A wide range of types and degrees of integration exist. Integration may use coercion or mutual consensus. Economic, political, military and social processes create a sense of coercion for group and individual participation, and the individual consents, if not voluntarily, then to gain respite from hunger and brutality, and to maximize well-being under difficult circumstances. Integration is a continuing process, a relationship maintained through continued interaction, rather than a final condition of society. The particular type of integration is affected by a number of factors, including whether the groups have common or discrepant goal definitions, their views on the legitimacy of the integrative forces, and the similarities of the cultures being integrated.

The characteristics of interethnic relations are perhaps most predominantly shaped by the nature of the forces that serve to integrate the groups. In contact between two groups of greatly different size, the relationship will usually be one of dominance by one group over the other. Forced integration may have varying degrees of legitimacy, with relationships involving coercive domination and integration of a politically subordinated minority representing one extreme. This makes conflict theory a fundamental perspective for understanding interethnic relations. Another extreme is represented by voluntary immigration, particularly those situations where the host society welcomes and values the immigrants who are culturally similar to the dominant cultural and social groups. The cultural congruencies of the two cultures in terms of core values, behaviors, objectives and other aspects of social life will facilitate integration (and its legitimacy).

Integration can produce many different types of relations between groups, including assimilation and amalgamation, where groups combine and mix cultural characteristics. Amalgamation occurs when, over time, the two groups become intermixed such that a new culture emerges. This amalgamation may be achieved through creating a synthesis of the two cultural groups and their beliefs and practices, or through one culture largely adopting practices of another. Assimilation may also occur where the total members of one group and their descendants are socially absorbed into the dominant cultural group by adoption of their cultural practices. But integration may also involve "integration at a distance," where the different groups in a common society maintain many divisions — cultural, social, economic, political, linguistic and others. This integration at a distance reflects the complementary principle of segregation.

Segregation

Segregation is a fundamental manifestation of the in-group versus out-group tendency. Without some form of segregation, the distinctiveness of groups in prolonged contact would disappear. Segregation involves the tendency for different cultural groups in the same society to live their own separated lives, compartmentalized apart from many aspects of other groups in the society. Segregation involves social practices that separate cultural groups along many social dimensions — place of residence, occupation, economic status, marriage partner, personal and social lives, etc. Many ethnic groups in the U.S. find their principal sphere of contact with the dominant society to be in work or school. Their personal lives within family and community are often separated from the lives of both the dominant ethnic group and other ethnic groups in society.

Segregation may take a wide variety of forms. Segregation is typically viewed as a process by which the dominant group separates the other groups from its spheres of activity. Segregation may reflect not only the limitations imposed by the dominant society, but also mechanisms relevant to the ethnic group's maintenance of in-group solidarity. Segregation may be self-imposed by a group in limiting its contact with others, a way of helping maintain its traditions and integrity. Self-segregation serves as a means of maintaining in-group boundaries, functions and social definitions, buffering immigrants from the larger society and permitting a gradual adjustment. The self-segregated ethnic community provides not only a source of social and personal relationships central to psychological stability, but also emotional and physical protection from the hostilities of the wider society. Different degrees of institutional self-enclosure and cultural group boundaries provide variation in terms of the nature of interethnic relations. What the respective group desires, their intergroup concordance and how they view each other are crucial aspects of the particular intercultural dynamic of integration and segregation.

Acculturation

Acculturation refers to the changes that occur as a result of intercultural contact. Acculturation is a very broad concept, designed to include the wide variety of changes that occur in both groups involved in the contact. Some authors use the term acculturation more narrowly to refer to the dominance by one culture and the loss of cultural characteristics and integrity. The term assimilation (see below) more appropriately refers to these more one-sided processes. Some authors have emphasized that acculturation largely involves one-way changes, imposed upon a subordinated group by a group with much greater power. Acculturation, or cultural change, also occurs to the dominant culture in the exchange. The dominant culture's changes may be minor, but attitudes, foods, work patterns, wealth and other aspects of the dominant culture may derive from the subordinated culture in the contact situation. Acculturation refers to the general process of change that occurs as a consequence of sustained contact between cultures. Both cultures will

change from prolonged contact and interaction. While most changes may occur in the cultural patterns of the smaller group as a consequence of contact, even the dominant group will change from the contact. Regardless of the nature of the contact, the interaction is communication that carries the seeds of change. Diffusion refers to the general process by which objects or ideas are transferred from one culture to another. In the context of contact between two cultures, a wide range of diffusions take place, some deliberate (e.g., manufactured goods, foods, political systems, loot) and others unintentional (e.g., diseases, ideas, stereotypes). Many factors influence the nature of the diffusion and consequent changes which occur as a result of acculturation, including the intensity and length of contact, the degree of power differences, the technological differences between the groups, the flow of goods and value between the groups, the presence of hostility and aggression between the groups, the cultural similarity of the groups in contact and the congruent or divergent goals of the groups. Generally, acculturation processes have their predominant effects upon the culture that is subordinate in the relationship. These changes may be so extensive that the subordinated culture loses its integrity and autonomy, either blending into the dominant culture through assimilation or persisting as a subordinated minority subculture.

Assimilation

In the broadest sense, assimilation is like acculturation in that it refers to the processes through which groups in contact change in response to one another. Assimilation is the processes through which groups in contact become more similar, generally involving a smaller or subordinated group adopting the characteristics of the larger and more dominant group. Assimilation as an end condition is where one ethnic group completely disappears as a distinctive culture as a consequence of its absorption into the larger group. Complete assimilation occurs when the total membership of one group "disappears" as their descendants blend into the dominant cultural group through adoption of cultural aspects of the dominant group and integration within the dominant culture's social system. Assimilation involving complete absorption of a subordinated ethnic group into the culture of the dominant social group has been widely espoused as the dominant culture's policy for ethnic adaptation in the U.S. Assimilation is the idea behind the "melting pot," a political ideology that encouraged the immigrant to blend into the culture of the European Americans.

Amalgamation

Amalgamation refers to a fusion of two groups to form a new culture. In most cases of intercultural contact where the power of the two groups is considerably different, amalgamation does not occur. Rather, the subordinated group is more likely to assimilate or maintain a distinct subcultural status. However, in some cases a mixture of two groups can and does occur. Amalgamation of two groups results from the mixing of the cultures to create a new culture that includes aspects of both of the contributory cultures. Amalgamation most likely can occur when the cultures and goals of the two groups and their members are sufficiently similar, such that over time the two groups harmoniously intermix to form a new culture. This amalgamation is generally achieved through a synthesis of the two cultural groups and their beliefs and practices. It results in a syncretism, a new hybrid culture that has an identity distinct from the parent cultures that gave rise to its development. True amalgamations are relatively rare in intercultural contact situations since the different power of the groups, as well as their strong tendencies to maintain their own group boundaries, tends to prevent such egalitarian mixing and synthesis.

Amalgamation was a fact of early American colonial life as English, French, German and other European cultures adapted to Native Americans and produced the American culture. African American culture too is an amalgam of distinct West African and Central African cultures plus the European American influences. Many types of amalgamations occurred in terms of food,

economic activities, political organization and expressive culture. As the different European immigrant cultures adapted together to the new ecological, social and political conditions in the New World, this gave rise to a new culture, the American culture. Examination of early society and culture in the American colonies illustrate that amalgamation occurred very early. The American was not British nor considered to be a European. Aspects of the early colonial society involved amalgamations of the German, French and English practices. Native Americans provided values, group orientations, and public principles that amalgamated with the ideas of the U.S. founders in creating a new form of government. In the frontier areas of Mexico and the U.S. there occurred various amalgamations of Spanish and Mexican cultures with those of Native American groups. The ranch culture of the American Southwest represents an amalgamation of the *norteño* culture of Mexico with that of the new European American settlers to the region. African cultural influences were also amalgamated in the early American culture. The survivals of African cultures in the U.S. were also transformed into the African American culture through amalgamation with aspects of the European American culture and society. Many of the diverse non-European ethnic groups that entered into the U.S. were ultimately amalgamated with the African American culture.

The practices of amalgamation present during the colonial period in the U.S. persisted through the American Revolution and into the early 19th century. But the two-way exchange of information and cultural influence was not as powerful once the Anglo-Saxon European American culture was established and became politically, socially, and economically dominant. Cultural amalgamation subsided as the new Anglo American culture began increasingly to reject foreign ways. The dominant political ideology that emerged was one of assimilation, in which the immigrant groups were expected to leave their own cultural characteristics and adopt those of the American culture.

Theories of Assimilation

Early work on assimilation presented it as a series of stages involving a linear progression from one culture and identity to another. Park, in his classic and influential study *Race and Culture* (1950), argued that immersion of a minority ethnic group into a larger society moved from the stage of contact to competition, which was resolved in an accommodation, and ultimately resulted in assimilation. But the evidence of actual intergroup contact and adjustment rejects simplistic universal stages. Some European immigrant groups did apparently follow similar stages, but many ethnic and cultural groups, particularly those defined as different races, were not allowed to finish the cycle to complete assimilation. Generations or centuries later, major barriers persisted, separating groups, especially those that were highly distinguishable on the basis of physical or cultural features. In the U.S. and societies around the world, many groups maintain separate identity rather than completing the proposed cycle of assimilation. Park's cycle of assimilation reflected the dominant political ideology of the U.S., assimilationist or "melting pot" ideals about what should happen to immigrant groups rather than what actually did happen in most cases.

Such idealized stages were also presented by Gordon (1964) in *Assimilation in American Life* that provided a more elaborate and detailed schema of the stages of assimilation (see Figure 5.3). Gordon's stages of assimilation further differentiated the process and emphasized that groups may remain at specific stages rather than go through the entire cycle to complete assimilation. But Gordon's view of the stages of assimilation also suffered from emphasizing a set of ideals rather than the actual processes through which some ethnic groups and individuals have proceeded. For instance, examine Gordon's first two stages, those of cultural and behavioral assimilation and structural assimilation. Cultural and behavioral assimilation is supposed to involve the change of cultural patterns to that of the dominant society. Such a simplistic representation of the culture and what is assimilated overlooks important facts. While extensive assimilation may occur with respect to work, individuals'/groups' domestic organization, religion and values may persist long beyond the economic assimilation. Cultural differences may persist after structural assimilation (integration into all economic levels). Aspects of behavioral difference and identity may also persist long after other aspects of structural assimilation, as manifested in the persistence of endogamous (in-group) marriage patterns of Jewish and other groups long after effective structural assimilation into the secondary relations of society.

Gordon's Stages of Assimilation in American Life

Stage of Assimilation	Characteristics
Cultural and behavioral	Adopt cultural patterns of dominant society
Structural	Primary group admittance
Marital	Intermarriage
Identification	Societal identification
Attitude reception	Lack of prejudice
Behavior reception	Lack of discrimination
Civic	Lack of value and power conflict

Figure 5.3 Gordon's stages of assimilation

On the other hand, sexual and conjugal relations may occur between groups without effective assimilation, as in the colonial relations between African Americans and European Americans that produced offspring identified as African American and not assimilated to European American culture. Intergroup sexual relations and offspring do not automatically create assimilation. Where the offspring of such unions are stigmatized with the identity of the lower-status group, even intermarriage may not result in cultural assimilation. Rather, it can result in structural segregation with an amalgamation of the traits from the dominant group within the cultural system of the subordinated ethnic or cultural group. The persistence of ethnic attitudes beyond prejudice and discrimination is reflected in the resurgence of ethnic pride and identity among the White ethnics once assumed to be completely assimilated. Substantial structural assimilation in both primary and secondary areas requires that there be considerable attitude and behavioral receptivity and a lack of prejudice and discrimination. While Gordon's schema provided a more detailed understanding of the different aspects of assimilation, it still emphasized the ideology of assimilation rather than reflecting the diversity of adaptations that actually occur in multicultural societies.

Aspects of Assimilation

Assimilation involves a range of processes in which individuals and groups adjust to external cultural influences. Rather than a single final condition, assimilation involves a number of kinds of outcomes. Assimilation may involve relatively minor internal adaptations a subordinated cultural group makes to the external cultural group that has structurally incorporated them into the lowest social strata. Or assimilation may entail complete cultural loss accompanying a group's thorough and complete assimilation into the dominant society and culture. Assimilation of groups involves a number of different dimensions of change — biological, cultural, linguistic, occupational, educational, economic, political, structural, psychological, etc. Assimilation may

proceed at different rates along these different dimensions. Marger (1991) illustrated this variability in his discussion of the biological, structural, cultural and psychological aspects of assimilation.

Biological Assimilation.
Biological assimilation refers to mixing of two distinct populations by producing offspring of parents from the different groups. While biological assimilation is frequently considered to follow other forms of assimilation, it can occur at the point of initial contact. Spanish gene pools began to be assimilated into the Native American populations shortly after contact, creating a new amalgamation, the mestizos. There was, however, little reciprocal gene flow. The Spanish women seldom bore children of Native American parentage that were assimilated into the Spanish culture. Biological assimilation was one directional. Similar processes occurred in the relationships between African American and European American populations in the U.S., where the offspring was legally defined as slave and Negro, and complete and mutual biological assimilation of two populations did not occur. Biological assimilation generally requires the development of extensive structural and cultural assimilation as well.

Cultural Assimilation.
Cultural assimilation generally refers to the complete adoption of the cultural traits (e.g., language, beliefs and values) of one cultural group by another. Complete cultural assimilation results in the relatively complete merger of the members of one cultural group into the other cultural group. Assimilation may occur because of the desire of one group to adopt the lifestyles of the dominant group, as well as because of pressure from the dominant culture to enforce assimilation. Dominant pressures in U.S. society have been towards this form of assimilation, often called "Anglo conformity," reflecting its emphasis upon conformity to the norms of Anglo American society. In spite of great pressure for conformity and assimilation of some groups, other groups have not been fully assimilated. Cultural assimilation may be a partial process in which

some aspects of the dominant culture are adopted (e.g., dress, education, work and occupation) while other aspects of the original culture are maintained (e.g., religion, holidays, primary networks). Other aspects of cultural assimilation may involve relatively complete adoption of the dominant culture by the subordinated group, while the subordinated groups nonetheless remains at the margins of the dominant group and the power structures of the society (e.g., African Americans who have been culturally assimilated into the patterns of European American culture and society but nonetheless experience discrimination and exclusion).

Structural Assimilation.
Structural assimilation refers to the incorporation of a cultural group into all of the different social and economic strata of the dominant society. Cultural assimilation has often been accompanied by structural segregation, the maintenance of economic barriers rather than structural assimilation and equality. Cultural assimilation does not assure structural assimilation, but rather tends to segregate different ethnic groups into economic strata. In the U.S., African Americans have been largely culturally assimilated into the patterns of European American culture and society. However, such cultural assimilation has not been accompanied with proportional structural assimilation of African Americans to all of the economic, social and political strata of society. Even though there are African Americans at all socioeconomic levels, they tend to be isolated in a parallel stratification system with little contact with their "economic peers" in the European American system of stratification. Complete structural assimilation occurs when all barriers to access — linguistic, educational, occupational, civic, political — have been eliminated and members of the different ethnic groups are found throughout the society's institutions and social classes. Structural assimilation may be partial, occurring with respect to specific spheres of social life, such as work and education, while segregation persists with respect to primary relations (marriage, family, kin, friendships and neighborhoods). The term integration has been used to refer to this process of structural assimilation, particularly in terms of the secondary institutional spheres of society. When complete structural integration or assimilation occurs, ethnicity ceases to confer minority status upon the individual. Integration can be compatible with the persistence of ethnicity if it no longer serves as a means of denying access. Such structural assimilation is found in culturally pluralistic societies where a balance of power between different groups prevents ethnicity from conferring a subordinated minority status. The elimination of structural impediments at the level of secondary relationships sets the stage for more complete assimilation at the level of primary relations, which may have begun prior to complete social acceptance and secondary structural assimilation.

Psychological Assimilation.
Psychological assimilation refers to changes in the individual identity of members of an ethnic group. Psychological assimilation occurs when individuals in what were once distinct ethnic groups no longer view their identity in terms of their historical culture of origin, but rather in terms of the ethnicity or nationality of the larger society to which they are assimilating. Once psychological assimilation has been completed at the group level, the group ceases to exist as a separate social, cultural and ethnic identity. While psychological assimilation normally requires other forms of assimilation, an individual may attempt psychological assimilation ("passing") long before other forms of assimilation have been achieved by the group as a whole. Such efforts at individual psychological assimilation may be rejected by the persistent discriminations of members of the dominant society, thwarting or delaying this process.

Factors Affecting Assimilation.
Factors internal to the group and found in the wider society affect a group's tendencies towards and success in assimilation. Assimilation is more likely to occur under circumstances that reduce the typical in-group versus out-group dynamics of intergroup relations. One of the most important factors affecting assimilation is the attitudes of the dominant group towards accepting

immigrants, and the attitudes of the immigrants towards adopting the host culture of the country. When acceptance of immigrants is high and the willingness of the immigrants to assimilate is high, then assimilation is most likely to occur. Acceptance and assimilation are also affected by cultural similarities between the groups. Differences as simple as language or religion can create major barriers to acceptance and assimilation. The resemblance of the physical and cultural characteristics of the immigrant groups the appearances and customs of the dominant culture facilitates assimilation. Conversely, obvious physical and cultural differences present formidable barriers and grounds for prejudices and discrimination. Whether or not the immigrations are voluntary, and whether or not the immigrants can return to their own country also affects acceptance. Groups whose immigration is voluntary tend to assimilate more easily than those groups who are involuntary immigrants (e.g., slaves), or those groups who were indigenous to a region and subsequently find themselves dominated by more powerful invaders. The greater adaptability of voluntary immigrants in part reflects the planned nature of their move, which enables them to deal with the new society more on their own terms. Slaves and subordinated and conquered peoples find themselves dealing with social and political systems that are imposed upon them rather than willingly selected. Whether or not immigrants can return also affects their attitude towards assimilation; greater options are available to those who may return. The arrival of relatively small groups of immigrants from the same cultural group also facilitates assimilation. The arrival of large groups at the same time tends to provoke xenophobic reactions from the previous residents. Small groups facilitate assimilation because they reduce the perception of threat and the possibility of the ethnic immigrants forming communities where their cultural patterns will persist. The factors of competition versus cooperation also affect a group's acceptance and assimilation. If obvious competition exists between groups, then the newcomers are not likely to be welcomed. But groups with skills needed by the larger society find assimilation facilitated.

Cultural Pluralism

Rather than assimilation, the dominant reality of modern societies with multiple cultural groups is some form of cultural pluralism, which involves the persistence of different ethnic and cultural groups within the same society. Cultural pluralism involves the maintenance of cultural identity, and functions in an atmosphere of sufficient tolerance to permit the continued presence of different cultural groups without high levels of manifested conflict and aggression.

Cultural pluralism, like assimilation, can take on a number of forms. Schermerhorn (1978) suggests that there have been at least four different uses of the term pluralism: ideological, political, structural and cultural. Ideological pluralism refers to situations in which a minority ethnic group wants to maintain their culturally distinct way of life within a multicultural society. This can also be called normative pluralism, in recognition of what people think ought to be the situation (as well as what de facto exists). Political pluralism refers to situations in which a number of autonomous interest groups affect societal political decision making; the numbers of the different groups and their balance of power keep any one group from dominating the others or the government. Political pluralism creates conditions in which the different ethnic groups are roughly proportionally represented at the different levels of the stratification system. Structural pluralism refers to the presence of a number of different cultural groups, each developing a parallel set of institutions. Structural pluralism involves structural segregation, with different amounts of political and economic power associated with the different cultures. Schermerhorn uses cultural pluralism to refer to cultural conditions of separate groups that set them off from the majority, but under conditions that are independent of the stratification system (e.g., Switzerland). True cultural pluralism exists when the different cultural groups participate in the same social institutions.

Cultural pluralism ideally refers to conditions under which there is mutual respect among the various cultural groups in a society. However, prejudice and hostility may persist among groups in a culturally pluralistic society. Cultural pluralism has been a *de facto* condition of U.S. society for centuries, almost since the inception of the original colonies where early intercultural relationships were often characterized by antagonisms and hostilities. While relations among the pluralistic cultures in U.S. society have become more tolerant, many people in the U.S. still feel strong antagonisms towards some ethnic and cultural groups. Discrimination has produced a structural pluralism for African Americans and other minority groups, and political pluralism has not been achieved at the national level. While the presence of multiple cultural groups in stable relations to one another make cultural pluralism a reality, some aspects of the ideal of cultural pluralism have yet to be achieved. The forms of pluralism in the U.S. have not eliminated prejudices and discrimination. To the contrary, these relations of pluralism include economic and social stratification systems in which relations of dominance and exploitation are part of the overall system of relations. Cultural pluralism may be accompanied by structural pluralism, where the different ethnic groups in the society are characterized by separate stratification systems within the group, and little interaction between the groups.

In cases where the power of different groups is relatively more balanced, cultural pluralism may create contexts in which several ethnic power groups collectively share power. Cultural pluralism may or may not be accompanied by conditions of structural assimilation, where the various groups participating equally in the various economic strata of society. In contrast to structural assimilation, the traditionally subordinated ethnic groups remain structurally segregated, lacking proportional representation in the upper economic strata. When cultural pluralism is characterized by the presence of structural inequalities that perpetuate the boundaries between the groups, it forms an ethclass, the intersection of ethnicity and class structure in the organization of society. Here ethnic groups occupy a specific level within the societal stratification system.

The major differences in types of pluralism include whether relatively equal status groups participate in *equalitarian pluralism*, or whether groups, separated by cultural and structural segregation, participate in a system of *inequalitarian pluralism* (Marger 1991). Although equalitarian pluralism has been achieved in some societies, it generally remains an ideal rather than a reality. In the U.S., the associated structural impediments have maintained a system of economic and social stratification. Structural segregation has led to the persistence of conditions of inequalitarian pluralism and the associated differences in economic resources and access to power. As a consequence, the differences between groups persist rather than disappearing in assimilation or amalgamation. Groups in a society characterized by inequalitarian pluralism may maintain intense intergroup interactions at the level of secondary social relations (work, school, etc.), while maintaining relatively complete segregation at the level of primary relations (friends, family life, neighborhoods). Societies characterized by inequalitarian pluralism may be much more segregated than in the U.S. A complete segregation of most secondary relations may exist as well, where different ethnic groups participate in different occupations, attend separate schools, use different health facilities and may completely lack access to the political system. The extreme of inequalitarian pluralism is manifested in societies characterized by caste systems.

Multiculturalism.

Multiculturalism is a societal condition in which many members of a society participate in substantial aspects of the cultural life of two or more cultural groups. The individuals themselves are bicultural or multicultural. Examples of predominantly multicultural communities, include bilingual Hispanic communities throughout the U.S. and the predominantly English-speaking populations found among many Native American groups. While most of these are considered ethnic or cultural communities, many members of these communities are actually bicultural, largely acculturated to both the behavioral norms of the larger society and their own culture. However, the presence of multicultural individuals in a culturally pluralistic society does not preclude antagonistic relations between various groups.

Multiculturalism has not been a highly valued part of American culture. Americans have tended to view themselves rather parochially and ethnocentrically, considering the English language and Anglo Saxon origin culture to be superior to others. Such attitudes do little to foster the kinds of relations necessary for effective functioning in multicultural societies. While the U.S. will persist as a culturally pluralistic society, the development of extensive multiculturalism among the dominant European American group seems far less likely — unless cultural competence becomes a valued social attribute among European Americans and societal institutions help instill such capabilities (e.g., through bilingual education for everyone). Thus far, multiculturalism in the U.S. has primarily involved members of the subordinated minorities becoming bicultural by learning to be participants in the dominant society. The development of bicultural minorities is often followed by assimilation rather than the maintenance of bicultural lifestyles and the further development of multiculturalism.

Summary

The U.S., like most societies, is not characterized by a single model of acculturation. Different groups have different objectives and modes of acculturation, and individual members may make different adaptations. For instance, African Americans were historically structurally segregated in the European American society, but some individuals of African American ancestry have "passed" as members of European American society. And while many African Americans have aspired to some form of societal integration under conditions of equalitarian pluralism, other African Americans have avidly promoted separatism. Given the diversity of groups in society and the individual variation within groups, most forms of assimilation have been present simultaneously. These differences reflect varying attitudes towards different groups, as well as different aspirations and opportunities of the cultural groups. Recognizing the diversity of individuals within ethnic and cultural groups and their variable responses to the dominant society is essential in effective adaptation to intergroup relations.

REFERENCES AND ADDITIONAL READINGS

Adorno, T. et al.1950. *The Authoritarian Personality.* New York: Wiley.

Allport, G. 1954. *The Nature of Prejudice.* Reading, Mass.: Addison Wesley.

Amir, Y. 1969. "The Contact Hypothesis in Ethnic Relations." *Psychological Bulletin* 71:319-42.

Atkinson, D., G. Morten and D. Wing Sue. 1983. *Counseling American Minorities A Cross Cultural Perspective.* Dubuque, Iowa: William Brown Company.

Becker, G. 1971. *The Economics of Discrimination.* Chicago: University of Chicago Press.

Bochner, S., ed. 1982. *Cultures in Contact.* Oxford: Pergamon.

Bogardus, E. S. 1931. *Fundamentals of Social Psychology.* New York: Century.

Brown, D.1991. *Human Universals.* New York: McGraw-Hill.

Fletcher, G. and C. Ward. 1988. "Attribution theory and processes a cross-cultural perspective." In Bond, Michael, ed. *The Cross-Cultural Challenge to Social Psychology.* Newbury Park, Ca.: Sage Publications.

Furnham, A. and Bochner, S. 1986. *Culture Shock.* London: Methuen.

Glazer, N. 1975. *Affirmative Discrimination: Ethnic Inequality and Public Policy.* New York: Basic Books.

Gordon, M. 1964. *Assimilation in American Life.* New York: Oxford University Press.

Jaspars, J. and M. Hewstone. 1982. "Cross-cultural interaction, social attribution and inter-group relations." In Bochner, S., ed. *Cultures in Contact.* Oxford: Pergamon.

Knowles, L. and K. Prewitt. 1969. *Institutional Racism in America.* Englewood Cliffs, N.J.: Prentice-Hall.

Marger, M. 1991. *Race and Ethnic Relations American and Global Perspectives.* Belmont, Ca.: Wadsworth.

Marsella, A. and P. Pedersen, eds. 1986. *Cross-cultural Counseling and Psychotherapy.* New York: Pergamon.

Merton, R. 1949. "Discrimination and the American Creed." In R. Maclver, ed. *Discrimination and National Welfare.* New York: Harper & Row.

Park, R. 1950. *Race and Culture.* Glencoe, IL: Free Press.

Phinney, J. 1991. "Ethnic identity and self-esteem: a review and integration." *Hispanic Journal of Behavioral Sciences* 13(2):193-208.

Rhinesmith, S. 1985. *Bringing Home the World.* New York: Walsh & Co.

Schermerhorn, R. 1978. *Comparative Ethnic Relations.* Chicago: University of Chicago Press.

Simpson, G. and J. Yinger. 1985. *Racial and Cultural Minorities.* New York: Plenum Press.

Taft, R. 1977. "Coping with unfamiliar cultures." In N. Warren, (ed.) *Studies in Cross-Cultural Psychology Vol.1*, pp. 125-153. London: Academic Press.

Vander Zanden, J. 1966. *American Minority Relations.* New York: Ronald Press.

Williams, T. 1983. *Socialization.* Englewood Cliffs. Prentice-Hall.

Winkelman, M. 1994. "Cultural Shock and adaptation." *Journal of Counseling and Development* 73:121-126.

———. 1998. *Ethnic Relations in the U.S.: A Sociohistorical Cultural Systems Approach.* Dubuque: Eddie Bowers Publishing, Inc.

<u>NOTES</u>

SELF-ASSESSMENT 5.1

SOCIAL DISTANCE

Social Distance: To Whom Do You Want to Relate?

The concept of "social distance," that is, how closely you are willing to relate to people of other ethnic groups, is a classic measure of prejudice and discrimination. The social distance scale was developed by Bogardus (1931) to assess the degree to which people were willing to establish social relations with members of other ethnic and cultural groups. Assessments of people's willingness to relate to other groups has been based upon a 7-point scale, as illustrated below, ranging from close (1) to distant (7). Individuals' unwillingness to relate to various groups has been taken as a measure of general ethnic prejudice. Social distance assessments have also been used to determine the relative status of different ethnic groups within the society. The classic use of this assessment asked about people's willingness to relate to the different major American ethnic groups (Black, Jewish, Mexican, Chinese, German, Irish, Italian, etc.).

Using the social distance scale, examine the nature of your own prejudices by assessing your feelings about your willingness to relate to several of these groups or others listed below.

Would you feel comfortable about a _____

     Marrying you, or your son or daughter?

     Being a member of your social group (e.g., club, church)?

     Living in your neighborhood?

     Being a member of your profession or a co-worker?

     Being naturalized as a citizen of your country?

     Being a visitor to your country?

     Being excluded from your country?

Islamic fundamentalist
Canadian
Native American
Hare Krishna devotee
Communist
Liberal
Arab
African American
European American
Serbian
Pimp or prostitute
Chinese
Persian
Transsexual
Briton
Russian
Hassidic Jew
Korean
Mexican

<u>NOTES</u>

Culture Shock
Have you ever experienced culture shock?

When and where?

What were your reactions?

How did you deal with the experiences?

Cross-cultural Contact
What are some of the other cultural groups with whom you have daily contact? Occasional contact?

What are the cultural factors that affect the interactions?

What are the social factors that influence the interactions?

Prejudices
What do you recognize as your principal prejudices?

What are your pet peeves or dislikes?

NOTES

What kinds of behaviors in other people particularly please you?

What kind of people do you go out of your way for?

What kind of people do you most dislike?

What kinds of behaviors in people of other cultures do you particularly dislike?

Attribution

Reflect upon a major U.S. ethnic groups (different from your own) and answer the following questions.

What are the characteristics of _____? What are the typical characteristics you associate with people of this group?

What do you know about _____ cultural norms for behavior?

What are the stereotypes your culture holds about _____?

What are the relationships of stereotypes to cultural norms? To prejudices?

<u>NOTES</u>

Accultuation and Assimilation
What have been acculturation influences upon you from other cultural groups?

Have you ever felt pressure to assimilate to the norms of a different cultural, ethnic or reference group? How?

NOTES

NOTES

CHAPTER 6

CROSS-CULTURAL AWARENESS, SENSITIVITY AND COMPETENCE

Overview

The recognition of the need to have cultural knowledge in order to effectively work with people of other cultures is the beginning of cultural awareness. This awareness may be superseded with the development of sensitivity to significant cultural features and a competency in developing relationships with people of other cultures. These personal developments that occur in the process of learning to deal with other cultures are the focus of this chapter. Achievement of cultural competence is addressed in the broader context of a general developmental model involving the replacement of the normal ethnocentrism with ethnorelative perspectives. This approach is based in recognition of the perspectives used by people of other cultures. The adoption of these perspectives of other cultures provides the basis for competence in addressing cultural differences; these perspectives also have implications for the nature of one's self, producing changes as one adapts to and integrates the influences of other cultures.

Objectives

Introduce general concepts related to cultural awareness, sensitivity and competence
Present classic notions about the stages of cross-cultural development
Illustrate major aspects of cultural sensitivity, competence and proficiency
Characterize cross-cultural development in terms of overcoming ethnocentrism and acquiring perspectives of ethnorelativism
Present strategies for development of ethnorelativsm
Illustrate major aspects of the transformation of self in the process of acquiring multicultural perspectives

Chapter Outline

Introduction: Cultural Awareness, Sensitivity, Competence and Proficiency
    Major Stages of Cross-Cultural Development
    Aspects of Cultural Competence
Toward Ethnorelativism: Stages of Intercultural Sensitivity
    Ethnocentric Stages
    Ethnorelative Stages
Developmental Approaches to Cross-Cultural Competence
    Ethnorelativism
    Multicultural Identity Development
References and Additional Readings
Self-Assessment 6.1: Cross-Cultural Development I
Self-Assessment 6.2: Cross-Cultural Development II

INTRODUCTION: CULTURAL AWARENESS, SENSITIVITY, COMPETENCE AND PROFICIENCY

The ways people change as a consequence of contact with other cultures is central to understanding the processes involved in developing cultural sensitivity and competence. The personal changes that occur as a consequence of cross-cultural contact were the foci of classic assimilation and melting pot theories, reflecting an approach in which the immigrant's adaptation to the dominant culture causes loss of personal culture and identity. As Chapter 5 illustrates in the discussion of assimilation, this process involves changes across a number of dimensions (personal, cultural, structural, identity, etc.). These classic assimilation models have been supplemented with perspectives on cultural competence that focus on the deliberate personal changes — alterations in the person's psychology (self, identity, attitudes, behaviors and beliefs) that enhance cross-cultural adaptations and relations. These personal changes involve a process of self-development during which the individual increases cultural capacities by moving beyond the limitations and models of their birth culture, replacing ethnocentrism with ethnorelative perspectives.

As fields of the helping professionals have deliberately engaged in cross-cultural skills as a part of professional development, recognition of the need for people to deal effectively with cultural differences has shifted from an emphasis on cultural *awareness* to recognition of the need for more sophisticated understandings and skills. Initial concerns with managing cultural differences by helping professionals that emphasized the importance of cultural awareness have come to be seen as inadequate, as one can be aware of culture differences and unable to deal effectively with them. Cultural *sensitivity* engages a more appropriate approach, one based on recognition of the need to change behaviors to be more effective in dealing with cultural differences. Sensitivity was also seen as inadequate, often involving one's own cultural concepts about what was sensitive rather than addressing what was important in the other culture. Cultural competence emerged as a concept that recognized the need to behave in ways that are appropriate in the other cultures. But, competence too, can be superseded in the development of more extensive capabilities for managing cultural differences, what Castro (1998) conceptualized as cultural proficiency, the ability to teach competence to others.

This chapter covers major aspects of the personal developments that occur in the process of learning to deal with other cultures. It begins with some of the classic notions about the major stages in the development of cultural awareness, and supplements these with more recent concerns about cultural sensitivity, competence and proficiency based in knowledge about other cultures and the ability to use intercultural skills to overcome the process barriers to effective cross-cultural relations. These achievements of cultural competence are placed in the context of a general developmental model involving replacement of the normal ethnocentrism with ethnorelative perspectives based in recognition of the perspectives of other cultures. These changes have implications for the nature of the self and its awareness of cultural influences.

Major Stages of Cross-Cultural Development

Anthropologists, sociologists, communication specialists, international managers, cross-cultural trainers and others have conceptualized similar stages in the development of cross-cultural competence, based upon their own experiences and those of others they have supervised. The stages of cross-cultural development range from an ignorance of and antipathy towards out-groups through varying degrees of appreciation of cultural differences, potentially culminating in multicultural competencies and identity (Hoopes 1979; Bandlamudi 1994). Members of dominant ethnic groups and minority groups may have different aspects in their trajectories of cross-cultural development (see Chapter 2), but nonetheless show similarities in the overall stages. These involve increasing awareness of cultural influences upon self and others and the ability to adapt effectively to these cultural differences in relating to others.

Pre-Contact/Ethnocentrism

People generally begin in an ethnocentric condition, ignorant of culture, the relation of self to culture, cross-cultural differences or historical and contemporary effects of racism. An exaggerated sense of cultural superiority impairs relations with other groups and limits awareness of cultural differences. Attitudes may be characterized by a belief in the "melting pot" (assimilation) and a naive "color blindness" (the belief that "everybody is the same").

Exposure and Dissonance.

Increasing contact and learning about other cultures can lead to several outcomes: guilt about racism, prejudice and discrimination and, consequently, personal efforts to change society; a defensive withdrawal and re-encapsulation into one's own culture, with increased justifications for racism; or paternalistic efforts to protect ethnic minorities or help change them. Exposure does not necessarily lead to development of cultural sensitivity or competency, but instead may increase dislike of other groups or a minimization of the significance of the differences (see "Universalism" below).

Cultural Awareness

Awareness of the importance of cultural differences and knowledge of their impact upon behavior is the beginning of intercultural adaptation and effectiveness. This awareness includes self-awareness of cultural values and their impact upon one's behavior. Awareness of cultural influences on beliefs, behavior and interpersonal relations helps reduce cross-cultural misunderstandings and provides a basis for developing appropriate approaches to culturally different others.

Cultural Sensitivity and Acceptance

Development of cultural sensitivity requires establishing relationships with members of other cultures in a learning and growth process, leading to culturally appropriate behaviors. Cultural sensitivity involves awareness of relevant cultural differences and the ability to accommodate to them through appropriate adaptations. Cultural sensitivity leads one to question one's own assumptions and replace them with assumptions from other cultures to appropriately interpret their members' behaviors. Cultural sensitivity recognizes both specific cultural characteristics and intra-cultural (within group) differences.

Cultural Competence

Cultural competence, an ability to work effectively with clients from a cultural group, based upon an understanding of cultural values, beliefs and behaviors. The culturally competent individual is capable of using knowledge of cultural priorities, communicating empathy and acceptance, being responsive to individual and community needs and working effectively with cultural groups to develop culturally relevant interventions. Cultural competence involves development of the personal skills to work effectively with people of other cultural groups, using appropriate behaviors and culturally appropriate attitudes to effectively bridge cultural difference. Cultural competence includes the ability to use culturally relevant communication skills, motivational strategies and organizational approaches (Castro 1998). Cultural competence implicates a personal bicultural development as one acquires a new sense of self derived from the ability to identify with and internalize the expectations of another cultural group based on their expectations and perspectives. At the level of institutions, it requires changing the organizational culture to make it more appropriate for the cultures that are served (see Table 6.1).

Biculturalism and Multiculturalism

Biculturalism involves developments where the individual is the internalization of two or more different cultures' expectations. This may or may not involve the ability to function effectively in those different cultures. Some biculturals are "marginalized," feeling a lack of identity and acceptance in either cultural group. Some are "middlemen," functioning effectively in two cultural groups, but keeping those cultural lives separate. Multiculturalists have a range of skills and perspectives that allow them to make effective adaptations to people from many cultural groups and the ability to mediate effectively between people of diverse cultures. Multiculturalists have the ability to move easily and fluidly between cultures, integrate their relationships across the groups and produce group benefits from a synergistic integration of cultures.

Cultural Proficiency

Cultural proficiency extends cultural competence in a social activist approach that involves the community in developmental projects that enhance health resources. This proactive approach engages the cultural group, health organizations and broader community in the design, development and delivery of culturally relevant services. Cultural proficiency includes the ability to teach and direct others effectively in the development of culturally sensitive and competent approaches. Cultural proficiency uses a "strengths approach" that recognizes community health and helping resources, and strengthens them through incorporating them in community health programs.

Principles of Organizational Cultural Competence

Policies of social work agencies reflect the expectations of the cultural groups they serve.

Public agencies support the alternative and complementary health services in their communities.

Public service organizations hire personnel at all levels of the organization who reflect the ethnicity and culture of the community.

Community groups are provided a say in policy, operations and practices of social service organizations.

Organization has advisory and review boards with representatives from all major ethnic groups in the area.

Organization's written educational materials are translated into the major languages of their community.

Organization provides services in the language that is most comfortable to their clients.

Professional staff solicits suggestions from community groups on how to improve their professional practice.

Table 6.1. Principles of Organizational Cultural Competence

Aspects of Cultural Competence

The ability to deal effectively with cultural issues is conceptualized by Castro (1998) in terms of a three-factor model involving capacity level, specialty area and specific cultural groups. Cultural capacity levels range from destructiveness (ethnocentrism), incapacity and blindness through cultural sensitivity, competence and proficiency. An individual's cultural capacities vary across different professional and specialty areas (e.g., assessment, intervention, teaching and research) and across different cultural groups. Specific professional skills are required for teaching as opposed to clinical evaluation or management. Cultural competency is group specific, and may even vary within ethnic groups. For example, one may be competent in relations with elder African Americans, but lack sensitivity in dealing with young African Americans.

The capacities of awareness, sensitivity and competence reflect increasing extent of the ability to deal effectively with cultural differences. Awareness provides the abilities to begin to adapt effectively to other cultures through knowledge of specific cultural information and skills for addressing the general barriers (e.g., process dynamics) to effective cross-cultural relations. Cultural sensitivity provides an informed response to cultural differences that may be superseded with cultural competence, based upon abilities to provide services effectively to people of other cultures. Cultural competence involves learning the personal skills that enable people to interact effectively with others in their culture. Cultural competence (or competency) may be superseded with cultural proficiency — the ability to transfer cross-cultural knowledge and skills to others.

Cultural competence includes behaviors, attitudes and policies that effectively address the effects of cultural differences and the need for intercultural skills. Cultural competence has at least three major dimensions:

1) Knowledge of the general dynamics of culture and cross-cultural relations
2) Skills in intercultural adaptation and relations
3) Culture specific knowledge of behaviors and beliefs of specific groups.

Chrisman & Zimmer (2000) characterize clinical cultural competence as also involving professional attitudes, clinical skills and knowledge of cultural systems. Developing the professional attitudes necessary for effective cross-cultural clinical relations begins with awareness of the generic dynamics of intercultural relations, including prejudice, ethnocentrism, cognitive attribution, culture shock, transference and discrimination. These ordinary but non-productive dynamics of intercultural relations need to be replaced with informed approaches that use cultural tools to understand clients and their health behaviors and beliefs. Clinical skills depend upon intercultural abilities for carrying out culturally competent assessments of both biological and cultural aspect of clients' presenting problems. Intercultural skills enable elicitation of clients' concerns and the negotiation of an acceptable treatment plan that incorporates both clients' and clinicians' needs and perspectives. Knowledge of cultural systems involves the ability to consider clients' concerns within the context of their family, community and the health resources they need; and the ability to function as a cultural broker in translating between clinical and client cultures. These skills require personal transformation to provide new perspectives that change how the person perceives and responds to others. Developing cultural competencies for effectively relating to particular cultural groups is generally beyond the reach of providers unless they spend long periods of time engaged with the culture in everyday life. Helping professionals are more likely to learn how to incorporate cultural knowledge into culturally sensitive approaches rather than develop complete cultural competency.

TOWARD ETHNORELATIVISM: STAGES OF INTERCULTURAL SENSITIVITY

Bennett (1993) characterizes the development of cross-cultural sensitivity and competence in terms of a general model of self-transformation that involves relinquishing aspects of our ethnocentrisms and acquiring perspectives of ethnorelativism. Ethnorelativism involves recognition that different cultures produce different realities and necessities. This recognition of cultural differences provides a basis for increasingly complex and sophisticated ways of experiencing cultural differences and accommodating them. Ethnorelative growth involves development of greater intercultural sensitivity as a function of personal change and cognitive expansion that provide the ability to construe differences in terms of cultural factors. The major aspects of Bennett's model of intercultural sensitivity are presented in Table 6.2. The overall development involves the suspension of ethnocentrism and the acquisition of perspectives and behaviors related to ethnorelativism. Bennett's model of intercultural sensitivity posits growth from ethnocentric stages of denial, defense and minimization to ethnorelative stages of acceptance, adaptation and integration based upon skills in contextual evaluation. Ethnorelativism allows one more effective ways of dealing with cultural difference by providing more accurate interpretations of those differences. These perspectives provide the rationale for new behavioral and evaluative approaches that further develop intercultural communication and relation skills. These recognitions of the cultural construction of reality involve the predictable stages described below.

Levels of Intercultural Adaptation

Ethnocentric Stages
      Denial: Isolation, Separation
            Blind ethnocentrism
            Denial of the relevance of cultural difference
            Maintenance of isolation or separation from other groups

      Defense: Denigration, Superiority
            Negative evaluation of differences
            Expressions of superiority of one's own group

      Minimization: Physical and Transcendental Universalism
            Minimization of fundamental differences across cultures
            "Everybody's basically the same," "treat everybody the same"

Ethnorelative Stages
      Acceptance: Respect Behavioral Difference, Respect Value Difference
            Behave in different ways depending upon whom you are with
            Other cultures' values are as worthy of respect and tolerance
            No universal standards for evaluating what is right or wrong

      Adaptation: Empathy, Pluralism
            View reality from the perspective of another culture
            Recognize many different cultural definitions of reality as equally valid

      Integration: Contextual Evaluation, Constructive Marginality
            The way situations are evaluated depends upon whom is involved
            Who you are and how you behave depends upon whom you are with
            One does not adhere to the values and beliefs of a particular group

Table 6.2. Bennett's Model of Intercultural Sensitivity

Ethnocentric Stages

Ethnocentrism involves the natural assumption of culturally encapsulated people that their own unconscious world view is reality. Ethnocentric perspectives underlie most of the problems in intercultural relations, producing a denial or minimization of cultural difference.

Denial

Bennett considers the purest form of ethnocentrism to involve denial, normally maintained through separation from others. This contributes to an ignorance of differences, a form of isolation, or psychological captivity, that is normally available only to culturally dominant groups. The denial phase involves a "blind ethnocentrism" in the sense of a total lack of awareness of cultural differences and their relevance. Others are reflectively evaluated from one's own cultural perspective. However, one's cultural perspective is not recognized as such, but instead seen as a normal, universally valid system of evaluation. An ethnocentric perspective ignores the relevance of cultural difference. Denial is normally maintained through isolation or separation from other groups.

Defense

Bennett refers to defense as "a posture intended to counter the impact of specific cultural differences perceived as threatening . . . to one's sense of reality and thus to one's identity" (pp. 34-5). The defensive reaction constitutes an intercultural development because it recognizes difference, but the threats that differences present lead to reactions to preserve one's own world view. Bennett characterizes denial as progressing through denigrating others to feelings superior to them. In some cases, defense produces reversal, a relatively rare phenomenon in which a person espouses attitudes of superiority in regard to another culture rather than attributing superior status to his/her own culture. For example, a minority person in the initial stages of identity clarification may still express the internalized

prejudicial ideas regarding his or her own culture that are part of the dominant culture's negative attitudes towards minorities. Denigration involves a negative evaluation of differences, normally attached to some notable out-group category, to which innate inferiority is attributed. The denigration attitude generally leads the individual to feel it is better to reduce contact between groups. The general process of devaluation of others (see the ethnocentric syndrome and authoritarian personality in Chapter 5) means that the general dynamics of ethnocentrism, rather than the specific negative stereotypes, need to be addressed. The other aspect of defense is the expression of superiority of one's own group, such as are manifested in nationalism and ethnic pride movements. This ethnocentrism embodied in social evolutionary theories and perspectives on "development," where other cultures are seen as being at lower stages than one's own society.

Universalism

Universalism involves minimization, a perspective that rejects fundamental differences across cultures, instead emphasizing human similarities — universals. It takes the individual beyond the negative evaluation of cultural differences and instead trivializes them. This aspect of intercultural development often is manifested in the idea that "everybody's basically the same" and that you should "treat everybody the same." This perspective remains naïve regarding the importance of cultural differences, ignoring of the fact that one's perspectives about human universality and sameness are based in one's own cultural assumptions. In the minimization stage, people often express the assumption that being one's "natural self" and expressing genuineness can produce success in intercultural relations. This level emphasizes the appropriateness of one's own cultural behavior in intercultural contexts, an ethnocentrism that reduces the ability to recognize and incorporate understandings of cultural differences. The minimization process may be manifested in a physical universalism, in which human physical and biological commonalities are emphasized, while the culturally unique aspects that direct behavior are ignored or discounted. In transcendental universalism, in spite of behavioral differences, one believes that all humans conform to some single transcendental principle. This is often embodied in religious universalism, in which a single god is believed to have created all humans and demand their adherence to the religious system the god represents. Transcendental universalism does recognize cultural differences and may emphasize learning about them in order to convey the presumed universal principles to which the person adheres.

Ethnorelative Stages

The ethnorelative stages are based in recognition of cultural relativism, i.e., recognizing that people's behavior is best understood in its cultural context, and that there are no absolute or culture-free standards for evaluating what is right or wrong. This ethnorelative position contrasts with the ethnocentrism of previous stages that bases judgments unreflectively on one's own cultural assumptions, world view and values. Values are seen not as fixed or inherent principles but, rather, are understood as the result of an ongoing process of locating and assigning meaning. Ethnorelativism instead attributes the meaning of cultural behaviors and differences to new categories of understanding based upon culture. An interest in differences emerges as the person seeks out cultural differences and their understanding.

Acceptance

Ethnorelativism engages an acceptance of others and adaptation to them through intercultural skills and appropriate behaviors. Bennett characterizes acceptance as acknowledging and respecting behavioral differences and value differences. Acceptance of behavioral differences tends to emerge first as one moves beyond recognition of superficial communication differences to recognition of more profound differences in nonverbal behavior and communication styles, including valuation of patterns of social-emotional expression and types of information exchange (e.g., direct versus indirect). Learning about cultural differences in unconscious emotional

expressions and other aspects of non-verbal communication leads to recognition of value differences and their significance. At the stage of accepting value differences, other cultures' values are understood and seen as worthy of respect and tolerance, even if one does not agree with those values or personally engage them. Value differences are understood as part of a cultural system and its organization of behavior and social life. Recognition of the relativity of cultural values provides a basis for enhanced intercultural sensitivity and the acceptance of others' world views. The recognition of others' perspectives enhances understanding of the relativity of one's own world view, producing greater cultural self-awareness. Central to these developments is the recognition that values as a process. Values are understood in terms of "valuing," an active process of assigning worth to a perception, rather than something one has. This allows one to develop new reactions to difference rather than taking personal offense. But attitudes favorable to other cultures do not necessarily produce an identity transformation and a conscious application of ethnorelativism. Bicultural identity results from prolonged living in the context of another culture, where one internalizes the different patterns of behavior and valuation and cultural frames of reference in ways that produce new forms of identity. This ability is generally very culture specific, resulting from the adoption of a new cultural frame of reference that allows effective interaction with another specific culture, but not necessarily a new attitude that enhances intercultural relations in general.

Adaptation

Adaptation involves making appropriate adjustments for interactions with people from other cultures, developing communication skills that allow expression and interpretation of meaning in cultural context. Real-life interaction with people of another culture provides developmental opportunities for producing new behaviors, thought and feelings. These interactions produce relationships that lead to an "internalization of the other," an identification with others' points of view that produces changes in identity. Empathy for the radically different "other" develops as one learns how to view reality from the other's perspective, a consequence of the intentional shift of interpretative and evaluative frameworks. Thinking and feeling like a member of the other culture begins through these processes and the abandonment of one's own habitual cultural frames of reference, using ethnorelative approaches to achieve understanding and acceptance of the other culture. These new frames of reference provide the ability to select among possible personal and cultural frames. This allows a recognition of many valid cultural forms and behaviors, creating a pluralism involving a philosophical commitment to the many different cultural definitions and constructions of reality. Bennett characterizes two dimensions of pluralism: (1) a general intercultural sensitivity from learning other world views in employing ethnorelative assumptions and (2) an "accidental pluralism" based in the cultures within which one has formed an identity, and not involving the general development of intercultural communication skills. This "accidental pluralism" may result in a negative attitude towards intercultural education training and the refusal to engage pluralism as a stage of self-development. Such individuals may remain with negative attitudes towards some other cultures in spite of their bicultural or multicultural identity and social skills. General intercultural sensitivity engages a general commitment to maintaining non-judgmental attitudes towards all cultural differences in order to maintain the openness and flexibility necessary to understand and adapt to differences.

Integration

Integration involves new perspectives that transcend the limitations of the previous cultural self, producing a new identity that incorporates the "other" and his/her culture. This stage of integration produces a person who defines his/her identity in relation to specific cultural contexts. Marginality, an experience of alienation from one's culture, may be a consequence. Contextual evaluation emerges as a skill for managing choice in the problematic contexts produced by ethnorelativism. Contextual evaluation is a skill that enables one to use self-awareness to make choices, to shift cultural context in evaluating situations, using a variety of cultural perspectives. Bennett links contextual evaluation to the ethnical developmental stages of "contextual relativism." The evaluation of context is key to decisions about whether a certain behavior is moral. Personal identity itself is also contextual, shifting as a function of situation, the context created by others and personal goals. Bennett suggests that this ability to engage situation-based identity, evaluation and behavior is the last stage of intercultural development for most people, and sufficient for most intercultural sensitivity. Constructive marginality may provide a subsequent stage of development of intercultural sensitivity, one where the individual attempts to suspend the use of cultural frames of reference, losing any sense of natural cultural identity. This person constantly questions assumptions and rejects absolute norms of what is right and wrong, operating outside of the framework of any specific reference group. Constructive marginals engage in the conscious creation of their own reality. This type of marginality differs from the classic concept of the marginal man in that the constructive marginal is prepared for this transformation in a way that does not produce a sense of disconnectedness and vulnerability that normally comes from losing one's cultural context for self-reference. Bennett considers constructive marginality as a powerful position from which to utilize skills in intercultural sensitivity, serving as a mediator without unreflective adherence to any reference group and capable of restraining excesses of ethnocentrism and value-based conflict.

Summary.

The process of developing greater capability in managing the interface between cultures goes through regular stages. As one's natural and naïve ethnocentrism gives way to knowledge about cultural differences, new capabilities emerge for managing the relationships between cultures. These capabilities can be learned by directing learning opportunities that promote change from one level to the next, producing a transformation of the self.

DEVELOPMENTAL APPROACHES TO CROSS-CULTURAL COMPETENCE

Bennett's (1993) general model of the stages of development of intercultural sensitivity characterizes it as a function of personal growth and enhanced abilities for dealing with cultural difference. The development of cross-cultural competence involves using the perspectives of ethnorelativism as a basis for interpretation of differences, a process of differentiation of people and cultures. Ethnorelativism is recognition that different cultures produce different realities. Ethnorelative recognition of the cultural construction of differences produces increasingly complex and sophisticated ways of experiencing and accommodating differences, construing them in terms of cultural factors. Bennett (1993:25) characterizes this development as "a kind of cognitive complexity, where greater sensitivity is represented in the creation and increasing differentiation of cultural categories." This personal development begins in recognition that one is actively engaged in "meaning making," in the construal of one's own world view. These new approaches contribute to a transformation of self and identity in the production of new personal cultural frames of reference. Transformations of self and identity move one beyond limited cultural frames of reference, thereby permitting enhanced management of cultural differences. Development from ethnocentrism through various stages of ethnorelativism can be achieved by providing learning experiences that lead one to the perspectives of the subsequent stage.

Ethnocentrism

Development from this stage can be based upon exposure to others that promotes a cultural awareness of those who are different. Individuals skilled in appropriately moderating interactions between cultures should mediate these interactions in order to avoid the likelihood of conflict and increased ethnocentrism. Exposure to information about other cultures is a good first step. This can include consideration of any aspect of the culture, although Bennett cautions against addressing major cultural differences as being too alarming and potentially exacerbating denial.

Denial, Denigration and Superiority

Addressing these stages of denial can be achieved by exposure to information that illustrates the importance and value of cross-cultural contact. A focus on the positive attributes of the other cultures involved is important. Bennett cautions that excessive focus on cultural differences or introduction of cultural relativism may be counter-productive at this stage, producing enhanced needs to withdraw, denigrate or express superiority. Instead, training should focus on commonalities found across cultures, particularly positive aspects. A sense of the essential humanness of all people can serve as an important counter to the sense of group superiority and denigration of other.

Universalism

Addressing physical universalism may be achieved by material which illustrates that physical aspects of humans and their biological needs are not met identically in all cultures, but rather are met in a cultural context that fundamentally shapes their characteristics. Illustrating cultural differences in gender, the culturally shaped aspects of sexual identity, can be a useful approach to show that culture, not biology, is fundamental to understanding human characteristics. Bennett characterizes the impediments at this stage of minimization as a "paradigmatic barrier" based upon absolute dualistic principles that impede recognition of relativity. To shift the person's framework, a cultural self-awareness must be developed, enabling people to place their own behavior in cultural context. This can lead to a reduction in assumptions about the universals of human behavior, and can be enhanced by exposure to material that illustrates major cultural differences in the meaning of certain behaviors and the significance of these differences. Direct personal interaction with persons from other cultures that illustrate these differences can be a significant impulse generating an awareness of the significance of differences.

Ethnorelativism

A variety of developmental opportunities are necessary for acquiring ethnorelative perspectives. These can include opportunities for interaction with people of other cultures in real-life situations, as well as training exercises. While training exercises can provide practice in communication skills and opportunities to develop behavioral competence, the real learning at the adaptation phase is "doing it" - in other words, prolonged interactions with others in real-life situations in their cultural context. Close personal relationships with others are an essential learning experience, providing the identifications that lead to an "internalization of the other as personal frame of reference."

Acceptance

The development of cultural acceptance involves acquiring another cultural perspective. Behavioral responses that incorporate cultural differences produce an affective response of appreciation and increased cognitive knowledge. These provide the basis for behavioral applications that lead to further development of intercultural communication skills. Acceptance of another cultural perspective contributes to development of identification with others' points of view, providing internalized reference points that produce changes in identity. The internalization of another culture provides an ability to select among possible frames of reference. This enables malleability in the construction of self, providing the basis for subsequent developments involving recognition that one constructs one's own identity through cultural processes. Bennett (1993:26) notes that "[I]ntercultural sensitivity increases as people consciously select and integrate culturally disparate aspects of their identities."

Adaptation

The adaptation phase involves the development of cultural competency, based in a number of processes: personal management and transformations, social skills acquisition, conceptual cultural learning and management of cultural differences. Ethnorelative development requires a cognitive engagement that addresses the affective reactions to the threats posed by differences to one's world view by acceptance of those differences as legitimate. The problems of choice and ethics raised by ethnorelativism can eventually be addressed by awareness of the different cultural frames of reference that can be evoked and their appropriateness for specific contexts and situations.

Integration

The development of the ethnorelative stage of integration is necessarily the product of many years of bicultural development and efforts to supersede the effects of any one culture. Long-term cultural immersion experiences and mediation of the differences and conflicts among the groups with which one identifies are necessary experiences for moving beyond habitual cultural frames of reference. The development of contextual evaluation skills involves practice in evaluating situations from a variety of cultural perspectives. Learning how to make evaluations in context is key, as is the ability to shift personal identity as a function of context and situation. Further development of constructive marginality involves the ability to suspend the use of cultural frames of reference and abandon any sense of natural cultural identity. This requires that one question assumptions constantly and reject absolute standards of right and wrong to produce frameworks outside the criteria of any specific reference group. The constructive marginal practices the creation of new realities and utilizes intercultural skills as a mediator without unreflective adherence to any reference group. These abilities and activities produce a transformation of the self.

Multicultural Identity Development

Bandlamudi (1994) investigated ways that people understand multiple cultural and social influences and their implications for the self. There are a range of understandings of the relationships of cultural context to therealization concept of self, behavior and thoughts. Bandlamudi illustrates the roles of self-concept construction and self-knowledge provided through the meanings created in social interaction. This reveals the interdependence of self upon concepts of the other in self-construction.

Bandlamudi's research with people of varying degrees of bicultural background and contacts reveals the fundamental role of cross-cultural relations in producing the cultural and cross-cultural aspects of the self. Bandlamudi proposes that there are five qualitatively distinct conceptual categories of identity development. These different conceptual categories of the self involve a shift from undifferentiated or global states lacking differentiation towards increasing differentiation and hierarchical integration of dialectical concepts of self and culture. The five major categories of relationship between self and the collective other that Bandlamudi posits are:

---

1) Non-relational subjectivism/objectivism
2) Relational-unilateral
3) Relational-bilateral
4) Multilayered/multifaceted
5) Dialogical/dialectical

Non-Relational Self

The non-relational self is not aware of self and its relation to culture. "[T]he [non-relational] self is either completely differentiated from the rest of society or totally submerged in it" (Bandlamudi 1994:468); people are typically viewed as either being all the same or all different. People with a non-relational self characterize themselves in terms of personal likes and dislikes, or in terms of interests or family, but they do not view themselves, or at least talk about, their own characteristics in terms of ethnicity, nationality, language or other groups. "[K]nowledge about self and society is seen as being obvious and self-evident, requiring no explanation. . . . The reasons for underlying causes for human behavior, thoughts, and thought processes, whether about self or other, are not given" (pp. 468-469).

Relational-Unilateral Self

The relational-unilateral individuals define their self in terms of a group identity and collective orientation, in contrast to the personal orientation of the previous level of self. The relational-unilateral self is capable of relating to various stratifying groups, but while capable of recognizing intergroup similarities and differences, is not capable of articulating the nature of the differences, nor of explaining how the cultural factors affect thought or behavior. The relational-unilateral self recognizes cultural differences, conceptualizing them in terms of the contrasting norms and values of different cultures. But this differentiation contrasts a differentiated self with an undifferentiated "other" (Bandlamudi 1994:471). This relational-unilateral view focuses upon ceremonial and ritualized aspects of culture and uses "essentialist" concepts. Culture is viewed as a determinant of behavior, but the relational-unilateral self analyzes only the outward behavior, not the influences of culture upon thought processes and values.

Relational-Bilateral Self

The relational-bilateral individual finds reasons for their behavior in cultural rules. The acquired cultural norms and rules are contemplated, their usefulness questioned and analyzed in relation to cultural institutions. But rather than accepting cultural traditions and norms at face value, they are rationally assessed in terms of their usefulness. But culture is understood as a given, a rule-governed entity and an authority regarding proper conduct, norms and values that the individual internalizes to guide their action. The relational-bilateral individual has an intertwining of self/other and self/culture, and the self and other are understood simultaneously in terms of shared meanings. The distinction between "I," the self as the knower, and me, the self as the known, is central. The individual understands his/her cultural rules and perceives them in relation to the dominant culture. The constant adaptations to the demands of different social environments produces a divided sense of identity. This division of identity between dominant and minority ethnic culture requires a constant adjustment to different contexts, leading the individual to feel as if he/she were "putting on an act" and having a "split personality." This alienation is experienced with respect to both their own ethnic home culture and the dominant culture.

Multilayered/Multifaceted Self

The multilayered/multifaceted individual recognizes multilevel complex processes derived from the relations between cultures and an increasing understanding of the levels of differentiation and integration within cultural systems (Bandlamudi 1994:477, paraphrased). This produces a complex self located within multiple cultural and social matrices. The self of the multilayered/multifaceted individual interacts with the aspects of self provided by the other. Intergroup differences are assessed in terms of underlying thought processes, and in terms of their sources and relevance. The analysis of self is in terms of context. The multilayered/multifaceted self is aware of the social sources of meaning and of the cultural processes that construct self and other through social interaction. There is not only an awareness of cultural influences, but also an effort to reject certain influences and norms. There is, nonetheless, a strong sense of identification with both specific ethnic identity and broader societal identity. There is an appreciation of both cultural origin aspects of the self without the feeling of a divided self (mediator). The multilayered/multifaceted self seeks out diversity and enjoys and appreciates it.

Dialogical/Dialectical Self

The dialogical/dialectical self experiences a breakdown of the division of self and culture in an interpenetration in which one recognizes that the self is located in a specific sociohistorical context that produces one's psyche. But the dialogical/dialectical self is characterized by beliefs that one can transcend those influences. One's self is understood as a historical being and the individual is aware of "historicity," the influences of the cultural matrix and the interconnectedness with others. Consequently the self is viewed as a relational being, a consequence of influences from the economic, social, political and ideological realms of culture. The self and society are recognized as creating each other in a dialectical process; consequently, the self is seen as in a state of constant evolution. At the dialogical/dialectical level, any proposition is considered in juxtaposition to contradictory considerations that enable individuals to understand the variability within their self.

These aspects of self-produced by different adaptations to multicultural influences reflect the diversity of ways in which one may adapt to cultural differences. Individual adaptations to intercultural relations involve a multiplicity of models across cultures, within a culture and within an individual across different life stages and situations. Gardiner, Mutter & Kosmitzki (1998) suggest a modification of the unilineal model of ethnic identity development. They also suggest a subsequent stage of multicultural interdependence in which sharing of new cultural experiences with one's own cultural group produces changes in one's ecological setting and one's culture. This stage differs from the independence stressed in other models by emphasizing the collective sharing of experience that can produce changes in the attitudes of members of one's own culture. These kinds of personal and group transformations can be expanded by a more directed approach to using cultural knowledge and cross-cultural perspectives to change one's understanding of and ability to participate in intercultural relations.

Summary

Anthropological principles are important for addressing barriers to cultural competency. Overcoming barriers at personal, interpersonal and organization levels requires a cultural systems approach, cultural self-awareness and emic perspectives. Effectively adapting to other cultures requires knowledge of cultural influences and the common barriers to cross-cultural relations. Cultural competency requires the use of cultural knowledge and intercultural skills to overcome intercultural barriers. This involves intercultural competency as an awareness of the dynamics of cross-cultural interactions and the ability to adopt perspectives that facilitate those interactions.

Cultural competencies include four major sectors:

1) Personal, including cultural self-awareness, personal management and cross-cultural adaptation skills;
2) Cognitive, including knowledge of cultural systems and beliefs and their impacts on behavior;
3) Interpersonal, particularly knowledge of intercultural process dynamics and cross-cultural skills; and
4) Professional skills in intercultural relations, relevant to specific activities.

Knowledge about cultural systems (Chapter 4), culture's impacts upon behavior (Chapter 3) and the dynamics of intercultural relations (Chapter 5) have been addressed. The appendix to this chapter provides you with another opportunity to evaluate your personal cross-cultural development with the self-assessment exercise "Cross-Cultural Development." The following chapter addresses personal management and cross-cultural adaptation skills and the development of interpersonal skills necessary for cultural competence.

REFERENCES AND ADDITIONAL READINGS

Bandlamudi, L. 1994. "Dialogics of Understanding Self/Culture." *Ethos* (22):160-193.

Bennett, M. 1993. Toward Ethnorelativism: A Developmental Model of Intercultural Sensitivity. In: Paige, Michael, ed. *Education for the Intercultural Experience*. Yarmouth, Maine: Intercultural Press, Pp. 21-71

Castro, F.G. 1998. Cultural Competence Training in Clinical Psychology: Assessment, Clinical Intervention and Research. In: A.S. Bellack and M. Hersen (Eds.), *Comprehensive Clinical Psychology* (10):127-140.

Chin, J. 2000. Viewpoint on cultural competence: culturally competent health care. Public Health reports 115:25-33

Chrisman, N. J., and Zimmer, P. A. 2000. Cultural competence in primary care. In: P. V. Meredith and N. M. Horn (eds.), *Adult Primary Care,* pp.65-75. Philadelphia: W.B. Saunders.

Fowler, S. M. and M. G. Mumford (ed.). 1995-1999. Intercultural Sourcebook: Cross-Cultural Training Methods. (Vols. 1 and 2). Intercultural Press

Gardiner, H., J. Mutter and C. Kosmitzki. 1998. *Lives Across Cultures Cross-cultural Human Development*. Boston: Allyn and Bacon.

Gropper, R. C. 1996. Culture and the Clinical Encounter: An Intercultural Sensitizer for the Health Professions. Yarmouth, ME: Intercultural Press

Hoopes, D. 1979. "Intercultural communication concepts and the psychology of intercultural experience." In M. Pusch, ed. *Multicultural Education: A Cross-cultural Training Approach.* pp. 10-38.

Kohls, R. L. and J. M. Knight. 1994. Developing Intercultural Awareness: A Cross-Cultural Training Handbook (Second Edition). Yarmouth, ME: Intercultural Press.

Kohls, R. L. and H. L. Brussow. 1995. Training Know-How for Cross-Cultural and Diversity Trainers. Adult Learning Systems.

Seelye, N. H. (ed.). 1996. Experiential Activities for Intercultural Learning. Yarmouth, ME: Intercultural Press

SELF-ASSESSMENT 6.1

CROSS-CULTURAL DEVELOPMENT I

Please respond to how you feel about each of the following statements with "NO" or "YES." After you have assessed your responses on the scales provided, compare them with your initial self-assessments in Chapter 1.

1. NO/YES   I am just a normal person, without any special cultural identity or characteristics.
2. NO/YES   My principal characteristics as a person reflect basic aspects of human nature.
3. NO/YES   Immigrants to the U.S. should be expected to keep their own values and customs.
4. NO/YES   People of a racial group are generally all basically the same.
5. NO/YES   True Americans are all basically the same.
6. NO/YES   My cultural group is superior to most other cultures.
7. NO/YES   My basic values and beliefs are based in ethnocentrism and prejudice.
8. NO/YES   The government should control minority groups for their own good.
9. NO/YES   There is only one correct way to behave if you are going to live in the U.S.
10. NO/YES   Cultures that do not have Christian values are basically immoral.
11. NO/YES   It would be better if people of different ethnic groups kept to themselves.
12. NO/YES   I would prefer to live in a community where foreigners are not allowed.
13. NO/YES   I think that we should treat everybody the same.
14. NO/YES   Minority groups would be better off if they "melted in" like everybody else.
15. NO/YES   I feel that we would be better off if we practiced "color blindness."
16. NO/YES   People from minority groups are poorer because of societal prejudice and discrimination.
17. NO/YES   People of specific races are all basically the same.
18. NO/YES   Differences in personal success generally result from different opportunities in life.
19. NO/YES   I think that religious punishments should be outlawed everywhere.
20. NO/YES   Cultural background basically determines the way that people behave.
21. NO/YES   Cultural differences are less important than humans' biological commonalities.
22. NO/YES   In spite of cultural differences, all human behavior is governed by the same principles.
23. NO/YES   There is only one true god who evaluates the morality of humans' behavior.
24. NO/YES   I am comfortable attending religious services of faiths other than my own.
25. NO/YES   What is normal behavior differs from one culture to another.
26. NO/YES   Other cultures' ways of behaving are as valid and legitimate as my own.
27. NO/YES   Politicians need to pass laws to help assure that foreigners do not change our country.
28. NO/YES   It is dishonest when ethnic minorities try to act as if they are like other Americans.
29. NO/YES   Everyone should have to learn about the cultures of American minority groups.
30. NO/YES   I behave in different ways depending upon whom I am with.
31. NO/YES   Islam is just as moral as Christianity or Buddhism.
32. NO/YES   People who practice animal sacrifice as part of their religion should be put in jail.
33. NO/YES   Cultures in which people eat dogs and cats are really evil.
34. NO/YES   Other cultures' values are as worthy of respect and tolerance as my own values.
35. NO/YES   There are no universal standards for evaluating what is right or wrong.

<u>NOTES</u>

36. NO/YES   Americans would be better off if we adopted some practices from other cultural groups.

37. NO/YES   In Muslim cultures women should generally appear in public only with their faces covered.

38. NO/YES   I have been able to show that I can view reality from the perspective of another culture.

39. NO/YES   There are many different cultural definitions of reality and morality that are equally valid.

40. NO/YES   It is important to me to be able to speak more than one language.

41. NO/YES   I have incorporated aspects of other cultures into my life and behavior.

42. NO/YES   I have established close friendships with people from other cultures.

43. NO/YES   You can relate better if you know a person's age, racial identity, education and social class.

44. NO/YES   My culture makes me really different from the people with whom I regularly associate.

45. NO/YES   I do not identify with the traditions of my parents and grandparents.

46. NO/YES   I would be embarrassed if my friends found out about the cultural background of my family.

47. NO/YES   I feel like I have a "split personality," that I am a different person at home than I am at work or school.

48. NO/YES   Some aspects of my parents' or grandparents' culture embarrass me.

49. NO/YES   Sometimes I feel like there are two different cultures fighting inside me.

50. NO/YES   I sometimes feel like I am "putting on an act" in order to fit in with others.

51. NO/YES   I feel more comfortable when I am with people from a culture different than my own.

52. NO/YES   I use the language and cultural behaviors in everyday life of groups other than my birth culture.

53. NO/YES   People in another cultural group have "adopted" me, considering me to be their own.

54. NO/YES   I can feel totally comfortable being in a culture different from my birth culture.

55. NO/YES   I can feel like a totally different person when I am with people of a different culture.

56. NO/YES   The way in which I evaluate a situation and behave depends upon who is involved.

57. NO/YES   There is no objectivity; I create my own reality.

58. NO/YES   I do not adhere to the values and beliefs of any one culture.

59. NO/YES   Whether or not something is immoral depends on the situation and who does it.

60. NO/YES   Who I am depends upon whom I am with.

61. NO/YES   Clients should be required to use English when seeking social services.

62. NO/YES   Services provided by employees of public agencies should always be provided in "English only."

63. NO/YES   I have an ability to work effectively with clients from a cultural group different from my own.

64. NO/YES   Policies of social work agencies ought to reflect the expectations of the cultural groups they serve.

65. NO/YES   Public agencies should use the same procedures for dealing with clients of all ethnic groups.

66. NO/YES   Public service organizations should be required to hire personnel at all levels of the organization that reflect the ethnicity and culture of the community.

67. NO/YES   I have solicited suggestions from community groups on how to improve my professional practice.

68. NO/YES   Public agencies should support the alternative health services in their communities.

69. NO/YES   Community groups ought to have a say in the policy and practices of social service organizations.

70. NO/YES   Social service agencies should have advisory and review boards that include representatives from all of the major ethnic groups in their service area.

71. NO/YES   Public agencies should translate written materials into the major languages of their community.

72. NO/YES   Social service agencies should provide services in the language most comfortable to their clients.

73. NO/YES   I engage in activities to make sure the rights of minority groups are protected from discrimination.

74. NO/YES   Developing cultural sensitivity in staff is the responsibility of government organizations.

75. NO/YES   I have trained people to use knowledge of culture to understand others, communicate empathy and use relevant skills in working with people from another culture.

NOTES

SELF-ASSESSMENT 6.1

SCORING

For each answer on your self-assessment, assign the value of "0" for No and "1" for Yes. Write the answer (0 or 1) to each question in the space beside the question number. Then add up the totals of your answers for each line, convert your answers where instructed and add the subtotals for an overall score for each scale.

Scale N = N1 + N2 = _____ (N Range = 0 to 12) **Normal/Ethnocentric;** Higher values indicate higher levels of ethnocentrism

N 1 = #1___ +#2___ +#4___ +#5___ +#6___ +#8___ +#9___ +#10___ +#11___ + #12____ = _____(N1)

N 2 = #3___ + #7___ = _____*   *If 0, N2= 2; If 1, N2 = 1; If 2, N2=0   + _____ (N2)

                                                          = _____ N

Scale U = U1 + U2 = _____ (U Range = 0 to 11) **Universalism;** Higher values indicate universalist assumptions rather than recognition of the importance of cultural principles

U1 = #13___ + #14___ +15___ + #17___ + #19___ + #21___ + #22___ + #23___   = _____ (U1)

U2 = #16___ + #18___ + #20___ = _____*If 0, U2= 3; If 1, U2 = 2; If 2, U2=1; If 3, U2= 0 _____ (U2)

                                                           = _____ U

Scale AC = B + V = _____ (AC Range 0 to 12) **Acceptance;** Higher values indicate higher levels of acceptance of other cultures

B1 = #24___ + #25___ + #26___ + #29___ + #30___   = _____ (B1)

B2 = #27___ + #28___*   *If 0, B2= 2; If 1, B2 = 1; If 2, B2=0   + _____ (B2)

V1 = #31___ + #34___ + #35___ =   + _____ (V1)

V2 = - #32___ + #33___* *If 0, V2= 2; If 1, V2 = 1; If 2, V2=0   + _____ (V2)

                                                           = _____ AC

Scale AD = E + P = _____ (AD Range 0 to 8) **Adaptation;** Higher values indicate higher levels of adaptation to other cultures

E = #36___ + #37___ + #38___ + #39___   = _____ E

P = #40___ + #41___ + #42___ + #43___   = + _____ P

                                                           = _____ AD

Scale M = _____ (M Range 0 to 8) **Marginalized;** Higher values indicate higher levels of experiencing a *marginalized* biculturalism

M = #44___ + #45___ + #46___ + #47___ + #48___ + #49___ + #50___ + #51___   = _____ M

Scale B = B1 + M = _____ (B Range 0 to 12) **Bicultural;** Higher values indicate higher levels of biculturalism

B1 = #52___ + #53___ + #54___ + #55   = _____ (B1)

                                                           + _____ (M)

                                                           = _____ B

Scale I = _____ (I Range 0 to 5) **Integrated;** Higher values indicate higher levels of ethnorelativism

I = #56___ + #57___ + #58___ + #59___ + #60___   = _____ I

Scale C = C1 + C2 + I = _____ (P Range 0 - 10) **Cultural Competence;** Higher values indicate higher levels of cultural competence

C1 = #63___ + #64___   = _____ (C1)

C2 = #61 + #62 + #65___* *If 0, C2= 3; If 1, C2 = 2; If 2, C2=1; If 3, C2= 0   + _____ (C2)

                                                           + _____ (I)

                                                           = _____ C

Scale P (P Range 0 to 10) **Cultural Proficiency;** Higher values indicate higher levels of cultural proficiency

P = #66___ +#67___ +#68___ +#69___ +#70___ +#71___ +#72___ +#73___ +#74___ +#75___ = ____P

<u>NOTES</u>

SELF-ASSESSMENT 6.2

CROSS-CULTURAL DEVELOPMENT II

Using the concepts of intercultural learning processes discussed and assessed above, reflect on your personal cross-cultural characteristics.

Ethnocentrism. What aspects of your life do you recognize as ethnocentric? What do you recognize as specific ethnocentrisms of your past? Are there racial, ethnic or cultural groups with whom you prefer not to interact?

Awareness. What are specific values and priorities of a culture different from your own and in direct conflict with your own values? How do you/would you deal with these?

Understanding. Examining the values of another culture identified in the previous question, explain why these different perspectives make good moral sense from the perspective of their culture.

Acceptance. What are some other cultures' ways of behaving that you accept as valid and legitimate as your own? Which cultures do you not accept as valid and legitimate?

Adaptive and Selective Adoption. What are aspects of other cultures that you have incorporated into your life, behavior and identity?

Biculturalism. Are there aspects of your life that are bicultural? If so, what are they? Is your biculturalism marginalized or integrated? If so, why?

Cultural Competence and Proficiency. Do you score on the scales of cultural competence or proficiency? How were you led to acquire these opportunities and perspectives? Are there things you can do to enhance your development of cultural competence? What are they?

NOTES

<u>NOTES</u>

CHAPTER 7

DEVELOPING CROSS-CULTURAL COMPETENCE

Overview
The ability to effectively work with people of other cultures involves a developmental process that depends upon the acquisition of certain skills and perspectives. This chapter outlines basic approaches for cross-cultural learning and adaptation, focused upon: intercultural effectiveness skills; anthropological understandings that functions as intercultural tools; the personal skills necessary for managing the stress, conflict and uncertainty of intercultural relations; and the interpersonal skills that reduce barriers to social communication and relations.

Objectives
Understand basic aspects of developing cross-cultural adaptation and competence
Understand skill areas for developing cross-cultural competence
Identify personal strategies and interpersonal skills necessary for cross-cultural competency
Identify skills involved in development of cross-cultural conflict resolution and management

Chapter Outline
Introduction: Cross-Cultural Learning and Adaptation
Perspectives for Cross-Cultural Adaptation
    Intercultural Effectiveness Skills
    Anthropological Understandings as Intercultural Tools
Personal Skills for Cross-Cultural Adaptation
    Stress Management and Culture Shock Adaptation
    Managing Personal Life-Transformations
    Managing Emotional Reactions: Self-Maintenance.
Interpersonal Skills for Intercultural Relations
    Language Barriers and Communication
    Establishing Personal and Social Relations: Understanding Social Interaction Rules
    Behavioral and Communication Styles
    Managing Cross-Cultural Conflict
    Developing a Multicultural Self
References and Additional Readings
Exercise 7.1: Interview Assignment

INTRODUCTION: CROSS-CULTURAL LEARNING AND ADAPTATION

There are ways to reduce the difficulties and conflicts that occur in intercultural relations. Success in intercultural relations requires preparation and knowledge that can be acquired through cross-cultural orientations that teach cultural self-awareness and more effective ways to mediate cultural differences in relationships. Fundamental to cross-cultural competence is knowledge about the general dynamics and processes of intercultural relations, such as the material provided in this text. These general orientations provide an understanding of culture, cultural relativity and the cultural and social factors determining behavior. Other aspects of general cultural orientations involve developing cultural self-awareness of one's values, prejudices and beliefs, since one's cultural biases intrude into intercultural relations and have powerful influences, especially when left unconscious. Understanding one's beliefs and prejudices helps reveal pre-conceptions that will block acceptance of other cultures.

Cognitive, behavioral and emotional learning experiences are necessary for acquisition of cross-cultural competencies. Cross-cultural competency requires combining knowledge with behavioral adaptations and emotional transformations. Cognitive learning of classrooms and structured experiences of training programs need to be linked to new behaviors and emotional reactions developed through social interaction in other cultures. If one is to be effective in cross-cultural relations, there is no substitute for the experience of relationships with people of other cultures in the context of everyday life, and the integration of this learning with the prior cognitive and analytic study of culture and social behavior.

Development of intercultural effectiveness requires a social learning approach that combines cognitive and behavioral approaches, in which new attitudes and cognitive orientations are integrated into behavioral and personal transformations. Development of cross-cultural capabilities involves resocialization through new patterns of social interaction that provide behavioral skills for effective personal and social relations, personal relations for learning and personal support, new reference groups for social identity and new social roles and attachments instilling new cultural attitudes and perceptions.

Case Studies, Role Playing and Simulations

A variety of methods can be employed to prepare oneself for the social interaction behaviors necessary for expressing social competence in other cultural settings. Case studies are used for specific cultural orientations, based upon the study of general ethnographies of a specific culture, or more narrowly focused upon analysis of reports of actual situations of typical cultural conflicts with people from a specific culture. Discussion of these processes, conflicts and possible solutions within a supportive group context provides trainees the opportunity to develop confidence in their own skills in developing culturally sensitive responses. These skills can be put into practice with role playing and simulation exercises. These involve structured and scripted interactions (e.g., "plays") in which some participants play roles designed to emulate the normative behavior in other cultures, and the learners are placed in the interactions with the challenge to adapt appropriate roles and behavior as expected in that culture. Role playing can be extended in simulation exercises involving the development of an operating model of a physical or social situation typical of another culture and getting the learners involved in the actual processes of the other culture's communication and behavior. The types of situations people will find themselves in, or the typical types of problems that people from their culture encounter, are used as the basis for the scenarios. This helps participants develop a better understanding of the roles they can play in various intercultural situations and the conflicts that may emerge because of different cultural expectations. Such exercises can provide the opportunity for the practice of appropriate cultural behaviors, exercise of intercultural communication and adaptation skills, development of skills in problem solution for situations typical of the other culture and exploration of reactions to and feelings about specific conflict situations.

These learning situations can be particularly valuable for future behaviors and self-management. In one of my training programs in which participants were placed in a prolonged (15-minute) situation of frustration of their assigned goals ("getting the job done"), one of the participants feigned a heart attack. Later in the debriefing he explained that if he had been in such a situation, he felt that this is what would have happened to him. Cultural role playing and interaction simulations enable participants to integrate cognitive knowledge, self-directed behavior and ongoing experience in a complementary manner. When provided with knowledgeable feedback and support and with the opportunity to process reactions and achievements, new cultural and social skills development in a manner that facilitates their direct transference to cross-cultural situations.

Fundamental tools for cross-cultural learning and adaptation are also found in the perspectives of anthropology, its methods for studying culture and its understandings of the implications of culture for managing intercultural relations. Cross-cultural communication studies have also identified a range of more specific concepts and skills necessary for cross-cultural success. This chapter reviews some of these skills that underlie cross-cultural competence. These include personal management and transformation strategies, as well as knowledge promoting the adoption of new interpretative frameworks, relational and communication patterns and management styles.

PERSPECTIVES FOR CROSS-CULTURAL ADAPTATION

There are many cultural and intercultural dynamics about which one must be aware in order to be able to adapt effectively to a range of cross-cultural settings. These include an understanding of cultural effects and the dynamics of intercultural interfaces. Cross-cultural competencies involve a variety of cross-cultural perspectives and intercultural effectiveness skills. Development of intercultural skills involves several general stages, beginning with awareness of differences, adjustment to their challenges and

adaptation of new behaviors leading to cultural competence. Adjustment involves maintaining one's own psychological well-being while accommodating differences, producing a harmonious relationship between self and the new cultural environment. Adaptation is concerned with long-term changes that enhance the ability to interact effectively with others in another culture and feel comfortable. Competence involves the ability to be effective and successful, based on the abilities to build relationships, communicate effectively, establish rapport, express empathy and generally avoid stress associated with the new culture. It generally means that there has been a degree of internalization of the other culture and a mastery of the language for social interactions. These achievements require cognitive expansion, behavioral adjustments and emotional adaptations.

Intercultural Effectiveness Skills

Key to effective functioning in a new culture is a range of skills that facilitate adjustment and adaptation. These skills are related to the ability of individuals to manage the changes that will necessarily occur in themselves as a consequence of exposure to the other culture, and the processes of adapting oneself to the new cultural setting. Studies of people making cross-cultural adaptations (Hammer, Gudykunst & Wiseman 1978; Abe & Wiseman 1983; Hammer 1987; Adelman 1988; Cui & Van den Berg 1991) suggest the following as central to intercultural effectiveness:

* Dealing with psychological stress and emotional reactions
* Being tolerant and accepting of cultural differences
* Expressing cultural empathy and understanding
* Behaviorally adjusting to the other culture's social system
* Developing cultural communicative competence
* Establishing and maintaining inter-personal relationships

The abilities needed for successful cross-cultural adaptation are reviewed by Kelley and Meyers (1995) in terms of four major areas: personal autonomy, emotional resilience, flexibility/openness and perceptual acuity. Successful cross-cultural adaptation requires knowledge of the self, an understanding of personal priorities that facilitate self-maintenance and avoidance of defensiveness. Self-awareness can play a role in setting realistic goals for adaptation and building upon personal strengths. Knowledge of the values of cultures or people you dislike and an understanding of why such values are important helps expand the ability to deal with people who are different. It is also important to address your emotional reactions to cultural differences, particularly the negative ones, and examine the underlying thoughts and evaluations related to the negative feeling. Success in another culture requires that we effectively manage negative emotional reactions and stress and reduce culture shock. A good strategy is to focus on maintaining a positive attitude, while being willing to experiment and take risks and finding humor in your difficulties and mistakes while adapting to the other culture. Attitude is part of a strategy of flexibility and openness, developing a non-judgmental attitude towards the other culture, particularly things that you find disturbing. The attitudinal approach involves seeking a cognitive understanding of the other culture's reasoning using cultural relativism to perceive their world view and its rationales. Relationships with people in the other culture are key to adaptation. Making friendships and learning how to behave appropriately in interaction with people from the other culture are foundational to learning appropriate behavior. This requires the development of perceptual acuity, learning about another culture's communication patterns, especially non-verbal and social interaction styles. This requires active listening to assure comprehension and appropriate expression, and learning how to read body language, gestures, contextual communication and emotional expressions.

These basic skills for intercultural adaptation can be organized in terms of cognitive orientations that help us understand and adapt to cultural differences, personal adaptations that enable the individual to deal with the different culture, and interpersonal adaptations related to the ability to person to be socially effective in the other cultural setting. Cognitive orientations provided by anthropological perspectives include cultural perspectives, cultural relativism, cross-cultural or etic perspectives and cultural characterizations versus intracultural variation. Personal skills focus on the management of stress, self-esteem, emotions and attitudinal orientations. Social skills are focused upon language and communication competence, appropriate social behaviors, conflict resolution and cultural competence management and negotiation skills. All of the above basic skills are detailed below.

Anthropological Understandings as Intercultural Tools

Anthropologists use several perspectives and methods to understand other cultures. These include the concept of culture, emic perspectives, participant-observer methods and cross-cultural (or etic) systems perspectives. These approaches provide a basis for bridging the gap between cultures.

Culture, Emic Perspectives and Cultural Relativism

The fundamental tool for cross-cultural relations is the notion of culture, the common patterns of learned behavior that characterize human groups. Cross-cultural effectiveness requires an understanding of the processes by which humans acquire culture, the effects of culture upon behavior and perceptions, and the role of culture in producing conflict in intergroup relations. Differences between cultures create problems in intercultural relationships that derive from an inability to understand one another. Fundamental to understanding other cultures is the emic approach, based upon the understandings that members of a culture have about their own culture and lives. It is an "insider's" view, an understanding of the other culture's perspectives, world view, values, assumptions and motivations.

Understanding the interpretations of cultural life from the perspectives held by members of the culture provides the basis for recognition that behavior is meaningful in cultural context. The emic perspective involves understanding another culture, and from their perspectives and assumptions. Cultural relativism involves recognition that human behavior is relative to the actor's culture and must be interpreted in that context if it is to be correctly understood. Cultural relativism tells us to interpret behavior within cultural context, which enables us to understand behavior as rational, intelligible and meaningful. Cultural relativism is the approach anthropologists use to develop emic perspectives and to understand culture-behavior relationships. Cultural relativism's recognition that behavior is meaningful in cultural context leads to an understanding that other cultures are as rational and valid as our own. Essential to this realization is the recognition that different cultures have different goals and values that are valid as our own values and goals are to us.

Cross-Cultural Etic Perspectives

The cross-cultural learner requires models and guidelines for investigating and continuously adapting to changing circumstances. To understand and adapt to another culture, one must have some understanding of how cultures are organized and how one can learn about and adapt to them. In addition to culturally specific emic approaches, anthropologists use comparative cross-cultural (etic) perspectives to understand the patterns of behavior of one culture in comparison to those of others. Anthropology contributes systematized cross-cultural models of the institutions of cultural systems to facilitate cross-cultural learning of the organizational dynamics of cultural behavior. These are derived from a synthesis of the commonalties found across cultures. These etic perspectives provide universal models of cultural systems to understand and explain dynamics found in a particular culture. These comparative or cross-cultural perspectives such as are found in the cultural systems and psychocultural models allow for identification of universals of human behavior and the variant ways in which these universal biosocial human needs

are met. General models of culture (Chapter 4) and of the relationship of culture to human behavior (Chapter 3) have been provided here. These systems perspectives recognize that human behavior is produced through the interaction of many different factors. Systems models address both micro-level (interpersonal) and macro-level (institutional) forces that affect human behavior, examining the wide range of influences that produce individuals, their unique and cultural characteristics and the ways in which they behave, feel and think.

Intracultural Variation: Cultural Characterizations versus Stereotypes

Some resist the attribution of cultural features to members of specific groups as stereotyping. In the process of viewing culture as forming common patterns of behavior, one must avoid stereotyping or viewing everybody in the culture as being the same. Cultural characterizations based upon normative behaviors provide an understanding of both typical patterns and variation within a culture. Cultures produce both common patterns of behavior that characterize their members and intracultural (within culture) variation in self, personality and social roles. Cultural competence includes an ability to respond to the culturally patterned differences reflected in age, generation, acculturation, class, gender, family roles, economics and other aspects of intercultural variation. Complex societies have even greater variation — occupational specialization, political position, educational — as well as different subcultures. Intracultural variation does not eliminate the importance of culture, but instead requires a more complex understanding of cultural influences.

PERSONAL SKILLS FOR CROSS-CULTURAL ADAPTATION

Cultural competency requires a range of learning experiences and personal adaptations. A variety of methods need to be employed as a basis for cross-cultural training, combining the teaching of general principles and cultural specifics with experiences and activities that promote self-awareness, behavioral adaptations and emotional transformations. Cross-cultural training procedures are available to learn how to adapt personally to situations one is likely to encounter (see Weeks, Petersen & Brislin 1985; Kohls & Knight 1994; Kohls & Brussow 1995; Gropper 1996; Seelye 1996; Fowler & Mumford 1999). Cognitive learning must add interactions with people in other cultures in everyday life, learning to express new attitudes and cognitive orientations that produce personal transformations. Personal changes include adopting development of cultural self-awareness, an attitude of willingness to change, acquisition of skills for managing cultural shock and associated emotional distress and restraint of cultural projection tendencies.

Personal Change and Transformation.
Developing cultural competence requires an effort to change personally, facilitated by awareness of the benefits. Cross-cultural contact produces strong emotional reactions and resistance to learning about and accepting cultural differences. Developing cultural competency requires adopting a positive attitude about working through the difficult personal challenges of intercultural adaptation. Fukuyama & Sevig (1999) characterize cross-cultural competency as requiring a deep personal passion and commitment that is shared with others and implemented in actions that interrupt oppression and identify opportunities to be proactive. The process of cross-cultural development produces changes in the self, a transformation process that leads to increasing identification with and internalization of others' points of view.

Cultural Self-Awareness.
Cultural competence requires recognition of one's own cultural characteristics and influences, particularly one's values, prejudices and beliefs, and their effects upon behaviors and attitudes. Cultural self-awareness begins with knowledge of one's own culture and its effects upon one's self, identity, preferences, patterns of behavior and characteristics of one's professional practice (for example see Chapter 5 on biomedical and nursing

professional cultures). Self-knowledge of one's own culture is most important because it underlies all of one's behavior, personal and professional. Self-awareness needs to include consideration of the nature and sources of one's attitudes towards other ethnic groups. Values assessments (see Self-Assessment 4.2: Values Assessments) are an essential part of developing cultural self-awareness and cultural competence, understanding how one's own cultural orientation affects relations with others. Cultural self-awareness provides a basis for anticipating and managing the conflicts that may be encountered with a foreign culture. Awareness of one's own cultural values helps suspension of the habitual tendencies to judge others with such cultural self-awareness, based on our cultural assumptions, also facilitating acceptance and understanding of other cultures.

Maintenance of Emotions and Self.
Cross-cultural contact produces stress, emotional reactions and resistance to learning about and accepting cultural differences. The challenging circumstances can make us lose self-esteem and our sense of personal efficacy. Adaptation requires management of these emotional reactions and stress, strengthening one's personal resources for dealing with cultural differences, developing a sense of self-efficacy through cognitive and behavioral coping strategies (Winkelman 1994). Physical stress management and maintenance of one's physical well being are important for cross-cultural adaptation. Emotional reactions that need to be managed include culture shock, involving physical, psychological, social, cognitive and emotional reactions to contact with another culture. Culture shock produces dislike of another culture and a desire to leave it, or even psychological disorders such as transient neurosis, paranoia and acute psychotic breakdowns. Effectiveness in cross-cultural relations requires recognition of cultural shock and taking steps to prevent it from undermining cross-cultural adaptation (see Winkelman 1995). This requires knowledge of likely provocative situations and means of reducing stress and conflicts through knowledge of cultural differences and likely sources of conflict.

Stress Management and Culture Shock Adaptation

Successful control and management of stress is central to working successfully in other cultures, especially in terms of adaptation and effectiveness. Major resources for dealing with cross-cultural stress (Walton 1990) include cognitive coping strategies based upon realistic expectations and the ability to engage in cognitive reappraisal; self-efficacy, derived from perceived control and the ability to view new situations as challenges rather than threats; and social support — family, friends and others who support needs for affiliation, affirmation, emotional caring, instrumental aid and information. Dealing with stress also requires an acceptance of the validity of the other cultural system embodied in empathetic understanding. The cultural differences require that we adjust behaviorally to function and meet our needs and be accepted by others, a significant factor in feeling self-efficacy. Perhaps one of the greatest producers of stress in foreign cultural environments is the inability to understand others and to make ourselves understood. Communication competence is not dependent solely upon language skills, but also upon comprehension of behavioral communication and the ability to initiate, establish and maintain relationships. In effective intercultural relationships with people of other ethnic groups, it is necessary to have an attitude of tolerance and empathy for their culture, and an awareness of the significant cultural differences, especially appropriate social behavior and display of respect. Social relations and human assistance are widely shown to be crucial to the process of cross-cultural adaptation. Social relations are crucial to one's sense of well being. These include provision of tangible assistance; validation of self-worth through affirmation, acceptance and assurance; and opportunities for expressing one's emotions, leading to understanding of the dynamics creating stressful situations. These general intercultural effectiveness skills can be supported and enhanced by a variety of understandings that enhance cross-cultural relations and adaptation.

The experience of the unknown and different causes stress. Even when cross-cultural contact is desired and enjoyable, it produces stress through novelty and the additional effort required to make sense of cultural differences. Effective cross-cultural relations require that one learn how to manage the stress that is exacerbated by the inevitable difficulties and conflicts of cross-cultural contact. Management of stress is central to cross-cultural adjustment, adaptation and effectiveness. Since ambiguity is a major source of stress, it can be reduced through understanding the cross-cultural adaptation process, developing accurate and realistic expectations and learning how to tolerate ambiguity. Effectiveness in dealing with stress requires that one recognize it is inevitable in cross-cultural relations and understand personal lifestyle activities that help reduce stress and utilize them in adaptation to the new cultural setting.

One aspect of stress induced by cross-cultural contact is culture shock, a profound physical, psychological, social, cognitive and emotional reaction to the experiences resulting from numerous stressors occurring in contact with a different culture. This ultimately leads to a crisis characterized by an extreme dislike of the foreign culture and a desire to leave it as soon as possible. Culture shock may induce a "transient neurosis," a temporary emotional disorder, with more critical cases having features resembling acute psychosis with paranoid features. Some form of culture shock is a normal reaction to a foreign cultural environment, but those experiencing culture shock generally do not recognize it, nor do they respond effectively to the problems created. The culturally pluralistic nature of U.S. society creates daily cross-cultural conflict for the members of diverse ethnic groups, including the dominant culture. To be effective in cross-cultural relations, one must recognize cultural shock occurrences and their nature and causes in order to prevent cultural shock experiences from undermining cross-cultural adaptation. This requires adapting personal responses and problem-solving strategies and developing ways to manage stress and problems in the new cultural environment effectively.

Although difficulties in adjusting to a foreign environment are often minimal in the first few weeks of the "honeymoon" or "tourist" phase, any amount of exposure to a foreign environment can produce culture shock. Virtually everybody who spends prolonged periods of time in contact with a foreign cultural environment experiences varying forms and degrees of culture shock. Culture shock is a multifaceted reaction to the stressors experienced in contact with a foreign culture. These include a variety of physiological reactions, psychological and emotional responses, social stresses and cognitive overloads. While milder forms of culture shock involve reactions of frustration, disgust, anger and sadness, the more severe forms of culture shock are manifested in acute psychotic reactions with paranoid features.

The lack of recognition of culture shock and ineffectiveness in responding to it with adaptive cognitive and behavioral strategies is a primary cause of inadequacies and failures in foreign assignments. Effectively managing the debilitating effects of culture shock require both pre-departure training and on-site transition support for resolving issues. Central to culture shock management is the awareness of the nature and causes of culture shock and a behavioral plan for effectively changing one's perceptions, feelings and reactions. Most people undergoing culture shock crisis lack an awareness of the nature and causes of their dilemma, instead blaming their local counterparts and the local culture for the problems they experience. Frequent characteristics of these culture shock reactions are frustration, tension, exaggerated disappointment, isolation, withdrawal, depression, anger, disgust, paranoia and physical and emotional illness. Serious cases of culture shock may manifest symptoms of extreme paranoia and acute psychotic reactions and breakdowns. The progress of culture shock from mild annoyance to extreme psychological breakdown may occur within hours of cross-cultural immersion. Effective preparation and support systems can help curtail or even eliminate culture shock reactions.

Successful control and management of stress is central to working successfully in other cultures, especially in terms of effectiveness and adaptation. Adjustment and effectiveness are functionally interrelated meaning that procedures for stress management should be incorporated into intercultural training (see Walton 1990). Since ambiguity is a major source of stress, reduction of ambiguity through developing accurate expectations and learning how to tolerate ambiguity is necessary for successful adaptation. A sense of control and reduction of ambiguity can be achieved by having realistic expectations about the foreign experience, understanding the cross-cultural adaptation process and having a clear understanding of job expectations. Dealing with stress requires that one first recognize stress; secondly, one must engage in activities — dietary modification, relaxation techniques, exercise and productive use of discretionary time — that enable the individual to deal more effectively with stress (Walton 1990:511). Among the major resources for dealing with cross-cultural stress are:

---

* *Self-efficacy:* derived from perceived control and the ability to view new situations as challenges rather than threats;
* *Cognitive coping strategies:* based upon realistic expectations of one's likely experiences and the ability to engage in cognitive reappraisal;
* *Social support:* family, friends and others who recognize one's needs for affiliation, affirmation of self-worth, emotional caring, instrumental aid, important information and inter-personal support; and
* *Communication competence:* the ability to understand others and to make ourselves understood, which includes not only language skills but also the ability to rely effectively upon bilingual personnel (translators) and one's own educated interpretations of social behavior, especially displays of respect.

Managing Personal Life-Transformations

To become cross-culturally effective, one must become "cross-cultural," a transformation of cultural identity that implies significant changes in the nature of self, personality, behavior and identity. These changes are gradual, piecemeal and selective in their breadth.

Attitudes Toward Change

Vital for cross-cultural adjustment and effectiveness, one's attitude about other cultures and commitment to changing one's self to make an effective adaptation. The adoption of new attitudes changes in previous attitudes, and the acquisition of new knowledge is a necessary part of effective cross-cultural adaptation. Cross-cultural effectiveness requires recognition of the benefits of being able to participate in relations with people from another culture and having a positive attitude about the challenges of cross-cultural learning experiences. A recognition that cross-cultural relations are challenging is essential for the commitment to make adaptations that are often difficult. Perseverance in the face of conflict, misunderstandings and difficulties is essential for developing cross-cultural competency. Another essential attitude is tolerance of personal differences and the ambiguities that characterize intercultural relations. The tendency to judge others has to be supplanted by an attitude in which we attempt to perceive and understand non-judgmentally the validity of others' points of view. This requires a suspension of habitual judgmentalness.

Overcoming Resistance to Cross-Cultural Adaptation

Reactions to cross-cultural experiences often involve strong emotional responses and resistance. Few people can accept the legitimacy of other cultures openly, completely and without reservation. Humans are cultural beings, and enculturation leads them to value and prefer the ways of their own cultures and simultaneously to reject the ways of other cultures. The socialization into one's culture and its values creates ethnocentrism — culturally based preferences — and, consequently, resistance to the acceptance of another culture. Human cultures are characterized by pervasive ethnocentrism as a normal aspect of being cultural. Ethnocentrism means that contact with another culture invariably leads to conflict with some deeply held notions about what is appropriate and correct, and hence resistance to acceptance and change. Because of conflict with one's values, there will necessarily be resistance

to many aspects of cross-cultural experiences and adaptations. Our sense of self, derived from our cultural influences and beliefs, resists the changes involved in adopting the behaviors of another culture and accepting their beliefs. This resistance to cultural differences has to be consciously addressed in order to reduce its interference with the cross-cultural adaptation processes. Cross-cultural effectiveness requires that one learn how to manage these strong emotional reactions in self and others, validating the legitimacy of such feelings, while recognizing them as impediments to cross-cultural development. This can be facilitated by developing self-reference groups in the other culture.

Developing Cultural Self-Awareness

To be cross-culturally effective, one must develop an awareness of one's own cultural characteristics and influences, particularly one's values, prejudices and beliefs, and their effects upon behaviors, feelings and attitudes. Otherwise, one remains naive to the influences that culture has on one's own behavior and incapable of being sensitive to the cultural influences upon others' behavior. By developing an awareness of one's own cultural influences, one can better appreciate the importance of others' cultures for their behavior, which will facilitate acceptance and understanding of other cultures. A number of different procedures can be employed in order to stimulate exploration of one's own cultural background and value systems and how they affect relationships with people from other cultures. Values assessments (see Self-Assessment 4.2: Values Assessment) are an essential part of cross-cultural training and cultural self-awareness. Bringing ones' own personal and cultural values into awareness allows for an examination of preconceptions that will block acceptance and understanding of other cultures. This chapter includes cultural self-awareness exercises and values' assessments that will help you develop an awareness of these cultural influences.

Cultural self-awareness provides a basis for developing an awareness of the primary value conflicts to be encountered in new cultural environments. Conflicts with other cultures are based in our own cultural expectations. If one is unaware of one's own values, then one is unprepared to manage potentially conflictive situations. Assessments of cross-cultural skills and attitudes important for cross-cultural communication (e.g., openness to new experience, cognitive flexibility) can be assessed to determine one's existing capabilities and the need for development of new skills for effectiveness in cross-cultural relations (see Kelley & Meyers *The Cross-cultural Adaptability Inventory* 1995). "Workbook approaches" based on a set of guided materials through which the trainee engages in directed exploration of personal experiences and intercultural communication resources, skills and perspectives (see Hoopes et al. 1979) provide assessment of the individual's experiences, preparation and motivation for cross-cultural effectiveness. Open-ended questions provide the basis for exploring fears, prejudices, expectations, problems, personal resources, values, behavioral and cognitive orientations and a context for planning for improved intercultural communication. Workbook activity can be initiated outside the group setting and provide the basis for subsequent group processing. Discussion with others provides a basis for developing an awareness of different styles and perceptions and can guide cognitive and empathic understanding of alternative points of views and new perspectives on social interaction.

Assessing Values Orientations

Understanding one's own values and the values of the cultures with which one interacts is a crucial tool for intercultural adaptation. Values are important as the principal cultural determinants of behavior, frequently embedded in unconscious assumptions and motivations. Values are culturally determined, emotionally charged priorities for decision making and social behavior that reflect the most important aspects of a culture's beliefs, goals and expectations. Values have an emotional commitment, and their violation creates emotionally charged responses. They become standards for action and the bases of attitudes, shaping perceptions and determining behavior. Values determine many needs we feel, affecting motivation and productivity. Values impact communication and what is attended to. Values

determine what is defined as a problem and how it should be solved. Values are intertwined with one's world view, generally with an important basis in religion. As a cultural embodiment of values, religion can have important impacts upon social behavior by providing ultimate justifications, demanding certain social relations and providing proscriptions and prescriptions about relationships to nature and other groups. Understanding the main values of a culture provides some global perspectives for understanding the impacts of culture upon behavior. Values reflect the overriding and widespread influences of a culture, providing guidelines for adaptations to many settings.

Managing Cultural Attribution and Projection

A consequence of enculturation is the acquisition of assumptions about what is normal and expected. A normal human tendency is to attribute meaning and significance to new situations based upon previous experiences and partial information. One aspect of this process is called the "self-reference criterion," using our own culture and personal dynamics as the basis for the projections we naively make for understanding why others behave the way they do. This use of our own personal dynamics as the interpretive framework for understanding others' behavior, motivations, feelings, etc. is normal. Such processes are a fundamental part of phenomena such as ethnocentrism, stereotyping and prejudices. Cross-cultural effectiveness requires that we overcome these cultural habits involving the use of "self-reference criteria," assumptions that the others' motivations, meaning and significance are the same as our own. While attribution processes cannot be abandoned altogether, success in cross-cultural relations requires that these tendencies be controlled by developing awareness of the intrusion of our culturally based values and beliefs. People of different cultures are more likely to be motivated by factors different from our's. Habitual aspects of projection during conflict lead us to attribute the reason for others' behavior to their (negative) personal traits. This attributional tendency has to be controlled in intercultural relations or conflicts will escalate. One should consciously adapt and apply a perceptual framework of *cultural attribution* (or cultural relativism), recognizing that culturally different actors are behaving in ways that are correct and meaningful from their cultural perspectives. It is necessary to adopt consciously a non-judgmental perspective to guide interaction with people from other cultures, and to recognize that their behavior is meaningful and reasonable in the context of their culture.

Managing Emotional Reactions: Self-Maintenance

It is virtually impossible to grow up without any negative attitudes, feelings or experiences from contact with people from other cultures. For many people, the experiences of intercultural contact have been so negative they have left a backlog of unresolved emotional issues that developed long before deliberate cross-cultural orientation began. The powerful emotional reactions that even simple intercultural training exercises can evoke indicate the importance of addressing these issues. A normal aspect of cross-cultural contact is emotional distress. Cross-cultural effectiveness necessitates managing the stress from the difficulties and conflicts of cross-cultural contact. Personal stress management procedures and cognitive orientations for realistic expectations about and mastery of the new environment facilitate adaptation.

Maintenance of one's personal emotional condition is essential for successful cross-cultural adaptation. This may be achieved through persistence in habitual activities used for stress management and maintenance of one's personal identity and sense of well-being. Problems in personal and emotional life caused by cross-cultural contact may also need to be addressed through reparative behaviors, activities that reestablish those vital aspects of oneself through enjoyable, self-renewing and self-validating activities (e.g., talking with friends, going to movies, sleeping or eating or other activities that are personally gratifying). Social support networks ameliorate a variety of stressors through validating self-worth, providing socioemotional bonds, and providing feedback and insight for

understanding cross-cultural situations. A variety of specific emotional reactions need to be managed, including increased stress, culture shock, cross-cultural conflict and resistance to change.

The ability to manage these emotional reactions is dependent upon knowledge of the provocative situations we are likely to encounter. This requires not only cultural self-awareness but, also, preparation for the conflicts likely to be encountered in contact with the other culture. Preparation for the management of conflict can be enhanced by the use of cultural assimilator, critical incidents and intercultural sensitizer materials (see Hoopes & Ventura 1979; Weeks, Petersen & Brislin 1985; Seelye 1996). These materials present prepared cultural conflict scenarios and provide a range of potential explanations of the behavior or conflict. For European Americans, these "contrast-American" exercises are designed to produce learning about one's values, attitudes, assumptions, cultural identity and behaviors that will most likely clash in interaction with people of different cultures. Contrast-American exercises prepare for managing cultural differences by presenting material focusing upon direct conflicts of American cultural expectations with the normal behavior of another culture. These contrast-American conflicts provide the basis for a critical examination of one's own cultural values, and offer material for learning about the cultural differences most likely to cause difficulties. These conflicts can be discussed in small group settings in order to reveal how one's own cultural assumptions and values lead one to misread the behavior of those from other cultures. Examination of the conflict enables participants to understand not only their own often-unconscious cultural assumptions, but also the legitimate and rational basis for the behaviors of others. This self-awareness and awareness of others' orientations provides the basis for a greater sensitivity towards and empathy for members of other cultures by understanding one's own and others' cultural frames of reference. These critical incident scenarios can be used to determine individual's preparedness for resolution of typical problems in specific cultures by assessing the individuals' readiness to respond in a culturally sensitive way to his/her specific norms for social interaction. Assessment of specific problem areas in cross-cultural social skills (e.g., appropriate empathy, respect, social interaction styles, other awareness, adaptability, acceptance of others, etc.) helps pinpoint where to work to improve intercultural competency.

INTERPERSONAL SKILLS FOR INTERCULTURAL RELATIONS

Specific interpersonal skills for cross-cultural competence include language and communication capabilities; appropriate relational, communication and management styles; and conflict management and negotiation skills. Cross-cultural adaptation also requires social support, other people we rely upon for affiliation, affirmation, learning, emotional caring, instrumental aid and information.

Language Barriers and Communication

Cultural competence requires management of language barriers. Culturally sensitive interactions may use interpreters, but requires skills in their effective management, particularly a differentiation of translator and interpreter roles. Cultural knowledge is key to interpretation, which goes beyond translation in placing the client's communication in cultural context to reveal its full meaning. For instance, if a patient verbally denies pain, but winces when touched, an interpreter would point out cultural reasons to accept the non-verbal indications rather than the verbal statement. Even when providers and clients share a common language, communication problems may nonetheless interfere with relations. Clients are often confused by the providers' professional terms that communicate within their profession but do not afford clear communication between them and all clients. Effective communication requires expression of medical, technical or legal concepts into terms intelligible to the patient. Competence requires an ability to express understandings and communicate respectfully in a culturally sensitive manner, based in knowledge of cultural preferences, including manner of addressing people and asking questions.

Listening and Attending.
Active listening is a primary tool through which anthropologists learn about the perspectives of other cultures; it involves attention to the speaker and an effort to place what they say in the broader context of their life. To be an effective listener, one has to refrain from judgments, using cultural relativism to understand communications in the context — personal, social and cultural — of the communicator. In provider-client relations, active listening functions to assist acquisition of the patient's perspective. Cultural competence requires active listening — an effort to grasp the meaning of the range of messages and feelings communicated by others. Physical attending uses the body to enhance receptivity to communications and to show others that you are focusing attention upon them. This requires knowledge of social interaction rules of the culture, including appropriate social distance and personal space, touching, culturally appropriate eye contact and other social dynamics. At the end of Chapter 1 there is an exercise to illustrate the different styles of relating.

Communication Style.
Appropriate communication with others often involves stylistic and non-verbal cultural norms regarding social and information priorities and aspects of interaction involving posture, interpersonal space, gestures, physical and eye contact, interpersonal space, tone of voice and timing. Communication style is more than words; it is also behavior and the underlying values. For instance, a direct communication style is offensive in cultures where social pleasantries and indirect reference to embarrassing situations are preferred. Major cultural differences in communication priorities regarding how messages are delivered contrast technical and relational approaches. Technical styles emphasize information and speaking directly, openly and honestly. Relational styles are concerned with harmony and respect, avoiding offense to dignity and reputation or

disturbing others' harmony. In relational cultures, communication serves the need to maintain appropriate human relationships. Verbal communication is frequently suppressed and emphasis placed upon maintaining socially appropriate moods, emotions and relations. Communication takes place through many different dimensions, including space, touch and emotions. These "non-verbal" mediums carry the bulk of information in communicative interactions; European American preferences for direct, verbally explicit messages may lead them to miss significant communication. For many cultures, a lack of a personal relationship may impede effective clinical consultation. Biomedical interpersonal relations styles exemplify the European American task orientation. This biomedical focus upon information relevant for diagnoses, a "doctor-centered" rather than "patient-centered" approach, contributes to patients' dissatisfaction. The traditional doctor-centered interaction style is authoritarian, dictatorial, self-protective and largely unskilled in counseling and communication techniques and attempts to control the interaction with the patient. Implementation of most treatment depends upon cooperative relations between provider and client. More effective communication can be achieved by adapting different styles; providers can reduce their image as uncaring, insensitive and arrogant by adopting client-sensitive styles of communication and using non-verbal mediums to assure and encourage patients.

Establishing Personal and Social Relations: Understanding Social Interaction Rules

Cross-cultural competency requires development of satisfactory relationships and friendships with people in the other culture. Relationships provide the personal interaction necessary for identification with the social "other" as a point of reference for one's own self and behavior. Participation in the daily life of the host culture with significant social others is essential for cultural adjustment and adaptation, providing the opportunity to learn social behavior patterns through observation and social exchanges. These social support networks can also ameliorate a variety of stressors through validating self-worth, providing opportunities for expressing emotions and providing feedback and insight for understanding cross-cultural situations. Social relations provide the context for cross-cultural resocialization necessary for acquiring cultural knowledge, attitudes and perceptions and a variety of *social interaction rules*. Normative expectations regarding the ways in which people interact.

Effective functioning in another culture requires the ability to understand a wide range of cultural behaviors. Cultural competence is based on the knowledge of meaning and communication, not only those involving verbal language skills, but also the ability to understand the meaning of a wide range of cultural behaviors or nonverbal communication patterns, the social interaction rules of everyday life. Social interaction rules involve behavioral patterns, the microlevel social behavior patterns and norms of a group, including styles of relating, communicating, socializing, reasoning, managing and negotiating across diverse roles and settings. These social interaction rules include behavioral communication forms such as gestures, gaze and postures; emotional communication rules and patterns; space and touch rules (proxemics and kinesics); paralinguistic conventions; interpersonal behavior patterns and rules; and patterns of social reasoning. Social interaction rules include both the rules we know consciously (e.g., how to greet people) as well as rules we may not consciously know (e.g., proxemics or interpersonal space, and lengths of pauses used in conversations). Effective cross-cultural relations and communication requires learning many culture-specific rules for contextual social behavior. Effective functioning in a social group requires manifesting a wide range of arbitrary behaviors and styles that conform to cultural expectations. Cross-cultural conflict often results from differences in the style of behavior. The ability to respond correctly to the behavior of people in another culture depends upon the correct interpretation of their behavior and its intent and meanings. The following lists some of the primary aspects of social interaction rules.

Social Interaction Rules

Language Codes and Dialects	Contextual Communication
Paralinguistic Cues	Metalinguistic Messages
Communication Style	Relations Styles
Greetings	Formality of Relations
Family Roles	Gender Roles
Respect	Personal Relations
Presentation of Self (Face)	Self-Disclosure
Emotional Communication	Proxemics (Space)
Kinesics (Touch)	Facial Expressions
Eye Contact	Gestures and Signs
Body Posture	Time Orientation
Learning Styles	Authority Relations
Decision-Making Processes	Persuasion/Argument Styles
Negotiation Approaches	Conflict Management
Power Distance	Work Values and Attitudes

Behavioral and Communication Styles

Humans in all cultures have structured interpersonal relations for communicating information, but the priorities, forms, foci and emphases in these relationships vary widely. Establishing effective interactions and engaging in culturally sensitive behaviors in relationships with people of other cultures requires an understanding of and adaptation to these differences.

Relational and Task Orientations

One of the most significant cross-cultural differences in behavioral priorities is in terms of the differences in the importance of communication and interaction that support interpersonal relations as opposed to technically oriented interactions that support task or work orientations. European American culture was traditionally work or task oriented, as manifested in what has come to be referred to as the foundational "Puritan ethic." Work was next to godliness and one of the major sources of self-concept and self esteem. This technical or task orientation is not a universally shared priority.

While in the eyes of some cultures Americans "live to work," for many other cultures "one works to live," but work is not the primary priority in one's life.

For many cultures, interpersonal relationships take priority over the demands of work. Development of personal relationships may come first, even in the context of work. For many cultures, one must know the person with whom one is working before effective work relationships can be established. For many North Americans, relationships and friendships are subordinated to the priorities of work and business. In the U.S., an instrumental or technical orientation directed towards work goals is valued over an expressive or relational orientation, which prioritizes the value of the processes of social relations — friendship, personableness and the affective/emotional aspects of communication. Furthermore, whether we like people personally is supposed to be irrelevant to our ability to carry out our job assignments. People in task-oriented cultures can work with others whom they do not like, while people in relationship-oriented cultures will not want to work with others with whom they do not have friendly personal relations. In these cultures, personal relationships are given the highest priority, and friends and family take priority over work.

One aspect of social behavior is how people relate to power differences: some cultures emphasize power differences and avoid powerful people (strong emphasis on power differences or hierarchy), while others minimize power differences, emphasizing equality (low power difference or egalitarian cultures). Hofstede (1984) refers to these ways of dealing with human equality and inequality as "power distance." In high-power- distance cultures, rank, status, power, prestige and wealth are emphasized, In cultures with high power distance, subordinates tend to accept the power differences as a natural part of life and do not consider themselves to be equal to their superiors. These cultures do not permit subordinates to disagree with superiors, placing a heavy emphasis on obedience, and have a strongly hierarchical and centralized authoritarian social structure. People often avoid those who have greater power and treat them with deference. European American ideals emphasize low power distance, tending to downplay status differences, as epitomized in the notion of equality and a rejection of hierarchy. Low-power-distance cultures prefer expert and legitimate power and tend to downplay the differences between bosses and subordinates. Respect for the individual, equality and freedom are important, and managers may expect their employees to bring suggestions to them. The relationships between people of high- and low-power-distance cultures may involve conflicts related to the perception that people are "too pushy" or "not assertive." These differences are also reflected in communications dynamics.

Communication Dimensions, Processes and Styles

Cultural values affect how messages are produced and delivered, and the priorities for that information. Problems in cross-cultural communication are frequent in contact between people from cultures that have a personal, personable, oral and relational style of organizing social behavior; and those from other cultures who operate with a priority on technical efficiency and information. Some of the communication patterns European Americans accept in interpersonal behaviors violate other cultures' concerns with harmony and respect. European American behavior patterns such as speaking directly, openly and honest or providing constructive criticism may be seen as very rude and a devastating blow to the dignity of others. A person who speaks openly may be seen as crude, uneducated, poorly mannered and lacking appropriate restraint. Cultures have different ideas about providing information that may be disturbing, and may avoid any statements that upset others' sense of harmony or offend their reputation. Complaints are taken as personal affronts in many cultures, and constructive criticism may ruin relationships. In relational cultures, communication is seen as serving the needs for maintaining propriety in human relationships, and emphasizes control of emotions and accommodation to other needs. Verbal communication is frequently suppressed, and an increased emphasis is placed upon maintaining socially appropriate moods, emotions and relations.

Communication processes take place through many mediums. In addition to the verbal medium, other communication modes include physical dimensions such as personal space, touch and olfaction; emotional expressions, including facial, gestural and tonal qualities of voice; social and behavioral dimensions; visual aspects, including dress, cosmetic appearance, gestures and context; and temporal contexts, such as timeliness and the distribution of events in time, including the pace of speech. These "non-verbal" mediums carry the bulk of information in communicative interactions, although they may occur mostly subconsciously. The European American preferences for "direct communication" involving verbally explicit messages often lead them to miss significant parts of the communication interaction. The very term "non-verbal communication" indicates how much we emphasize speaking over the behavioral aspects of communication.

Cultures emphasizing dependence upon context and implicit understandings are referred to as "high context," while those emphasizing explicit verbal statements to communicate meaning and organize activities are "low context." European Americans are a low-context communication culture, with most of the information in the explicit verbal code. High-context communication cultures understand most of message in the physical context or internalized in common understandings. High-context cultures will avoid getting directly to the point, and may avoid verbally communicating information of a negative or disagreeable nature altogether, instead allowing context to implicate the messages that are socially undesirable. Low-context cultures emphasize technical aspects of the situation and tend to interpret misunderstandings as related to a problem with information. In contrast, high-context cultures emphasize the affective, personal and emotional dimensions of the interaction, and tend to interpret misunderstandings as related to problems of an expressive, affective or personal nature.

Recognizing such communication differences can provide the basis for more effective communication interaction and an appropriate focus on the interpersonal dimensions of difficulty instead of mistakenly assuming it has to do with failed technical expertise. In contrast to the direct communication styles exemplified in European Americans' "straight talk" is an indirect style concerned with the needs and reputation of a group, including harmony. Concern with interpersonal dynamics of group harmony emphasizes the use of an ambiguous and imprecise verbal code in which important information is embedded in what is left unsaid or manifested in behavioral channels. Cultures valuing indirectness may avoid saying no, instead using ambiguity to circumvent conflict, even giving answers that satisfy desires of the receiver at the cost of the truth. Other differences in communication patterns reflect the relative importance of information versus expressiveness. Instrumental and technical communication styles emphasize the use of the exact language necessary to get the message across, neither more nor less than is needed to assure that the speaker is understood. These styles are characterized by the use of sender-oriented language patterns, goal-oriented processes and an emphasis on technical information. In contrast to this "information-only" orientation are the elaborate communication styles that use a rich and expressive language, including embellishment or exaggeration of the facts. This flowery language often irritates people who favor technical styles, while its expressiveness and excessive praise meets the needs of relationship-oriented cultures.

Management of Self and Others.
The managerial adaptations required to function effectively in cross-cultural environments are reflected in what Harris & Moran (1991) 0refer to as the "Global Manager" in their *Managing Cultural Differences.* The "Global Manager" is a cosmopolitan, intercultural communicator who can lead cross-cultural adaptation and cultural change in work and organizational settings and create cultural synergy. The global manager must be culturally self aware and interculturally sensitive, a cross-cultural performer who can adjust to diverse work cultures and individuals. The global manager is a leader who can operate in a pluralistic cultural environment and is flexible enough to be able to adapt to people of different backgrounds. Cultural sensitivity is the basis for a concerted effort to acquire relevant knowledge about the effects of culture upon behavior and use this awareness as the basis for effective relationships with culturally diverse individuals and groups. The global manager understands the culturally conditioned nature of his/her own and others' behavior and the impact of culture on communication and relations. The global manager is capable of managing cultural influences and differences, and can adapt his/her management style to the individual as well as to local practices and situations. The global manager is able to apply cultural understandings to the peculiarities of motivation of people from the cultures involved. The global manager can move between work cultures and business practices, effectively dealing with people of different backgrounds and behaviors. The global manager combines all of these capabilities in the creation of cultural synergy, integrating different cultural potentials into a system with common benefits exceeding the potentials of the individual cultures.

The Universality of Human Relations Management.
Managers who unconsciously privilege their own cultural assumptions will have problems because

Universalist Assumptions	Other Culture Orientations
Express doubt	Portraying competence
Take input from subordinates	Maintain privilege and hierarchy
Be honest	Save face, honor
State clear expectations	Be controlling, indirect
Encourage subordinate independence	Emphasize collective needs
Determine responsible parties	Maintain group, harmony
Encourage participation	Hierarchical division of labor
Share credit	Maintain prestige, power

American Human Relations	Contrastive Cultures
Speak cheerfully to people	How to maintain position, authority
Smile at people	What do smiles mean? when are they appropriate?
Call people by their name	Formality (titles)
Be friendly and helpful; assist people	Role expectations, interference
Be cordial	Personable and friendly
Be genuinely interested in people	But do not ask about wife, daughters, money, health
Be generous with praise	Not exposing people to special attention
Value other's opinions	You want me to make decisions, pay me your salary
Be alert to give service	Social role expectations

of differing cross-cultural assumptions. This is illustrated in Harris and Moran's review and critique of an international management-training program that suggested a universal human relation approach based on a participatory management style. The universal assumptions listed above on the left are contrasted with dominant value orientations found in other cultures.

While human relations perspectives in management have been widely touted as a solution to intercultural relations, they are not globally applicable due to cross-cultural differences in social behavior and expectations. Human relations management theories reflect the expectations of the North American culture that has developed these ideas. Alongside the American Human Relations perspectives listed above are conflicting expectations found in other (contrastive) cultures.

Managing Cross-Cultural Conflict

Conflicts are inevitable in intercultural contact because these problems are based upon different priorities and an inability to understand one another. Conflicts and misunderstandings will happen, so it is necessary to utilize actively approaches to minimize them. A key perspective is realizing that differences do not mean that someone is wrong. Instead of finding fault and escalating conflict through personal blame, the cultural rationales behind people's behavior must be understood. We can reduce conflict by making an effort to identify the learned cultural factors that influence each individual's behavior. The normal tendency to escalate conflict through personal blame (or attribution; see below) can be replaced by a conscious decision to understand the other culture's rationale for their behavior. Central to cross-cultural adaptation is an understanding of the nature and causes of conflict between people of different cultures. Virtually anything can cause cross-cultural conflict. Preparedness for this conflict and the implementation of behaviors and attitudes for constructively solving these problems is essential for effective cross-cultural adaptation. Even if we can resolve intercultural conflicts, adapting to another culture is not an easy task. There are many obstacles to effective performance in another culture — language barriers, culture shock, misunderstandings, prejudices, etc. Recognition of these problems and developing effective means of overcoming these challenges are essential to successful cross-cultural adaptation. Chapter 5 addresses some of the sources of these conflicts and strategies for overcoming deep-seated cultural tendencies that lead people into conflicts.

Management of the conflict process can be impeded by both personal psychological barriers, and interpersonal conflict style barriers. There are many dimensions of difference in terms of how conflict is handled: passive avoidance, active attention, interactive collaboration, compromise, competition or active confrontation. Important factors include the culture's evaluative views of conflict, the social values that prevail in terms of how conflict is managed and communication and decision-making strategies.

In cross-cultural relations, Americans often seek explanations about a conflict at the level of the technical interaction. However, most of the time, conflicts derive from the interpersonal relations rather than the technical issues. While North Americans tend to be direct and confrontative in conflicts, many other cultures have alternative means of handling disputes and conflicts, including being indirect or avoidant, apologizing even when they are not at fault or seeking the services of mediators or go-betweens to minimize loss of face. A vital priority for North American companies is recognition that our cultural tendencies tend to escalate conflict. Our frank discussion of differences, directness in identifying problems, looking to blame responsible parties and legal responses all escalate conflict, especially in cultures that practice conflict avoidance and "face-saving" maneuvers.

Conflicts and disputes may be managed, where there is an effort to reduce the impact of the conflict, or they may be resolved when a solution regarding the source of the conflict is determined and implemented. We can extend our ability to avoid or manage intercultural conflict successfully through a series of steps, including (1) recognizing sources of conflict, (2) developing

procedures for preventing and successfully resolving conflict and (3) gaining knowledge of the cross-cultural variation in styles of manifesting and managing conflict. Conflicts may have both manifest aspects (that which people recognize as the problem) and latent or hidden elements (either a hidden agenda or sources of culturally or personally based conflict of which neither party is aware). Conflicts may be happening even if neither party recognizes that there is a conflict. The conflict may remain implicit, hidden, unarticulated and unrecognized. Because of unconscious dynamics underlying the behaviors producing the conflicts, the person's social ego may be unaware of what is causing the problems. The conflicts are manifested as dislike, irritation, discomfort, etc., without recognition of the source of the problem.

Avoidance and resolution of conflict requires a recognition that conflict can be caused by any aspect of cultural behavior, including emotions, nonverbal communication, values and beliefs, personal space, dress and appearance, time norms, learning styles, work habits, management styles and so on. The normal reaction to conflict is personal attribution, blaming the other party in the conflict for the problems. The personal attribution approach will escalate conflict as parties accuse one another of being responsible for the conflict. An alternative approach to cultural attribution anticipates conflict, but instead of attributing the conflict to personal factors, the underlying cultural factors causing the dispute are recognized as fundamental. Instead of blaming the other person, understanding the nature of the hidden cultural agenda becomes the priority. This then enables the individuals involved in the conflict to seek cultural reasons for each other's behavior and then work out the conflict based on this understanding. Similar approaches are recommended for managers who have to deal with "difficult employees"; understanding the other parties' reasons for their behavior generally provides a perspective from which to see the reasonableness of the other parties' concerns. Cross-cultural problem solving describes problems or conflicts from the perspectives of the two cultures involved and develops an understanding of how both perspectives are correct. This awareness of possible solutions from each of the cultural perspectives provides the awareness of basis for identifying a synergistic solution integrating the two perspectives.

Cross-cultural problem-solving skills are necessary for adapting to the cross-cultural context because they provide a means of reducing conflicts. Understanding the inevitable conflicts from the point of view of the host culture is fundamental, and requires "bracketing" or setting aside one's own cultural definition of the situation and problems. A key method for resolving cross-cultural problems and conflict consists of understanding problems and conflicts from the point of view of the other culture, suspending one's own cultural definition of the situation and problems. Resolution of cross-cultural problems can be achieved by identifying, describing, analyzing the problem from *both* cultures' points of view in order to develop a synergetic solution that combines both cultures' concerns and perspectives. In addition, developing a perspective from a third culture's point of view is often a useful way of developing alternative solutions and the detachment necessary to accept different perspectives and avoid conflicts. These perspectives require that we inhibit the normal tendency to see the world from our own culture's point of view.

Mediation of Conflict

Successful interaction with people from other cultures requires that we understand different means of resolving disputes, utilizing styles of conflict management found cross-culturally. Many societies use mediation and other informal means of settling disputes instead of relying on legal systems, as is typical in North America. Mediation can be defined as a process of intervention between different parties regarding a conflict, with the purpose of achieving a settlement of conflict by reconciling the different interests through compromise. Mediation is typically achieved through the services of a third party who assists the parties in reaching a mutually acceptable resolution of their conflict in a manner consistent with their interests and needs. While a mediator

is often defined as a disinterested, impartial third party who is without power or authority, this may not be true in other cultures. Conflicts at a personal level may be addressed through an intermediary or go-between who attempts to resolve the differences between disputants without the conflicting parties' having to engage in face-to-face interaction. This saves face, reduces hostilities, helps prevent escalation, allows for outsiders to provide solutions, etc. Where disputes occur between members of the same group, a respected member of the group may be asked to mediate between the disputants and seek a resolution acceptable to both parties without an escalation of the conflict that face-to-face contact can create.

To be effective in using mediation, we have to recognize conflict, conflict styles and appropriately seek assistance. Cultures differ considerably in the ways in which they manifest, manage and resolve conflict. Conflict styles contrast in the following ways:

* Control or forcing style characterized by direct confrontation, imposition, arguments and attempts to resolve conflicts through the use of power (very American);
* Non-confrontational and soothing style emphasizing a reduction or an avoidance of conflict through indirectness or withdrawal and with a concern for relationships and approval of others;
* Issue style associated with "negative self face" or protection of one's reputation or autonomy; and
* Solution oriented style integrating the needs of the different parties into a mutually acceptable solution.

A central issue in conflict resolution is the concept of "face," involving the social presentation of self — claims that one makes for one's social representation and which one expects others to accept and validate in the course of social interaction. Cultures have a variety of rules about "face work" maintenance that must be recognized in determining how to manage conflict.

Developing a Multicultural Self

Success in cross-cultural relations requires a desire to learn about the new culture and to change consciously and adapt to function effectively within it. Cross-cultural adaptations require changes in emotional reactions, personal behavior, socially defined roles and reference groups. Learning to behave and react in new ways will impact one's sense of self (e.g., men hugging other men without sexual or homophobic reactions) and necessarily lead to the creation of a new sense of self and identity. Managing cross-cultural relations requires adaptations in personality and the development of personal comfort with new culturally defined roles that go along with changes in cultural behavior and reference groups. As one changes one's emotional reactions, developing new behaviors and identifications, a transformation of oneself will necessarily occur. Learning to function in another culture involves a form of personal development, and effective cross-cultural adaptation inevitably leads to changes in personal and social identity as a consequence of the relationships developed with others in the culture. Cultural adaptation requires manifesting social and expressive behaviors that are understood in the host culture. These new behaviors will bring about changes in the individual. Successful cross-cultural adaptation means that one becomes bicultural, integrating one's original identity with a new identity created in interaction with the new culture. One cannot become a competent intercultural communicator and establish effective cross-cultural relations without developing multicultural aspects of the self. Accepting new ideas, manifesting new behaviors and undergoing new experiences will change the individual. To produce personal intercultural effectiveness, one can facilitate self-transformation through personal behavior based on Harris and Moran's "Global Manager" model. This person seeks to develop intercultural communication skills, leading cross-cultural adaptation and cultural change in work and organizational settings. The global manager understands the culturally conditioned nature of his/her own and others' behavior, and consequently adapts his/her self-expression and interaction style to the local circumstances. In moving between different cultures, styles and individuals, the global manager combines new influences in a cultural synergy that transforms him or her as a person. Key to this transformation is the development of self-awareness of one's values and their cultural sources.

Summary

Success in intercultural relations requires a desire to want to do what it takes to succeed in learning about a new environment and to prepare consciously and deliberately for successful adaptation. One must make a commitment to do what is necessary to change, adapt and transform oneself beyond one's current cultural limitations. Wanting to learn about other cultures and improve one's intercultural adaptation requires a commitment to personal development. Flexibility and openness to the ideas of the other cultures and development of a positive regard are essential. Cross-cultural relationships are a part of the cross-cultural adaptation and learning process. The sources of our learning and ultimate source of guidance in becoming cross-culturally proficient and competent are relationships with people of that culture. The ability to establish rapport with the people of the culture is the basis for cross-cultural competency, with relationships of personal harmony and mutual benefit across the cultural barrier being the essence of cross-cultural competency and intercultural skills. Cross-cultural competency is a continual process of learning and adaptation that transforms one from a culturally encapsulated individual into a multicultural and culturally pluralistic self. Because of the diversity of cultural groups found in the U.S. today (as well as virtually every society of the world), cross-cultural competency requires a continual process of learning and adaptation. We have to continue to learn, adapt and acculturate to new cross-cultural contexts as life in all parts of the world continues to become more culturally pluralistic. Furthering multicultural adaptation and cross-cultural competence depends upon general cultural orientations to the dynamics of intercultural interaction and adaptation. The fundamental aspects and patterns of cross-cultural interaction and adaptation provide the basis for understanding the social dynamics to which we must adapt.

REFERENCES AND ADDITIONAL READINGS

Abe, Hiroko and Richard Wiseman. 1983. "A Cross-Cultural Confirmation of the Dimensions of Intercultural Effectiveness." *International Journal of Intercultural Relations* 7:53-67

Adelman, M. 1988. "Cross-Cultural Adjustment A Theoretical Perspective on Social Support." *International Journal of Intercultural Relations* 12(3):183-204.

Bochner, S., ed. 1982. *Cultures in Contact.* Oxford: Pergamon.

Brislin, R., K. Cushner, C. Cherrie and M. Yong. 1986. *Intercultural Interactions A Practical Guide* Sage: Beverly Hills.

Casse, P. 1982. *Training for the Multicultural Manager.* Wash., D.C.: Sietar.

Casse, P. and S. Deol. 1985. *Managing Intercultural Negotiations.* Wash., D.C.: Sietar International.

Cui, G. and Van den Berg, S. 1991. "Testing the Construct Validity of Intercultural Effectiveness." *International Journal of Intercultural Relations* 15(2):227-241.

Fisher, G. 1980. *International Negotiation A Cross-Cultural Perspective.* Yarmouth, ME: Intercultural Press.

Furnham, A. and S. Bochner. 1986. *Culture Shock.* London: Methuen.

Hammer, M. 1987. "Behavioral Dimensions of Intercultural Effectiveness: A Replication and Extension." *International Journal of Intercultural Relations* 11(1):65-88

Hammer, M., W. Gudykunst and R. Wiseman. 1978. "Dimensions of Intercultural Effectiveness An Exploratory Study." *International Journal of Intercultural Relations* 2:382-393

Harris, P. and R. Moran. 1991. *Managing Cultural Differences.* Houston: Gulf Publishing.

Hofstede, G.. 1984. Culture's consequences, international differences in work-related values. Beverly Hills: Sage Publications.

Hoopes, D. and P. Ventura, eds. 1979. *Intercultural Sourcebook Cross-Cultural Training Methodologies* Wash. D.C.: Sietar International.

Kelley, C. and J. Meyers. 1995. *The Cross-cultural Adaptability Inventory.* Minneapolis: NCS and Yarmouth, ME: Intercultural Press.

Kohls, R. and J. Knight. 1994. *Developing Intercultural Awareness.* Yarmouth, ME: Intercultural Press.

Kluckhohn, F. 1961. *Variations in Value Orientations.* Evanston, Ill.: Row, Peterson and Co.

Landis, D. and R. Brislin, eds. 1983. *Handbook of Intercultural Training*, Vols. 1-3. New York: Pergamon.

Seelye, N., ed. 1996. *Experiential Activities for Intercultural Learning.* Yarmouth, ME: Intercultural Press.

Walton, S. 1990. Stress Management Training for Overseas Effectiveness. *International Journal of Intercultural Relations* 14(4):507-527.

Weeks, W., P. Petersen and R. Brislin, eds. 1985. *A Manual of Structured Experiences for Cross-Cultural Learning.* Wash. D.C.: Sietar International.

NOTES

EXERCISE 7.1

INTERVIEW ASSIGNMENT

In order to learn about another culture, select an ethnic or cultural group different from your own whose members you can encounter. Next, organize what you know about the group. In particular, write down:

a) Your preconceptions about the common stereotypes associated with the group,

b) Your view of the actual cultural characteristics of the group, and

c) The dominant social interaction rules that characterize the group.

Then interview at least three people from that ethnic or cultural group. In the interview, determine the following:

a) How do the people of this group view themselves as a cultural group, in terms of their social group characteristics and psychology, particularly in terms of how they are different from your ethnic group (or the European American/White culture)?

b) How does this group views your ideas of the cultural characteristics of their group?

c) What should be known about the culture, psychocultural dynamics and social interaction rules of this group to enhance relations with them?

NOTES

NOTES

CHAPTER 8

CROSS-CULTURAL WORK IN THE HELPING PROFESSIONS

Overview

The need for cultural awareness, sensitivity and competence are recognized in a variety of professional areas, social work as well as the other helping professions. These issues of the knowledge and skill base for effective professional practice are illustrated in this chapter. Cultural competency is necessary for effectively professional performance in social work, as well as education, nursing, medicine, public health, psychology and counseling, the criminal justice system and management in all areas.

Objectives

Illustrate how cross-cultural awareness, sensitivity and competence are used in a variety of helping professions.

Illustrate some major ways in which cultural competence is used in education

Address some principal aspects of cultural competence in the health services

Discuss principal aspects of cultural competence in psychology and counseling.

Show how cultural sensitivity is incorporated in the legal system.

Describe cultural competence in occupational social work and management

Chapter Outline

Introduction: Cross-cultural Contexts in the Helping Professions
Social Work and Education
    Ethnic Sensitivity in Social Work Education
    Social Work in Schools
Cross-Cultural Issues in Contemporary Education
Cross-Cultural Issues in Social Work in the Health Services
    Social Work in Public Health
    Cross-Cultural Issues in Medicine and Nursing
Cross-Cultural Issues in Psychology, Counseling and Psychotherapy
    Adaptations to Barriers to Cross-Cultural Therapy
    Family and Child Welfare Services
Cultural Factors in Criminal Justice
    The Cultural Defense in Criminal Law
Multicultural Management in Occupational Social Work
    Cross-Cultural Perspectives in Administration
References and Additional Readings
Self-Assessment 8.1: Cross-Cultural Interactions

INTRODUCTION: CROSS-CULTURAL CONTEXTS IN THE HELPING PROFESSIONS

Cross-cultural competency is involved in the professional activities of social workers and many helping professionals. Interactions with clients of different cultural backgrounds occurs in virtually all areas of work in the public and private sectors, including governmental agencies, health education and services programs, child and elder care centers, hospitals and clinics, counseling services, schools and other educational programs, businesses and the judicial and correctional systems. Because cultural differences are produced by not only by ethnicity, but also by class, gender, professional training, education, organizational cultures and other social aspects, cultural issues are involved in all relationships with individuals, groups, institutions or communities. Cultural differences between ethnic groups and professionals are further complicated by organizational cultures of agencies and organizations. Cultural factors are central to the diverse problems helping professionals address, including individual social functioning and adjustment, personal pathologies and social deviance, personal care, family dysfunction and community problems. This chapter reviews some of the major areas of social work practice to illustrate the fundamental role of culture in addressing the needs of clients and their communities. The principal areas addressed here are social work in education; clinical social work and other applications in the health fields; psychology, counseling and child welfare; criminal justice; and occupational social work.

SOCIAL WORK AND EDUCATION

Cultural knowledge and cross-cultural skills are required in educational settings. Not only must the social work student and other helping professionals be educated, but the diverse groups of clients with whom social workers, teachers, nurses, physicians and public health professionals

work also need cultural competence and cross-cultural skills education. Social workers have a long history of work in school settings, where relations between ethnic groups has stimulated concerns about ethnic sensitivity.

Ethnic Sensitivity in Social Work Education

The necessity of education for culturally sensitive approaches in social work has been recognized by the Council on Social Work Education in its accreditation standards, which state the expectation that schools of social work make special efforts to enrich the cultural dimensions of social work education. Social work programs must provide students with multicultural perspectives in order to assure quality human services. This includes a culturally relevant curriculum in education, inclusion of a culturally diverse faculty and staff in programs and organizing social work agencies with culturally sensitive services and procedures. Social work programs have begun to address the need for their students and workers to understand their own cultural backgrounds and how they effect social work, an essential first step toward engendering cultural sensitivity and effective cross-cultural relations. This includes addressing the culture and social traditions of social work as a profession. The history and cultural traditions of social work, along with its values, beliefs and training and socialization processes, must be critically assessed, understood and modified if social work is to be both culturally sensitive and culturally relevant in a culturally pluralistic society.

Social work programs have been integrating knowledge about ethnic and cultural differences and cross-cultural adaptations derived from the other social sciences in order to develop a systematic basis for providing cross-cultural perspectives in teaching, training, research and practice with diverse cultural communities. Outlines of the fundamentals for incorporating cross-cultural understandings into social work education and practice are found in texts such as Green's (1982) *Cultural Awareness in the Human Services*; *Collaboration: The Key* (1989), edited by Gonzales-Santin, which provides insights into creating culturally sensitive relations with Native Americans in the Southwest and a Model Curriculum on Indian Child Welfare, and in Lum's *Social Work Practice and People of Color* (1996). These cross-cultural perspectives call into question some traditional assumptions of social work practice. For example, traditional assumptions of the dominant European American culture about the "normal" family system (e.g., the nuclear family) have to be abandoned in working with other cultural groups with different family structures. The failure to develop cross-cultural perspectives has caused serious problems for some groups. For instance, Native Americans have had their children removed and placed in foster homes because social workers felt that a child was abandoned and neglected, in reality, the social worker failed to recognize the child's appropriate cultural residence with extended family members.

Perspectives promoted in curricula for culturally sensitive social work education and practice have emphasized the classic anthropological approaches. These include cultural relativism — understanding cultures from their own perspectives, values, opportunities and points of view — and the comparative approach which uses cross-cultural perspectives to understand commonalities and differences in human needs and behavior. It is necessary to understand others on their own cultural terms, in relation to the overall dynamics of their cultural systems, and in regard to their culturally shaped perceptions of opportunities and desired goals. These approaches lead social workers to understand that what is valued by people of other cultures may differ fundamentally. In sharp contrast to the classic melting pot approach, which tried to ethnocentrically force a model of Anglo conformity on the diverse cultural groups, culturally sensitive approaches in social work recognize that the strength, social integrity and mental health of clients, their families and their communities are best served by reinforcing the traditional cultural institutions that organize people's lives, provide community support and give them meaning and value. Being an effective social worker with culturally different clients requires that one know and understand the existing social organization and cultural values that make people's lives meaningful. Guided with such cultural knowledge, the social worker can provide services that enhance their client's sense of well being, and provide the self and cultural pride and empowerment necessary for successful resolution of problems. Operating from a paradigm of cultural sensitivity and relevance requires solutions framed in terms of the client's cultural background, community relations and social opportunities and alternatives provided by the client's own culture and community.

Cultural knowledge and cross-cultural skills are necessary for social workers to provide competent and appropriate social services to cultural communities and avoid ethnocentric behaviors. Without cross-cultural understandings, one acts from the assumptions and values of one's own culture, which is inappropriate for relations with people from other cultures. Consequences of cultural ignorance are ethnocentric, critical and condescending attitudes, and the inability to effectively provide needed services to clients, who are misunderstood and alienated. Without cultural competencies, social workers are likely to be part of the problem, rather than providing solutions to the difficult situations that their clients face. If social services are to strengthen the abilities of clients to care for themselves, clients' cultural systems, including family life and community organizations, must be involved in ways that enhance their functioning. The ability of the social worker to foster such relations depends upon an understanding of these cultural systems. Culturally sensitive social work also requires an understanding of a number of phenomena, such as race, culture, ethnicity, minority, socialization, acculturation and assimilation.

Ethnically sensitive social work requires a proactive approach, one based upon cultural self-awareness and preparation for cross-cultural interactions. Rather than just a course in "cultural sensitivity training," self- and cross-cultural awareness requires a range of cross-cultural learning experiences. Learning about the cultural dimensions of interaction requires cognitive, affective and behavioral experiences in daily interaction with the ethnic group, in addition to books and classroom instruction. The social work process of establishing empathetic relations and rapport with clients is based upon cultural norms and expectations. This means that a simplistic application of "helping skills" and "human relations approaches" will not suffice; instead, culturally appropriate approaches based on ethnically specific social interaction patterns and appropriate emotional (affective) and behavioral responses are necessary. Culturally sensitive social work requires cultural skills acquired in daily relations with members of the ethnic group, not just in the context of casework. Such experiences provide the basis for *cultural competence*, the ability to behave in ways consistent with social expectations about competent behavior within the client culture. Green discusses the steps a social worker should take to develop such competencies. Ethnic competence includes openness to the culture's characteristics, a commitment to systematically learning about the other culture and a commitment to utilizing cultural resources as a means of cultural empowerment and to maintain cultural integrity. To achieve cultural empowerment and maintain cultural integrity requires knowledge about the cultural community and its sources of values and social strength. It also requires a commitment to advocacy in an effort to recognize and change the cultural factors embedded in social work institutions that may perpetuate discrimination and ethnic insensitivity.

Culturally sensitive approaches in social work have reconceptualized the role of the social worker in relation to the ethnic clients and communities. These new models of the social worker as advocate and broker are designed to replace the classic approaches of counselor and regulator. A key difference is that the social worker comes to understand the problems from the clients' perspectives and as a consequence of conditions in the wider society, rather than blaming the client and attempting to change the client to fit the models of the dominant cultural group. The advocate role addresses the wider societal conditions and the ethnic group's relationships with the dominant groups that produce problems. The advocate's services then focus on changing societal conditions that contribute to client problems rather than just trying to change the client. The advocate's approach

requires that the social worker be aware of the institutions of the larger society and how they affect the lives of minority ethnic groups. Advocates then often lead efforts to change institutions such as health care facilities, educational institutions and job training programs to redirect programs to better meet cultural group needs. The broker role recognizes that the wider societal conditions may be a source of client problems, and the social worker then serves as a mediator between the client and the social institutions that exacerbate, or can alleviate, the client's difficulties. Brokers may represent clients to agencies, as well as assist their clients in adopting social skills and forms of behavior that facilitate their success in dealing with the institutions of the dominant society. In essence, the broker role involves both being a cultural mediator, and teaching clients more effective bicultural skills and intercultural relation styles. Both goals obviously require an understanding not only of cultural patterns, but of societal and intercultural dynamics as well. The social worker as broker needs to learn new behaviors to utilize intercultural social skills necessary in cross-cultural relations.

Social Work in Schools

Hendricks (1997) points out that knowledge of client culture and social class is central to service delivery in school settings. The gap between home culture of the client and the culture of the school system creates many problems and barriers to success. The cultural gap makes the roles of cultural mediator, broker and interpreter between family and the school system a central responsibility of the social worker. This mediation is particularly crucial because the student will invariably acculturate more rapidly than the parents, producing additional intergenerational and intercultural conflicts within the family system. Failure to recognize the acculturation of the child, the traditional norms of the family and culture and their conflicts with the broader social values and norms will exacerbate problems. An accommodation between the different value orientations is necessary in order to reduce tensions and conflict, encourage the child's learning and adaptation to the school system and engage the parents in a mutually supportive relationship with their children and their school system. Failure to achieve effective mediation places children at risk of failure and drop out without ameliorating the acculturation-induced conflict with their parents.

A central feature of culture is language; it plays a central role in adaptation to the school setting. The fundamental role of language in social competence results in marginal performances in school for those children whose dominant language is not English. Language-insensitive evaluations have often tracked children into classes for the learning disabled, developmentally delayed or mentally retarded when their cognitive capacities were far above those levels. Formal test content and testing procedures have a wide range of cultural values and assumptions embedded within them, making "culture fair" assessments of intellectual capacity a challenge.

Awareness of one's own values, those of one's culture, and those of the social work profession are essential for developing a sensitivity to the circumstances and responses of foreign language speakers in U.S. school systems. The expectations for "normal" parental involvement in interaction with the teacher involve deeply embedded cultural values that may not be shared by parents in other ethnic groups. Traditional respect for teachers, authority or other experts often preclude the parents asking questions or seeking clarifications necessary for effective participation in their children's educational adjustments. Effective school social work must not only address the gap in parents' understanding and their lack of assuredness in relating to school professionals; it is also necessary to address institutional features that inhibit effective participation and development of the foreign language student. To provide competent and ethnically sensitive services in schools, social workers must consider the impact of professional, personal and cultural assumptions about bilingual skills, normal development, acculturation, the relative value of education, acceptability of intervention processes, questioning and clarification, empowerment and autonomy, family obligations and the importance of group heritage and identity.

Cross-Cultural Issues in Contemporary Education

The cross-cultural and interethnic issues in contemporary society have created many new opportunities and needs for the culturally sensitive social worker. They range from issues about how to instruct culturally diverse students effectively to questions about educational policies and the mission of schools in our society, including how to help a wide range of professions adapt to cultural pluralism through appropriate training. While ethnic minorities have been systematically excluded from many opportunities in the broader society, including educational institutions, U.S. Supreme Court decisions have forced intercultural relations in schools, making them one of the earlier areas in which cultural differences and relations have been addressed. Beginning with decisions related to the "Lemon Grove Incident" in California in the 1930s and *Brown versus the Board of Education* in Kansas in 1954, and following with the *Lau versus Nichols* case in 1974, court rulings have established students' rights to an equitable education. Supreme Court rulings have established that teaching students in an incomprehensible language was a violation of their civil rights, and have also required integration of educational facilities, bringing the issues of how to adapt to cultural differences to the forefront of societal concerns.

The presence in classrooms of children speaking different languages and lacking basic competencies in English led to some of the first contemporary concerns with cross-cultural issues in education. While bilingual education issues have their origins deep in U.S. history, organized bilingual programs going back to the early 1800s faced nativist and anti-foreigner sentiments that led to laws outlawing instruction in any language other than English. By World War I, bilingual education had been virtually eliminated in the U.S., but increasing cultural pluralism of the U.S. during the 1960s made bilingual education a pressing public issue once again. The necessary inclusion of children of different cultural groups within the classroom has led educators to grapple with the issue of how to manage the complexity of a multicultural society and school system. This involved not only language training for teachers and students but, more significantly, training in cultural competencies and knowledge as well. While bilingual and multicultural education have had many opponents who insist upon instant assimilation and an "English- only" policy, the multicultural present and future of the U.S. has led many educators to address the question of what kind of education should be provided for participation in a multicultural society.

One of the motives for developing bilingual and multicultural education curricula was the recognition that students of many ethnic groups were not being provided with successful education experiences. The public education systems have failed to educate large segments of many of the ethnic and cultural groups in society, as evidenced in low high school graduation rates. Rather than taking the traditional approach of blaming those groups who do not succeed in schools as being responsible for their own failure, the multicultural approach to education has increasingly accepted that it is the teachers' and institutions' responsibility to assure the success of the diverse ethnic groups that enter the school systems. The challenge is to develop educational programs that engage the student and overcome cultural and social barriers to educational success.

Societal Benefits from Multicultural Education.
While justifications for culturally sensitive education have often focused upon the benefits for ethnic minority groups, such understandings are short sighted. There is a pressing need for all Americans, regardless of their ethnicity, to be able to participate effectively in their society and economy. The educational success of all ethnic groups in our society is a vital self-interest for all Americans. The low success rates of many ethnic groups in the educational system is not just a problem for them and their groups. The widespread failure of some ethnic groups in the school system is a burden and loss to all members of society. School dropouts contribute little to the economy, and their future contributions to a high-tech economy are minimal, making them more likely to burden the economy in terms of welfare costs, the criminal justice system, health care, and many other areas. Similarly, they are less likely to

contribute to the tax base, Social Security funds or the educated work force that the U.S. needs in the future. The benefits of culturally sensitive and effective education are not just for the recipients, but for all of society, since it helps to assure productive members rather than institutionalized failures.

Multicultural education programs today represent a range of approaches and goals that reflect the diversity of society and the various ways of learning to adapt to cultural pluralism. Roles of teachers and social workers include preparing students for living in and understanding multicultural society. Like the bilingual and multicultural teacher, social workers, too, have become intercultural mediators who assist students, staff and parents in adapting to different cultural settings. Many of these cultural barriers are the structures of schools and classrooms, where traditional culturally derived teaching styles conflict with learning styles of other cultures. While the traditional teacher imparted an ethnocentric monocultural curriculum, the teacher of today has to balance the presentation and understanding of a variety of cultural groups. The traditional curriculum emphasizing assimilation to Protestant Anglo Saxon norms is not appropriate for adaptation in a culturally pluralistic society; today multicultural understandings are necessary. The need for recognition of and adaptation to cultural pluralism means that social workers have roles in assisting teachers in their adaptations to become multicultural and capable of relating and communicating across cultural barriers. Social workers have to be effective cross-cultural mediators to facilitate others' cross-cultural adaptations; otherwise, they are likely to be part of the problem rather than part of the solution of how to manage multiculturalism effectively for societal benefit. Only people with cross-cultural perspectives and skills can be effective purveyors of multicultural education.

U.S. cultural pluralism raises questions about the roles of schools and social workers in educating all students and professionals for relationships with members of the different cultures found within the U.S. Effective participation in a culturally pluralistic society requires an understanding of the different ethnic groups and phenomena basic to the study of culture and society. Central to these efforts is understanding the nature and role of ethnicity in American society and its effects upon numerous social phenomena from the economically impoverished underclass to the minority success stories. Education about the diverse ethnicities in the U.S. is fundamental in enabling people to end the cultural encapsulation that makes cultural differences a barrier to the effective functioning of a culturally pluralistic society. Cross-cultural education is a necessary part of learning how to relate effectively to this human diversity and develop a positive regard for and appreciation of the potentials embodied in the diverse cultures of the U.S. and the world. Banks' *Teaching Strategies for Ethnic Studies* (1987) examines the many dimensions of education necessary for effectively living in a multicultural society.

Part of that preparation involves recognition of the slanted views of history conventionally provided in the U.S. educational systems. American history has been written largely as the history and development of the Anglo Saxon Americans, and from the perspectives of their descendants and other European Americans. Other ethnic groups have not traditionally been portrayed as playing an important role in the development of the U.S., although they have contributed to it quite substantially (Winkelman 1998). These contributions have been systematically overlooked in the accounts written from the perspectives of those who historically dominated the social institutions of the U.S. The time has come for a fuller accounting of U.S. history, a history that is being reconceptualized, expanded and enhanced by the diverse ethnic and cultural traditions and voices that have created it. This "rediscovery" and recognition of the historical contributions of diverse ethnic groups to the formation of the contemporary U.S. is a central aspect of developing crucial cultural knowledge and cross-cultural competencies. These recognitions force us to a new understanding of what it means to be an American and a broader conceptualization of what constitutes American history, traditions and culture. This book provides a contribution to developing these broader perspectives.

CROSS-CULTURAL ISSUES IN SOCIAL WORK IN THE HEALTH SERVICES

Social work has a long history within medicine, going back to the 19th-century foundations of public health, and to the professional foundations of social work in the early 20th century, with the establishment of medical social work. Today there are many different roles for the social worker in health care, including primary health care centers, health maintenance organizations (HMOs), emergency rooms, family practice, community health centers, out-patient programs, public health education programs and private clinics. Health care applications are considered one of the major areas of future expansion for social work; the dramatic growth of ethnic minority populations makes knowledge of the cultural factors affecting health and treatment central for the social worker's effective application of professional skills.

Social workers need to use cultural knowledge and resources to recognize and address the roles of environmental, social, interpersonal and emotional factors in illness and recovery. Systems frameworks provide perspectives for integrating knowledge of the effects of biological, environmental, psychological, social and cultural impacts upon the client. Addressing the psychosocial impacts of illness requires an integration of the patient into a support system that is fundamentally cultural in nature. Cultural factors structure family relations, roles and responsibilities; social networks and community relations; and desired goals and outcomes of treatment and rehabilitation. A central role of the social worker is the coordination of family, social networks and community resources in the care of the patient. The social worker's role in coordination of diverse services and resources includes efforts to obtain needed services for clients to assist them in addressing the social factors related to illness; and in coordinating diverse resources necessary for comprehensive care of the patient (e.g., doctors, nurses, therapists). Cultural factors affect issues such as appropriate providers, acceptable procedures and desired outcomes of treatment. Illness also contributes to family dysfunction, the dimensions of which will be cultural in terms of their consequences. Assisting the family's coping with the patient's illness requires knowledge of family dynamics, strengths and weaknesses. Addressing these broader cultural dimensions includes consideration of religious, spiritual and metaphysical concerns of clients and their families. It also relies upon an ability to mobilize existing community structures and resources to address conditions afflicting a cross-section of the population, for example, chronic illness, lifestyle problems and consequences of social disintegration. Since social problems are basic to illness and recovery, social workers can play a role in the total care of patients by addressing these factors, especially through communicating their significance to others. The person-in-environment and systems perspectives basic to social work provide models for investigating and describing the multiple factors affecting the onset of disease, its consequences and factors affecting recovery. Social workers have a range of roles in health care that are based in assessment of cultural factors, including appraisal of the impact of environmental and psychosocial factors, enhancing collaboration among health care services and professionals to meet client need, engaging the family and social network's participation in care and serving as a broker linking the patient to appropriate resources. Social work's systems perspectives can play a central role in integrating understanding of the environmental, social and cultural determinants of well being into the predominantly biomedical paradigms of medicine.

Social Work in Public Health

A long-standing and central aspect of social work within health care is in the interface with public health. The historical foundations of social work and public health are intimately intertwined because of the fundamental role of social and cultural factors in disease spread and prevention. The role of poverty and other social problems in the incidence of disease and illness was recognized as requiring changes in housing, working conditions, economic resources and health care. These improvements in living conditions are as important to the health of ethnic minorities today as they were to the impoverished working classes of 19th-century England where these causal relationships were first established.

Public health today utilizes the skills of many different professions; social workers play roles in linking these diverse professionals with the ethnic clients' needs and community resources. Contemporary concerns with promotion of healthy behaviors and primary prevention through education, screening and appropriate diagnosis and treatment all require cultural sensitivity. The role of cultural factors in exposure to disease, seeking help for and communicating about conditions and responses to recommend treatments provide the context for social work contributions to providing culturally sensitive health care. As public health programs shift towards an increased concern with prevention and the promotion and maintenance of health, cultural knowledge and sensitivity has become increasingly important. The emphasis of prevention on collective social action means that an awareness of cultural patterns of behavior is fundamental. Cultural factors are central to the major areas addressed by preventive public health in concerns with behaviors, lifestyle, environmental relations and the organization of health care institutions and programs. Culture is a major determinant of risk behaviors embodied in behaviors and lifestyle, while environmental relations and health care organization is fundamentally concerned with intergroup relations affected by cultural factors.

The public health model's recognition of the multiple determinants of prevention makes the social work perspectives based in ecological and systems models and biopsychosociocultural interactions particularly useful. Cultural factors are central to the public health approaches of enhancing individual and community strengths, particularly the utilization of community resources and interpersonal social support networks. Efforts to reduce stress must recognize the personal, and hence cultural, nature of the interpretations that lead to stress reactions. Bloom's (1995) review of the major technologies of primary prevention practice and the associated paradigms involves a plethora of cultural factors:

appropriate education, "natural" caregiving, community and societal change and "coordinated and integrated action involving all levels of intraindividual, interindividual and group or organizational systems and the physical and cultural contexts involved" (p. 1896). Social workers address these contexts and their interaction in schools, employee assistance programs, recreational programs, substance abuse programs and a variety of agency settings. Bloom points out that in regard to ethnic minority groups, these primary prevention services require special sensitivities in developing community-based programs that incorporate ways to address the specific culture's strengths and weaknesses and its values and perspectives.

The three principal foci of prevention — primary, secondary and tertiary — all have major cultural dimensions. Primary prevention of contact with disease conditions requires changing patterns of behavior. Secondary prevention concerned with early diagnosis and intervention requires providing education and encouraging health care utilization patterns, often necessitating changes in habitual cultural behaviors. Tertiary prevention concerns of rehabilitation must address cultural factors in understanding family and community support networks, as well as culturally contextualized goals for rehabilitation. Pubic health activities in primary care contexts involve social workers in roles in assessment and counseling, as liaisons to community organizations, in performing community health assessments, in planning and administering health services, in providing health education and in developing public policy (Oktay 1995). Primary health care involves the "first contact" with health services; the cultural factors mediating people's presentation for and acceptance of such services makes cultural sensitivity necessary, not only in serving the ill, but also in assuring their timely and adequate treatment to reduce risk for the population in general. Treatment is not merely physical care, but a social and culturally mediated interaction where conflicts result in low levels of compliance. "Because patients' and their families' beliefs about health, lifestyles, health practices and cultural patterns all play a role in patients' compliance with treatment, it is important for

practitioners to have good communication skills and knowledge of their patients' *culture* to encourage patients to comply with treatment and to prevent chronic illness through effective health education. . . . In the coming years, the understanding of *cultural* factors and their contribution to health care will become increasingly important to the delivery of effective health care in this country" (Oktay 1995:1890, emphasis added). While the identification of cultural factors has been traditionally the providence of anthropologists, it may be social workers who have the primary role in communicating these factors to health care teams and in educating health care providers regarding providing culturally appropriate services.

Cross-Cultural Issues in Medicine and Nursing

Nursing has adapted to ethnic concerns in the health care context over the last half a century, with the establishment of transcultural nursing. Cross-cultural medicine has also come to the forefront as physicians have come to recognize that the effective practice of medicine cannot be achieved unless the health care practitioners understand the culture of their patients and establish effective cross-cultural relations. Transcultural nursing and cross-cultural medicine emphasize that the patient's culture affects numerous aspects of the medical interaction, including presentation for treatment, reporting of symptoms, communication about illness, conceptualization of problems, understanding diagnoses, compliance with treatment plans and the process of healing. Social workers with ethnic knowledge can have an important role in assuring more effective utilization of medical resources by facilitating communication about and management of illness (as opposed to disease); and through coordination of diverse healing resources, including the patients' own family and community-based cultural healing resources.

Communication is necessary for effective medical treatment of virtually all conditions, since compliance with treatment, including self-care after discharge, is necessary. Without effective communication with patients, their effective participation is not possible. Cultural factors are central to a primary problem facing doctors — the compliance of patients with medical recommendation. Low rates of compliance with medical advice are directly related to two-way communication failures: the provider's understanding of patient complaints, and patient's understanding of medical plans and the rationale for them. Effective medical practice requires that health care providers understand the patient's concerns or the rapport necessary for compliance will not be established. The doctor's technically correct diagnosis and effective treatment plan may be ignored if it is meaningless to the patient and fails to address his/her concerns. Patient-provider relations invariably require cross-cultural communication skills, even if both are from the same ethnic group, since medicine uses a specialized vocabulary not shared by the general population. Emotional aspects of medical communication are also problematic in cross-cultural relations. While doctors have been taught to communicate emotional neutrality, patients from many cultures consider emotional rapport to be necessary for relationships and understanding. If appropriate emotional communication is not established, other aspects of the communication process may be ignored. This means that social workers can play a central role in mediating between the conceptual and communications systems of health care providers and their culturally different populations, using skills of cross-cultural communication and intercultural mediation to assure an effective bridging of the different cultural realities. This requires knowledge of the client's conceptual frameworks.

Illness and Disease.
Effective communication includes not only language, but also the conceptual framework which patients use to understand their conditions and their treatment. The terms illness and disease have been used as a conceptual framework for differentiating between what patients experience and what doctors diagnose, respectively. Disease is the medical perspective that sees health problems as being the consequence of a biological organic dysfunction. Illness is what the patient

experiences, including not only physical manifestations, but also the personal, cognitive, social, emotional and spiritual changes that result from health maladies. The patient's experience of illness generally has limited correspondences with the physician's concepts of disease. Patients' experience of illness is tied to cultural meanings, and their experience of distress may be the result of personal, social and cultural consequences rather than biological dysfunction. If medical models and explanations in terms of disease are not sufficiently congruent with the patient's perceptions of his/her illness, then non-compliance, and consequently ineffective treatment, is highly likely. Being able to communicate with the patient within the symbolic system he/she understands and accepts is essential for achieving compliance. Effective communication requires not only understanding the language but also the cultural system of meanings used to conceptualize health and illness conditions. Cultural rather than medical beliefs generally dominate most patients' conceptualization of health problems. A central aspect of cultural conceptualizations of illness are represented in "culture-bound syndromes" or "folk illnesses" that represent culturally specific ways of conceptualizing the experienced reality of illness and communication about the illness process. While these systems of explanation may include religious and supernatural components, they are the cultural symbols representing the linkages of emotions and physiology, the cultural language of illness and healing. Patients' conceptualization of and communication about their illness experiences are often limited to their own cultural conceptualizations of illness, making knowledge of them vital to effective health care provision.

The Health Beliefs and Explanatory Model.
The recognition that patients experience health problems through their own cultural systems led to the development of the health beliefs model (see Becker 1974). This proactive response in the public health sector was designed to identify patient's conceptualiztion and decision-making models as central components of both preventive and treatment actions. The health beliefs model

is designed to provide a comprehensive framework for the psychological, social and cultural factors that influence health behavior. It includes beliefs about health, illness, sick role behavior and treatment. It recognizes that what determines health behavior is the individual's beliefs about the condition and the available courses of action, rather than the medical view of the physical conditions and appropriate responses. The physician-anthropologist Arthur Kleinman (1980, 1988) has articulated the health beliefs' model as an "explanatory model." Explanatory models about the nature, causes, meaning, treatment and cure of illness/disease episodes are held by both the physician and patient, and must be bridged by the health care providers to assure compliance. Kleinman indicates that in order for the medical consultation to be effective, there must be an effective bridge between the physician's perceptions of disease and the patient's perceptions of illness. Kleinman suggests health care providers must understand and incorporate a number of aspects of the patient's explanatory model, including their beliefs regarding the cause of disease (why?); timing and onset of symptom(s) (why now?); pathophysiology of the disease (what are causes and consequences?); the natural history of a disease (what is consequence of disease if left untreated?); and appropriate treatments (what should be done?). What is done from patient perspectives invariably involves concepts lying outside of the medical model.

Lay and Folk Health Sectors

While health care providers typically conceive of treatment options within the context of their medical models, they must also be aware of cultural beliefs and practices regarding illness that provide a range of additional health resources often employed by patients. Before, during and after medical treatment, patients utilize resources from a lay or popular sector and the folk sector. The popular sector primarily involves family knowledge and resources regarding what to do about health care. Its decision-making processes about what to do may include ignoring symptoms or seeking folk or biomedical services. The popular domain of health knowledge constitutes

the first level of recourse in a hierarchy of resources potentially available to the sick person. It also constitutes the primary context within which decisions are made about health care utilization, including the utilization of biomedical resources. The folk sector, often discussed as complementary, alternative or unorthodox medicine, involves a variety of forms of healing that are institutionalized in cultural traditions, but which do not form part of the official medical system. These include midwives, spiritual healers, herbal doctors and many other healers often labeled as involving magical, religious or superstitious practices. These traditions provide important services, many of which have well-established empirical effects both in terms of physical medicine (e.g., midwives, masseurs, herbalists) and psychological treatment (e.g., spiritualists healers, witch doctors).

The folk healer sector generally provides a holistic, culturally relevant approach to health concerns. Patients from cultures with well-established health traditions often take a pluralistic approach to treatment, simultaneously utilizing both biomedicine and folk healers. If the biomedical health care providers fail to understand these cultural resources, several problems may result. The different health sectors may provide conflicting treatments or treatments whose effects compound one another to dangerous levels. Understanding folk and popular remedies is important to make sure that treatment complications do not arise, as well as to assure that cultural and community resources are being used effectively to support the patient's treatment and recovery. Social workers have a role in the mediation of these diverse resources. Physicians and patients differ in their health beliefs and views of appropriate resources. In order for clinical consultation to be successful, patient and physician must share information, with the patient's explanatory model (illness) translated into the physician's explanatory model (disease), and vice-versa. Then a treatment program can be prescribed which is acceptable within the patient's explanatory model. Non-compliance results when the gap between them is not effectively bridged. Enhancement of patient relations and communication depends upon health care providers becoming sensitive to the cultural conceptual frameworks of their patients, especially their health beliefs. Social workers can play a role in mediating these realities through the use of both ethnic knowledge and cross-cultural skills.

Mental Health and Drug Abuse

Social work's commitment to addressing the causes of mental illness and its amelioration through preventive and treatment programs requires social and cultural knowledge in addition to the traditional psychosocial and psychiatric perspectives. Addressing mental health concerns within public health and social work involves education, crises services and community-based out-patient services (Moroney 1995), all of which must be concerned with cultural factors in their conceptualization and delivery. While medicine often attempts to reduce patients' complaints to a biological dysfunction, cross-cultural perspectives illustrate that health maladies that people face have social and cultural dimensions as well. While client conditions may be medically diagnosed in terms of the dominant psychiatric classification schemas (e.g., the *Diagnostic and Statistical Manual IV*), social workers have the opportunity to reframe the client's conditions in terms of cultural systems of meaning.

A central feature of programs to address mental health needs has been the development of community mental health centers designed to provide comprehensive mental health services. The charges to these centers to provide services for the underserved has made minority groups a primary target group for receiving this assistance. The federal mandates to these centers require cultural sensitivity and knowledge for their effective implementation. Their responsibility, and that of social workers, to provide appropriate services requires that they educate other health professionals regarding the care of ethnic populations, based on knowledge of cultural factors affecting health and social behavior. The provision of specialized mental health services must take into consideration the psychocultural dynamics of the individuals in order to provide effective screening. Culturally specific forms of normal behavior, deviance and psychopathology need to be recognized. Recognition of cultural and social factors is also essential for assessing socially induced problems associated with minority status (e.g., prejudice), as well as culturally specific afflictions. Provision of appropriate services requires knowledge of cultural and community structures and the ability to utilize these as part of a rehabilitative support system. The dependence of mental health upon appropriate social relationships makes knowledge of cultural patterns of social relationships and behavior and the means of integrating the client into such networks a central skill for the social worker. The central role of outpatient clinics in rehabilitation makes knowledge of community resources and cultural patterns of behavior vital to the development of appropriate facility structures and activities. The need for community developments to prevent mental health problems and resolve them makes knowledge of the broader societal values, structures and political processes an essential tool for effective advocacy.

These community-based developments are critical for addressing the central contemporary health problems of drug abuse. The relationship of drug abuse to family dynamics, interpersonal relations and community conditions make cultural knowledge an essential element of treating the individual and resolving broader relationships that support his/her conditions. Impact of drug abuse upon families extends the social worker's concerns to addressing their disorganization and the cultural support systems that can reinforce family functioning. The need for prevention and diversion activities to discourage initiation of drug use requires an understanding of culturally rewarding alternatives. Cultural norms supporting drug use (e.g., alcohol use associated with concepts of manliness) illustrate the need for community intervention and support if patients are to achieve sustained abstinence. The social factors promoting drug use require the development of intervention programs that recognize the cultural contexts within which drug use recruitment occurs so as to provide culturally specific prevention programs aimed at vulnerable populations. This is exemplified in the anti-smoking campaigns that contextualize their message in a manner appealing to their youthful target audiences.

Major public health concerns today such as maternal and infant health problems, malnourishment, teenage pregnancy, crime and violence, substance abuse and AIDS disproportionately afflict ethnic minority groups, illustrating the fundamental need for culturally aware and ethnically sensitive public health prevention approaches to the problems affecting these individuals, their communities and the public well being. Social workers need cultural knowledge to develop appropriate prevention and treatment services to ethnic communities, and guidance to the multidisciplinary teams that characterize contemporary public health. Their cultural understandings can also help assure appropriate utilization of services, as well as reduce burdens upon health providers by preventing ineffective over-utilization resulting from misunderstandings. The increasing focus on disease *prevention* and the importance of social environment and lifestyle have required community-based health programs and increased the necessity of cultural knowledge and sensitivity. Community organization strategies and citizen involvement necessary to make such programs successful requires the ability to relate effectively to ethnic communities in forming partnerships with health and social service agencies. The success of community programs requires the use of cultural knowledge and skills in the elicitation of community involvement and ultimately its empowerment to participate in social change. The social components of disease also require social reforms that link community needs with a range of private and governmental agencies, making the social worker's roles of brokering and advocacy central to the collaborations necessary for success.

The shift in the private health care systems to HMOs and their emphasis on managed care and prevention has expanded opportunities for medical social work, particularly in the prevention of disease through health education and promotion. These settings also expand the opportunities for social workers to play a role in screening patients, particularly with respect to environmental, social and familial factors affecting health. This is reflected in the clinical social work speciality, where roles include diagnosing patient's conditions within a biopsychosocial framework that specifically considers environmental, cultural, behavioral and affective components, in addition to psychosocial effects, upon disease, illness and disability. This requires a range of cultural knowledge and skills, including cultural health beliefs and self-care practices, symptom recognition and importance, norms regarding the disclosure of health conditions and the roles of family and family members in illness responses and the interpersonal relationships of care. Knowledge of cultural patterns is essential for prevention programs, education, diagnosis and treatment through the linkage of clients with diverse resources. The final goal of rehabilitation of clients requires knowledge of culturally acceptable roles, the meaning of the affliction within the individual's ethnic community, the impact upon psychosocial functioning and psychocultural dynamics and the goals for ideal self-concept and social functioning.

CROSS-CULTURAL ISSUES IN PSYCHOLOGY, COUNSELING AND PSYCHOTHERAPY

Concerns of ethnic sensitivity and intercultural relations have been addressed in cross-cultural counseling and psychotherapy, one of the earliest and most important applications of cross-cultural perspectives within the social services. The development of cross-cultural counseling and psychology largely stems from the ethnic resurgence of African Americans and other ethnic groups in the 1960s. This ethnic revival awakened psychology from an ethnocentric slumber and began a transformation of the discipline. This cross-cultural contact within the U.S. stimulated the development of the fields of cross-cultural counseling and psychotherapy and the incorporation of cultural knowledge and cross-cultural skills into their practice. More recently, the methodological implications of cross-cultural perspectives have also begun to impact academic psychology, particularly social and developmental psychology. Additional aspects of cross-cultural applications in psychology include cross-cultural industrial psychology and training, as well as education, testing and assessment, international students, acculturation and cross-cultural relations (see Brislin 1990).

Awareness of U.S. cultural pluralism resulted in an increased concern by counseling professionals with the application of their profession across various ethnic groups. The concerns were with how cultural factors affected therapeutic processes. Problems are encountered in therapeutic interactions when culturally alien goals, values and practices are imposed upon people of other cultures. This turned critical attention to the cultural assumptions within the discipline of psychology, making it apparent that psychology represented a cultural enterprise that embodied cultural assumptions about what was normal and abnormal, how therapeutic relationships should be established, how treatment should proceed and what its goals were. Psychotherapy had been assumed to have a universal applicability that was easily shown not to be the case. The challenge to the therapist was to determine which aspects of the therapeutic approach were applicable in other cultural milieus, and which aspect of therapy had to adapt to cultural aspects of the client. Therapy for a culturally distinct group must integrate the values and goals of that culture.

Furthermore, cross-cultural counseling came to recognize that its practices had served as a tool of the status quo in subordinating minorities, serving to oppress ethnic minorities through imposing European American cultural assumptions and values. For example, vocational counseling had served as a tool of the status quo in directing minorities into lower-class occupations. Educational counseling had failed to appreciate cultural factors affecting school participation or to understand how to overcome the structural inequalities and forms of institutional prejudice that blocked ethnic minorities' efforts toward academic achievement. Psychological counseling had frequently not only failed to meet ethnic and cultural needs, but had actually been counter-productive to well being, blaming individuals for problems that were a consequence of class relations and oppression. Psychotherapeutic approaches directed towards changing the individual, who was characterized

as socially or personally deviant, presumed the need for an adherence to the norms of the dominant group. Those who failed to conform to the dominant standards were considered to "have" or "be" problems rather than recognizing the causes in broader social factors. Cross-cultural psychology rejected the traditional assumption that client's problems were a result of personal disorganization, and instead focused on the institutional and social factors that caused individual dysfunction. The shifts in perspectives required to address this oppression were mirrored in social work's theoretical movement away from psychodynamic theories to social psychological, person-in-environment and systems perspectives.

The cross-cultural counseling approach rejected the notion that ethnic groups were culturally deviant, deprived and disadvantaged. Rather, it pointed to cultural criteria of normalcy and the sociohistorical and contemporary social conditions that created conditions afflicting minority groups. As cross-cultural psychology addressed the cultural biases implicit in Western counseling and psychotherapy, it began to develop new approaches cognizant of the psychocultural characteristics of diverse ethnic groups in the U.S. Cross-cultural psychology developed perspectives distinct from the classic therapy approaches where history and the personal past were identified as the source of problems. Recognition that aspects of ethnic psychology were a consequence of historical factors and relations with dominant socioeconomic and political groups led to an emphasis on helping the client alter his/her environment and learn how to cope with inequality. Cultural relativism rather than pathology had to inform psychology if it was to develop relevance for people from other cultures.

Cross-cultural perspectives in counseling also emphasized the perspective that cultural factors must be recognized and adopted in establishing therapeutic relations. Traditional counseling approaches were rejected because of their basis in middle-class European American values, without a recognition of the different cultural values appropriate for people from other cultures. Counseling processes that depend upon self- disclosure, insight and verbal expressiveness and disclosure of family problems reflect values not shared by many other cultures. The cultural values of the client and reference group must be assessed in order to select appropriate treatment modalities and goals. The therapist must not only accommodate techniques to the client's culturally based expectations, but must be aware of the pervasive impact of the norms and values of the U.S. middle class on psychotherapy and counseling. The American values of "rugged individualism" and the need for individual efforts to improve one's psychological condition were replaced with perspectives emphasizing that therapy must help minorities alter their environment and social conditions. The cross-cultural counselor helps the client adapt and selectively adopt rather than assimilate, shaping the social milieu to support the individual rather than making the individual change to the dominant norms.

Cross-cultural therapy's approach to giving ethnic clients the skills to change their social world required that the therapist understand the cultural norms, values, beliefs and opportunities within minority cultural systems and their interaction with the dominant society. Study of the psychologies of different U.S. ethnic groups led to recognition of psychological differences reflecting culturally different patterns of normal behavior. Awareness of cultural differences in norms and values led to a realization of the inaccuracy of standard psychological assessment tools in assessing culturally different clients. Culturally inappropriate concepts of what constitutes normal behavior, interpersonal expectations and mental illness may lead counselors to view as abnormal client behaviors that are normal and accepted within their own culture (e.g. different cultural expectations on passivity, disclosure, motivation, family relations, etc.). Therapy with individuals from different cultures also requires an understanding of the indigenous categories of illness belief and treatment and their relationship to wider cultural values.

Cross-cultural psychology contributed to the recognition that cultural factors were always part of psychotherapy, although they were not generally explicitly recognized. Therapy always involves processes outside of both the therapist's and client's consciousness, but cultural differences add additional dimensions, since cultural assumptions about the world and normalcy vary. Understanding culture and its impacts is essential for effective psychotherapy, since all interactions have cultural components. Also essential are understanding cultural differences and how they are manifested in the processes of therapy and intercultural contact and communication. Appropriately adapting to the effects of culture includes not only recognizing the normative characteristics of people from specific groups, but also recognizing relevant dimensions of variation within groups. Effective cross-cultural psychology requires that the therapist knows the variation within a culture and use such knowledge as a basis for relating to clients as individuals, not stereotypes.

This recognition of a need for cultural knowledge in therapy raised fundamental questions about how those in helping relationships can work with and assist those who are culturally different. The development of cultural awareness and sensitivity triggered greater changes than European American therapists anticipated. Some ethnic psychologists demanded that cultural knowledge be considered an ethical imperative in treating ethnic clients — one cannot ethically do cross-cultural counseling or therapy without cultural knowledge and awareness. Knowledge of psychological dimensions is not sufficient; knowledge of values and broader aspects of culture and society are necessary for an effective therapeutic relationship. Relevant factors include unconscious patterning by cultural factors; societal effects such as racism and discrimination; economic effects on opportunity; and sociocultural effects on personality, occupation, value structures, behavioral patterns and expectations, communication patterns and indigenous psychologies.

Adaptations to Barriers to Cross-Cultural Therapy

Assessments of utilization of counseling and psychotherapy services by ethnic minorities indicate a general underutilization in spite of indicators that these groups suffer from greater psychological distress and are in greater need of counseling and therapeutic services. The underutilization has been recognized to be a consequence of social, cultural and institutional barriers to access. Cross-cultural therapy faces special problems from cultural barriers, as well as from more complex process variables that are part of every counseling relationship. Some barriers are economic and social, while others are interpersonal (e.g., prejudice, misunderstandings, lack of identification, culture-bound values, nonverbal and contextual modes of expression, cultural values on self-disclosure and norms about emotional expression and restraint).

Process-Oriented Problems.
Many of the ordinary processes of psychotherapy such as resistance, transference and counter-transference have different dimensions in cross-cultural context. What is traditionally interpreted as client "resistance" to therapeutic interactions and direction must be reinterpreted in a cross-cultural counseling as the therapist's failure to understand the reasons for the client's behavior. Different cultural definitions of the situation and concerns must be used as the context for interpreting reactions rather than assuming resistance. Transference, the projection of previous experiences onto the counselor, is likely to have additional aspects in the cross-cultural therapeutic setting because of the client's likelihood of viewing the counselor as a member of the majority group with whom conflicts and problems have occurred. The therapist must address not only the ordinary transference problems, but also problems that result from a history of interethnic relations. Counter-transference, the projection by the therapist onto the client as a result of previous experiences, is compounded by the therapist's previous experiences with members of the client's ethnic group. The therapist holds stereotypes, beliefs and experiences related to the client's groups that, unavoidably, influence relations with the client. Prejudices generally manifest in terms of lower evaluations of functional status. In order to deal with the counter-transference reactions that occur in the therapy setting as a result of unconscious attitudes, the therapist should develop cultural self-awareness and other cultural awareness to assess the distortions and miscommunications in the therapy process. Both therapist and client engage in an intercultural attribution process that can be effectively addressed only with cultural self-awareness.

Atkinson, Morten & Sue (1983) suggest that there are five principal characteristics of culturally effective counselors:

1) Self-knowledge, especially of value assumptions;
2) Awareness of cultural aspects of counseling;
3) Understanding of sociopolitical impacts on minorities;
4) Ability to accept the client's symbolic world; and
5) A variety of skills and theories for appropriate application.

Understanding one's own cultural values, beliefs, behaviors and self-identity is an essential aspect of effective cross-cultural counseling. Cross-cultural relations and communication skills are required for the intercultural relations necessary for cross-cultural therapy. Cross-cultural relationships require understanding the culture's norms about verbal and non-verbal communication styles, especially social interaction patterns (e.g., eye contact, touch, personal space, relationships, self-disclosure, etc.) that have important effects upon the therapeutic process. The therapist must have more than just tolerance for differences, but must also be committed to supporting diverse ethnic adaptations found in a culturally pluralistic society. Adaptation to cross-cultural counseling requires decentering from one's own culture and overcoming the stereotypes of other cultures. The cross-cultural therapist must understand the cultural factors affecting the client in his/her day-to-day living situations. These perspectives are necessary in order to help the client understand something of the nature of the cross-cultural situation in which he/she exists and how to cope with and adapt to cultural differences. Adequate knowledge of another culture requires diverse participation in the everyday life and activities of the people whom the therapist counsels. This requires a form of ethnographic study, not merely book learning or counseling session exposure. These kinds of experiences can be acquired through internships, community service learning and study-abroad programs.

Social Psychology as Cultural Psychology.
Although academic psychology has traditionally ignored the implications of cross-cultural psychology, there is evidence indicating the need to address cross-cultural issues in all of psychology, including social psychology. Social psychology as currently presented in the U.S. would be more truthfully characterized as the "social psychology of middle-class European Americans." However, social psychology has not addressed the specific historical, cultural and sociopolitical factors derived from the specific characteristics of these Americans and their social behavior. Cross-cultural psychology as a discipline has been critical of social psychology for its failure to establish that the theories are generalizable across cultures, rather than merely assuming the universality of findings. The development of a mature social psychology requires addressing the issue of what aspects of its findings are universal and which are culturally specific. Only cross-cultural research can provide the answer to these questions and determine just what is the "psychological unity of humankind."

The culturally specific aspects of social behavior are illustrated by cross-cultural differences in basic constructs of social psychology (e.g., internal-external control, personal and social motivations, collectivism versus individualism, conformity and anti-conformity). This illustrates the fundamental importance of culture in determining dispositions and social behavior. The emphasis on individualism, rationalism, directness, self-interest, personal gain and other factors characteristic of the dominant culture in the U.S. is countered in other cultures by group loyalties, limited goods and needs, indirectness, emotional control or expressiveness and other social values

that would undergird different rationale and philosophies for social behavior. Cross-cultural communication and relations studies illustrate that these differences are manifested in numerous areas, indicating the differential importance of social relations versus technical information; individual versus group responsibility; direct versus indirect styles of communication; authoritarian versus participative managerial styles; normative, intuitive, factual and analytical styles of negotiating; and modes of leadership. Important cultural differences exist in terms of groups and their role in social life, including why they are formed, how they affect social life, the extent to which new groups can be created and the role that groups play in change. Since groups are fundamental to social life, social psychology must address the cross-cultural variation in how groups affect social life.

There is such extensive variation in human behavior that claims to the universal patterns of behavior or complex psychological processes are open to question. Cross-cultural research is essential in order to establish the universality of postulated social psychological processes and theories. Cross-cultural research is likely to continue to show the limitations of generalizations derived from research in a single culture. Social psychology has been described as suffering from an insularity and narrow focus resulting from traditional approaches to defining its problems. Research in other cultures can free theories from traditional constraints embedded in the cultural assumptions about motivations, values, causes, meanings, etc. Cross-cultural data not only provides a wider variation in behavioral phenomena, but also broader conceptions of the self and psychological structures. These cross-cultural psychological differences are recognized in the emerging field of cross-cultural developmental psychology.

Cross-Cultural Developmental Psychology.
The integration of cross-cultural perspectives into psychology is exemplified in Gardiner, Mutter & Kosmitzki's (1998) *Lives Across Cultures: Cross-Cultural Human Development.* Their research illustrates the necessity of cross-cultural data and perspectives for understanding the nature of

human development and as a means of decentering the ethnocentric Western biases inherent in most contemporary and classic psychological theories of development. These culturally specific perspectives for development and social behavior are necessary to avoid an ethnocentric imposition of dominant norms and instead develop ethnic sensitivity and awareness of cultural specificities in client relations. The cross-cultural study of human development is necessary to test the generalizability of theories that claim universality, and to discover the broader social and cultural patterning of human behavior. Only then can psychological theories of human behavior be applicable to interpretation and guidance of clients' behavior. Traditional developmental and social psychology do not provide those perspectives, instead constituting an "indigenous psychology" of middle-class North Americans, or perhaps a little more generally, the more affluent of the Western world.

Family and Child Welfare Services

One of the classic foci of social work and one of its most important contemporary application is service to children and families, where cultural sensitivity is central to social workers' effectiveness. Addressing issues of neglect, physical and sexual abuse and violence are central concerns. These services may be provided through material resources, shelters, counseling centers and home visits, but ultimately the services are provided to families. Given the central role of the family in the physical, psychological and social welfare of children, social workers must know how to work effectively with families to strengthen their roles. Social work has been one of the professions most concerned with family maintenance for many reasons, including the disproportionate reliance upon social welfare by families experiencing a variety of disruptions. Social workers are often faced with the challenge of helping to establish effective family relations among people who have had little success in maintaining these basic social units. Central to social work's concerns in this area are the protection of children and the provision of

resources necessary for their adequate development, the maintenance of effective family operation and subsistence and resolution of spousal and other family discord. Meeting these goals requires cultural knowledge, especially since these problems are disproportionately found among impoverished ethnic minorities, where unmet economic needs produce increased family dysfunction.

The contemporary dictates of social work practice emphasize the service to children through the maintenance of their family systems by an emphasis on their strengths. This requires that the social worker understand the cultural family system and how to reinforce its system of ideal relations. This involves not only maintenance of the ties with the parents, but also with the extended family and immediate community. This requires knowledge of culturally specific family roles and relationships and the nature of the wider community and its institutions and practices. The integration of the relationships and resources from these many different levels — immediate and extended family, community and social institutions — requires that the social worker understand both the client family and specific sociocultural systems and their relationship to the institutions of the larger society.

Cultural factors play a number of important roles in family and child welfare services. While the family is a universal of human social life, the specific form of the family, its various statuses and roles and their functions are highly variable. Cultures have specific expectations about the functions of family members and their appropriate behavior that often conflict with the norms of the dominant culture. The cultural differences in gender roles include concerns with parental roles, outside work and household responsibilities, discipline, dominance and decision making, health behavior, self-care and many other social behaviors. Acculturative changes make parent-child relations particularly salient sources of family problems. Acculturative changes also produce and exacerbate spousal conflict, where the differences between traditional cultural norms and dominant society's sex roles can create additional strain between spouses. Awareness of these differences is essential for culturally appropriate intervention plans. Awareness of these differences can be particularly important for the "modern liberated" feminist social worker whose ideas about appropriate social roles for men and women may have departed significantly from the more traditional patterns. The normal tendency is to impose upon others' our own ideas about what is appropriate. Changing patterns of behavior contributing to female oppression (e.g., females subordinated in domestic arenas) may be important issues to consider in addressing client problems and changing behaviors. However, these recommendations should not be made as unconscious cultural ethnocentrisms (e.g., liberated women are better off), nor without consideration of cultural norms and the implications for the female client of challenging them. Encouraging "liberated" behavior without assessment of the potential consequences (e.g., reprisals) and plans to prevent this may place clients at greater risk. Protection of women from traditional practices of physical abuse, and re-adjustment of men's normative behaviors to the legal expectations of the dominant society are important issues in helping immigrant families effectively function in their new social milieu.

The removal of children from their natural families and their placement with foster families is a long-standing aspect of social work practice. These practices are generally based upon the assessment that the child is in serious risk or danger, and that the family is incapable or unwilling to care for their child. These assessments have often been made without considering the relevant culturally specific forms and ideals of care. Views of family disorganization and child abandonment may reflect the inappropriate imposition of the norms of the dominant society rather than the cultural reality of the child and family. In many cultures, extended families and elder females, particularly grandmothers and aunts, are considered primary caregivers. The extensive out-adoption of Native American children has led to federal laws mandating placement within the tribes to reduce further cultural disintegration created by removal through adoption or foster care. Issues of "race"-specific adoptions have also been raised in the context of African American children being raised

by Anglo American families; often concerns are with the practical issues of the adequacy of the "white" family to prepare a minority child to deal with the reactions of a racist society. The skills necessary for addressing the special issues of "bi-racial" families are an important part of the social worker's services.

Cross-cultural issues are also raised in the context of child-care services, where providers from one culture care for children from other cultural groups. A wide range of conflicts can emerge from the cultural differences in values regarding the appropriate way to rear and treat children (see Gonzales-Mena 1993). Conflicts and dissatisfaction with the quality of care provided by parents or staff can arise from different views of appropriate attachment, indulgence, activity, independence, sleep and feeding schedules, reinforcement and punishment. Conflicts frequently emerge in provider-client relations because of the differences between them on issues such as feeding on demand versus feeding on a schedule. Cultural differences based upon concerns about meeting children's needs versus spoiling them or meeting adults' needs can place families and service providers in conflict. Concerns about independence (e.g., self-feeding) often conflict with concerns about cleanliness or wasting food. For some cultures, feeding children is a means of appeasement and tranquilizing the child, while others reject the notion that food should be used to comfort. The issue of toilet training so important in transitioning children to child-care centers appears irrelevant from the perspective of cultures where parents, not children, are toilet trained. Parents learn to recognize the cycles of the child and subtle signs of impending need to eliminate, and take the child to the appropriate place. The management scheduling of sleep cycles for children range from cultures that attempt to instill a rigid schedule to those where the infant's sleep patterns accommodate to family activities and adult schedules. The European American pattern of separate sleeping quarters for infants diverges dramatically from common patterns found in other cultures where infants sleep with their mothers, continuing a day and night pattern of constant contact with the mother or other caretakers. These intense patterns of contact reinforce an immediate response to infant needs, including hunger and discomfort. Cultural factors also play an important role in discipline practices, which may produce conflicts with the current norms of the dominant society. The recent development of interpretations in the dominant society regarding physical punishment as criminal abuse are not shared by all American ethnic groups, where punishment may be seen as an important way of building character and respect and alerting children to social boundaries and the racism threatening their survival. Social workers may need to provide counseling regarding acceptable forms of discipline and parental authority to help prevent problems with the criminal justice system.

Gonzales-Mena (1993) suggests that in addressing such parent-provider conflicts one takes a deliberate approach that examines the source of one's and others' values, particularly recognizing the parents' perspective, acknowledging the discomfort that cultural differences produce for both parties, accessing whether practices are harmful for the child or dysfunctional in the context of the family's cultural goals and establishing a dialogue to negotiate the differences and share power in decision making. Rather than viewing other cultures' practices as deviant or deficient, they need to be recognized in terms of a culture's (historically) adaptive responses to universal human needs. These approaches recognize that the practices of socialization produce very different outcomes for normal human development, and that service providers need to adapt to these expected outcomes in establishing effective cross-cultural relations and providing culturally sensitive services.

Culture and Reproductive Status.
Another area of potential cross-cultural conflict regarding gender roles has to do with appropriate age for marriage and/or reproduction. Dramatic cultural differences exist in what is considered marriageable age, ranging from as young as 12 or 14 years old for females to the early 30s for males. Cultures also differ considerably in what is considered to be an appropriate age differential between spouses, but there is apparently a universal preference for husbands being older than wives. While the difference is typically only a few years for the European American culture, for other cultures it may approach a decade or more. These cultural differences can cause legal problems when the age gap, combined with early age of marriage, produces mating patterns that violate U.S. laws regarding statutory rape. For example, under the Mexican constitution, a female may marry at 14 years of age, or younger if pubertal and with parental consent. A lack of cultural awareness and ethnic sensitivity can produce serious legal and personal problems when common-law couples from Mexico, whose age differences constitute statutory rape under U.S. law, immigrate to the U.S. and find themselves engaged with social service or legal agencies. Such patterns have been repeatedly reported among Hispanic couples, especially Mexican Americans in southern California. The importance of the family unit, spousal support for the wife and the father role for their children has led many social workers and their agencies to take culturally sensitive approaches in supporting the integrity of the family system rather than prosecution that would destroy families and lives. Such culturally sensitive approaches reflect the consideration of cultural differences, as well as cultural and cross-cultural legal differences (see Cultural Defense below).

CULTURAL FACTORS IN CRIMINAL JUSTICE

The concerns cultural pluralism raises are central issues in American politics and the criminal justice system. The disproportionate representation of ethnic minorities in the criminal justice and prison systems of the U.S. directly reflects the importance of both social and cultural factors in addressing and resolving pressing contemporary social problems. The different realities of ethnic cultural groups also produce challenges to a legal system based upon the assumptions of what is "reasonable for the ordinary person."

Gang violence in urban areas reflects the intersection of social and cultural factors, where relations with the broader society contribute to the importance of cultural mechanisms that reinforce gang formation. While gang behavior concerns Americans as a whole, its effects are primarily inflicted upon their own ethnic communities, making the problems of gangs multiply embedded in cultural contexts. The role of gangs in providing a reference group for youth reflects both the disaffection with structures of the wider society and a lack of fulfillment of interpersonal needs within legitimate institutions and their own communities. Research illustrates that gangs may play a significant factor in adolescent socialization, particularly when other supports are lacking. Investigations of the origins of gang membership and the functions of gangs reveals their true nature to be somewhat different from the stereotype of a criminal organization. Gang membership and behavior reflects societal relations and individual needs that have combined to make gangs adaptive organizations that also have positive functions, rather than just the primarily criminal functions typically ascribed to them in the popular press.

Based on over a decade of study, Moore and Vigil (1989) conclude that "gang activities revolve primarily around normal adolescent concerns: peer respect and approval, security and protection, group support and acceptance, and age and sex role identification" (p.28). Their research indicates that gangs provide a context for development during the adolescent period when other institutions alienate the individual. Gangs meet social and personal needs, providing a context for clarification of aspects of personal identity, particularly roles and support for youth having difficulties in making the transition to adulthood, creating a context for realizing strivings for self-identity. Gang membership may also constitute a statement against conformity to the dominant culture, with gangs operating as a subculture which provides an alternative to the dominant society's values. The institutionalized prejudice and failure in schools, combined with the lack of effective familial and community reference groups, enables gangs to provide an alternate frame of reference for social support and self-esteem. Addressing gang problems requires the development of meaningful cultural alternatives to gang membership within the

community, providing additional culturally relevant ways of fulfilling the needs that they meet.

Social workers address gang problems within a variety of contexts — schools, hospitals, law enforcement agencies, court systems and outreach programs. Escalating gang problems are mute testimony to the ineffectiveness of most large-scale efforts to resolve these problems. The importance of community intervention approaches and alternatives is well recognized; these require cultural knowledge and the engagement of the community. The administrative roles of social workers in correctional programs provides the opportunity for changing existing programs to intervene more effectively in communities to prevent gang recruitment and violence and to provide effective alternatives to continued participation and recidivism. These alternatives must be cognizant of the social and cultural realities gang members and potential recruits face. In-group relations and inter-group conflict play major roles in gang dynamics, particularly recruitment, making cultural knowledge central to programs of effective resistance. Rehabilitation programs must also address these social and cultural pressures and provide meaningful alternatives, which must be culturally sensitive if they are to be successful responses. The community relationships that support gang recruitment and the social needs that make gangs important social groups must be addressed at community levels and in terms of meaningful cultural alternatives. These necessarily involve environmental and community interventions which require cultural knowledge and a variety of intercultural skills. Self-esteem issues that motivate gang participation must be addressed within the cultural milieu to provide meaningful alternatives. The central self-concept issues underlying gang participation require an appreciation of cultural perspectives on self, other and society and the implementation of systems perspectives to incorporate effectively multifactorial approaches to addressing these social problems.

An important factor affecting gang behavior and delinquency is relationships between local communities and law enforcement agencies.

Social workers have been taking increasingly important roles in mediating these relations and in training law enforcement officials in the cross-cultural perspectives and sensitivities necessary for effective relationships with the members of ethnic communities. Social workers in the criminal justice system also play significant roles in assisting judges, prosecutors and probation officers in understanding the circumstances facing individuals by conveying information about their total social and cultural environment. Their appreciation of the significant family, kin and community relationships provide important information contributing to appropriate placement, restrictions and rehabilitation. Effective prevention and rehabilitation requires changes in social networks and cultural patterns of behavior. By using cultural knowledge and systems perspectives, social workers are better equipped to address the familial, interpersonal, peer, educational and other influences affecting long-term development. Only with cultural knowledge can rehabilitation be achieved through a community re-integration that supports adaptive patterns of behavior. Social workers' ability to appreciate the individual circumstances in cultural context, as well as affect, cognition and behavior, provides them with crucial information relevant to the disposition of court cases. In this capacity, social workers are increasingly functioning as expert witnesses affecting the disposition of criminal cases. Their understanding of cultural factors affecting behavior can provide important insights into behavior and appropriate disposition of offenders, as illustrated in the concept of the "cultural defense."

The Cultural Defense in Criminal Law

Cultural factors have received increasing attention in criminal defense proceedings, manifested in the popularly recognized "cultural defense" (Lyman 1986; Notes 1986; Sams 1986; Sheybani 1987; Rentelen 1993; Winkelman 1996; this section is largely summarized from Winkelman). The cultural defense refers to criminal defenses in which cultural factors motivating a defendant's

behavior are considered relevant to establishing motive, state of mind, and mitigating and extenuating circumstances. Because cultural pluralism has been at the foundation of American society, there has been a responsiveness of law to diversity (Norgren & Nanda 1988). This is exemplified in long-standing features of the American legal system that permit inclusion of cultural factors in establishing excuses and mitigating and exculpating circumstances. Cultural defense is not recognized as a specific defense, but cultural factors can be considered in the context of traditional defenses.

Uses of the cultural defense have been highlighted by coverage in major newspapers of the cases of Asian immigrant defendants (e.g., *Los Angeles Times*, *Wall Street Journal*). Parent-child suicide (*oyako-shinju*) was attempted by a Japanese woman living in the U.S., who followed the traditional practice of suicide rather than living in the shame and humiliation of her husband's marital infidelity. While the mother was saved, the children drowned, leading to first-degree murder charges. Instead of an explicit cultural defense, a psychological defense based on insanity and emotional illness led to plea bargaining to reduced charges of voluntary manslaughter and a one-year prison sentence, with immediate release for time already served. The outcome was similar to typical Japanese adjudication of such situations as involuntary manslaughter and imposing a light suspended sentence. This reflects the functioning of the cultural defense via consideration of cultural factors in the negotiations of the charges and sentencing. Other cases have involved the Hmong tradition of marriage by capture (*zij poj niam*) as a culturally legitimate form of matrimony. This was traditionally preceded by ritualized male flirtation, with the female responding through exchange of tokens and joint social activities signifying acceptance of the courtship. When the man comes for his bride, however, the women is traditionally required to protest, but her refusal is viewed as culturally prescribed and construed as acceptance. The man ignores the (presumably) mock objections, kidnaps her and consummates the marriage. The need for a recognition of cultural factors in such cases in the U.S. is illustrated by the problematic nature of prosecution: prosecutors have been forced to drop most cases because the victim appeared to accept the marriage and declined to press charges.

There has been, however, widespread vocal and public opposition to acceptance of the cultural defense, especially in well-publicized cases where the traditional cultural norms justifying abuse of women have been argued to be exculpating circumstances. Others have suggested that the cultural defense operate far more frequently in prosecutors declining prosecution of mothers who commit child abuse in punishing their children according to traditional norms. A frequently voiced objection to the cultural defense is that it allows foreigners to do something a native-born citizen could not. The popular notion of the cultural defense is often a misleading view of the cultural factors of relevance to legal deliberations. The use of the cultural defense does not allow the foreigner rights not available to the citizen, but presents cultural information to make the same rights available to the foreigner as to the native-born citizen (Winkelman 1996). Cultural factors provide the foreigner with the same provisions of the legal code by illustrating the cultural context within which legal factors such as reasonableness, state of mind, provocation, presumption of facts and extenuating and mitigating circumstances operate. Recognition of the cultural defense and cultural pluralism, which supports our societies' emphasis on equality, is consistent with American cultural values and respect of human rights, self-esteem and identity (Notes 1986).

While legal authorities differ in opinion as to the precise applicability of cultural factors in legal defense, there is a general consensus that their applicability is largely in establishing the defendant's "state of mind" (*mens rea*), and in terms of the category of legal defenses called excuses. The traditional category of excuses includes recognition of personal characteristics as an excuse for criminal behavior, or to establish mitigating circumstances. Cultural factors may provide evidence about the actor's "state of mind" during a crime, a requisite factor in determining the actor's culpability. Crimes are generally considered to have both physical and mental components, legally known as the *actus reus* — the guilty act, and *mens rea,* the mind at fault, the

guilty culpable state of mind, which is a required mental condition generally needed for criminal guilt (Sheybani 1987:752-3). These mental factors are central in differentiating between whether or not a crime occurred, or the various degrees of a crime, for instance, different types (degrees) of homicide. The Model Penal Code assesses specific states of mind in defining the elements of murder versus manslaughter. "The Model Penal Code section 210.2(1)(a) focuses the inquiry on the defendant's subjective state of mind...Certain factors...mitigate a criminal homicide to the lesser offense of manslaughter. Under Model Penal Code section 210.3(1): 'Criminal homicide constitutes manslaughter when: (a) it is committed recklessly; or (b) a homicide which would otherwise be a murder is committed under the influence of extreme mental or emotional disturbance for which there is reasonable explanation or excuse. *The reasonableness of such explanation or excuse shall [sic] be determined from the point of view of a person in the actor's situation under the circumstances as he [or she] believes them to be*'" (Sheybani 1987:757, 759, emphasis added).

Excuses are a category of defenses that have been long recognized in criminal law in establishing liability, or seeking exculpation based upon some disability of the defendant. Excuses and their grounds are part of the definition of *mens rea* requirements. Excuses constitute recognition that the act of the defendant was unlawful, but seeks to "forgive the actor because she lacked the requisite culpability" (Notes 1986:1296). Although they have not generally been widely accepted, they have been used successfully, and recently in new ways (e.g., defenses of brainwashing and "rotten social background," battered-spouse defense and Vietnam veteran defense).

Defects of knowledge constitute excuses because lack of knowledge constitutes the lack of adequate *mens rea*. In contrast to the truism that "ignorance of the law is no excuse" is the fact that ignorance of the law does constitute a defense when it negates the mental state necessary for a crime to have occurred. The Model Penal Code provides that "Ignorance or mistake as to a matter of fact or law is a defense if: (a) the ignorance or mistake negates the purpose, knowledge, belief, recklessness or negligence required..." (cited in Sams 1986:338). Cultural factors could lead to a "mistake of fact" which would negate criminal intent. This is because the defendant's subjective state of mind, resulting from cultural beliefs and societal norms, can be considered in determining misunderstanding of the situation and consequences, as opposed to criminal responsibility. Legal systems have found acquittal, absolution or insanity in cases where defendants killed devils, witches or supernatural beings — in human form. The mistake of fact argues that the client lacked the requisite mental state — intention and knowledge of consequences of acts.

Nonresponsibility is an excuse and extenuating circumstance when one could not be expected to act otherwise, given inadequate capacities for judgment and choice. The law has recognized this in the legal insanity defense, where mental illness prevented someone from conforming to the law. The *Harvard Law Review* (Notes 1986) suggests that the cultural defense in the context of the insanity plea strains the definition of mental disease to the point unlikely to be accepted. This is particularly likely to be true when the definition of mental disease is limited to those defined by the *Diagnostical and Statistical Manual of the American Psychiatric Association*. The broader view of mental illness incorporating the concept of "folk illness" and "culture bound syndromes" is necessary to incorporate effectively cultural factors within the traditional insanity defenses (Winkelman 1996).

The role of cultural factors in a criminal defense have been limited to specific areas of traditionally accepted defenses: *mens rea* or state of mind; mistake of fact as to circumstances or consequences of behavior, duress and non-responsibility because of constraints on will, immaturity and insanity. Cultural factors can be used to reduce charges or mitigate punishment by establishing certain mental states, the actor's situation and perceptions and extenuating circumstances. Cultural factors may establish the defendant's state of mind at the time of the crime, indicating, for example, lack of knowledge or cultural factors that may have contributed to provocation or diminished capacity. Cultural

imperatives for behavior and culture-bound behavior disorders or folk illness may establish grounds for an insanity excuse or show that a person may not be in control of his/her conduct. Cultural factors are also widely accepted in determining the defendant's character and background during the penalty phase.

Societies predicate criminal laws and sanctions upon their own cultural norms about reasonableness (Lyman 1986). A person from a different culture might not be able to exhibit the rationality and practical reason expected in another culture. An important utilization of cultural perspectives lies in orienting the defense and jury to the cultural factors that may establish both the normalcy and deviancy of an individual's behavior. The writer's experience and reflection on legal considerations of the factors supporting a cultural defense indicate that those in the legal profession — like most people — lack a full appreciation of the extent to that cultural factors affect behavior, cognition and emotion, creating the personal circumstances that are extenuating factors under legal codes. As social workers become increasingly involved in expert witness work, their appreciation of environment, community and person-in-situation provides them with perspectives for interpreting how cultural factors and experiences may constitute mental and personal states that would be legal grounds for reduced charges or leniency.

The predominant consideration of these factors of cultural defense has depended upon the discretion of prosecutors and judges. This lack of procedural safeguards and guidelines may result in inconsistencies in treatment and differential bias against some minorities; social workers involved in the criminal justice system may help prevent these injustices by presenting relevant cultural knowledge. Effectively presented cultural background material can help juries serve justice by understanding causal factors involved in an individual's intent, as well as cultural factors leading to duress, non-responsibility or mental insanity. Some of the primary cultural factors that social workers can address in providing a basis for equal justice under law are covered in Winkelman (1996).

MULTICULTURAL MANAGEMENT IN OCCUPATIONAL SOCIAL WORK

Skidmore, Thackeray & Farley (1997:253, 259) characterize "social work in the work place [as] on the cutting edge of practice.…[T]his emerging field is one of the most important for the profession." A wide variety of contexts and services characterize social work's involvement in the occupational setting. Human services departments and their employee assistance programs deal with a variety of emotional, behavioral, social and psychological problems. These programs are not only humanitarian or service oriented, they are also cost-effective in that such programs promote a healthy and effective work force. The focus upon employee problems and effective social functioning means that an understanding of their cultural background is essential. The need to address both institutional and individual requirements makes the environmental and systems perspectives of social work a powerful tool. A central resource of the occupational social worker is a range of community institutions and programs that can be utilized to resolve problems, making cultural and community knowledge an essential aspect of job skills. Since employee problems are not strictly work related, but derivative from the broader context of their lives, an understanding of community strengths and weakness is an essential component of occupational social work.

While many factors have contributed to this development of occupational social work, cultural pluralism is a primary driving force. The intensified contact between different cultural groups in the work place has made management of intercultural contact an important growth area of occupational social work. The importance of adapting to cultural factors has been long recognized in international relations and business; these same insights are being increasingly applied to administrative and management concerns here in the U.S. These needs for cultural knowledge and cross-cultural competencies in the U.S. workplace derive from many factors, beginning

with the U.S. being a part of a global village, an interdependent world system where domestic and foreign relations are inter-linked. Numerous aspects of management within the U.S. have important cross-cultural dimensions derived not only from the need for U.S. companies to operate in the international arena, but also from the presence of foreign international businesses and workers in the U.S. and the increasing proportion of the ethnic work force. The shift in U.S. demography has created dramatic changes in the composition of the U.S. work force. Five out of six new workers entering the work place in the next decade will be ethnic minorities and women. The demographic shift predicted for the mid-21st century indicates that the ethnic minorities of today will constitute the majority of the U.S. The hiring, training, promotion, retention and management of a culturally diverse work force has already created difficulties for the traditional manager. The cultural diversity of the U.S. means the manager must develop skills for relating to people across numerous dimensions of diversity — ethnicity, age, sex, education, disability, values, family status, etc.

Domestic business issues include the need to understand how cultural factors affect work behavior, how to manage an increasingly multicultural work force, and how to relate to the foreign nationals working and owning companies in the U.S. These require cross-cultural knowledge and intercultural relations and communication skills. Understanding of culture and intercultural dynamics can help solve work problems and provide business benefits in a multicultural world. Businesses today not only have to address cultural issues related to cultural pluralism, but also the consequences of the passing of the industrial paradigm to a service economy orientation based upon information and communications. These entail a dramatic revision in assumptions, concepts, and models that require a massive reorganization to adapt to the new technoeconomic paradigm and cultural pluralism. Even within the context of U.S. operations, different local and business cultures and the consumer preferences of different communities and regions of the country require cultural awareness and adaptation. Marketing to the diverse cultural and ethnic groups is an increasing concern. The long-recognized special market of African Americans in terms of cosmetics, beauty aids, dress styles, foods, movies, music and other items have been extended to recognition of other ethnic markets as well. Even the ethnic markets themselves are becoming differentiated with different Spanish-language greeting cards marketed for different U.S. Hispanic markets (e.g., east coast Puerto Rican or Cuban versus Southwest Mexican American). Not only are particular products for ethnic markets an issue requiring cultural adaptations, but there is a need recognized for different marketing approaches and products featured for different cultural groups. For example, the cultural values of some groups suggest the need to market based upon family appeal rather than long-term guarantees, which may not motivate buyers with short-term or fatalistic expectations.

Cultural factors are important in many issues involved in managing a multicultural work force and meeting the needs of cultural markets. Management involves diverse social behaviors such as communication, authority relations, leadership, decision-making, planning, organization, controlling resources, performance appraisal and motivation. The traditional management approaches to these issues have been based on Anglo American concepts, as is illustrated well in cross-cultural business perspectives. Culturally pluralistic societies' need to relate to different cultural groups requires a multicultural management approach. Internal variation in society means that managers have always needed multicultural management skills as embodied in the concept of "Different Strokes for Different Folks." Changing demographics and work force means "managing diversity" has become a major issue for the 21st century. Flex management has become a crucial tool, encouraging the manager to recognize the need to treat different people differently. Success in culturally diverse work environments can be enhanced by an appreciation of the importance and value of individual differences and a realization that diversity can be an asset if properly managed. Transforming personnel and organizations to take advantage of the

opportunities of cultural diversity is crucial. Culturally and personally appropriate motivators and evaluations are essential for building relationships with employees and obtaining optimal productivity and commitment, recognizing individual and cultural differences to match people with tasks based upon skills and dispositions. Companies' needs for consultants and trainers to prepare their managers and employees for effective utilization of the multicultural work force has created additional opportunities for social workers with cross-cultural perspectives and intercultural skills.

Comparative or Cross-Cultural Management.
According to Harris & Moran (1987), all management is multicultural, involving cross-national relations or cultural or subcultural differences based upon ethnic, class, age, sex, religion or other beliefs, values and assumptions. Rather than the classic management or "human relations" approaches, effective cross-cultural management requires adoption of a perspective "human resources development." Human resources development approaches assume that people are interested in meaningful work and that the right environment will produce creative and motivated workers. This is different from the human relations approach, but insufficient for managing cross-cultural situations since it still includes many of the typical human relations assumptions which embody European American values, rather than cross-cultural perspectives. What is necessary is a comparative management approach based upon knowledge of the similarities and differences found cross-culturally and in different social contexts. The comparative manager is eclectic and synergistic, modifying his/her approach depending on the characteristics of specific people and contexts in order to participate effectively in a variety of cultural settings and optimize their managerial potentials. Comparative management includes a macro approach to the sociocultural factors in the external environment; a behavioral approach to microlevel factors such as cultural attitudes, perceptions, values and management philosophies; and an open systems perspective that analyzes organizational and individual behavior with respect to task,

organizational and sociocultural environments. The cross-cultural management approaches indicate that universal principles of management do not exist and that organizational culture varies widely, making awareness of different management approaches and organizational principles essential skills for effectively working in multicultural environments.

Cross-Cultural Perspectives in Administration

Understanding the role of culture in behavior has numerous contemporary applications in the areas of administration in private firms, government agencies and public institutions, especially in education, health and human services, human relations, the criminal justice system, community development, labor and public relations and many others. Besides serving the administrator or manager of a culturally diverse work force, or the advocate or change agent, cross-cultural skills are needed for implementing evaluation research and impact and needs assessment for ethnic communities, marketing and consumer behavior, new product development, planning and policy research and organizational change to adapt to the changing economic and social environments. The utilization of cross-cultural perspectives provides tools for understanding how institutions function and relate to a culturally diverse population.

Since management effectiveness requires cross-cultural perspectives, businesses are turning to anthropological perspectives and methods derived from industrial, business, organizational and corporate anthropology to deal with work-related situations and problems. These fields are primarily concerned with problem-solving activities in private sector organizations, including understanding cultural structures and internal dynamics, environmental interaction/relations, the cultural context of behavior and organization and organizational culture and functions. They also have applications in public organizations and bureaucracies, including creating, maintaining and changing organization cultures to adapt to changing environments. The dramatic changes in the U.S. population and social work clientele

require such changes in the traditional cultures of social work agencies.

Public Administration.
Cultural perspectives are necessary in public administration. Housing projects, community renewal and rehabilitation of neighborhoods generally require the interaction of distinct cultural or subcultural groups. Success requires the development of community-based solutions that assess the social consequence of programs, develop means of maintaining the vital aspects of the neighborhood and assure the rights of the existing community. Human resources administration in urban areas necessitates the accommodation of needs of different and often conflicting cultural groups. Cultural factors permeate responsibility for managing programs, project planning, problem solving, policy development and inter-agency coordination. Correctional facilities that largely house inmates from the U.S. minority groups require assessments of and adaptations to the cultural nature of their wards and the different (and often conflicting) cultural groups they represent. The successful management of these multicultural groups requires the identification of the cultural problems and conflicts, and the development of solutions based upon an analysis of the underlying cultural assumptions and their effects upon social behavior and perceptions. Cultural factors are concerns in all public services, particularly health and human services.

Organizational and corporate culture provide the fundamental structuring of all business activities whether or not the managers and employees are aware of it. In the current era where work cultures and national cultures are undergoing rapid change, understanding the nature of organizational culture and how to shape it has become a crucial issue for business in terms of effectively utilizing multicultural work forces and transforming organizations to assure their survival. In order to operate with awareness of the cultural factors affecting organizational behavior, it is necessary to become aware of the organizational patterns, their effects upon performance and how to change them when necessary.

The concept of organizational culture is useful in terms of analyzing and understanding the work environment, whether encountered overseas or in one's own society. By focusing on the structure of the organization and its relationships to the many systems and environments with which it interacts, a company is better informed in terms of how to manage the cultural factors functioning (or malfunctioning) in its system. Organizational culture is the system of beliefs and rules for behavior that structure the activities of an organization and provide the procedures and means for achieving success. Organizational culture involves values, myths, heroes, rituals and symbols that integrate work place behavior and maintains it across shifting personnel; it profoundly affects organization, behavior, decisions, promotions, planning and other work behaviors, including analysis, problem solving and adaptation to the environments (Deal & Kennedy 1982). Because of changing environments, organizations need to modify and create their cultures deliberately to meet the needs created by those changes. The manager can adapt to these needs by understanding and deliberately creating organizational characteristics that foster the potentials of diverse groups and individuals in the multicultural clientele and work force. Such adaptations are imperative for social work agencies to adapt to cultural pluralism.

In *Managing Cultural Differences,* Harris and Moran (1987) suggest that cross-cultural relations demand a "Global Manager" — a cosmopolitan, intercultural communicator who can lead cross-cultural adaptation and cultural change in work and organizational settings and create cultural synergy. The global manager must be interculturally sensitive and a cross-cultural performer who can adjust to diverse work cultures and individuals. Global manager is a leader who can operate in a pluralistic cultural environment and is flexible enough to be able to adapt to people of different backgrounds. Cultural sensitivity is the basis for a concerted effort to acquire relevant knowledge about the effects of culture upon behavior and use this awareness as the basis for effective relationships with culturally diverse individuals and groups. The global managers understand the culturally conditioned nature of

their own and others' behavior, and the impact of culture on communication and relations. Global managers are capable of managing cultural influences and cultural differences, and can adapt their management style to the individual and local practices and situations. This enables the global manager to be an effective intercultural performer and to apply cultural understandings to the peculiarities of motivation of people from other cultures. The global manager can move between different work cultures and business practices, effectively dealing with people of different backgrounds and behaviors. The global manager combines all of these capabilities in the creation of cultural synergy, integrating different cultural potentials into a system with common benefits exceeding the potentials of the individual cultures.

Summary

The growth in the U.S. population of various ethnic groups has created a cultural pluralism that has already impacted virtually all aspects of society. The shifting ethnic composition of the U.S. has been projected to change virtually all institutions of society, including schools, communities, social services, health care, businesses and government. These changes have become a focus of interethnic conflict and political confrontation in American life. As ethnic minorities form the plurality of many urban areas, urban politics take on new dimensions and alliances. Political conflicts of the future are already emerging in the schools and boards of education of urban areas and states where different ethnic groups, most notably African Americans and Hispanics, are vying for power. Political battles are already being fought over the calls for a new curriculum that represents the history, contributions and experiences of the diverse ethnic groups that have participated in the founding of the nation and that existed before the U.S. was founded. History and current conflicts clearly indicate that America's cultural pluralism is not typically characterized by harmony and cooperation, but rather by conflict and problems. There is a clear challenge for all Americans to learn how to participate more effectively in the culturally pluralistic society in which we live.

Success in today's world requires social, cultural and cross-cultural expertise. Culturally sensitive management efforts range from planning, recruitment and training, to organizational development and creation of multiple models for relations, communication, management and negotiation. Such knowledge can assist one in rising beyond cultural limitations, avoiding ethnocentrism, and effectively utilizing the potentials of cultural diversity. Cross-cultural perspectives are important sources of information for overcoming culture-bound tendencies, permitting one to take advantage of the opportunities and benefits resulting from effective participation in multicultural environments. Social workers need to use such skills and perspectives in transforming their organization, and can play a central role in assisting others to transform their management and interpersonal behaviors to be more effective participants in an increasingly multicultural society. Indeed, the improved participation and interethnic relations has the potential to benefit all of society. This book is a contribution towards that goal, one based upon the realization that understanding other cultures and the dynamics of cross-cultural relations will facilitate productive interethnic relations.

REFERENCES AND ADDITIONAL READINGS

Education
Banks, J. 1987. *Teaching Strategies for Ethnic Studies*. Boston: Allyn and Bacon.
Colangelo, N., C. Foxley and D. Dustin, eds. 1979. *Multicultural Nonsexist Education A Human Relations Approach*. Dubuque, Iowa: Kendall/Hunt Pub.
Diaz, C. 1992. *Multicultural Education for the 21st Century*. Washington, D.C.: NEA Professional Library.
Dodd, C. and F. Montalvo,. eds 1987. *Intercultural Skills for Multicultural Societies*. Washington, D.C.: Sietar
Edwards, Richard, Editor-in-Chief. 1995. *Encyclopedia of Social Work 19th Edition*. Washington, D.C.: National Association of Social Workers Press.
Fulginiti, J. 1986. "Ethnography in school administration." *Practicing Anthropology* 8(3-4):20-21.
Hendricks, C. 1997. *The Child, the Family and the School: A Multicultural Triangle*. In Congress 1997:37-60.
Lynch, J. 1989. *Multicultural Education in a Global Society*. New York: Falmer Press.
Porter, R. and L. Samovar. 1991. *Communication Between Cultures*. Belmont: Wadsworth Publishing Company.
Sleeter, C., ed. 1991. *Empowerment Through Multicultural Education*. Albany: SUNY Press.
Takaki, R., ed. 1987. *From Different Shores Perspectives on Race and Ethnicity in America*. New York: Oxford.

Business
Akhabs, S. 1995. "Occupational Social Work" In Edwards 1995:1779-1786.
Beyer, J. and H. Trice. 1993. *The Cultures of Work Organizations*. Englewood Cliffs: Prentice Hall, Inc.
Copeland, L. and L. Griggs. 1985. *Going International*. New York: Random.
Deal, T. and A. Kennedy. 1982 *Corporate Cultures: The Rites and Rituals of Corporate Life*. Reading, Mass.: Addison-Wesley.
Harris, P. and R. Moran. 1987. *Managing Cultural Differences*. Houston: Gulf.
Kotter, J. and J. Heskett. 1992. *Corporate Culture and Performance*. New York: Free Press.
Raelin, J. 1986. *Clash of Cultures: Managers and Professionals*. Boston: Harvard Business School Press.
Terpstra V. and K. David. 1991. *The Cultural Environment of International Business*. Cincinnati: South-Western.

Health and Social Services
Atkinson, D., G. Morten and D Sue. 1983. *Counseling American Minorities A Cross-Cultural Perspective*. Dubuque, Iowa: Wm. C. Brown.
Becker, M., ed. 1974. *The Health Belief Model and Personal Health Behavior*. Thorofare, N.J.: Charles Slack, Inc.
Bloom, M. 1995. *Primary Prevention Overview*. In: Edwards 1995:1895-1905.
Bond, M. ed. 1988. *The Cross-Cultural Challenge to Social Psychology*. Newbury Park, Ca.: Sage Publications.
Brink, P. 1976. *Transcultural Nursing: A Book of Readings*. Englewood Cliffs, N.J.: Prentice Hall.
Brislin, R. ed. 1990. *Applied Cross-Cultural Psychology*. Newbury Park, Ca.: Sage Publications.
Capers, C., ed. 1992. *Culture and Nursing Practice*. Gaithersburg, MD: Aspen Publishers.
Downes, N. 1994. *Ethnic Americans for the Health Professional*. Dubuqu: Kendall/Hunt.

Galanti, G. 1991. *Caring for Patients from Different Cultures: Case Studies From American Hospitals*. Philadelphia: University of Pennsylvania Press.

Gonzales-Mena, J. 1993. *Multicultural Issues in Child Care*. Mountain View, Ca.: Mayfield.

Gonzales-Santin, E. ed. 1989. *Collaboration: The Key*. Tempe, AZ: ASU School of Social Work.

Green, J. 1982. *Cultural Awareness in the Human Services*. Englewood Cliffs, N.J.: Prentice-Hall.

Heelas, P. and A. Lock 1981. *Indigenous Psychologies: The Anthropology of the Self*. New York: Academic Press.

Kleinman, A. 1980. *Patients and Healers in the Context of Culture*. Berkeley: University of California.

Kleinman, A. 1988. *The Illness Narrative. Suffering, Healing and the Human Condition*. New York: Basic Books.

Lenninger, M. 1978. *Transcultural Nursing*. New York: Wiley.

Lenninger, M., ed. 1991. *Culture Care Diversity and Universality*. New York: National League for Nursing.

Lum, D. 1996. *Social Work Practice and People of Color*. Pacific Grove: Brooks/Cole Publishing Co.

Marsella, A. and P. Pedersen. 1981. *Cross-Cultural Counseling and Psychotherapy*. New York: Pergamon.

Marsella, A. and G. White, eds. 1984. *Cultural Conceptions of Mental Health and Therapy*. Boston: Reidel Publishing.

Moore, J. and J. Vigil. 1989. "Chicano gangs: group norms and individual factors related to adult criminality." *Aztlan* 18(2):27-44.

Moroney, R. 1995. *Public Health Services*, In: Edwards 1995:1967-1973.

Oktay, J. 1995. *Primary Health Care*. In: Edwards 1995:1887-1894.

Pederson, P. ed. 1987. *Handbook of Cross-Cultural Counseling and Therapy*. New York: Praeger.

Skidmore, R., M. Thackeray and O.W. Farley. 1997. *Introduction to Social Work 7th Edition*. Needham Heights, Mass.: Allyn and Bacon.

Simons, R. and C. Hughes, eds. 1985. *The Culture-Bound Syndromes*. Boston: Reidel Publishing.

Triandis, H. and W. Lambert, eds. 1980. *Handbook of Cross-Cultural Psychology*. Boston: Allyn and Bacon.

Politics and Social Life

Barker, L. 1992. *Ethnic Politics and Civil Liberties*. New Brunswick, N.J.: Transaction Publishers.

Burgoyne, E., ed. 1985. *Race and Politics*. New York: H. W. Wilson Co.

Ellis, C. 1992. *A Nation of Strangers*. New York: Morrow.

Kadish, S. 1987. "Excusing Crime." *California Law Review* 75(1):257-289

Kosmitzki,?? 1998. *Lives Across Human Development*.

Lyman, J. 1986. "Cultural Defense: Viable Doctrine of Wishful Thinking." *Criminal Justice Journal* 9:87-117.

Nieto, S. 1992. *Affirming Diversity: The Sociopolitical Context of Multicultural Education*. White Plains, NY Longman.

Norgren, J. and S. Nanda. 1988. *American Cultural Pluralism and Law*. New York: Praeger.

Nordquist, J. ed. 1992. *The Multicultural Education Debate in the University*. Santa Cruz: Reference and Research Services.

Notes. 1986. "The Cultural Defense in Criminal Law." *Harvard Law Review* 99:1293-1311.

Renteln, A. 1993. "A Justification of the Cultural Defense as a Partial Excuse." *Southern California Review of Law and Women's Studies* 2(2):437-526.

Sams, J. 1986. "The Availability of the Cultural Defense as an Excuse for Criminal Behavior." *Georgia Journal of International and Comparative Law* 16:335-354

Sheybani, M.-M. 1987. "Cultural Defense: One Person's Culture is Another's Crime." *Loyola Los Angeles International and Comparative Law Journal* 9:751-783

Trager, O. ed. 1992. *Americas Cultural Minorities and the Multicultural Debate*. New York: Facts on File.

Winkelman, M. 1996. "Cultural Factors in Criminal Defense Proceedings." *Human Organization* 55(2):154-59.

<u>NOTES</u>

SELF-ASSESSMENT 8.1

CROSS-CULTURAL INTERACTIONS

Using a recent magazine or newspaper as your source, describe a situation involving an interaction between different ethnic groups in the society.

Who are the groups involved and what is the nature of the interaction?

Are there problems associated with the interaction?

Are there cultural factors associated with the problems? Problems reflective of the dynamics of intercultural relations?

Are benefits derived from the interaction?

What kinds of misunderstandings occur (or are likely to occur) between the groups involved?

What cultural knowledge might facilitate the interaction?

What would you do or recommend be done to enhance the mutual benefits to be derived from the interaction?

NOTES

INDEX